OXFORD
UNIVERSITY PRESS
AUSTRALIA & NEW ZEALAND

LEADERSHIP

CONTEXTS AND COMPLEXITIES IN EARLY CHILDHOOD EDUCATION

SECOND EDITION

MANJULA WANIGANAYAKE | SANDRA CHEESEMAN
MARIANNE FENECH | FAY HADLEY | WENDY SHEPHERD

Oxford University Press is a department of the University of Oxford.
It furthers the University's objective of excellence in research, scholarship, and education by publishing worldwide. Oxford is a registered trademark of Oxford University Press in the UK and in certain other countries.

Published in Australia by
Oxford University Press
253 Normanby Road, South Melbourne, Victoria 3205, Australia

First published 2012

Second edition 2017

Reprinted 2018, 2019, 2021

National Library of Australia Cataloguing-in-Publication entry

Creator: Waniganayake, Manjula, author.

Title: Leadership: contexts and complexities in early childhood education/Manjula Waniganayake,
Sandra Cheeseman, Marianne Fenech, Fay
Hadley, Wendy Shepherd.

Edition: 2nd edition.

ISBN: 978-0-19030-936-7 (paperback)

Notes: Includes bibliographical references and index.

Subjects: Educational leadership.
Early childhood education—Administration.
Education, Preschool—Administration.
Organizational effectiveness.

Other Creators/Contributors:
Cheeseman, Sandra, author.
Fenech, Marianne, author.
Hadley, Fay, author.
Shepherd, Wendy, author.

Edited by Sandra Balonyi
Cover design by Visionary Creative
Text design by Jennai Le Fai
Typeset by Newgen KnowledgeWorks (P) Ltd, Chennai, India
Proofread by Sarah Russell
Indexed by Nikki Davis
Printed in China by Leo Paper Products Ltd.

The Honourable Quentin Bryce AD CVO

Foreword

By The Honourable Dame Quentin Bryce AD CVO

to Leadership: Contexts and Complexities in Early Childhood Education (Second Edition)

Leadership in Early Childhood programs is demanding and complex. It calls for professional skills and personal qualities of the highest order. Every day the role brings a myriad of challenges: responding to government initiatives, legal responsibilities, needs of young children and their families, and the well-being of staff. In addressing these demands, early childhood leaders must be efficient administrators as well as excellent communicators, strategists and advocates for children.

This revised edition continues to explore these dimensions in some detail and with reference to recent reforms in the governance of early childhood settings and developments in contemporary approaches in theorising educational leadership. In its comprehensive analysis and discussion, readers are given insight into the practical demands of leading early childhood settings in Australia. The voices of leading practitioners in this second edition illustrate the professional expectations and the personal satisfaction gained from an understanding of the importance of leadership roles and responsibilities in early childhood contexts.

The authors have expanded their discussion and analysis with their inclusion of current reflections on modern theory, and their appreciation of the complexities of enacting leadership in practice. This has resulted in the inclusion of leaders already engaged in working with children and families living in different locations across our country. New voices are added to emphasise diversity in approaches to leadership.

The range of roles and responsibilities of a strong and effective leader are dealt with in detail. Perspectives presented in this book will enable today's leaders—especially those new to the role—to have a deeper appreciation of the knowledge, skills and qualities needed to be strong and effective leaders. This book does not gloss over the challenges of leadership but confronts them in a way that supports wise and responsible decision-making.

Sound, thoughtful and wise leadership makes a difference to the quality of the education and care given. Good leadership creates environments in which children, families and staff can thrive. There is, for example, a new chapter on 'places and spaces for adults for thinking and learning' which explores the value of providing suitable retreat spaces for staff in early childhood settings.

In recognition of the rapid pace of change impacting the lives of today's children and families, a further new chapter looks at the implications for leading organisational change in the early childhood context. At the heart of this book is recognition that quality of the leadership has a profound effect on the quality of the services for children, families and community.

It is a book that is comprehensive in its approach to leadership. It is practical and inspirational in its detailed analysis and exploration of the professional judgment and decision-making required of strong and competent leaders, and acknowledges the ethical responsibilities of the role.

June 2. 2017.

CONTENTS

LIST OF FIGURES

LIST OF TABLES

LIST OF LEADERS IN PRACTICE BOXES

Visit Oxford Ascend for interviews with selected practitioners

LIST OF ACRONYMS

ACECQA	Australian Children's Education and Care Quality Authority
ACTU	Australian Council of Trade Unions
ACYP	Advocate for Children and Young People (NSW Government)
AGM	annual general meeting
AITSL	Australian Institute for Teaching and School Leadership
AM	Member of the Order of Australia
ARACY	Australian Research Alliance for Children and Youth
ASG	Australian Scholarships Group
ASPECT	Autism Spectrum Australia
ALGA	Australian Local Government Association
CCCCNSW	Community Child Care Co-operative NSW
CEO	chief executive officer
COAG	Council of Australian Governments
DEC	Department of Education and Communities
DECS	Department of Education and Community Services
DEEWR	Department of Education, Employment and Workplace Relations
ECA	Early Childhood Australia
ECEC	Early Childhood Education and Care
EI	emotional intelligence
EPPE	Effective Provision of Pre-school Education
EYLF	Early Years Learning Framework
FDC	family day care
GDP	gross domestic product
GPS	global positioning system
HRM	human resource management
ISA	Inclusion Support Agency
LDC	long day care
LGA	Local Government Area
MACS	Multifunctional Aboriginal Children's Service
MP	Member of Parliament
NAEYC	National Association for the Education of Young Children
NCAC	National Childcare Accreditation Council
NESA	New South Wales Educational Standards Authority
NGO	non-government organisation
NIFTeY	National Investment for the Early Years
NPQICL	National Professional Qualification in Integrated Centre Leadership
NQF	National Quality Framework
NQS	National Quality Standard

OECD	Organisation for Economic Co-operation and Development
ORIC	Office of the Registrar of Indigenous Corporations
OSHC	outside school hours care
PSTANT	Preschool Teachers' Association of the Northern Territory
QIAS	Quality Improvement and Accreditation System
QIP	Quality Improvement Plan
RDO	rostered day off
RLC	reflective learning circles
RTO	registered training organisation
SCAN	Supporting Children with Additional Needs
SME	small and medium enterprises
SWOT	Strengths, Weaknesses, Opportunities and Threats analysis
TAFE	Technical and Further Education
UN	United Nations
UNCROC	United Nations Convention on the Rights of the Child
UNICEF	United Nations International Children's Emergency Fund (now United Nations Children's Fund)
UTSCC	UTS Child Care Incorporated
WEL	Women's Electoral Lobby

WEBSITES OF PEAK ORGANISATIONS

Australian Childcare Alliance (ACA): www.australianchildcarealliance.org.au

Australian Community Children's Services (ACCS): www.ausccs.org.au

Australian Research Alliance for Children and Youth: www.aracy.org.au

Community Child Care Co-operative NSW: www.ccccnsw.org.au

Early Childhood Australia (ECA): www.earlychildhoodaustralia.org.au

Family Day Care Australia (FDCA): www.familydaycare.com.au/index.php/main/Home#M55

National Association of Mobile Services for Rural and Remote Families and Children (NAMS): www.nationalmobiles.org.au

National Association of Multicultural and Ethnic Children's Services (NAMECS): www.namecs.com.au/component/content/frontpage

National Council of Social Services (NCOSS): www.ncoss.org.au

National In-Home Childcare Association (NICA): www.nica.org.au

National Out of School Hours Services Association (NOSHSA): www.netoosh.org.au/noshsa

NSW/ACT Independent Education Union: www.ieu.asn.au

Occasional Child Care Association—National (OCCA Nat): www.occasional-child-care.com.au

Playgroup Australia (PA): www.playgroupaustralia.com.au

Secretariat of National Aboriginal and Islander Child Care (SNAICC): http://snaicc.asn.au

Social Justice in Early Childhood Group: www.socialjusticeinearlychildhood.org

United Voice: http://unitedvoice.org.au

IN ACKNOWLEDGMENT

Students constantly remind us that leadership in the early childhood context is a very complex and provocative concept. Your questions and struggles to understand organisational structures, policies, processes and the political landscape, prompted the original writing of this book. As authors, we have also again benefited from the generous support of many who enabled the finalisation of this second edition as noted in this acknowledgement.

Firstly, we sincerely thank the thirty individuals who willingly and freely gave their time to discuss and document their perspectives on key leadership matters for inclusion in our book. They are experienced early childhood teachers, educators and advocates for young children and their families, who live and work in a variety of settings located in different parts of Australia. Their perspectives are presented as 'Leaders in practice' throughout the book and bring authenticity and vibrancy to the discussions.

Virginia Artinian
Andrew Bagnall
Dennis Blythin
Jane Bourne
Deborah Brennan
Angela Chng
Candace Fitzgerald
Alicia Flack-Konè
Leanne Gibbs
Tonia Godhard
Michelle Gujer
Christine Knox
Jodie Knox
Daniela Kavoukas
Rhonda Livingstone
Karen Martin
Brigitte Mitchell
Marina Papic
Karen Palmer
Jennifer Ribarovski
Carrie Rose
Anthony Semann
Colin Slattery
Lisa Syrette
Angela Thompson
Sylvia Turner
Benjamin Walker
June Wangmann
Sally Whitaker
Sarah Woods

To the readers of this book, it is important to know that writing is often a solitary task; however, this book is a celebration of collaboration, collegiality and tenacity as each writer sought to overcome the challenges of balancing academic work with the needs of family and chapter writing deadlines. Each writer is indebted to the team for maintaining enthusiasm at various times, for keeping abreast of editing and reviewing chapters, and for providing extra support where needed. As authors we are also indebted to **Marjorie Lewis-Jones** for meticulously checking chapters, references and the glossary in formatting the manuscript for consistency. Marjorie's quality control and generosity of time enabled us to present a clean manuscript to the publishers in a timely manner.

To Oxford University Press, for commissioning this book and entrusting us to write a second edition, thank you for extending us this honour. In particular, we express our personal thanks to **Katie Ridsdale**, Senior Publisher, who led the team from Oxford, for her leadership, punctuated by thoughtfulness and wise advice. Likewise, to **Samantha Brancatisano**, Development Editor, for her understanding, efficient follow-up and generosity of time in coordinating various aspects of the production. To **Sandra Balonyi** and **Jennifer Butler**, who worked closely with us during the final stages of diligently editing the manuscript through to production. Sandra's care and patience was immensely appreciated. We commend all at OUP—including those who assisted us in the background unknown by name to us, for upholding high standards in publishing throughout.

We were also once again honoured by **Dame Quentin Bryce** for agreeing to write the Foreword to this revised second edition of our book. Thank you for your continuing support and interest in our writing.

We are confident that the work undertaken in revising and extending this edition has been well worth the sacrifices made by everyone involved in order to complete the book that you now hold in your hands. We trust that you, the reader, will find this book a useful resource and an inspiration for your role as an intentional leader in EC settings.

Manjula, Sandra, Marianne, Fay and Wendy

PUBLISHER'S NOTE

Oxford University Press publishing in Australia delivers quality teaching and learning resources that lecturers demand, students need, and educators refer to in their practice.

This second edition of *Leadership: Contexts and Complexities in Early Childhood Education* reflects our continued commitment to the advancement of scholarly knowledge and its impact on professional learning. We are indebted to the reviewers involved in our blind peer review process for their valuable guidance in the development of this new edition, as well as to all those who reviewed the original book proposal and manuscript. The second edition contains two new chapters, and several additional features including annotated online references and podcasts with some of the Leaders in practice featured in-text elaborating on their perspectives. Taken together, the new inclusions and revised chapter contents have enriched this second edition significantly.

This book is grounded in the authors' understanding of the work of early childhood educators as leaders, and reflects their skills and expertise in bringing together theory and evidence-based teaching practice. It contains original ideas on findings from early childhood studies conducted by the authors, as well as new insights on contemporary leadership literature relevant to the early childhood sector.

We expect that readers will discover in this book creative and critical ways of thinking about early childhood leadership. By prompting reflection on the issues raised, we hope it will assist readers to achieve their goals, becoming effective leaders who work intentionally with children and their families in diverse and complex contexts.

ABOUT THE AUTHORS

The same team of authors of the first edition of this book came together to prepare this second edition. Manjula, Sandra, Fay and Wendy are all early childhood academics employed at the Department of Educational Studies at Macquarie University, Sydney, Australia. Marianne now works at the University of Sydney. Their shared passion and commitment to promoting early childhood leadership and quality early childhood education for young children, as captured in this book, continue to fuel their teaching and research.

Professor Manjula Waniganayake (PhD, BEd (EC—Hons))

Over three decades, Manjula has been involved in the early childhood sector as a teacher, a parent, an advocate, a policy analyst, a teacher educator and a researcher. She was awarded an Honorary Doctorate from the University of Tampere, Finland for her scholarly contribution to the advancement of Early Childhood Leadership. She believes in diversity and social justice, and values learning from others within Australia and beyond. The research monograph *Thinking and Learning about Leadership: Early childhood research from Australia, Finland and Norway,* published in 2015, reflects her global interests in connecting early childhood research with policy and practice.

Dr Sandra Cheeseman (PhD, PGCinRM (EC), BEd (EC), DipT (EC))

Sandra is a lecturer in social policy, management and leadership. She brings to this role extensive experience as an early childhood teacher, director and senior manager. She has worked in a range of early childhood settings and leadership positions. Following many years as a director of community-based long day care centres, Sandra moved to the role of professional development coordinator for a large not-for-profit provider, later taking on the role of deputy chief executive officer. She has extensive experience in the management and day-to-day running of a range of early childhood settings and has broadened her expertise to the area of social policy through her involvement in a number of peak organisations. Sandra's current research is looking at the role of room leaders in infant/toddler rooms. She always strives to make clear the connections between research and practice and engages students in critical thinking about their practice.

Dr Marianne Fenech (PhD, MMgt, BSocWk)

Marianne is a senior lecturer and director of Early Childhood programs at the University of Sydney. Marianne is passionate about quality early childhood education for young children, particularly those from marginalised backgrounds. Her teaching and research focus on effective early childhood settings through strong management and leadership, and her vision is for a quality and equitable system of early childhood education in Australia. Marianne has expertise in early childhood policy, the regulation of early childhood services, quality early childhood education, and parents as childcare consumers. She has published extensively in these areas and is currently the lead researcher on an Australian research council–funded study investigating personal, public and policy influences on parents' childcare decision-making.

Marianne is chair of both the NSW/ACT and national Early Childhood Teacher Education Councils.

Dr Fay Hadley (PhD, MECh, BECE)

Fay is a senior lecturer and director of Initial Teacher Education programs at Macquarie University. Fay's expertise is in leadership, mentoring and working with diverse families. She has been researching in these areas for the past 10 years. In 2008, she was awarded the Early Childhood Australia Doctoral Thesis Award for her PhD, which investigated the relationships between families and early childhood staff in long day care settings. Prior to completing her PhD, Fay was a teacher and a director in long day care centres in New South Wales and the ACT. Since 2004, she has been a member of the editorial sub-committee of the *Australian Journal of Early Childhood* and is also currently the chair of the publications committee for Early Childhood Australia.

Wendy Shepherd (MECh, BEd (EC))

Wendy is the director of the Mia Mia Child and Family Study Centre and has more than 30 years of experience in leading early childhood programs. The position of director/lecturer has combined a practical and academic career with practice informing research and research informing practice. In her current work as an early childhood lecturer, she draws on her direct experience in a variety of early childhood settings and schools. She has consistently contributed to early childhood policy reform as an invited member of key government advisory committees and as an advocate for young children and their families. She has written journal articles and book chapters on the topics of legislation and regulation, child development, environments and young children and the arts. She keeps abreast of current issues in early childhood, and is involved in a range of professional development activities and inquiry-based research projects involving early childhood practitioners in Australia and overseas.

PREFACE—HOW TO USE THIS BOOK

Our book has an unashamed call for *intentional* leadership. It mirrors the concept of 'intentional teaching' introduced in the Australian Early Years Learning Framework (DEEWR, 2009), a key driver of early childhood policy reform in this country. To ensure appropriate implementation of curriculum reform, the Australian government has called on educators to demonstrate active leadership, particularly in relation to pedagogy and cultivation of sustainable partnerships with parents and the community. Accordingly, early childhood policy developments in Australia are used as a backdrop to illustrate complexities of understanding leadership implementation in early childhood settings.

In this second edition, there are 15 chapters arranged under two parts:

- Part 1—Contexts of Leadership
- Part 2—Leadership in Context.

Part 1 provides an orientation to the various contextual dimensions of early childhood leadership. These chapters are focused on 'big picture' issues that give shape to early childhood leadership, and include discussion of early childhood policy, legislative frameworks, quality standards, advocacy, governance, pedagogy and leading organisational change.

Part 2 deals with the application of leadership within early childhood settings. These chapters address perennial areas of importance including the development of sound relationships with families, engagement with community and the creation of effective workplaces, as well as a focus on other relatively new leadership dimensions including social entrepreneurship and succession planning.

Two brand new chapters have also been added to this second edition. One of these focuses on a persistent theme—leading change—and the other examines the easily forgotten aspect of spaces and places for adults' thinking and learning. Convergence of materials from some chapters has enabled us to emphasise the importance of professional communication and strategic planning. Collectively, the 15 chapters in this book can assist tertiary students and practitioners engaged in early childhood matters to critically understand and actively engage with the macro and micro contexts within which they may work as intentional leaders.

In each chapter we follow a similar format whereby **learning objectives** and **key concepts** are identified at the start as a way of guiding the reader to consider the content in an orderly manner. We draw on research we have conducted that has not been previously published, while also referring to published research and scholarly writing of both early childhood and education writers in Australia and overseas.

Each chapter contains definitions of key concepts discussed within that chapter. These concepts have been compiled as a glossary for easy reference as a single list presented in alphabetical order. Here we wish to also highlight the way in which we have used some common terms/words throughout the book:

- *Early childhood*: The international definition of 'early childhood' typically embraces from birth to eight years of a child's life. In this book, however, our discussions typically refer to young children aged birth to five years participating in government regulated and approved prior-to-school settings. The words 'early childhood' may not always appear in the text when referring to a setting/centre/profession/sector/organisation, unless required to clarify and/or emphasise a particular point being discussed.
- *Early childhood educator*: For ease of reference and consistency with Australian policy documents the term 'early childhood educator' or 'educator' is used when referring to early childhood personnel employed to work with young children and their families in prior-to-school settings.
- *Early childhood programs and settings*: Early childhood programs are those aimed at enhancing the learning of young children (birth to five years) within a setting that is accountable to the Australian government's National Quality Framework (ACECQA, 2011a) or operates as a multifunctional Aboriginal children's service. The words 'programs' and 'settings' are used interchangeably as appropriate to the discussion.
- *Early childhood sector or profession*: These terms refer to the professional contexts where early childhood educators are employed and/or are active as advocates.

Our book has been enriched throughout with the incorporation of **Leaders in practice** narratives, which reflect the diversity across gender, culture, age and the expertise of those working in a range of early childhood settings located in different states and territories in Australia. Their perceptions, ideas and recommendations are grounded in first-hand experiences and authentically foster meaningful engagement in leadership matters. We note that out of the 30 leaders in practice embedded in this edition, 24 are brand new. As an additional feature in this second edition, we have also collated audio recordings that are accessible as podcasts with 10 of these practitioners. These recordings cover the content included in the book and more, which we had to edit out of the book due to space limitations. In this way, we can also provide our readers direct access to the practitioners who have enriched this book in so many ways.

To engage the reader proactively, we have inserted a new feature labelled **Pause – Reflect – Act** throughout each chapter. These practical tasks serve to illustrate the duality of thinking and doing—an important learning and teaching strategy for readers of this book that will be useful to unpack with a peer and/or as a team. We have also included an additional element identified as **Online resources** and these comprise websites, and audio-video resources such as podcasts, relevant to the focus topic of each chapter. Please note, however, that while we have tried to include relatively reliable sources as far as possible, access to online resources can vary over time and this is beyond our control. Overall, the updated and restructured chapters have strengthened the discussions on leadership matters we explore.

We trust that this book will provoke and challenge you to think and question the way you look at and/or engage in leadership matters within your early childhood setting and beyond.

Manjula, Sandra, Marianne, Fay and Wendy

PART 1
CONTEXTS OF LEADERSHIP

1 CONCEPTUALISING EARLY CHILDHOOD LEADERSHIP

CHAPTER LEARNING OBJECTIVES

After studying this chapter you will understand that:

- Leadership is complex and contextual, and can change over time and place.
- Leadership is a professional responsibility of educators working in early childhood (EC) settings.
- Much is known about the work of leaders, and EC leadership theorising is progressing well.
- Leadership implementation brings together the three elements of the person, the place and the position.
- Demonstrating intentional leadership takes courage, learning and collaboration with others.
- EC leaders play a pivotal role in implementing quality programs for young children.
- EC leadership is underpinned by ethical practice.

Key concepts

intentional leaders
professional growth
spheres of influence

Overview

Leadership is a professional responsibility of educators implementing quality early childhood (EC) programs. In Australia, reinforced by government policy reform, there is an increasing sense of purpose and excitement in taking up leadership responsibilities in the sector. Being an EC leader is challenging as well as rewarding. The necessity to act purposefully and ethically becomes evident as leaders recognise the importance of strategic planning from a long-term perspective. This book introduces the notion of 'intentional leadership' as a way of conceptualising or imagining contemporary leadership practice in EC settings. The discussion is situated within an increasingly regulated EC sector and includes a consideration of EC settings as enterprises imbued with social responsibilities and as sites for advocacy and activism. We will show that intentional leaders are courageous, and can demonstrate leadership through considered and deliberate actions and effective interpersonal and workplace communication. Using research on the conceptualisation and application of a variety of leadership approaches, we will discuss the complexities of implementing intentional leadership in everyday practice.

Contexts of EC leadership

Leadership is a socio-cultural construct (Coleman & Earley, 2005; Hujala & Puroila, 1998; Hujala et al., 2013) that is underpinned by the beliefs and values of a society, community and organisation. This means that there are differences in the way that educators in Australia, Finland, China or Russia, for example, would define early childhood leadership and explain its significance. How leadership is practised can also vary between organisations in the same country and over time. These differences may arise because of, for example, the EC organisation's philosophical approach to EC education and leadership; the number of university-qualified teachers they employed; or the diverse mix of children and families using the setting at a particular time, in a particular community. For example, a preschool in a small rural community may be seen as an important place for community gatherings. Educators could actively demonstrate leadership by initiating conversations with families about matters that concern young children's education such as integrating technology into children's learning. As there may be lots of centres in neighbouring suburbs, it can be more challenging to create a unique community focus within a single centre located in a large city.

Awareness of the local community, as well as the needs and interests of children and families at their centres, can enhance the way leaders work within their settings. Major events within a country and/or developments overseas can also influence the performance of leadership responsibilities locally. For example, natural disasters such as bushfires and floods can have a dramatic effect on communities, including the destruction of children's homes and childcare centres. Likewise, the impact of the resources mining boom in Australia, for instance, can be felt across the country, including increasing employment in remote rural regions in Queensland and Western Australia. The extent to which such developments are temporary or long term must be considered in the provision of EC programs in these regions. Some situations, such as a sudden outbreak of a contagious disease in a centre or a runaway car hitting a childcare centre and damaging sections of the building, are unpredictable. When dealing with an unexpected crisis or changing community needs, educators can demonstrate leadership by adopting a planned approach.

It is not a new understanding and there is an abundance of literature affirming 'the critical responsibility of a leader's role and functions' in leading change (Rodd, 2013, p. 182). Consistently, this literature has emphasised the importance of understanding three aspects comprising first, the contexts of leadership activities; second, the people involved in each situation; and third, the interconnectivities between them. As stated by Ladkin (2010, p. x), such an awareness reinforces leadership as 'a collective process, in many ways not reducible to "the leader"' or one individual. Importantly, this approach indicates the changing focus of leadership theorising from looking at the individual with a designated leadership position to focusing on a more collective approach where leadership is distributed within an organisation, and relies on relationships (Mujis et al., 2004; Rodd, 2013; Thomas & Nuttall, 2014; Waniganayake et al., 2015). This discussion on examining EC leadership from the perspective of people, places and positions is developed further in this chapter and throughout this book.

Arriving at an appropriate definition of the words 'leader' and 'leadership' that can be applied to EC contexts has proved difficult (Rodd, 2013; Thornton et al., 2009; Waniganayake,

2011). Widespread use of these terms across a range of media, from the popular press to scholarly publications, adds to the confusion. Everyone has an opinion about 'good' and 'bad' leaders and what constitutes successful or unsuccessful leadership. Moreover, failure or the lack of leadership is presented as an explanation when things do not work out according to plans. This begs the question posed by Hogan (2015): 'Are we expecting too much from our leaders?' Within this context, emerging interests in focusing on teacher leadership in Finland (Heikka et al., 2016) and Norway (Hognestad & Boe, 2015) present diverse approaches to enacting leadership in distributed ways.

Pause–reflect–act 1.1

- Write your definition of leadership by reflecting on your experiences and understandings before you read this book.
- Collect three to five definitions of leadership from popular media using both print and online sources. Critically reflect on what is similar and different about these definitions.
- If you can read publications written in a language other than English, include these in your analysis and share the learning with peers. Explore the question: to what extent can cultural beliefs and values influence leadership definitions?
- Are we expecting too much from our EC leaders today? What evidence do you have to support your response one way or the other?
- Consider to what extent your personal perspectives of leadership align with public perceptions about leadership reflected in the media accounts.

An individual leader's personality—including their dispositions and style of leadership—can also influence the way their behaviour is perceived and assessed by others. Various typologies of characteristics of EC leaders began appearing in the 1990s (see Rodd, 2013), but these models are yet to be verified through longitudinal research. Some believe that 'leaders are born and not made' and others feel that attending a leadership course is sufficient to acquire leadership skills. These discussions are sometimes aligned with leadership enjoyed by kings and queens by virtue of being born into a royal family. Notions of royalty and its associated leadership responsibilities do not, however, fit with professional leadership functions performed by those such as educators working in EC settings.

About ten years ago, Thornton et al. (2009, p. 5) stated that 'the monocultural nature of writing on leadership' published in English reflects the culture-bound nature of leadership. Today, however, although written in English, research by scholars from Scandinavia (see Hard & Jónsdóttir, 2013; Waniganayake, Rodd & Gibbs, 2015) and Hong Kong (Ho, 2011), for example, is extending the EC leadership knowledge base by taking into account the cultural contexts of their homelands. Research based on the employment of educators and leaders from culturally and linguistically diverse backgrounds, however, remains unexplored and

intentional leaders are educators who demonstrate courage in implementing leadership responsibilities in ethical ways. They act purposefully, learning and finding ways to collaborate with others to achieve collective goals.

for further discussion on educational leaders in Australia, refer to chapters 2 and 6.

requires addressing particularly within multicultural societies such as Australia. Importantly, **intentional leaders** are expected to bring together the differing beliefs, values and attitudes of everyone involved in an EC setting with the aim of creating a harmonious organisational culture built on respect for diversity.

National and international policy reforms reflect government interests in EC leadership as a workforce improvement strategy (see, for example, Organisation for Economic Co-operation and Development (OECD), 2012; Productivity Commission, 2011b). Governments across the world have responded to an increasing evidence base about the importance of the early years by actively engaging in EC policy reform (OECD, 2006, 2012, 2015). It is widely accepted that if Australia is to realise its reform aspirations for the EC sector, attention must be given to up-skilling the EC workforce and, in particular, it is necessary to upgrade its leadership capabilities (COAG, 2009b). In responding to this challenge, the Australian government is uniquely positioned in the OECD countries in mandating the appointment of educational leaders in EC settings in this country.

Pause–reflect–act 1.2

Make a list of people whom you consider to be leaders in EC.

- Reflect on your reasons for identifying these individuals as leaders. In your opinion, to what extent have their personal characteristics (personality, age, sex, ethnicity, and so on) and their professional backgrounds, including their EC qualifications, skills and experience in the sector, influenced their leadership capabilities?
- Make the time to have a conversation with these leaders, to ask them about their own perceptions and experiences of leadership. These conversations can provide insights on alternative ways of working as leaders in EC.

Intentional leadership

The notion of 'intentional leadership' frames the discussion of leadership matters in this book. This builds on the definition of 'intentional teaching' that is described in the Australian Early Years Learning Framework (DEEWR, 2009, p. 45), which 'involves educators being deliberate, purposeful and thoughtful in their decisions and actions. Intentional teaching is the opposite of teaching by rote or continuing with traditions simply because things have "always" been done that way'. Likewise, intentional leaders are educators who engage in ethical practice by implementing leadership responsibilities in positive, purposeful ways with respect, care and compassion. Such leaders demonstrate courage in their decision-making and find ways to collaborate with others to achieve collective goals in moving the organisation forward. That is, in a rapidly changing policy environment, the frequency of making decisions impacting on the lives of young children and their families requires leaders to appreciate the complexities of their working environments and demonstrate a willingness to learn and inform others within their organisation so that everyone is abreast of evolving developments. Accordingly, Semann (2011, np) calls on educators to 'reimagine, dream and visualise a future landscape of hope and success'. This view is based on the belief that intentional leaders can demonstrate authenticity because they are 'deeply aware of how they think and behave and are perceived by others as being aware of their own and others' values/moral perspectives, knowledge and strengths' (Avolio & Luthans, 2006, as cited in Semann, 2011).

Reflecting on contemporary research evidence on EC leadership, it is possible to identify three enduring relational constructs that underpin intentional leadership in practice:

- *Leadership and vision*: Leadership literature has consistently affirmed the link between leadership and vision. In outlining their vision, intentional leaders demonstrate a capacity to think clearly and strategically about future possibilities and foster optimism and hope for the imagined future.
- *Leadership and learning*: Leaders epitomise a love of learning by actively and continuously engaging in self-development. By proactively facilitating and strategically investing in professional learning and development, intentional leaders promote thinking, questioning and critical reflection within their own organisations and beyond.
- *Leadership and connectedness*: Intentional leaders articulate their ideas in ways that others can understand and seek collaboration to make a difference by working together. They 'adopt a cognitive approach to organisational culture, making explicit the "rules" and ways of working, and *deliberately* [emphasis in the original] adopting them, rather than leaving it to chance and hoping that these will be learnt through practice' (Coleman & Earley, 2005, p. 33). This is particularly important in multi-ethnic societies such as Australia, as leadership can assist in bringing together people with diverse beliefs, values and attitudes by placing the emphasis on the best interests of children.

These relational constructs signify the essence of intentional leadership activity. That is, intentional leaders have the capacity to address these relational constructs in an integrated way. This means having a vision that others can easily see in the way the leader works every day. It also requires leaders to demonstrate their philosophical approach to achieving high-quality EC education for all children. In a broader sense, the leader's beliefs and values can reflect their thirst for learning and interest in actively engaging with others for the purposes of advocating for children's interests.

In promoting intentional leadership it is also necessary to draw attention to the 'dark side' of leadership, which consists of destructive and harmful elements achieved 'through the abuse of power and self-interests of the leader' (Slattery, 2009b). Discussion or publication of difficulties encountered by those experiencing workplace bullying, racism and discrimination are rare within this sector (Waniganayake, 2011). However, based on research carried out in EC settings in Australia and Iceland, Hard and Jónsdóttir (2013, p. 321), respectively, found evidence that EC educators avoided conflict and in some cases there are actions that silence debate. The strong expectations of conformity required through the discourse of niceness and the ethic of care can demand that staff seek agreement and adherence to these expectations rather than engage in open and robust debates for fear of conflict.

see chapters 4, 5, 13 and 14 for a wider discussion on leadership as it relates to strategic planning.

chapters 2, 3, 6 and 15 look at broad policy concerns including staff qualifications and staff:child ratios.

look at chapters 4, 5, 9, 12, 13 and 14 for more on the importance of organisational philosophies and strategic plans.

see chapter 8 for the exercise of effective communication and an ethical use of power.

collaboration between all stakeholders in the EC setting is explored in chapters 4, 10, 11, 12, 14 and 15.

These findings may surprise some, while others may disagree or deny the existence of conflict or discord within EC settings run by 'nice ladies'. If leadership is about creating positive change, then acting with courage and compassion by being proactive in enabling everyone to feel a sense of security and belonging is a priority for intentional leaders.

Effective leadership can be found in organisations that uphold children's rights and interests as a priority. The work of intentional leaders within these organisations may be framed along six foundational principles as follows, and these are developed in subsequent chapters of this book:

- using diverse resources, beyond the basic minimum standards required by government regulations, especially in the pursuit of advancing staff qualifications and staff-to-child ratios
- having a well-developed organisational philosophy and strategic and operational plans that are embedded in the everyday practices of all staff at the setting
- upholding a commitment to creating a socially just environment for children and adults at the setting, regardless of class, culture, religion, language, sexual orientation, marital status or any other individual and community variables
- having a vested interest and commitment to collaborating with others—children, colleagues, parents and the community—in respectful ways using effective communication
- practising ethical entrepreneurship, where the organisation pursues financial viability with the express intention of delivering high-quality programs for children and their families
- advocating for high-quality EC education policies and practices that aim to foster the potential of every child.

These six principles underpin the contents of this book, as can be seen in the discussion of various ideas and issues examined in subsequent chapters. The next sections in this chapter comprise a discussion based on some key considerations regarding the practice of EC leadership within contemporary contexts.

What do we know about EC leadership?

When tracking the history of EC leadership research, evolving developments over time have been documented in texts by Rodd (2006a; 2013) as well as Ebbeck and Waniganayake (2004). Publications written by Mujis et al. (2004), Nupponen (2006b) and Dunlop (2008) also provide a quick summary of previous research from a global perspective. Reflecting on developments that have taken place over the past three decades, six key themes that denote current understandings about EC leadership are as follows:

- *Definition of leadership*: There is no definitive way of describing or explaining leadership. While EC scholars have often lamented this absence of an agreed authoritative definition (see Ebbeck & Waniganayake, 2004; Rodd, 2006a; Siraj-Blatchford & Manni, 2007), the extent to which a single standard definition of leadership is appropriate is highly contestable because of the diversity of organisational settings where EC leaders work. If you believe in diversity, standardised definitions lack purpose and can also limit creativity and innovation in leadership practice, and as such, the search for a universally accepted definition has little or no value.

- *Separation of the relative constructs of administration, management and leadership*: The discussions on the extent to which these three concepts are similar and different is both historical and contextual. Ebbeck and Waniganayake (2004) developed a typology aimed at unpacking these concepts in relation to the roles and responsibilities, skills and dispositions of leaders. It is also possible to see cultural nuances of privileging one concept over another in different countries. Administration work, for example, is highly valued in the USA whereas in the UK it is often regarded as routine tasks (Coleman & Earley, 2005, pp. 6–7). While there continues to be tension between management and leadership functions, the focus on administration appears to have been subsumed as a function that everyone, including leaders, must do.
- *Leadership functions*: The nature of work performed by leaders in terms of functions or tasks as well as roles and responsibilities received a lot of attention in early research conducted in the 1990s. The increasing demands and complexities of the workplace within EC settings today require a deeper level of exploration of leadership functions. The potential for duplication of roles and responsibilities can be minimised by adopting clear job descriptions and a better understanding of each other's functions within the same organisation. New research on teacher leadership (Heikka, Halttunen & Waniganayake, 2016; Ho & Tikly, 2012) is of interest as this acknowledges teacher agency more explicitly.
- *Leadership qualities*: The notion of leadership dispositions or personal attributes of EC leaders was first studied by Rodd (1994). There are numerous leadership typologies that include lists of preferred personal characteristics of EC leaders (see, for example, Aubrey, 2007; Ebbeck & Waniganayake, 2004; Rodd, 2006a). There is a general perception articulated by Rodd (2013, p. 33) that 'the leader's personal qualities have a significant impact on followers because they affect a leader's general approach to people and goals'. However, recent research exploring the qualities of EC leaders is difficult to locate.
- *Leadership growth*: The nature versus nurture debate on leadership suggests that some believe leaders are born while others favour the belief that with training and experience anyone can become a leader. These beliefs are not mutually exclusive. Research in the 1990s (Hayden, 1996; Rodd, 1997) shows clearly that those appointed as centre directors in the past had little or no specific training in management and leadership. Today, leadership and management units are mandated in initial EC teacher education degree courses, and there are lots of professional development programs available on leadership skill preparation. The impact of these training opportunities on leadership practice has not yet been fully explored by contemporary research.
- *Leadership silences on matters of culture, class, gender and sexual identities of EC educators*: Although more women than men are employed in the EC sector, the implications of women leading women (or men) has not been researched to date. There is also little or no research on the extent to which staffing arrangements in EC workplaces reflect the

ethnically diverse communities they are located in and what impact this could have on organisational leadership. Similarly, variability of leadership according to an employee's socio-economic status, relative to education and income, also requires investigation. Anecdotal evidence indicates that there are informal divisions among educators working in a single centre on the basis of who has university or vocational education qualifications. Absence of a recognised career path with adequate financial remuneration matching the level of qualifications achieved can also exacerbate tensions within a staff team.

Pause–reflect–act 1.3

Read the story of Leela and her family and reflect on the questions below.

> Leela's mum came to your long day care centre through a government initiative aimed at helping single parents to find paid employment. Leela is nine months old. She has two older siblings at school. It has been two years since the family escaped from the political unrest and violence in their homeland. Leela's mum wanted to find a job so that she could provide for her children. She had not used centre-based EC programs with her older children and was finding it difficult to be separated from Leela, her new baby. When you explained Leela's family context to the staff in the baby room at your centre, they were also anxious about their responsibilities in caring for Leela.

- As a leader, how will you use your leadership skills and understandings to respond to Leela and her family, and to the concerns of the centre staff?
- Which leadership qualities can you use to demonstrate empathy towards families with complex challenges?
- Write a profile of your ideal leader, identifying their key roles and responsibilities. Which of these will you use when working with your colleagues?
- You can revisit these reflections after finishing this book or on completion of your studies to see how this profile might be revised in light of your new understandings about intentional leaders.

Theorising EC leadership

Rodd (2013, pp. 45–60) provides a potted history of the grand theories influencing the development of theorising EC leadership. More specifically, those such as Bloom (2003), Hayden (1996) and Ebbeck and Waniganayake (2004) have used business studies and school leadership literature by Sergiovanni (1984) and Harris (2009) respectively, to explore the nature of leadership within the EC sector. Despite the contextual differences between these disciplines, Mujis et al. (2004) concur that there is much to be gained from active collaboration in researching and theorising across discipline boundaries. More than a decade ago, these authors also claimed that theorising about EC leadership 'is limited' (p.159). There is, however, a growing body of literature showing a healthy progression in theorising EC leadership, aligned closely with the changing nature of EC practice. In appraising the conceptual landscape to date, Nicholson and Maniates (2016) identified four shifts in theorising EC leadership as follows:

- *Leadership as positional authority*: those employed as centre directors have traditionally followed a 'command-and-lead' approach based on job title and position within the organisation. As such, decision-making was hierarchically driven with the final authority vested at the top levels. Effectively, this approach 'positioned leaders as managers' (Nicholson & Maniates, 2016, p. 70) and the resulting confusion between leadership and management responsibilities continue to present problems today.
- *Leadership as specialist knowledge*: Kagan and Bowman (1997) introduced the notion of specialisation in their five faces of leadership by focusing on a specific area such as pedagogy, community, and advocacy, as explained in chapter 15. Others have expanded these specialisations, and Nicholson and Maniates (2016, p. 71) assert that expanding 'the boundaries of what is recognised as leadership in our field' has enabled the development of leadership as 'a more inclusive construct'.
- *Leadership as distributed and relational*: conceptualisations of distributed ways of leading EC settings emerged in the 2000s and were perceived as being reflective of the collaborative ethos of EC settings. According to Rodd (2013, p. 48) 'distributed leadership theory falls broadly under the category of transformational leadership', and given its popularity today, this discussion is expanded below.
- *Leadership as continual negotiation of uncertainties*: expanding responsibilities and increasing complexities of contemporary leadership work, does not always fit within linear logical ways of enacting leadership. Calls by those such as Davis, Krieg and Smith (2015), and Murray and McDowall Clark (2013) for alternative perspectives that can deal with ambiguities, tensions and uncertainties are pushing the theorisation of EC leadership through poststructuralist lenses.

This brief overview reflects how EC leadership theorising has moved from the privileged positioning of one individual as a leader to a more inclusive socially constructed phenomenon, embedded within the practice of leadership. Opportunities for collaboration are emerging in the examination of distributed leadership approaches and are beginning to attract the interest of diverse EC scholars. Within a distributed frame of reference, leadership activity is dispersed over different aspects of a particular organisation, system or situation (Harris, 2009). The process of leadership decision-making thereby moves beyond a single leader to a group, conceptualised in a way that is meaningful at the local context of each setting. The way in which individuals implement distributed leadership may be described along **spheres of influence** reflective of the professional boundaries based on an area of expertise or authority

spheres of influence
reflect how leadership enactment can inspire and impact others. Within an organisation, leadership responsibilities may be formally defined in individual staff job descriptions. Individuals may also influence others through inspiration, encouragement and/or by demonstrating leadership informally in everyday work.

and control the leader may have, and therefore be able to inspire and impact the work of other educators within the same organisation. Within distributed leadership theorising there are, however, no set limits about the 'openness of the boundaries of leadership' (Bennett et al., 2003, p. 7) and in any one setting there could be any number of leaders. Heikka, Waniganayake and Hujala (2013) also discuss how distributed leadership approaches placed emphasis on leadership practice rather than on leadership roles being performed by various individuals. Accordingly, when reflecting on staff interactions, as stated by Harris and Spillane (2008, p. 33) 'it is the nature and quality of leadership practice that matters'. As can be seen, this reinforces the shift in focusing leadership analysis away from the individual, to the structures and processes of enacting leadership.

Discussions about distributed leadership began appearing in EC literature in the 2000s (Aubrey, 2007; Ebbeck & Waniganayake, 2004; Fasoli et al., 2007; Mujis et al., 2004; Rodd, 2006a). The conceptual model of distributed leadership initially developed by Waniganayake (2000, cited in Ebbeck & Waniganayake, 2004) advocated the centrality of knowledge-based leadership. The underlying aim of this model was to facilitate leadership in areas in which the leader is knowledgeable and competent and therefore able to guide decision-making in an informed manner. Essentially, distributed leadership 'reflects a participatory and decentralized approach to leadership' and it 'relies on building relationships' as well as 'team work' (Ebbeck & Waniganayake, 2004, p. 35). As such, it represents a flatter organisational structure where leadership responsibilities are shared among multiple stakeholders located at different levels of the organisation. Within this framework, the effectiveness of leadership is reliant on the nature of interactivity between people, places and positions, and the creation of interdependency within the organisation. Thus, Harris (2013, p. 12) explains this as 'leadership that is shared within, between and across organisations'.

Due to misconceptions arising from the popularity of this approach, Harris and De Flaminis (2016, p. 144) were moved to declare that 'distributed leadership does not imply that everyone is a leader or that everyone leads'. They also assert that there is no blueprint or roadmap on distributed leadership that could be applied universally. In addition, they caution against the naivety of presuming that 'any form of distributed leadership practice is inherently good or automatically associated with positive outcomes' (p. 143). In declaring that 'distributed leadership is not automatically democratic', Woods and Woods (2013, p. 3) also call for a deeper level of exploration to 'address issues of purpose and power' (p. 16) in the application of distributed leadership. As in every case of leadership enactment, the demonstration of ethical practice must be assessed locally where the impact is felt deeply. Overall, the potential value of distributed leadership approaches rests on developing a collaborative organisational culture where there is a sense of trust and organisational cohesion.

Much of the evidence on distributed leadership, however, draws on research conducted in schools (Harris, 2008; 2009; Spillane, 2006; Tian et al., 2015; Torrance, 2013). Therefore, it is difficult to know the extent to which these findings can be applied to EC settings which are more likely to be driven by a play-based pedagogy and curriculum. In contextualising distributed leadership within EC education, Heikka, Waniganayake and Hujala (2013, p. 39) highlighted the need 'to ensure that the difficulties encountered by school leadership scholars are minimized or eliminated' in seeking conceptual clarity. Research on distributed approaches applied within EC settings, however, demonstrate the complexities of this task (Colmer, 2016a; Heikka & Hujala, 2013; Kangas, Venninen & Ojala, 2015). This work is also expanding as hybrid models such as the conceptualisation of distributed pedagogical leadership by Heikka (2014) through its application in Finnish EC settings. Likewise, in exploring pedagogical leadership in EC settings in New Zealand, participants 'found sense in third generation activity theory as a tool for understanding the centre as a system collectively focused on the achievement of shared objects (or tasks), rather than as a collection of individuals'. (Ord et al., 2013, p. xi). This section by no means provides a comprehensive review of relevant research on distributed leadership, but is sufficient to illustrate emerging research focusing exclusively on the work of leaders in the EC sector.

Pause–reflect–act 1.4

Do you agree or disagree with each of the following statements? Give two or three reasons to support your view.

- Not everyone can teach or lead.
- You can be an excellent teacher and be a poor leader.
- There can be more than one leader in an EC centre.

In your reflections consider possible prerequisites for distributing leadership within an EC setting.

Elements of leadership activity

There is a large body of research evidence (see, for example, Aubrey, 2011; McCrea, 2015; Rodd, 2013) to support the notion that leadership is multifaceted and can evolve over time. Based on this knowledge base, the implementation of leadership in professional work can be examined by looking at how three basic elements, comprising the *person*, the *place* and the *position*, come together, as shown in Figure 1.1.

- *The person*: People involved in leadership work are shaped by their personality as well as their beliefs, values and attitudes about leadership. Likewise, an individual's demographic features such as their age, sex, ethnicity and family background—as well as their professional qualifications, skills and experience in the sector—can also influence their demonstration of leadership. By being aware of their strengths and weaknesses, and by taking steps to purposefully engage in learning continuously, intentional leaders strengthen their leadership capabilities from a long-term perspective.
- *The place*: This is the professional setting where leadership is being implemented. Organisational characteristics such as its size, the number of staff employed, the children and families attending the centre, its age and history of establishment, its

Figure 1.1 Leadership elements

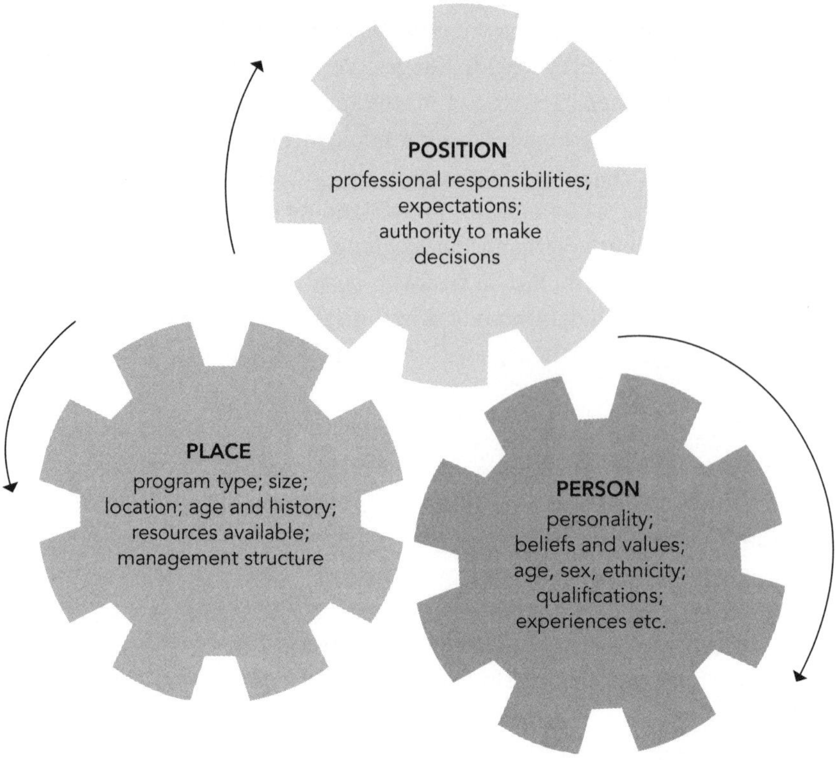

location (for example, being one of three centres at a university campus), the resources available and its ownership or management can all contribute to how leadership is practised in a particular setting. These organisational elements impede or advance the nature of relationships among the people at the setting, both children and adults, and thereby impact on the organisational culture that is being created and the quality of programs being implemented.

- *The position*: This refers to the formal authority and responsibilities allocated to a leader within an organisational setting. Sometimes described as the span of influence, the extent of leadership authority an individual may have in making professional decisions can be built into their job description. In this way, expectations of leaders may be defined either broadly or specifically and used to assess their effectiveness in carrying out their job. In Australia, under the National Quality Standard within Quality Area 7, for example, there is an expectation that staff performance will be regularly evaluated using an individual development plan (ACECQA, 2017, np).

chapter 4 looks at connections between governance and leadership within EC settings.

When implementing leadership, consider the integration of the three elements of the person, the place and the position. It is, however, difficult to predict whether a particular one or two of these elements will be more important when enacting leadership. For example, it is possible that anyone can demonstrate leadership informally or without an official position, such as when an unexpected situation arises where someone needs to step into the role of a leader. In these circumstances, the individual's personal characteristics, as well as the setting, timing and other people involved in the situation requiring leadership, can influence what actually happens and what decisions are made by the leader. Overall, the extent to which both formal and informal leadership is recognised, valued and fostered is dependent on both the individuals and the characteristics of the organisation.

Pause–reflect–act 1.5

Thinking about your own experiences of leadership, apply the three elements of the person, the place and the position to analyse what happened during a particular situation where leadership was demonstrated.

- Draw a diagram identifying the particular characteristics of each of the three elements that applied in this situation.
- Reflect on how these three elements came together (or not) in demonstrating leadership.
- Reflect on the factors that contribute to how leadership is understood and practised in EC settings.

Pivotal role of leadership in EC settings

It has long been argued that EC leaders play a pivotal role in EC settings (Bloom & Sheerer, 1992; Ebbeck & Waniganayake, 2004; Nupponen, 2006b; Rodd, 1994). An accumulating body of empirical evidence has continued to support this view, demonstrating the value-added benefit of having effective leaders in EC settings (Lower & Cassidy, 2007; OECD, 2015; Rodd, 2013; Sylva et al., 2004b). Collectively, these studies show that leadership can positively impact on the quality of the centre as a workplace, the quality of education provided and the developmental outcomes achieved by children over time.

as discussed in chapters 5 and 8, ethical entrepreneurship is an essential component in today's EC settings.

To date, there has been no specific longitudinal research on studying the impact of effective leadership in EC settings. However, the renowned 'Effective Provision of Preschool Education' (EPPE) study in the UK (Sylva et al., 2004b) is a longitudinal study that investigated the impact of participation in formal EC settings on the development of children aged three to seven years. Its findings suggest that strong leadership was a key characteristic of EC centres providing effective programs. In this study, centre quality correlated with the leader's EC qualifications: the higher the qualification the more effective the leader and the higher the quality of education provided. As such, this research affirmed that educators with a university degree in EC can be effective leaders.

turn to chapters 7, 8, 11 and 12 for a discussion of the importance of advocacy in EC education.

Pause–reflect–act 1.6

From your observations and professional experiences as a student and/or educator in EC settings, identify examples that show:

- connections between effective leadership and program quality
- how educators in leadership positions demonstrate effective leadership
- how respect for diversity is being reflected in leadership work.

Consider the extent to which your observations and experiences reflect the research findings on leadership. Refer to the references cited in this book for some appropriate readings. Identify potential gaps in the research, and develop questions that you may want to pursue as a researcher.

A focused discussion on professional growth is also presented in chapter 15.

There is now sufficient research (Aubrey, 2011; Bretherton, 2010; Colmer, 2016a; Rodd, 2013; Sylva et al., 2004b) conducted in various countries to show that leadership manifests in a clear vision and philosophy that is shared by all staff; curriculum development with a strong educational focus; opportunities for continuous **professional growth**; clear policies and procedures; and program innovation. These aspects can influence quality provision directly, as well as indirectly, as reflected in staff retention and enhanced job satisfaction. In Australia, in the *Guide to the National Quality Standard* (ACECQA, 2011c), for instance, leadership is one of seven quality areas used to accredit EC settings for quality purposes. In this way, leadership is endorsed as a professional responsibility of educators, demonstrating a clear alignment between research, policy and practice.

professional growth
educators can continue to develop their capacity to lead through participation in a range of professional activities and support, as discussed throughout this book.

In the *Guide to the National Quality Standard* (ACECQA, 2011c, p. 171), the pivotal role of leadership is defined in the following manner:

- creation of a positive organisational culture
- having an in-depth understanding and knowledge of EC learning and development
- empowerment of others
- adaptability to change and fostering continuous improvement
- establishment of a skilled and engaged workforce.

In keeping with this approach of linking leadership with professional responsibilities, this book also embraces the challenges of reframing EC leadership 'as sustainable professionalism' as discussed by Fasoli et al. (2007, p. 244). This means adopting a long-term perspective whereby intentional leaders demonstrate how they

> carefully seek out and allow key common issues to come into focus. Often what then becomes important is not an immediate fix to solve the problems, but a new way of thinking about the problem. This approach tends to generate new kinds of questions which lead to new kinds of actions never before imagined within bounded communities. (Fasoli et al., 2007, p. 244)

Accordingly, the content covered in this book aims to contribute to the process of generating new leaders in EC who will embrace the challenges of the twenty-first century with confidence, courage, optimism, compassion and resiliency.

In the absence of a prescribed list of agreed leadership functions, key roles and responsibilities of leaders in EC settings are defined locally, and this is considered appropriate given the contextual nature of leadership enactment. Importantly, responsibility for pedagogical planning and development—as well as program or curriculum implementation—are the core functions that require specialist expertise in EC education. Managing and supporting staff is only one aspect of the overall centre administration and requires oversight by leaders on a day-to-day basis. This work also includes budgeting and business plans, as well as broader strategic planning for the future. Inclusion of support for staff professional learning and development is a critical component of these plans. The placement of advocacy and activism functions that relate to external relationships has been an integral component of the work of EC professionals over time (Ebbeck & Waniganayake, 2004). These functions involve external stakeholders such as educators working at other centres, health professionals who work with young children and people in the wider community. Advocacy and activism, however, are at risk because of the lack of time due to the increasing demands on EC leaders to focus more on accountability, quality assurance and the internal operational matters of their EC settings.

Within Australia, concerned about the potential loss of professional autonomy through compliance based practices, Sims and Waniganayake (2015) call on EC educators and leaders to resist by rethinking the purpose of education, by asking critical questions and by facilitating dialogue that can transform leadership practice. In cultivating new ways of leading in EC, it is also no longer a matter of needing 'more' leaders because we must also seek 'more kinds of leadership' (Kagan & Hallmark, 2001) that reflect the diverse challenges encountered within our communities.

Leadership and ethics

Being an intentional leader is more than just performing the responsibilities specified in a job statement. A manager may be expected to focus on the staff and the regulatory responsibilities that impact on the day-to-day activities of the centre. A leader, on the other hand, is a visionary, and is therefore expected to be future oriented. Typically, these characteristics may be reflected in the philosophy and strategic directions of the centre. Adoption of ethical practices that align with research showing strong links between quality outcomes for children by employing well-qualified educators, for example, sits well with an intentional leader who believes in prioritising their work in the best interests of the children.

Focusing on leadership within schools, Duignan (2006) argues that 'educational leaders have an ethical responsibility to optimise learning opportunities and outcomes for their students by helping create organisational learning environments that are visionary, authentic, ethical, strategic, people-centred and motivational' (p. 7). This notion of ethical leadership has been explored more widely by researchers such as Schminke, Ambrose and Neubaum (2005), who suggest that leaders influence the ethical culture of the organisation. More specifically, their research found that this influence is related to the leader's ability to transfer moral reasoning into actions. In organisations where the moral perspectives of the leader and other staff did not match, there were higher levels of employee dissatisfaction and higher staff turnover. Leaders who express ideas in relation to morality reflect deep engagement with community values, beliefs and ideals which may manifest as leadership duties and obligations (Sergiovanni, 1992). In this way, consciously and deliberately, intentional leaders create and reinforce an organisational culture centred on learning and collaboration with children and their families.

Being an ethical leader means taking a stand and explaining the reasons that underpin your decisions, based on a consideration of prevailing community values and beliefs about a particular issue. This is not always easy, as seen in Pause–reflect–act 1.7.

Pause–reflect–act 1.7

Almost daily, you will receive pamphlets and brochures from businesses interested in securing a market for their products through the staff and families at your centre. Some advertisements offer a percentage of income from the sales generated through your centre. Over time, these sales can provide a steady income for your centre to pay for support staff and additional resources. Some parents are critical that selling chocolates, for example, contradicts the nutritious food policy of the centre. Other parents have commented that it is not appropriate to support certain companies they deem unethical; and others felt that staff were spending too much time administering these promotions. In response to community criticism, you have at least four options to consider as a way forward:

- Option 1: Stop all advertising—no longer allow business promotion as a revenue raiser.
- Option 2: Allow some advertising by carefully selecting the businesses on a case-by-case basis.
- Option 3: Allow some advertising by creating an annual list of preferred businesses.
- Option 4: Allow all advertising without any limits.

Define the ethical issues and underlying values that are presented in each option.

As an intentional leader, consider the consequences of each option for the centre and select the option you will adopt. Give your reasons.

In an increasingly market-oriented workplace, leaders are expected to deliver productivity through efficiency, assessed typically through financial measures. Intentional leaders, however, seek to

> strike a proper balance between performance management and creating conditions for efficacy in the workplace. Inspiring the commitment of people at all levels of education to the core task of learning is a high moral purpose that distinguishes leadership and management in education from that in other fields. (Oldroyd, 2005, p. 206)

There have been significant advances in the knowledge base of EC education, and the professional status of educators has moved on from being merely 'nice ladies who love children' (Stonehouse, 1989) to becoming dynamic and vibrant leaders (Rodd, 2013). Moreover, as Fasoli et al. (2007, p. 244) have noted, consideration of distributed approaches to leadership in EC is enabling a shift in thinking 'about what it means to be a professional away from being an expert and towards being an agent or facilitator of change'. As such, it is important that intentional leaders take the time to reflect and understand existing approaches to EC practice, theories, research and policy so that they may move forward with wisdom and courage, as will be discussed in more detail in the chapters that follow.

Hard and Jónsdóttir (2013, p. 321) have also noted that a culture of teamwork or collaboration does not guarantee or reflect equity or fair play, and instead could reinforce an institutionalised pattern of negative behaviour where some educators were 'being marginalised by one's peers' (ibid.) for standing out from the crowd. There is also no point denying either the power of those who hold a position of leadership or the potential danger of abusing positional power or esteem within the sector or within individual EC settings. Solutions to these challenges can be found, both as individuals and collectively, by taking action to demonstrate one's commitment to inclusion, equity and justice in EC settings. More research is also urgently needed to better understand relationships between staff, leaders and management, and the use of power, privilege and authority within EC settings. Importantly, it is anticipated that an intentional leader '[will] be inclusive; [will] learn from others; doesn't always have the answers and solutions; listens to and with others; [and] places ethics at the core of their work' (Davis, Krieg & Smith, 2015, p. 144).

In this way, intentional leaders demonstrate their capacity to contribute to community building by remaining focused on nurturing the best interests of the next generation of citizens. There is, however, much to learn yet about EC leadership in theory and in practice. The main aim of this book is to engage readers in a continuing dialogue, through active reflection, to seek better ways of conceptualising and advancing leadership in EC as appropriate for the twenty-first century.

Pause–reflect–act 1.8

- While reading this chapter, what questions about EC leadership emerged for you? When reading the subsequent chapters in this book, consider whether we have addressed these questions.
- Using the 'Key references' list at the end of this chapter and networking with other leaders from diverse contexts, including other professional backgrounds, may also assist you to engage more deeply in the content we have covered in this book.

Chapter summary

This chapter introduced leadership contexts through an examination of contemporary understandings found in scholarly publications based on leadership in schools and EC settings. It also provided an orientation to the notion of intentional leadership that frames the content covered in this book. It explained how leadership as a professional responsibility of educators has been endorsed by government policy in Australia. By providing an orientation to existing theory and research-based knowledge on EC leadership, this book aims to contribute new understandings of EC leadership relevant for new leaders in the twenty-first century.

Key references

Aubrey, C. (2011). *Leading and managing in the early years*. (2nd ed.). London: Sage Publications.

This book explores EC leadership concepts and characteristics based on a study involving early years leaders in the UK. It contains research instruments that may be of assistance to those interested in designing leadership studies in the future.

Harris, A. (2009). *Distributed school leadership: Evidence, issues and future directions*. Sydney: Australian Council of Educational Leaders.

In this brief monograph, Harris synthesises evidence on distributed leadership as applied within school settings. It provides a useful introduction to the concept of distributed leadership and introduces some of the key scholars who write about distributed leadership.

Nicholson, J. & Maniates, H. (2016). Recognising postmodern intersectional identities in leadership for early childhood. *Early Years: An International Research Journal*. 36(1), 66–80. doi:10.1080/09575146.2015.1080667.

In scoping the conceptual landscape of theorising EC leadership, these authors make a strong case for developing postmodern theorising by linking professional identity and leadership development.

Rodd, J. (2013). *Leadership in early childhood* (4th ed.). Crows Nest: Allen & Unwin.

First published in 1994, this fourth edition includes research on contemporary concerns such as working in multidisciplinary teams, mentoring and coaching. This is an essential text, written by a key pioneer in EC research on leadership, providing a comprehensive coverage of pertinent content.

2 THE AUSTRALIAN POLICY CONTEXT

CHAPTER LEARNING OBJECTIVES

After studying this chapter you will understand that:

- Australian EC policy is driven by a complex range of socio-political issues, both domestic and international.
- EC education is political and leaders require a sound knowledge of the socio-political context of teaching.
- Policy in the EC sector is influenced by a range of professional disciplines including education, health and welfare.
- EC teachers are leaders and advocates within this broad context with the capacity to influence policy reform.

Key concepts

Australian Constitution	policy
politics	productivity agenda

Overview

The EC context in Australia is characterised by a diversity of settings responding to an ever-changing socio-political landscape. Of significance in the Australian context is a political system framed by three tiers of government, including eight separate state and territory jurisdictions, all of which have some involvement in the provision of EC programs. This situation contributes significantly to a complex policy environment with often disparate approaches to funding, regulation and accountability. The continuing growth of commercial for-profit services along with an increasing interest in the early years by charities and welfare agencies has seen a range of new players establish themselves in the EC landscape, bringing new governance structures and challenges to the policy framework.

The introduction of Australia's National Quality Framework (NQF) has been an attempt to streamline some of this complexity and strive for a national system that is consistent for children and families across all jurisdictions. The complexity of establishing a nationally consistent framework for EC education and care cannot be underestimated. Australia is the only country in the world to date to attempt to bring together this number of separate jurisdictions into one cohesive national quality framework for EC.

Largely prompted by an increasing international interest in the early years and Australia's poor ratings on a number of international benchmarking reports, Australia has reconsidered its policy approach to EC provision. Along with this has been a reinvigoration in commitment to reconciliation and an imperative to be more inclusive of Aboriginal and Torres Strait Islander perspectives across all policy areas.

Since the announcement of the EC reform agenda in 2007 and the introduction of the National Quality Framework in 2012, Australia has experienced somewhat unprecedented political changes. There have been multiple changes of government, and a number of changes in the prime minister and senior ministers responsible for education. Over the past decade, the Early Childhood Education and Care (ECEC) portfolio has seen a number of reports and inquiries as well as ongoing attempts to amend the complex system of funding and support to Australian families. This chapter provides a contextual overview of the policy landscape to assist the reader in better understanding the complexity and links between broad social policy agendas and the day-to-day leadership of EC settings.

Why do I need to know about politics?

politics
is the art and science of government; affairs of the state and civics.

policy
is a statement of intent that can guide decision-makers about how to direct resources to achieve an intended outcome. Policy also reflects the political ideology and beliefs of the group with power to make decisions.

The study of leadership and management is now an integral part of most EC teacher preparation programs. A common question asked by many students studying EC education is why they need to study **politics** and **policy**. What does this have to do with being a teacher? Why am I expected to know about government and political issues? These questions typically end with the remark, 'I hate politics!'

Indeed, even when practising as managers and leaders in an EC setting, politics and policy can seem peripheral to an educator's day-to-day practices and responsibilities. This chapter addresses these questions and concerns, and provides a contextual backdrop to the work of EC leaders. The chapter provides information to pique readers' interest in the broader context of education within a political agenda and empowers EC leaders to be informed advocates for children, families and themselves.

It was the Brazilian educator and theorist Paulo Freire who proclaimed that teaching is a political act. His interest in social justice and his publication *Pedagogy of the Oppressed* (1972) considered the way in which power and politics shapes experience and often life outcomes according to the philosophical positions of those with power to make decisions about education. The Australian policy context influences just about everything relating to teaching and learning in EC settings. Governments determine the level of qualification a teacher or educator needs; they can establish Acts of parliament and standards to 'ensure' quality; and they influence what children will and won't learn, through curriculum documents and the articulation of learning outcomes. Government policies also have a bearing on which children access which EC services.

Teachers need to understand the intent and extent of all legislation and policy affecting their work and critically examine policy requirements in the context of their own EC setting. In addition, knowledge of the policy framework enables teachers to contribute their understandings of the EC context when policy is being reviewed or reformed. In a democracy such as Australia, teachers' contributions to government consultations on matters of standards, curriculum or funding are essential to inform governments of the realities of teaching and the experiences of children as they learn. Teachers are also well placed to inform parents of policy issues and agendas, so that they too can contribute to the policy-making process.

What is policy?

Policy is constructed and understood in a range of ways. It is more than simply the decisions of government articulated in a policy document. Bridgman and Davis (2004) explain that 'policy is the instrument of governance, the decisions that direct public resources in one direction but not another. It is the outcomes of the competition between ideas, interests and ideologies that impels our political system' (p. 3). Policies relating to EC are generally covered in the areas of social or public policy. This policy area covers a broad range of government issues including welfare, education and health—in short, the matters that affect the well-being of the population.

Policy can be understood in two ways (see Welch 2010):

- *As text:* the documents that inform educators and leaders about the provisions that are available for children, families and educators. Social policy manifests in different provisions: family payments; legislation; services; funding to services; and information and resources for families and services. Leaders' provision of quality EC programs will be influenced by their knowledge about, access to and use of these provisions.
- *As discourse:* illuminates values and agendas of government—expresses the priorities and the ideological drivers to political decisions about policy. Intentional leaders need to critically engage with policy discourse and consider whose interests are best reflected and how policy might be applied in their local contexts in ways that ensure children's interests are met.

Being a critical reader of policy both as text and as discourse equips leaders to participate in policy debates and act as advocates for the children and families with whom they work.

The Australian context

In any discussion about the history of EC in Australia it is important to acknowledge that Australia's first people—the Aboriginal and Torres Strait Islander people—had successful and sustainable ways of caring for and educating their children that were grounded in the local knowledge of the environment, the transference of important cultural traditions and respect for wise elders and the natural elements. As Martin (2007a) explains, 'Aboriginal worldview is structured in a way that embraces and is expansive of relatedness' (p. 20). Children learnt important life skills and knowledge through this relatedness. While this learning and teaching approach has sustained one of the world's oldest living populations, much damage has been done to the preservation of such knowledge and, along with Australia's rapid population growth through immigration, distinct understandings of Aboriginal and Torres Strait Islander ways have been lost for many. In this era of reconciliation it is important that educators seek to understand Aboriginal and Torres Strait Islander 'ways of knowing'. (For more information about this, go to www.8ways.wikispaces.com and see other resources in the Key references list at the end of this chapter.)

The past 200 or so years have seen Australia shaped by a history of immigration that has resulted in a culturally diverse population. In more recent times, Australia has grappled with global unrest and the increasing numbers of refugee families seeking asylum in Australia.

Policy relating to asylum seeking children and their rights to care and education continue to be a highly contested area of Australian political debate. In addition to these human elements of diversity, the island continent takes in an array of geographic and climatic differences requiring responses to local conditions, an important factor when designing EC programs that can accommodate diverse conditions and needs of communities. Funding schemes for EC programs must take account of the needs of rural and remote communities that do not always fit neatly into streamlined funding models based on urban populations. Once again consider how Australia's diverse landscape, geography and society have contributed to a diversity of EC service provision and funding.

Formalised approaches to EC education and care in Australia began soon after European settlement and are a relatively recent phenomenon. The development of differing service types have emerged in response to changing societal, cultural and economic circumstances. It is important for EC leaders to appreciate the historical context from which current policies have emerged. Knowledge of the historical context contributes to an understanding of where today's leaders have come from and what has been learnt along the way. Such an understanding enables leaders to recognise and contribute conversations that will drive innovation.

Government in Australia

In addition to the historical context, understanding of EC policy requires knowledge of the Australian political system. Australia is known as a constitutional monarchy. This means that Australia remains part of the British Commonwealth but has sovereignty over decisions and rulings vested in the **Australian Constitution** (Commonwealth of Australia, 1900). The Australian Constitution establishes the British monarch (at present Queen Elizabeth II) as the Head of State. The Queen's representative in Australia is the Governor-General. Within a constitutional monarchy, these official positions are appointments rather than elected officials and in the main act as figureheads rather than enacting powers over the nation. The Constitution establishes Australia as a democracy and sets out the structure of Australian governments and requirements for the election of officials who hold power to make laws and set the policy direction for the country.

Australian Constitution establishes the framework of the three main political institutions—the legislature, the executive and the judiciary—the relationships between them, and the powers of the Australian government in relation to the states and territories.

The Australian system of government is fashioned on the British model of dual houses of parliament known as the Westminster system. The lower house, or House of Representatives—also known as the people's house—is made up of individuals elected to represent regions or areas of Australia. They are known as members of parliament or MPs. The political party that holds the majority of seats in this house forms government and leads the country for the elected term. The upper house, or Senate, is also known as the house of review. Members of this house are known as Senators and are elected to represent their state or territory. Legislation must pass through the Senate for review and scrutiny by a rigorous committee system before being returned to the lower house to be adopted as law.

In Australia, legislation can be proposed by any member of parliament and put forward in the form of a bill to be made law. Under this system of laws created by elected members of parliament, the people have the capacity to suggest or recommend legislation. In a democracy, the people also have the opportunity to oppose and recommend changes to legislation. It is this system of government that provides opportunities for professionals such as teachers to have a say, contribute to government consultations and speak out when they have concerns about the impact of legislation on a particular group or individual.

The Australian government system is characterised by three tiers of government: the Australian government, state and territory governments, and local governments (also known as local councils). Each tier of government holds different responsibilities under the Australian Constitution. The Australian government, also known as the Federal or Commonwealth government, has constitutional responsibilities for national issues such as immigration, social security, higher education, foreign trade, social welfare and defence of the nation. The Australian government also collects revenue through the taxation system and distributes funding according to government priorities and policy decisions. The eight federated states and territories have autonomous governments that take responsibility for issues such as school education, health, local infrastructure and law enforcement. The third tier of government is local government. These are established by the state and territory governments and take responsibility for local planning and traffic issues, and the provision of local services such as public libraries and some children's services.

in chapter 7, it is proposed that this advocacy work is integral to the practice of an intentional leader.

Each of the three tiers of government plays some role in the provision of EC education and care services. This has resulted in a complex and multilayered system of EC provision often described as a 'patchwork' (Press, 2006) of services. Historically, the separation of responsibilities across the three tiers of government has resulted in uneven and at times poor distribution of services with significant variation in the quality and availability of programs for young children (Press, 2006). Policies vary from state to state on fundamental issues such as the school starting age, the qualification requirements for those working with young children and the cost to families for various services. Since 2007 the Australian government has taken steps to provide a more consistent national approach to EC education.

the Australian government's approach to quality in EC education is outlined in chapter 3.

Through the Council of Australian Governments (COAG), there has been a concerted effort to nationalise policies for young children in an attempt to ensure a more equitable distribution of good-quality services for all Australian children. COAG is an intergovernmental forum comprising the prime minister, state premiers, territory chief ministers and the president of the Australian Local Government Association (ALGA). Their charter is to address issues of national importance to all Australians. (For more information about COAG go to www.coag.gov.au.)

Pause–reflect–act 2.1

Think about how EC portfolio responsibilities of governments have been arranged. Historically, Australia has separated government responsibility for EC matters between the ministerial portfolios of 'Education', 'Social welfare' and 'Community/Human Services'.

- What do you consider to be the various strengths and weaknesses of locating EC matters in each of these portfolios?

- Reforms initiated since 2007 have seen a shift in responsibility for EC matters to the Education portfolio. What do you think will be the advantages and disadvantages of this move?
- Do you agree/disagree that EC matters should be located within the education portfolio? Give your reasons.

Creating policy from legislation

Once legislation has been passed, the work of enacting the legislation is usually passed to the relevant area of the public service or government department for implementation. In the case of EC this will often be within the ministerial portfolios of Education or Community/Human services. It is the responsibility of the relevant government department to interpret the legislation, allocate funding to achieve the aims of the policy and articulate how the legislation will be realised. It is at this point that governments often initiate consultations with the sector to gather responses and refine policy directions.

Broad-based consultations are generally publicly advertised and call for written responses. At times, more targeted responses are sought from peak children's services organisations. These 'peaks' will often call on their members to contribute field-based views on how a policy might impact on a setting or a region. This is an important time for EC leaders and educators to engage with the opportunity to contribute to the policy development process. Being a member of a peak organisation is a good way to not only contribute to such consultations but also to learn from others about different EC contexts. *In Leaders in practice 2.1, Tonia Godhard AM shares some of her many experiences of involvement in a range of advocacy campaigns. Her work with peak organisations is an example of the effective influence that leaders can have when working with a united voice.*

LEADERS IN PRACTICE 2.1

Tonia Godhard AM

Early Childhood Consultant, Sydney (NSW)

My interest in EC policy and advocacy started soon after I graduated. I was invited to attend an international conference in London, where I planned to work. At this conference I met and heard from people from many nations who were passionate about quality experiences for young children and support for families. I began to develop a better understanding that what I had learnt about and observed in services in Australia was in fact a right of very few young children in the world. Upon my return to Australia I was fortunate to work with a 'master teacher' who mentored me and showed how when working as a teacher in a centre we could be informed about policy and its impact on young children's experiences and teaching in EC settings. This included learning something about the opportunities available for practitioners to play a role in influencing policy and helping those outside the profession, including families, to understand the importance of the early years.

Thus, I became an advocate in my work as a teacher in an EC centre and in my contacts with the local community. I soon realised that if I wanted to be involved in trying to promote better quality services for all young children at the level of government policy then I would need to be a member of a group where members shared similar values. Early in my career I became a member of the Australian Preschool Association, which is now Early Childhood Australia (ECA). This shaped my belief that to be effective in influencing policy, active membership of advocacy groups is an important way to share one's passion with colleagues and to work together over an extended time to achieve commonly held views for change. Over the years a lot of the advocacy work I have been involved with has related to policies which centred on maintaining or improving the quality of education and care services for young children and trying to enable universal access to high-quality services, including making them affordable. Some key things I have learnt from my journey so far include:

- the influence that leaders can have and therefore the need to be well informed about the context in which any change to policy is being sought
- the development of strategic alliances
- the use of multiple strategies in a planned approach to achieving change
- the role of evidence and practitioner wisdom.

The following gives a brief description of some Australian policies that I have been involved with over the years that relate to improving the quality of children's services. I discuss these in relation to two key points I think are important when striving to influence policy. The first is a strategic and planned approach and the second is understanding the context, along with building relationships and alliances.

1 Multiple strategies and a planned approach

It is essential that any policy change that is being sought can be clearly and succinctly expressed even though there is a need for multilayers of information behind the key message. I was a member of a taskforce set up by the New South Wales government to make recommendations around a change from a one-to-five ratio of staff for under two year olds to a one-to-four ratio. The report with recommendations was completed but included a minority report from one member of the taskforce. The members involved in the majority report agreed that a further campaign was required so the matter did not slide off the government agenda. Community Child Care Co-operative (NSW) took on a facilitating role and established a planning group with a commitment to the change. This not only reduced the workload of an already very busy group of people, but enabled the sharing of strengths and interests. Some people had important media contacts, others were happy to speak to the media and others could work on keeping practitioners involved and informed. There were meetings with the minister, the opposition and senior bureaucrats. Strategies to raise the profile of the campaign included a march to Parliament House, and extensive use of the media including press releases, appearances on television and radio, and stories in local and state-wide newspapers. The slogan 'one to four make it law' was catchy and an easy message to then explain and to use in gaining publicity.

2 Context, relationships, strategic alliances and evidence

In 2013, the Productivity Commission was asked by the Commonwealth government to undertake an Inquiry into Child Care and Early Learning. The inquiry had a number of objectives including examining and identifying future options for:

- childcare and early learning that supports the workforce participation particularly of women
- a system that addresses children's learning and development needs
- a system that has financially sustainable funding arrangements to support more flexible, affordable and accessible quality childcare and EC learning.

The EC sector, after becoming aware of the inquiry, was first involved in reading an Issues Paper circulated by the Productivity Commission, which made it clear that consultation was an essential part of the process, including written submissions to the issues paper and later to a draft report, attending public hearings and providing evidence. The sector was quick to recognise the need to work together to develop common positions where possible and to assist each other in providing evidence to support positions being put forward. All major advocacy groups had it on their agenda, and strategic alliances were formed to work together first in identifying common principles that needed to be promoted and argued for by all groups in such a wide ranging inquiry.

As the process proceeded, it became apparent where the greatest threats to the rights of children and the quality of services lay. One of these was a threat to the requirement to have qualified staff working with under two year olds in services with little or no recognition of the importance of a planned program. The minister had said in a forum attended by many national and state-wide advocacy groups that training was not required and lots of grandparents would love to work with this age group. This was then followed by an interim report from the Productivity Commission saying there was a lack of evidence to support a requirement for qualified staff to work with this age group and in particular EC teachers.

The strategic alliances that had been formed then worked on responding through written submissions, giving evidence at hearings and at individual meetings with members of the commission. Help was sought from academics and others who were researching in this area and who were familiar with the research evidence. They also put in submissions and attended and gave evidence at public hearings. It was acknowledged that the input of other disciplines was essential, so forums were organised and commission members were invited to hear the views of a wide range of professionals with expertise in areas including economics, health, political science and social policy. At the same time, services were also involved in advocacy informed by the peak group of which they were a member.

It sounds simple, but the reality of change is that it is a complex process and as an individual you are listening to a diversity of views. Gaining consensus to move forward as a group requires pragmatism, and a willingness to compromise while learning from the views of others. For me, the test was, 'Will what we are arguing for be in the best interests of young children?'

Pause–reflect–act 2.2

- It is sometimes difficult to see how a new graduate teacher might contribute to the broader policy context. What are some of the key ways you can begin to build your confidence and engagement in higher level policy agendas?
- Tonia speaks of the importance of strategic alliances. What other areas of education, or family and community services, do you think might make good strategic partners?
- What might EC teachers need to know or understand if they are to be seen as valuable contributors to multi-disciplinary strategic partnerships?

Policy in the EC context

The Australian EC sector is characterised by a diversity of service types with a mixed market provision. Influenced strongly by the experiences of Britain, Australian EC settings were fashioned on either the nursery school model or the day nursery model (Moss & Pence, 1994). The nursery schools generally catered for children aged three to five years and were designed as a preparation for full-time school. The day nursery model was generally aimed at children whose parents were in the paid workforce. These settings traditionally focused on the health, welfare and care of children. In contemporary Australia we now see a melding of these two models along with the introduction of other service types such as family day care and occasional care.

There do, however, remain deeply entrenched, and at times artificial, demarcations between service types that have been brought about largely by the differing responsibilities of the three tiers of government and the shifting priorities of the eight state and territory jurisdictions. This has resulted in uneven funding arrangements and inconsistent requirements for the qualifications of staff who work with young children. These damaging demarcations are continuously debated and there have been many attempts to break down these barriers, which often find EC services competing against each other for available funds or promoting the worthiness of one service type over another. Despite the intent of the NQF to bring a more nationally consistent approach to EC provision, it remains the case that a child's experience in an Australian EC setting, the hours they will spend in the setting and the qualifications of the staff they will come into contact with, is more dependent on their parents' paid employment status than a policy commitment to what is in the best interests of children.

EC settings

The EC years in Australia are generally understood to cover the period from birth to age eight. During this period, children will likely engage with a range of different service types that include various prior-to-school and full-time school settings. As mentioned previously, this range of service types has emerged over time in response to social change and political agendas. It is not unusual for children in Australia to experience a number of transitions from one service type to another in their first eight years of life. Currently, each state and territory has a different policy on school starting age and parents are given considerable choice in many jurisdictions to determine the best time for their child to begin full-time school. Generally speaking children in Australia start full-time school somewhere between their fourth and sixth birthday. In the year prior to starting full-time school, each child can access 15 hours each week of a preschool program, for a maximum 40 weeks of the year. This program, known as 'universal access', is supported by government but is not necessarily free, nor is it compulsory (Australian Government, Department of Education and Training, 2016). The program can be delivered in a range of EC settings and must be delivered by a university qualified EC teacher.

Children under the age of four years usually access service types such as long day care, family day care or occasional care. The following table provides a profile of the main types of EC prior to school settings that can be found across Australia. Table 2.1 reveals the complexity of the Australian EC program mix.

Historical decisions and multi-jurisdictional input mean that the context of EC settings in Australia is quite difficult to navigate. The OECD report *Starting strong II* (2006), recognised this complexity in the Australian system. Among its general recommendations was the need for a national policy approach with a centralised ministry with responsibility for EC policy to overcome the difficulties of such a disparate system. Australia's response to this recommendation was in part recognised by initiating the National Quality Framework (NQF) and establishing a national body—The Australian Children's Education and Care Quality Authority (ACECQA)—to oversee its implementation (Cheeseman & Torr, 2009).

Why are governments involved in EC?

The education and care of young children is increasingly viewed in Australia as a shared responsibility between the family and the state. While the rearing of young children is primarily considered the private responsibility of the family, governments are increasingly motivated to be actively involved in funding and monitoring the provision of services for young children and their families. The impact of involvement in EC programs goes far beyond the personal gain to each child and family. Governments invest in EC because this contributes to:

- *increased workforce participation:* and therefore greater economic returns for the country
- *a more educated future workforce:* the importance of good experiences in EC is now well recognised as contributing to positive life outcomes
- *prevention:* early intervention and compensatory programs that fill gaps in what the family might be able to provide are recognised as preventing later problems such as social dysfunction, substance abuse and incarceration
- *the reproduction of cultural values:* perhaps previously the role of the extended family and church, the EC setting can contribute to developing a spirit of community and citizenry (Dahlberg, Moss & Pence, 2007).

Table 2.1 Types of EC settings in Australia

Type	Description
Long day care	Long day care (LDC) is a centre-based form of childcare service. LDC services provide all-day or part-time education and care for children aged birth to six years who attend the centre on a regular basis. Centres typically operate between 7.30 am and 6 pm Monday to Friday for 48 weeks per year so that parents can manage both the care of their children and the demands of their paid employment. LDC centres are required to deliver an educational program for children. Centres are run by private companies, local councils, community organisations, individuals, non-profit organisations or by employers for their staff.
Preschool/Kindergarten	Preschool is a planned sessional educational program primarily aimed at children three to five years of age prior to commencing full-time schooling. Preschool programs are usually play-based educational programs designed and delivered by a degree-qualified EC teacher. Operating hours are comparable with schools, generally being 9 am to 3 pm during school terms. All states and territories provide funding for eligible children to access a preschool program in the year prior to school entry. In Tasmania, Victoria, Western Australia and Queensland, the preschool year is known as kindergarten. Preschools are located at government and non-government school sites or local community venues. Many long day care settings incorporate a preschool program.
Family day care	Family day care (FDC) is where an educator provides education and care in their own home for other people's children. FDC is aimed at children aged from birth to six years who are not yet at school, but may also be provided for school-aged children. Educators can provide care for the whole day, part of the day, or irregular or casual care. In many states and territories, these educators are required to be registered with an FDC scheme. An FDC scheme supports and administers a network of educators by monitoring the standard of care provided and providing professional advice. In some states and territories, FDC educators may operate independently of a scheme.
Outside school hours care	Outside school hours care (OSHC, also known as out of school hours care, OOSH) programs provide recreational activities and care for primary school aged children (typically aged five to 12 years). They are available during, before and after school hours, during school holidays (vacation care) and on student-free days when the school is closed to enable all teachers to participate in professional development work. OSHC settings are usually provided from primary school premises such as the school hall and/or playground. They may also be located in childcare centres, community facilities or other OSHC centres located near the primary school. These programs are often provided by parent associations or not-for-profit organisations.

Occasional care
Occasional care is a centre-based childcare program catering for children aged from birth to five years who attend on an hourly or sessional basis for short periods or at irregular intervals. This type of setting is used by parents who do not need childcare on a regular basis but would like someone to look after their child occasionally; for example, if they have to attend a medical appointment or take care of personal matters. Occasional care is often provided as a stand-alone service, within LDC settings or preschools, at sport and leisure centres, and at shopping centres. Occasional care is sometimes referred to as crèche.
Multifunction Aboriginal Children's Services (MACS)
These services were established in recognition of the fact that many Aboriginal children do not participate in mainstream EC programs. MACS provide opportunities for local communities to design and operate their own culturally appropriate EC settings. A range of health and social welfare programs are often incorporated into the service delivery at these settings.
Mobile children's services
These services can provide preschool or long day care programs. Staff usually travel to a rural or remote community, bringing with them resources and equipment to provide educational activities for children. Venues include community halls, churches or local parks. Mobile services are an important feature of EC provision in the many remote and isolated communities throughout Australia.
Playgroups
These can include informal groups of parents, who come together for their children to play in a peer group. There are also now a number of supported playgroups, often run by charities and welfare agencies and funded through a range of government programs, to support parents and children, in particular those considered to be vulnerable. These funded playgroups are seen by some governments as a 'soft entry' approach to engaging young families in community programs where interventions can be initiated as and when needed.

Source: Adapted from EC Development Steering Committee, 2009, pp. 2–3.

Australian government involvement in EC provision

Historically, government involvement in EC has changed in accordance with changing priorities, social pressures and the political ideology of the government of the day. As Brennan and Adamson (2017) note,

> Broadly, Labor governments adopt a more inclusive approach, with all children being entitled to some subsidised care and education; the Coalition parties, by contrast, are more likely to promote child care primarily as a lever to influence labour force participation (p. 318).

An example of shifting government policy can be seen in the provision of childcare during World War II (1939–45). At that time, the Australian government supported and funded the provision of childcare to enable women's workforce participation towards the war effort. Following World War II and the return of soldiers to Australia, the government reduced its involvement in childcare and offered women incentives to leave the paid workforce and return to domestic duties. Support for childcare was consequently reduced and women's workforce participation actively discouraged through government policy and incentives. Childcare policy stagnated until the resurgence of the women's movement during the 1960s and 1970s when both the McMahon Coalition Government and the Whitlam Labor Government embarked on an ambitious plan to respond to growing international evidence that quality EC education improved the developmental outcomes of children (Brennan & Adamson, 2017).

Supporting centre-based not-for-profit providers to expand EC provision, there was an increase in community-run preschools for children aged three to five years. This was also a time of significant social change, with women more than ever before desiring professional careers and paid employment in addition to their parenting responsibilities.

Subsequent governments have variously focused on increasing the supply of services so as to increase Australia's productivity through an expanded workforce (Pocock & Hill, 2007). During the 1980s and 1990s, the Hawke/Keating Labor Governments extended this commitment by promoting policies that encouraged for-profit (including corporate) providers to enter the EC market. This approach sought to shift responsibility for the provision of EC services, particularly work-related long day care, away from the direct provision by government to the commercial sector. The subsequent Liberal/National Coalition Government, led by John Howard, further developed this policy approach, which was consistent with the Howard Government's ambition for smaller government under its economic rationalist agenda. These policy shifts have seen a dramatic change in the ownership and operation of EC settings across the country. By the mid 2000s more than 70 per cent of childcare was provided by the private sector, with a major proportion of this ownership under the governance of companies listed on the Australian Stock Exchange. Pocock and Hill (2007) declare that this represents a shift in the way education and care programs were delivered and understood, with providers obliged to meet shareholder expectations as well as the needs and desires of children and families. The 2009 collapse of two of the major publicly listed childcare companies in Australia has thrown into question the wisdom of such a policy (Brennan & Adamson, 2017).

The release of the 2006 OECD *Starting strong II* report highlighted Australia's poor comparative performance on a range of indicators for EC in relation to other OECD countries. Australia ranked poorly on measures of participation rates in EC programs, legal entitlement to a prior-to-school provision, and public expenditure on EC services for children aged from birth to six years (OECD, 2006). Equally concerning was UNICEF's 2008 Innocenti Report Card 8, comprising a league table of EC programs in economically advanced countries. In this report Australia achieved only two of ten benchmarks considered to be a 'set of minimum standards for protecting the rights of children in their most vulnerable and formative years' (p. 2).

> The agreed aspiration is that children are born healthy and have access, throughout EC, to the support, care and education that will equip them for

> life and learning ... This is critical to achieving long-term participation and productivity gains for Australia. Schooling and skills development must be improved now, and must start early as children are the nation's future. (Productivity Agenda Working Group, 2008, p. 2)

productivity agenda
Government plans that focus attention and resources on national outcomes. Children are considered worthy of investment for the contribution they will make to a future productive nation.

Situating EC education and care within the **productivity agenda** is a significant consideration in the Australian policy framework. A productivity agenda positions children for their potential as future citizens and aims to develop dispositions, skills and culture that support the long-term aspirations of the nation. Critics of such policy—for example, curriculum theorists—argue that when learning is geared towards future outcomes it can limit or contain educational possibilities. As Olsson (2009) asserts, curriculum in this sense can translate into '... an apparatus of taming instead of a place for learning' (p. xix). The political nature of learning and teaching means that teaching is never neutral. 'What counts as legitimate knowledge is the result of complex power relations, struggles and compromises among identifiable class, race, gender and religious groups' (Apple, 1992, p. 4).

Pause–reflect–act 2.3

- What do you see as the advantages and disadvantages of situating EC education within a nation's productivity agenda?
- Is this the only way to ensure a future productive citizenry?
- How do you see the productivity agenda reflected in the work of EC leaders on a day-to-day basis?

Governments tend towards funding and supporting the goals and aspirations that will achieve their policy objectives, but are also mindful of policy approaches that will work politically in their favour. Policies must appeal to the electorate in order for the government to be re-elected after each term. Devising policies that directly impact voters tends to have more influence on voter behaviour than policies that are more generalised.

In recent times, Australian governments have tended towards funding models that can be described as 'consumer side funding'. This approach stands in stark contrast to the way that many other public facilities such as schools are funded—at the service end (or supply side). Consumer side funding gives governments maximum control over the distribution of funding and enables a much more competitive market to operate. There is limited need to negotiate with the institutions involved about funding conditions and individual families have little power to argue for better quality standards. Consumer side funding is attractive to the electorate because consumers can see the direct benefit that they receive. Such an approach is seen as politically palatable and easier to promote as a government benefit to individual consumers.

In Leaders in practice 2.2, Professor Deborah Brennan talks about her interest in the EC policy landscape and the ways in which she has contributed to informing policy direction and analysing the impact of policies on the lives of children and families. Deb's work highlights the importance of understanding policy in the context of government agendas and societal change. An understanding of the policy context is essential for teachers as advocates for children and families.

LEADERS IN PRACTICE 2.2

Professor Deborah Brennan
Social Policy Research Centre,
University of New South Wales, Sydney

Why are you interested in early childhood policy?

I became interested in EC policy during the Whitlam years, when I was an undergraduate at the University of Sydney. As well as studying politics and philosophy, I spent a lot of time going to demonstrations and marches and debating issues in the student union. I stumbled across the issue of childcare through my involvement in women's liberation. The second wave of feminism was organised around a series of demands, including 'free childcare'. One of my lecturers suggested that I write an essay on this topic as part of a course on public policy, and I was quickly hooked! I really enjoyed being able to study an issue that was unfolding in the media and on campus, and a 'hot topic' in public debate. As part of the course, I had to explore the different ways that various actors framed the issue of childcare and how this opened up a range of contested policy solutions. A few years later I did a masters degree in Childhood Studies with Professor Jacqueline Goodnow at Macquarie University. Jacquie was an incredibly inspiring teacher and instilled in me a lasting appreciation of the importance of the child's perspective in public policy. Later still, I undertook a PhD in political science (back at the University of Sydney) where I investigated the changing ways in which women had mobilised around the care and education of children since the late nineteenth century.

How does the broader policy context interact with/affect ECE policy?

EC connects with numerous other aspects of social policy—housing, income support, health and education, for example. That is part of its fascination for me. Even population ageing, for example—strange as it may seem—is connected to EC. How does this occur? As populations age, a shrinking proportion of the population is of workforce age and personal income tax revenue declines. At the same time, a growing proportion of the population is made up of older people who require expensive health care and income support. For many governments, the easy way to generate more tax revenue to pay for these measures is to encourage (or push) more working-age people into paid work. This can lead to a narrow, instrumentalist approach to EC, in which the promotion of labour force participation, rather than promoting children's well-being and development, becomes the guiding rationale.

What are other countries doing that contrasts with EC policy in Australia?

Forward-thinking countries are doing three things that contrast with Australia's approach to ECE. They are:

- introducing child-based entitlements to early learning and care that are not based on whether or not parents have paid work
- investing in the skills of the workforce and paying educators properly
- ensuring that a fair proportion of services remain in the non-profit sector.

Many European countries take a holistic approach to family policy, enabling parents to move seamlessly from well-supported parental leave, to a guaranteed place for their child in an early learning and care service and then ensuring that they have access to reduced hours of employment, time off to care for sick family members and other practical supports. Australia, by contrast, puts each of these issues into a separate box—and often pits one service or benefit against another.

How have you attempted to inform EC policy directions through research and discussion papers?

Throughout my career, I've tried to conduct research that will have an impact on policy and, at the same time, be accessible to a broad audience. My first book, co-authored with Carol O'Donnell, was called *Caring for Australia's Children: Political and Industrial Issues in Australian Child Care*. Carol and I tried to put the wages and working conditions of EC educators onto the agenda and to make connections with broader policy debates around the funding of EC. I developed this theme and also tried to provide a nuanced historical understanding of the politics of EC policy in my next book, *The Politics of Australian Child Care: From Philanthropy to Feminism*. Since then I've published numerous reports, papers and articles relating to gender and social policy and have made submissions to just about every Australian government inquiry into EC and related policy areas. I strongly believe in staying connected with a range of people, both inside and outside the sector, in order to avoid being caught in a single, narrow perspective. EC is a vital and wonderfully interesting area of public policy and of everyday life. I feel fortunate to have stumbled into this area all those years ago.

Pause–reflect–act 2.4

- What is your view about studying policy and politics as part of a teacher education course?
- How has your childhood and upbringing influenced your views about politics?
- Why is it important to teachers to have an understanding of the broader policy context?
- How might an understanding of government intentions and motivations impact on your work as an EC teacher and a leader?

The Australian government's reform agenda for EC

Growing international awareness of the importance of the early years, the influence of the various international reports and the change of federal government in 2007 ushered in a new era for EC in Australia. Immediately following its election, the Rudd government initiated a number of ambitious reforms to the EC sector. These reforms picked up on many of the recommendations of the OECD *Starting strong II* report (2006), including the introduction of a national approach to policy through:

- the National Quality Framework (NQF), which included nationally consistent standards for quality, known as the National Quality Standard (NQS)

- a commitment to provide all Australian children with EC education in their year prior to full-time school, known as 'universal access'
- a national Early Years Learning Framework (EYLF) to support educators in developing curriculum appropriate for young children (EC Development Steering Committee, 2009).

In order to achieve these goals, it is widely recognised that there is a need to increase the EC workforce and, in particular, strengthen its leadership capabilities. A range of workforce strategies also formed part of the policy platform to address current weaknesses.

National Quality Standard and enhanced regulatory arrangements

The intention of the reform agenda was to streamline the state and territory regulatory processes and strive for national consistency in standards for all EC education and care provision. There is now a National Quality Standard (NQS) that addresses both structural and process elements of EC program quality (ACECQA, 2011c). This was a highly ambitious proposal and required the agreement of all jurisdictions (states and territories) about what constitutes quality outcomes for children. Given the significant historical differences between the state/territory jurisdictions—particularly in relation to requirements for qualifications of staff and ratios of staff to children—reaching agreement that is nationally accepted and cost-effective has proved challenging for the Council of Australian Governments (COAG). There remain a number of jurisdictional anomalies and exceptions that have been carried forward under grandfathered (or quarantined) clauses for the foreseeable future.

A quality rating system

Along with this new regulatory and quality framework, the Australian government has introduced a stratified rating system. The dual aims of this system are to provide parents with reliable information about the quality rating achieved by each setting, and to have a goal of continuous improvement by making explicit where the setting's strengths and weaknesses lie. This policy approach aims to provide parents and communities with more specific detail about the quality of a service, while at the same time encouraging services to strive for the highest rating, thus positioning themselves as more desirable in the competitive marketplace. Such a system works both as an accountability mechanism for services in receipt of public funds and as a way of monitoring the performance of free market operators. It also has the added benefit of demonstrating a commitment to transparency and access to information about quality issues.

see chapter 3 for more detail on the NQS and the rating system.

A national Early Years Learning Framework

A key component of this reform agenda was the launch of the Early Years Learning Framework (EYLF) in 2009. Developed as a guide to curriculum for those working with children from birth to five years and their transition to school, this was a landmark development as it is the first

Australian national curriculum document for children prior to full-time school. Importantly, government commitment to such a learning framework was a political acknowledgment that children learn from birth and that a government endorsed guide to curriculum is a key tool for supporting their learning. While a number of Australia's states and territories produced early years curriculum documents during the 1990s, it was the EYLF that consolidated a commitment to a more comprehensive accountability for children's learning in prior-to-school settings.

Central to COAG's EC reform agenda, the EYLF was introduced with the intent to

> ... guide EC educators in developing quality EC programs in a range of EC education and care settings ... It will outline the desired outcomes for children in ECEC settings across the birth to five age range, including the year before formal schooling, and enhance their transitions to school. (Productivity Agenda Working Group, 2008, p. 27)

As an integral part of the NQS, EC settings are accountable for their use of the EYLF as a guide to their curriculum development and are required to demonstrate under the NQS how their programs contribute to children's learning in five specified learning outcomes (DEEWR, 2009). Under a system requiring educators to show evidence of children's learning, there is a danger that the EYLF will be viewed not so much as a tool for reflection and rich curriculum development than as a technicist tool for demonstrating accountability. The authors of the EYLF have encouraged educators to resist attempts to reduce the document to an accountability tool and to be critically reflective about how any document—no matter how well intended—can be misused (Sumsion et al., 2009). It is important that EC educators are knowledgeable about the political intent of initiatives such as the EYLF and engage in professional dialogue and debate that contribute to wise and ethical practice.

in chapter 6, intentional leaders are urged to utilise professional judgment and confidence, and meaningfully utilise the EYLF to plan effectively for children's learning.

Indigenous initiatives aimed at 'Closing the Gap'

The reform agenda also identified that Aboriginal and Torres Strait Islander children are the most vulnerable group of children in Australia (COAG, 2009a). Gaps between health outcomes, school retention rates and mortality rates for infants between Indigenous and non-Indigenous children are getting wider (COAG, 2009a). Government policy to reduce the gap in developmental outcomes between Indigenous and non-Indigenous children is a key component of the COAG reform agenda. Recent revisions of the Closing the Gap policy have resulted in a renewed National Partnership Agreement between the states/territories and the Australian government. This initiative has two main targets, which have been agreed to by COAG (Australian Government Department of Prime Minister and Cabinet, 2016). They are to:

- halve the gap in mortality rates for Indigenous children under five within a decade, (by 2018);
- achieve 95 per cent of all indigenous four-year-olds enrolled in EC education by 2025.

In order to achieve these goals the Australian government is distributing additional funds to each of the state and territory governments to undertake targeted work. As part of the National Partnership Agreement, the aim is to bring all Indigenous services under the scope of the NQS. Many Indigenous services—particularly those in rural and remote regions—have previously not been required to meet the National Quality Standard. While this is a significant step in improving the learning experience of Indigenous children no matter where they live, it is indeed an ambitious policy and will require long-term commitment by present and future governments to achieve the set targets. One feature of Indigenous policy in Australia has been the fluctuating political commitments impacted on by changes in ideological approaches of various governments in power. When policy initiatives are short term or inadequately supported by resources, they are less likely to be successful. The expanding evidence base showing the long-term impact of Indigenous children's regular attendance at preschool has been a persuasive factor in the government's continued interest in funding the Closing the Gap initiative (see, for example, Arcos Holzinger & Biddle, 2015).

Universal access to EC education with a university-qualified EC teacher

As noted earlier, another element of the EC reform agenda is the policy providing universal access of 15 hours of preschool education for all Australian children in their year before full-time school. This policy recognises the important contribution that a preschool program (which can be delivered in a range of EC settings) plays in the transition to full-time school and the opportunities that participation in an EC program affords young children in the long term. Such policies emanate from EC research that can persuade politicians to invest in a particular policy program.

The employment of university-qualified teachers to deliver these programs sees an overall improvement across Australia in the qualifications required of those delivering this component of the EC program. While it has been commonplace for EC teachers to be employed in preschools/kindergartens, it is now a requirement under the Universal Access National Partnership Agreement that all EC settings providing the universal preschool program must employ a university-qualified teacher.

Strengthening the EC workforce

Increasing the supply of qualified teachers and educators in the sector has been another key tenet of the national reform agenda. Staff wages, work conditions and limited career paths are key barriers to a stable, qualified workforce and thus to the provision of high-quality education for young children and to the meeting of NQS staffing requirements (Productivity Commission, 2011b). To address these issues, the Rudd government introduced free education for students undertaking a Diploma in Children's Services qualification and opened up additional Commonwealth supported places for students studying for a university EC teaching degree. It is important to note that these strategies were aimed at increasing the supply of qualified EC staff, but there have been no attempts to consistently improve the wages or working conditions of EC educators in an attempt to retain them in the prior-to-school sector. Fenech, Giugni and Bown (2012) also note that while the reform agenda has brought some improvements to the qualifications and conditions of EC educators, there is still significant improvement required to match international best practice benchmarks. This is a critically important area for policy attention, as a well-educated and stable workforce underpins the success of the reform agenda.

At the time of writing this second edition, we are some five years on from the introduction of the NQF. Many gains have been made for children and families as NQS data shows that overall quality in Australian EC settings is improving (ACECQA, 2016). Policy initiatives have resulted in improved ratios for children under two years and improvement in the qualifications of educators, now requiring all educators to hold a minimum vocational credential. The national approach to quality standards and a focus on continual improvement remains a commitment of the states, territories and Australian government, and work continues to achieve nationally consistent standards to a broader range of EC settings. Many areas of the NQF remain contested with an ever-present focus on costs and affordability. The Australian government continues to puzzle through the complexities of funding and resourcing an equitable and cost-effective EC provision and the challenge of supporting a suitably qualified workforce that is fairly remunerated. To date the vision for an Australian model that privileges the rights of children to high-quality EC education and care provision remains a work in progress.

Pause–reflect–act 2.5

The current workforce policy of the Australian government might be described as limited in that it does not address some of the key factors known to inhibit the growth and stability of the EC workforce.

- What do you see as the key barriers for people considering a career in prior-to-school settings?
- As an EC leader, what might you argue for at the setting level to attract and retain good staff and counter the limited nature of this policy?

Chapter summary

Australian EC provision is directly impacted by government agendas and political ideology. Political interest in EC has increased over the past two decades, largely in response to research and economic arguments that public investment in ECEC results in productivity gains for the nation. The diversity of service types and the historical differences between the eight state/territory jurisdictions has led to a fragmented system that is complex and at times difficult to navigate. EC leaders with a sound knowledge of the policy framework can contribute to and influence future policy directions. They also play an important role in interpreting and clarifying policy to families. Intentional leaders play a key role in ensuring that policy directions are interpreted and enacted with children's best interests in mind.

Key references

Productivity Commission. (2011). *Early childhood development workforce: Research report*. Melbourne: Australian Government. Retrieved from www.pc.gov.au/inquiries/completed/education-workforce-early-childhood/report

The report of the Productivity Commission's investigation into the EC workforce in Australia provides a comprehensive overview of the national policy landscape with a focus on the current strengths and weaknesses of the workforce responsible for EC programs.

Productivity Commission. (2014). *Childcare and early childhood learning: Overview*. Inquiry Report No. 73. Canberra: Australian Government. Retrieved from www.pc.gov.au/inquiries/completed/childcare/report

This is the final report of Productivity Commission Inquiry in Childcare and Early Learning. It provides the most recent overview of policy relating to ECE in Australia along with the Commission's recommendations. The report highlights the complexity of the Australian EC system and the many competing agendas that shape the policy landscape in Australia.

Purdie, N., Milgate, G. & Bell, H.R. (Eds.). (2011). *Toward culturally reflective and relevant education*. Melbourne: ACER Press.

A useful book outlining issues in Aboriginal and Torres Strait Islander education. Assists the reader to understand the key issues for Indigenous policy and the role of teachers in 'closing the gap'.

Online resources

Australian, state, territory and local government

This website provides an overview of the Australian government system and is essential reading for international students or those who have limited knowledge of the Australian government context.

www.gov.au

3 | LEADING FOR QUALITY

CHAPTER LEARNING OBJECTIVES

After studying this chapter you will understand that:

- What quality EC education looks like will vary according to a centre's vision and philosophy and the context within which the centre is located.
- Intentional leaders meet legislative requirements to complement commitment to the centre's vision and philosophy and support the centre's provision of quality education.
- Leaders and educators are accountable to international conventions, professional and industry standards (including teacher registration and accreditation), and legislative requirements, including the National Quality Framework (NQF).
- A strong understanding of the NQF will enable leaders to use this framework to support quality ECEC.
- Intentional leaders strive for ongoing quality improvement.
- Intentional leaders read the NQF critically and meet its requirements by exercising professional judgment and autonomy. To this end, intentional leaders are also able to clearly and confidently articulate what they do and why they do it.

Key concepts

accountability
legislative frameworks
professional and industry standards
professional autonomy
professional judgment
quality

Overview

legislative frameworks are laws and regulations that educators are legally required to comply with.

The **legislative frameworks** that EC educators are accountable to have a major impact on quality practice. These legislative frameworks can inform and guide educators' practice in ways that support quality education and quality improvement. Legislative frameworks can also confine approaches to quality EC education and be in conflict with professional and local community beliefs and values, as reflected in a centre's vision and philosophy. This chapter proposes that intentional leaders will have a sound working knowledge of relevant legislative frameworks and will use these frameworks to actively support their own professional philosophy as well as the needs and interests of children, families and staff. To this end, this chapter provides an overview of current legislative frameworks—notably the National Quality Framework (NQF)—relevant to EC settings in Australia. It then highlights the critical roles professional judgment and professional autonomy play in a leader's application of legislative frameworks and provision of quality EC education for young children. Given that legislative requirements are not static, this core knowledge and skills base will enhance a leader's capacity to actively engage with legislation they are accountable to, both now and in the future.

Introduction

Thinking about quality EC education can be exciting for leaders and educators. '**Quality**' has connotations of providing education and care that is of value and that makes a positive difference to the lives of children and families. In contrast, thinking about laws, regulations and accountabilities can seem far from exciting. They may seem peripheral to the 'real work' educators do and a burden on leaders' valuable time. Viewed in this way, meeting accountabilities can become a 'tick the box' exercise: something that has to be done to meet the requirements of regulatory authorities.

quality education promotes children's rights, inclusion, development and well-being. What quality EC education looks like can vary among settings, in accordance with the philosophy and local context.

This chapter proposes that understanding and meeting accountabilities is intricately linked to providing quality EC education. Conversely, providing quality EC education necessitates the meeting of educators' legal and professional accountabilities. Intentional leaders will situate their accountabilities within the context of the quality setting they are striving to be. That is, they and their team will meet their accountabilities in a contextually meaningful way, giving due consideration to their vision, philosophy, mission, community context, and the needs and interests of the children and families they are working with.

What follows is an overview of the accountabilities leaders and educators in EC settings must meet. Intentional leaders approach these requirements critically while exercising **professional judgment** and professional autonomy. In this way, intentional leaders are far from passive recipients who feel compelled to meet their accountabilities. Rather, they are active in ensuring that they and the centre staff meet their accountabilities in meaningful ways to support their provision of quality EC education.

professional judgment is drawing on one's professional philosophy, professional knowledge base and understanding of a given situation to make informed decisions that are considered to be quality practice.

Quality EC education

The body of research that has investigated quality in EC settings has produced generally accepted understandings as to what constitutes the key elements of quality (Huntsman, 2008; Myers, 2004; Sims, 2007; Vermeer et al., 2016). Structural indicators or 'inputs' (Myers, 2004, p. 15) pertain to the measurable and regulatory aspects of a centre's environment and are said to provide the foundation for quality. These include staff qualifications, with teacher qualified staff generally correlating with higher quality ratings (Seung-Hee et al., 2013; Sylva et al., 2004a; Whitebook, 2003); staff:child ratios; group sizes; adequate indoor and outdoor space; and health and safety provisions. The presence of these structural elements is said to facilitate process contributors of quality. Process contributors reflect the quality of a child's experience and include the presence of stimulating, child-centred and play-based developmentally appropriate programs; warm, frequent, responsive interactions between staff and children; and parental involvement. Increasingly, governments in Australia and internationally have implemented legislation that requires EC settings to meet benchmark structural and process standards. This regulatory approach to ensuring quality follows research which has demonstrated that the presence of these structural and process elements enhances children's cognitive, language and socio-emotional development. Such development is considered indicative of a quality EC setting.

Some critical commentators (Cannella, 1997; Dahlberg et al., 2007; Farquhar, 1999; Grieshaber, 2000, 2002; Moss & Pence, 1994; Novinger & O'Brien, 2003) question such perspectives and approaches to quality in EC settings. For these commentators, quality is a relative construct that cannot be objectively prescribed. To do so, they argue, diminishes how complex 'quality' is, in light of multiple and changing local contexts. This is particularly the case when 'quality' is reduced to the meeting of externally determined regulatory requirements. For example, an overemphasis on documentary evidence that focuses on children's development may compromise perspectives such as those valued in Indigenous communities; namely, that children are capable and can actively contribute to the community context in the here and now, not when they are 'developed' (Hutchins et al., 2009). Another example is the excessive risk management of children's play, which can compromise learning and development (Little & Sweller, 2015; Shepherd, 2004; Wyver et al., 2010).

Accountabilities are a legitimate and necessary means of supporting the provision of quality education for young children. However, it is imperative that intentional leaders consider critically and apply their accountabilities in ways that are consistent with their vision for quality, their professional philosophy and their local context. In a case study exploration of six externally rated high-quality centres (Harrison, et al., 2008), for example, the director at a rural centre in New South Wales explained they had deliberately decided they were not going to install soft fall in their outdoor play area. Being a centre in a drought area, staff considered it important that the outdoor environment reflected their community context and, in keeping with their philosophy, provided authentic play experiences for the children. While a dusty, dry outdoor area was not particularly aesthetically pleasing, staff considered it to be nonetheless safe and resisted a practice that other centres in the area deemed fitting to their provision of a safe environment.

Overview of legal, regulatory and professional accountabilities for EC settings

Providing quality EC education requires leaders and educators to understand and meet the myriad legal, regulatory and professional requirements for which they are accountable. Figure 3.1 provides a conceptual illustration of these accountabilities.

At the outer-most layer are *international treaties*. Policy makers and citizens are obliged to adhere to a treaty—in legislation, policy and everyday practice—when it is signed and ratified by a country's government. Relevant to early childhood is the United Nations Convention on the Rights of the Child (UNCROC) (United Nations (UN), 1989), which Australia signed and ratified in 1990. The UNCROC stipulates 54 universal rights children are entitled to, and determines that these rights must be provided for, promoted and protected by law. Under the UNCROC all children are equally entitled to rights in three areas:

- *Participation:* children are regarded as active and contributing members of society.
- *Provision:* children are entitled to the means that will assure their survival and development.
- *Protection:* from physical and psychological harm, including discrimination and all forms of neglect and exploitation.

Figure 3.1 Conceptualisation of the requirements of leaders and educators

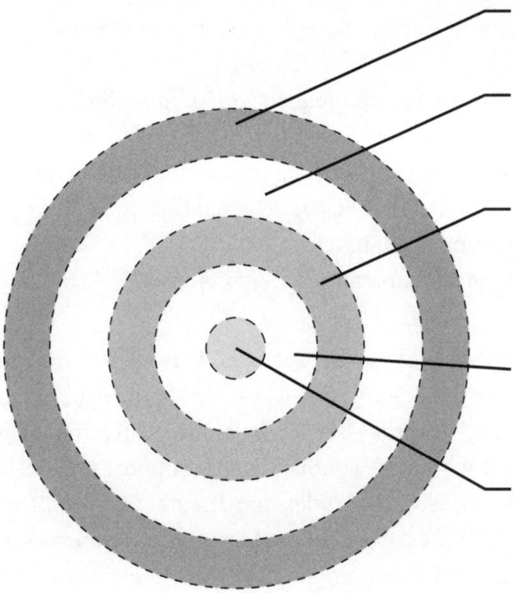

International treaties

Legislation and regulation that educators and others must comply with

Standards and professional codes that promote best practice in early childhood and other settings

Legislation and regulation specific to early childhood settings

The early childhood setting

Pause–reflect–act 3.1

The Australian Human Rights Commission and Early Childhood Australia (2015) published a three-year Statement of Intent that included principles and practices aimed at supporting EC educators' inclusion of these rights in their everyday practice. A number of action points are included in the report based on children's right to be heard; be free from abuse, neglect and violence; and be able to thrive. The report also encourages educators to promote children's rights to the broader community and to have their voice heard in the collection of data relevant to them.

- Read and reflect on the report's action points for educators.
- What image of the child underpins these actions points? Is this image similar to or different from the image you hold of young children?
- Can you find evidence to show that your professional philosophy and practices, and those of staff at the setting where you are working, reflect the action points highlighted in the report? In which areas are you doing well? In which areas could you aim to improve?

The next broad category of accountabilities that educators are required to comply with are *legislation and regulations that they but also others outside of early childhood must comply with.* These requirements include laws and regulations pertaining to:

- children and families—for example, state and territory child protection legislation (such as the *NSW Children & Young Persons (Care and Protection) Act 1998*); and federal legislation concerning parenting orders and child welfare (for example, the *Family Law Act 1975*)
- the effective management of a centre—for example, federal occupational health and safety law (such as the *Model Work Health and Safety Act 2011* and accompanying regulations); financial management law: taxation, superannuation and insurance (for example, the *Income Tax Assessment Act 1997*; *Superannuation Guarantee (Administration) Act 1992*; and state and territory public liability law)
- industrial relations and the employment of staff (*Fair Work Act 2009*; *Anti-discrimination Act 1977*; *Workers Compensation Act 1987*).

While these requirements are not specific to EC settings, it is critical that intentional leaders are aware of their legal responsibilities under these laws and regulations. This set of accountabilities can support quality directly—for example, by protecting children from harm—but also indirectly by enabling workplace conditions that support staff well-being.

professional and industry standards are best practice, as deemed by industry or professional bodies, and are legally enforceable only if incorporated in legislation or regulation.

Educators are also accountable to professional codes and standards relevant to children, families and EC settings. Importantly, these codes and **professional standards** are generally guides for best practice and are not legal requirements. Specific to EC is Early Childhood Australia's *Code of Ethics* (ECA, 2016). This Code promotes eight professional principles—a strengths-based and individualised view of children; from birth, children are citizens with rights; pedagogical practices based on professional decision-making that is informed by specialist knowledge of EC and the consideration of multiple perspectives with families and communities; support of equity and belonging; relationships with children that are marked by respect, responsiveness and reciprocity; play-based learning; and practitioner enquiry and research—and establishes expectations of professional practice and behaviour in relation to children, families, colleagues, the profession, and the community and society. All EC leaders have a responsibility to ensure that this *Code of Ethics* (ECA, 2016) guides their own and their team's practice and decision-making.

Increasingly, EC teachers are required to meet professional teaching standards so as to be accredited and eligible to teach in an approved EC education service. Teacher regulatory authorities are responsible for ensuring that graduate and practising teachers meet seven professional standards across three key domains of teaching: professional knowledge; professional practice; and professional engagement (Australian Institute for Teaching and School Leadership (AITSL), 2014). An animated overview of the Australian Professional Teaching Standards and their intended benefits is available at www.youtube.com/watch?v=iuKceiCvMEg&feature=player_embedded (AITSL, 2012). Teachers can be awarded accreditation at one of four key stages: Conditional or Provisional Accreditation, Proficient Accreditation, Highly Accomplished Accreditation and Lead Teacher Accreditation. Through these standards and stages teacher accreditation is designed to support the development of a teacher's professional practice, an idea that is further explored in Chapter 15.

Other **industry standards** inform safe practices in EC settings. These include playground surfacing, play equipment, healthy eating and sun safety standards. It is important to note that educators are generally not legally required to comply with these standards and codes, unless they have been included in a specific law or regulation. In these cases the standards outlined must be enforced.

Moving closer to the centre context is the next category of accountabilities: legislation and regulations specific to the provision of quality EC education. These requirements are embodied in the National Quality Framework (NQF) (ACECQA, 2011a) and will be discussed in detail in the next section.

Although represented separately in Figure 3.1, the dashed lines between each layer of **accountability** are indicative of how one requirement may fit multiple accountabilities. For example, adherence to the UNCROC (UN, 1989) and the Code of Ethics (ECA, 2016) is required in the NQS (ACECQA, 2011c). Collectively, these requirements can and should inform the everyday practices of an EC setting in ways that enhance quality education for young children. To this end, a strong grasp of these legal and professional accountabilities should be evident in a centre's policy documents. As will be discussed later in the chapter, how these requirements are applied may vary from centre to centre, as we argue that an intentional leader will exercise professional judgment and meet these accountabilities in ways that are consistent with their vision and philosophy, and their community context.

accountability implies that educators are answerable to children, families, the community and governments. This means being professionally responsible, and meeting legislative frameworks and relevant standards in providing quality EC programs.

Pause–reflect–act 3.2

- From your experience and knowledge, brainstorm a list of legislation, regulations and professional standards that you have complied with. In what way(s) do you think each requirement contributes to quality EC education?
- Reflect on one setting in which you have worked. Can you think of any examples where meeting these requirements took into consideration the centre's vision, philosophy and community context?

The National Quality Framework (NQF)

As discussed in Chapter 2, the development of the NQF was one of a number of key reforms instigated by the Council of Australian Governments (COAG) through its National Partnership Agreement on the Quality Agenda for Early Childhood Education and Care (COAG, 2009b). The intent of the NQF is to drive consistent and improved quality standards and practices across the country. Significantly, the NQF is a streamlined national approach that for the first time brings the regulation and assessment of EC services across Australia under the one system. The NQF includes a national legislative framework consisting of the National Law and National Regulations; a National Quality Standard (NQS) consisting of seven quality areas; the Early Years Learning Framework (EYLF); and a national quality assessment and rating process (ACECQA, 2011).

The *Education and Care Services National Law Act 2010* (Commonwealth of Australia, 2010a) and its associated Education and Care Services National Regulations (New South Wales Government, 2016) legally mandate the NQF. Under this Act the NQF became effective on 1 January 2012 and is a legal accountability for all educators in long day care centres, preschools/kindergartens, out of school hours care services and family day care. The Australian Children's Education and Care Quality Authority (ACECQA), located in Sydney, works collaboratively with a regulatory authority in each state and territory to implement the NQF in a nationally consistent way across the country. These individual state and territory regulatory authorities are specifically responsible for service approvals, monitoring and quality assessment. Additional details on the roles and responsibilities of ACECQA and regulatory bodies, and on the national law and regulations, can be found at www.acecqa.gov.au/welcome and from the Australian Children's Education and Care Quality Authority (2014). It is critical that intentional leaders have a strong working knowledge of both legislative requirements and clearly understand their responsibilities under each.

In addition to the National Law and Regulations there are three key components of the NQF. First is the Early Years Learning Framework (EYLF) (DEEWR, 2009). As discussed in Chapter 2, the EYLF is a curriculum framework document designed to guide educators' planning, implementation and evaluation of quality EC programs. The EYLF describes the principles, practice and outcomes essential for supporting and enhancing young children's learning from birth to five years of age, as well as their transition to school. The EYLF has a strong emphasis on play-based learning and recognises the importance of children's communication and language (including early literacy and numeracy) and social and emotional development.

how pedagogical leadership can be exercised using the EYLF is explored in chapter 6.

The principles, practice and learning outcomes of the EYLF are intended to support implementation of the National Quality Standard (NQS) (ACECQA, 2011c), the second key component of the NQF. The NQS incorporates seven quality areas, with each area comprising two to three standards. These standards express expected outcomes, which are operationalised into a number of contributing elements. The standards for each quality area, effective February 2018, are outlined in Table 3.1.

The NQS provides flexibility for centres to meet these quality areas in ways that take into consideration the particular cultural and community context within which they are operating. In doing so, however, leaders and educators are expected to be guided by the six principles that underpin the NQF (Commonwealth of Australia, 2010a, Section 3.3):

- The rights and best interests of the child are paramount.
- Children are successful, competent and capable learners.
- Equity, inclusion and diversity are essential values.
- Australia's Aboriginal and Torres Strait Islander cultures are valued.
- The role of parents and families is respected and supported.
- Best practice is expected in the provision of education and care services.

Table 3.1 NQS quality areas and accompanying standards

Quality Area	Standards
1 Educational program and practice	1.1 The educational program enhances each child's learning and development 1.2 Educators facilitate and extend each child's learning and development 1.3 Educators and co-ordinators take a planned and reflective approach to implementing the program for each child
2 Children's health and safety	2.1 Each child's health and physical activity is supported and promoted 2.2 Each child is protected
3 Physical environment	3.1 The design of the facilities is appropriate for the operation of a service 3.2 The service environment is inclusive, promotes competence, and supports exploration and play-based learning
4 Staffing arrangements	4.1 Staffing arrangements enhance children's learning and development 4.2 Management, educators and staff are collaborative, respectful and ethical
5 Relationships with children	5.1 Respectful and equitable relationships are maintained with each child 5.2 Each child is supported to build and maintain sensitive and responsive relationships
6 Collaborative partnerships with families and communities	6.1 Respectful relationships with families are developed and maintained and families are supported in their parenting role 6.2 Collaborative partnerships enhance children's inclusion, learning and well-being
7 Governance and leadership	7.1 Governance supports the operation of a quality service 7.2 Effective leadership builds and promotes a positive organisational culture and professional learning community

Source: ACECQA, 2017.

Pause–reflect–act 3.3

Consider the seven quality areas of the NQS and their associated standards. Given your own experience, do you consider that the quality areas and their associated standards are indicative of what contributes to quality EC education?

Draw a mind map with 'Quality Early Childhood Education' written in the centre. Now add seven offshoots using seven different colours, each one representing one quality area of the NQS. For each quality area add further offshoots (in the same colour), which will be their respective standards. Now consider how you might go about ensuring that you and the staff at your centre meet each of the Standards you have listed. Aim to add as many elements for each standard as possible, again using the same colours for each quality area.

Once you have completed your mind map, read through pages 10 to 11 of the *Guide to the National Quality Standard* (ACECQA, 2011c).

- How do your elements compare with the 40 elements of the NQS?
- To what extent do the principles of the NQF and your centre's philosophy underpin the elements you have identified and that are listed in the NQS?

How well a centre is meeting the NQS is also determined by a third key component of the NQF: the national *assessment and rating system*. In each state and territory an approved regulatory authority conducts these assessments and determines appropriate ratings for each quality area and for the centre overall. The regulator's assessment is based on the centre's compliance and rating history; examination of the centre's quality improvement plan (discussed below); discussions with staff; sightings of supporting evidence such as centre policies and program planning and evaluation; and observations of centre practices. Table 3.2 lists the five rating levels and what each means in terms of the standard of quality a centre is providing.

Following assessment, a centre receives a rating for each of the seven quality areas, and an overall service quality rating (ACECQA, 2011b). These ratings must be displayed in the centre and are publicly available on the ACECQA, MyChild and Starting Blocks websites (the latter two websites being government information websites for parents). To meet the quality standard benchmark—the NQS—settings must first meet all elements within the one standard, and then meet all the standards within a quality area (ACECQA, 2011c).

chapters 4 and 5 consider governance and strategic planning and development matters respectively.

The intentional leader will consider what rating level is feasible and desirable for their centre to attain. For example, will current resources support quality practices that exceed the NQS? How might the centre's vision and strategic organisational development inform the rating that staff, parents and management aim to attain? In what ways do the centre's governance and management structure support or limit the centre's capacity to achieve standards of practice that exceed the NQS benchmark?

Table 3.2 Overview of the NQF rating system

Rating Level	Equivalent Standard of Quality
Significant improvement required	Received if at least one quality area is assessed as posing a major risk to children's health, safety and well-being and thus is not meeting the minimum National Quality Standard. The centre is at risk of being closed if, in conjunction with the Regulatory Authority, they do not demonstrate immediate improvement.
Working towards National Quality Standard	Received if the centre demonstrates that it is on a trajectory to attaining the National Quality Standard. No quality area is rated as requiring significant improvement.
Meeting National Quality Standard	The centre is meeting or exceeding the quality benchmark in all seven quality areas, though not sufficiently to receive a higher rating.
Exceeding National Quality Standard	The centre exceeds the National Quality Standard in at least four Quality areas, with at least two from quality areas 1, 5, 6 or 7.
Excellent	Centres that receive an Exceeding rating for all seven quality areas can apply to ACECQA for an excellent rating. This rating will be given to those centres deemed to be leaders in the field.

Source: Adapted from ACECQA, 2011b, Part 3.2, p. 44; Education Council (2017).

Responses to questions such as these will inform the development of the centre's Quality Improvement Plan (QIP) which, as noted above, must be prepared for the purposes of the NQS assessment process (New South Wales Government, 2016. Part 3.1, Section 55). The QIP must include a self-assessment of the centre's provision of quality practice against the NQS and the National Regulation. In addition, it must include the centre's philosophy statement and highlight areas for improvement.

The intentional leader will ensure that critical reflection on centre quality drives the completion of the QIP. Importantly, critical conversations will be held with children, staff, parents and management about what quality in each Quality Standard should and could look like. These collaborative, reflective conversations will be ongoing, so that quality and quality improvement are at the forefront of everyday thinking and planning, rather than something that is forgotten once the centre has been assessed and rated.

In these processes the intentional leader will give thoughtful consideration to the future of the centre: where it is heading, how it might get there, what strengths it has to draw on, and what areas warrant further development. These considerations will be made with reference to the centre's vision, mission and philosophy and the community context within which the centre is located. The requirement to develop and constantly reflect on a QIP is an opportunity that can inform the leader's future-oriented thinking and planning.

see chapter 5 for a discussion of developing an organisational vision, mission and philosophy.

Pause–reflect–act 3.4

Read ACECQA's *Guide to Developing a Quality Improvement Plan* and the Quality Improvement Plan template (both can be retrieved from www.acecqa.gov.au/quality-improvement-plan_1).

- Thinking about the approaches and practices of a centre you have experience working in, complete the QIP template for that centre in one NQS quality area.
- In completing this task, on what basis did you decide what the centre's strengths were, where improvement was needed, and what goals were set?
- To what extent did the template help you reflect on the centre's approaches and practices in this quality area?
- Did you find aspects of the centre's approaches and practices in this quality area that were not covered in the respective standards and elements in the NQS?

Leaders in practice 3.1 shows how Sarah Woods, Director of Port Hedland Early Learning Centre in WA, uses the NQF as an intentional leader to drive the provision of quality ECE at her centre.

LEADERS IN PRACTICE 3.1

Sarah Woods

Director, Port Hedland Early Learning Centre (WA)

Originally from the UK, my passion and enthusiasm for driving quality outcomes for children led to 13 years' experience working across Education, Inclusion, Community and Early Years settings in three different countries. My professional philosophy helps me in my approach to lead staff teams and work collaboratively with families and communities to improve quality outcomes for children. It now finds me as director of YMCAWA Port Hedland Early Learning Centre, a not-for-profit remote LDC facility in WA for children aged six weeks to five years. We believe every child is unique, capable and curious and work together to create safe and inclusive environments which are based on child interests. We conduct ourselves alongside the four core values of Honesty, Respect, Responsibility and Caring to promote Early Years Education and Care, resulting in a successful transition to school.

For me, international treaties such as the UNCROC and legislative requirements such as the NQF are not tools to be only referred to in the event of an impending assessment and rating process, or tools to be used only by management. Practitioners who are truly passionate and dedicated to improving quality outcomes for children should know, live and breathe these documents. All children, regardless of background, age, disability, nationality, religion or gender are uniquely capable, and as educators we should continually strive to improve quality with them. The EYLF and NQS are requirements to be celebrated in early education and care settings as they support quality improvement and in several cases help identify practices we all do effectively every day as strengths!

Inspired by the Reggio Emilia approach to learning, I use the NQF to support and encourage educators to drive their own quality practices, enabling them to be co-learners and collaborators with each child. Educators are supported with their professional development and practice in a number of ways, such as the provision of access to online PDs, training sessions, ongoing role modelling and daily communication around quality practice, and an in-depth probation/appraisal process. Observation of practice and professional development reviews alongside the educators are conducted by myself and the pedagogical leader, where clear targets are mutually agreed and set to ensure quality provision is a continuing practice. Educators in turn then role model these practices to their colleagues and to children, which in turn creates a number of positive outcomes. For example, our respectful, reciprocal and responsive dialogues with children and families help us form collaborative partnerships which enable children to self-direct their own learning!

The development and review of our Quality Improvement Plan (QIP) helps us to further drive quality practice. We share our QIP with families and ask for their feedback on our practices through a range of different media, taking into account barriers such as English as an additional language and family access to technology. The regular meetings which take place between the director and educators to celebrate what is working well and to strategise ideas for further quality improvement and our monthly staff meetings enable the EYLF to be explored on a regular basis. For example, the agenda at staff meetings is broken down into the seven National Quality Standards. These then become open topics for review and reflection, and the improvements are then added to our QIP. Most importantly, however, we ask children to share their thoughts and feelings with us on a daily basis to promote the principles, practices and learning outcomes in the EYLF and to continually drive child-led quality!

The underlying values of the NQF are supported by the principles underpinning the EYLF and the five Learning Outcomes. These provide educators with valuable resources against which children's development can be identified. Supporting the educators to use the EYLF and to follow our own YMCA approach to learning then enables them to document this development through observations. The critical reflection of these observations enables extension of learning and supports each child's future development. The EYLF planning cycle is broken down into Question, Plan, Act and Reflect. It's designed to show programming doesn't have to be difficult and can be so rewarding—keep it simple, make it effective—and basing it on the expressed needs of the child is the key!

Rome was not built in a day! Quality practices take time and effort to build. However, there is a lot of support to help drive Quality. The support I gained from understanding all aspects of the NQF has helped drive my own professional and quality practice. My own experience of the assessment and ratings process was really positive and I found it to be an excellent opportunity to celebrate strengths within the centre and also focus on areas and formulate exciting plans for continuing quality improvement. I was delighted when our centre recently achieved an overall rating of 'exceeding' the National Quality Standard.

Pause–reflect–act 3.5

- In what ways does Sarah use the NQF to support her centre's provision of quality EC education?
- What did you learn from how Sarah engages with centre stakeholders in the review and development of her centre's Quality Improvement Plan?
- Review the underlying principles of both the NQF and the EYLF. How might these inform your professional philosophy and practice?

Quality from whose perspective?

Quality and accountability are intrinsically linked. As noted earlier, providing quality education requires critical consideration and application of relevant accountabilities. While the NQF is likely to support quality practice, intentional leaders need to consider the extent to which the NQF will support their own vision and philosophy about what it means to provide quality EC education for young children. As both a legal accountability and a discourse, the NQF can shape educators' thinking about 'quality'. Indeed, national and international research and academic commentary have suggested that regulatory requirements can shape and confine educators' professional practice (Chalke 2013; Fenech, 2007; Moss 2006; Osgood 2006; Woodrow & Busch, 2008).

chapter 7 considers the National Quality Framework as a discourse.

Intentional leaders ensure that they and the staff at their centre meet the requirements of the NQF. But they will also ensure that this compliance is meaningful—that it is not merely a 'let's make sure we pass the test' exercise. To this end, intentional leaders will not feel overwhelmed by the NQF, nor fearful of the assessment and rating process. They will approach both with confidence, in the knowledge that their centre team is on a trajectory informed by their vision, mission and philosophy towards high-quality education that is continually being refined as new families and children enter the centre community. Two examples that follow illustrate the value of thinking about quality as going beyond simply adhering to regulatory requirements. The first examines ratio and teacher requirements, and the second considers EC settings as sites that facilitate social inclusion.

see chapter 7 for a discussion on critically reading government policy and provisions.

According to COAG (2009b) the NQS was intended to ensure high-quality and consistent EC education and support ongoing quality improvement in settings across Australia. It is crucial that intentional leaders critically reflect on whether this is the case at their respective centres. Consider the regulatory staff:child ratios outlined in Table 3.3 (sourced directly from Fenech et al., 2012). For each age group NQS ratios are compared with (i) state regulatory standards that have been grandfathered (protected) and thus will continue to be legally enforced, and (ii) evidence-based recommendations from Early Childhood Australia (Press, 2006). The table shows that NQS standards meet evidence-based recommendations for only two out of five age groups. Questions for intentional leaders to consider are, 'What ratios will (or would) they seek to implement, and why?'

Table 3.3 Differing expectations on staff:child ratios

Age of Child	NQS Standards	Grandfathered Standards	Early Childhood Australia's Evidence-based Recommendations
Birth–12 months	1:4	N/A	1:3
13–24 months	1:4	N/A	1:4
25–35 months	1:5	VIC = 1:4	1:5
3 years	1:11	NSW, SA, TAS, WA = 1:10	1:8
≥ 4 years	1:11	NSW, SA, TAS, WA = 1:10	1:10

Source: Fenech, Giugni & Bown, 2012.

Requirements for qualified teachers pose similar questions for intentional leaders. Research undertaken in Australia (Fenech et al., 2010a) and overseas (Siraj-Blatchford & Manni, 2007) highlights the direct and indirect contribution of a core of EC teachers to quality EC education. Benefits included pedagogical leadership; a learning community where mentoring, support and collaboration occur in individual rooms; and across the centre; and staff stability. In some cases the employment of teachers above regulatory requirements was an outcome of intentional leaders who advocated for high-quality standards (Fenech et al., 2010a).

Juxtaposing this research is the NQF requirement for only one EC teacher per centre licensed for more than 25 children. (New South Wales Government, 2016, Division 5, Clause 130). Centres licensed to enrol fewer than 25 children are only required to have access to an EC teacher for at least 20 per cent of their operating hours. Given these scenarios, the intentional teacher can consider what their approach to staffing qualifications will be. What factors will support or inhibit their employment of EC teachers, as required by the NQF, but also beyond what is required? What mix of staffing qualifications will best enable the centre to live out its philosophy and strive towards its mission and vision? How might the intentional leader advocate for recommended teacher and ratio standards in their centre and more broadly in the sector?

chapter 7's focus on advocacy leadership can inform thinking about these questions.

Of course, the intentional leader's implementation of regulatory requirements such as ratios and qualified staff, in keeping with the centre's philosophy, is not straightforward. Issues such as teacher shortages, affordability, the management structures under which a centre operates and budget constraints can limit a vision for high quality.

chapters 5 and 13 consider how an intentional leader can strive to strategically plan for quality through, among other strategies, staffing practices and budgeting.

A second area that illustrates the importance of leaders utilising the NQF through the lens of their vision and philosophy is social inclusion. More than 30 years of research investigating quality in EC settings has primarily and consistently conceptualised quality EC education as education that enhances children's developmental outcomes (Fenech, 2011). This focus is, of course, a critical aspect of quality EC programs, and thus a key agenda of the NQF. Thinking about quality EC education more broadly, however—as, for example, encompassing social inclusion—may require approaches and practices that exceed NQF requirements.

In Leaders in practice 3.2 we read the perspective of Sylvia Turner, an experienced director of an EC centre in Sydney, New South Wales and recipient of the 2014 Australian Scholarships Group National Excellence in Teaching award, owing to her 'inspirational leadership'. In her profile, Sylvia shares her perspective about inclusion as an integral component of the quality she and her staff provide for children at their centre.

Visit Oxford Ascend to hear more from Sylvia.

LEADERS IN PRACTICE 3.2

Sylvia Turner

Director, Tigger's Honeypot Childcare Centre, University of New South Wales, Sydney (NSW)

I often wonder if growing up being different has not only built resilience within me but also the strong drive for inclusion, respect for diversity, and the importance for all to feel a sense of belonging and to have their voice acknowledged and represented.

Growing up I had to hide my cultural background—well, at least I thought I did. There was no space for being 'other'. It was assumed, I guess, that all of the children at preschool celebrated Christmas. We were all light skinned and spoke English. My mum would take me in to preschool each day and collect me, so the teachers never met my dad, never heard his thick accent. I have never asked my mother, but I do wonder if there were questions on the enrolment forms back then asking about culture or language. Perhaps there were, and perhaps my centre just wasn't sure about what to do with this knowledge—what to do about this 'otherness'. So, as a young child, I sat and listened and learnt the language of Christmas and Santa. I found a way to fit in. Eventually we moved to a suburb with cultural diversity. It took some time but eventually I felt safe, and understood.

As a teacher, and as an adult generally, my vision is for a peaceful world, one where everyone is safe, where we all feel a sense of belonging and connectedness, where we are understood and respected for who we are. It is ambitious, I know, but visions after all are meant to be aspirational—why not go for gold! With this in mind I try to make decisions that work towards this dream. I try to humanise decisions that need to be made while at the same time ensuring that they fit within the many frameworks within which I, as an EC professional, need to work.

As the director of an ECEC centre, a thorough knowledge of the regulatory requirements for my work is not only critical to ensure compliance, but can be a great tool too for pushing boundaries and going beyond. While some components within the NQF are black and white, there are many that are grey—that can be interpreted to best meet the needs of all families and children to work with equitable practices. I am conscious that I am now in a position of power and that I have an incredible legal responsibility for other people's children as well as for my own team of staff. My aim is to use my position to push boundaries so that there are better outcomes for all, and to ensure that I do my very best in relation to my responsibilities. This can only be done with an understanding of the frameworks within which I am required to work.

My centre's philosophy is a useful tool for backing up inclusive practice, and I am often debating with others the rights of inclusion for many 'othered' families or children, whether it be family type, ability, cultural heritage and so on. I find that being open from the outset about inclusion provides a safe space for prospective new families or staff; it reduces the likelihood that they feel that they need to be silent.

When questioned about our centre practices around inclusion, I always respond by saying how important it is to us that no child is silenced into pretending that they are anyone but who they are, or their family is anything other than what they are. I respond that we want children to grow up confident and proud of who they are. I love that I can also use the NQF to back up such practice to say that we are actually required to ensure inclusion and respect.

I am required to use the guiding principles of the NQF to inform my practice. My vision reflects these principles and I am grateful for their existence to support my practice. One of my favourite guiding principles is 'to ensure equity and inclusion'. I believe we are only limited by our own vision and commitment to social justice as to how we can use this principle to support decision-making. I can choose to use the NQF as a 'tick the box' or can truly and deeply engage within the requirements to work towards a vision of inclusion and respect. I will continue to use the NQF as a tool to challenge biases and break down stereotypes within the curriculum and whole-of-centre practice.

Pause–reflect–act 3.6

Take a few moments to reflect on Sylvia's profile and what you believe quality EC education for young children is.

- What does it look like?
- What does it value; for example, child development, inclusion, equity, children's rights ...?
- How might you use the NQF to support your ideal of what quality EC education is?
- What else will enable quality EC education at your centre?

Go to oxfordascend *to hear Sylvia's thoughts.*

Professional judgment and professional autonomy: essential tools in an intentional leader's repertoire

In the current regulatory climate, the challenge for intentional leaders is to engage with the NQF in ways that maximise its capacity to support quality practices. To do this will require professional judgment and professional autonomy. Together, these attributes mean that an intentional leader will not aim to meet the National Regulation and the NQS in a vacuum. Rather, and as has been alluded to in this chapter, the intentional leader will meet their accountabilities mindful of their professional vision and philosophy, their professional knowledge base (theoretical and technical) and their understanding of a given situation (for example, knowledge of the child, family and staff involved; and local context). With this collective knowledge, they will make informed decisions that are considered to be quality practice and in the children's best interests. Practising this way requires professional autonomy: having the freedom and being trusted to exercise professional judgment, and taking responsibility for the decisions made. Significantly, the NQF is premised on the principle of 'earned autonomy' (COAG, 2009b, pp. B–4). This means that the higher the quality rating a centre has the less it will be subject to formal and informal assessment visits from the regulatory authority, and thus the more scope it will be given to exercise professional judgment.

professional autonomy is being trusted with freedom to exercise professional judgment and take responsibility for making professional decisions.

Exercising professional judgment and **professional autonomy** is the hallmark of a professional (Sachs, 2003). Given a leader's legal and pedagogical responsibilities, it is appropriate and critical that they practise as professionals, not technicians. An analogy to illustrate this point is that of a GPS (Cheeseman, 2009). A leader who uses the NQF as a GPS—to take them to where they need to go without having to apply any thought to the matter—is like a technician who unthinkingly approaches their practice in a simplistic manner. In contrast, a leader who uses the NQF as a road map will practise intentionally and professionally, giving due consideration to the many factors that can impact on where they might like to go and what would be the best route to take.

see chapter 6 for a full discussion on pedagogical leadership.

Adopting a professional 'road map' approach necessitates intentional leaders having a strong working knowledge of all aspects of the NQF. A theme to emerge from the aforementioned research that investigated teachers' perceptions of the impact of the regulatory environment on their provision of quality EC education (Fenech, 2007) was that teachers' anxiety about regulations and accreditation could be attributable to their familiarity (or lack thereof) with these requirements. Some teachers appeared to rely on 'Chinese whispers'; that is, their knowledge of the requirements was second-hand. In contrast, teachers who were familiar with the requirements approached them with 'practical wisdom' (Goodfellow, 2003). These teachers read and re-read the requirements themselves, discussed what they might mean in practice at staff meetings, and explored which areas were 'black and white' (clear and not negotiable) and which were 'grey' (not clear and thus open to interpretation). They interrogated all areas and exercised professional judgment in light not just of the requirements, but of their more extended knowledge base and experience.

Chapter summary

Educators in EC settings are responsible for myriad legal and professional accountabilities, including the NQF. Intentional leaders will regard NQF requirements as critical to their knowledge base and thus one aspect to consider in their provision of quality EC education. Accountabilities such as the NQF will not be the key driver of an intentional leader's practice and provision of quality EC education. Rather, intentional leaders will exercise professional judgment and autonomy and meet their NQF responsibilities in ways that are consistent with their centre's vision, mission, philosophy and local context.

Key references

Dahlberg, G., Moss, P. & Pence, A. (2007). *Beyond quality in early childhood education and care: Languages of evaluation* (2nd ed.). London: Routledge.

This text provides a critical perspective on how 'quality' has been and can be otherwise conceptualised in EC policy and practice settings.

Fenech, M., Giugni, M. & Bown, K. (2012). A critical analysis of the National Quality Framework: Mobilising for a vision for children beyond minimum standards. *Australasian Journal of Early Childhood*, 12(4), 5–14.

This article provides a critical analysis of the NQF that intentional leaders can draw on to think about their provision of quality EC education.

Shepherd, W. (2004). Children's services: Dangerous places for children? *Rattler*, Autumn, 23–6.

This article offers a leader's perspective on the complexities of regulatory compliance in light of her vision for quality EC education. While over a decade old, the leadership issues raised in this article are still relevant today.

Online resources

National Quality Framework resources

These resources comprise guides to the NQF, the National Law and National Regulations, the NQS and developing a QIP. Published by the Australian Children's Education and Care Quality Authority (ACECQA, 2011), they are essential reading and provide clear explanations of leaders' and educators' accountabilities.

www.acecqa.gov.au/national-quality-framework

National Quality Framework videos and podcasts

ACECQA's website also has a range of videos and podcasts for educators that explain the NQF and can be used to reflect on and improve quality practice.

www.acecqa.gov.au/national-quality-framework/nqf-video-resources

4 LEADERSHIP AND GOVERNANCE

CHAPTER LEARNING OBJECTIVES

After studying this chapter you will understand that:

- Governance structures and processes outline authority and accountability arrangements.
- There is a close relationship between leadership decision-making, management structures and the governance of EC settings.
- Governance arrangements can apply at local, national and global contexts of EC education.
- The principles of good governance influence effective leadership.
- To ensure inclusivity, human rights principles underpin how governance is implemented.

Key concepts

duty of care
governance
government
management structures
mixed economy

Overview

Governance refers to the formal authority and accountability arrangements established within an EC organisation. How centres performed their core functions of learning and teaching with young children and their families is reflected in their governance arrangements. Good governance can be achieved by defining decision-making within a human rights perspective. Governance arrangements can have both immediate and long-term consequences for quality delivery of EC programs. As a framework for guiding leadership decision-making, governance arrangements can be an important resource for intentional leaders in their work.

Governance involves looking at both structures and processes of how an organisation functions in delivering its services according to its set objectives. Within Australia, EC organisations are managed under a variety of governance structures. For example, look at the NQF Snapshot Q3 (ACECQA, 2016, p. 7) for the distribution of different types of management structures of approved services around Australia. Management structures influence how governance is established and the different arrangements for achieving quality provisioning. For instance, the same 'Snapshot' shows that the highest proportion of approved services (54 per cent) rated as 'Exceeding NQS' were managed by state/territory and local governments (ACECQA, 2016, p. 11). Given the paucity of published research, this chapter presents a 'big picture' approach to governance of EC settings. Our aim is to raise awareness and understanding and thereby enable leadership thinking and action for good governance.

What is governance?

Governance arrangements provide guidance for leaders about their level of authority and shared accountabilities when overseeing the work of an EC setting. The word '**governance**' is, however, not well understood within the EC sector and this may be in part due to the limited research and writing on this topic (Neuman, 2005; Vitiello & Kools, 2010). Derived 'from a Greek word that means "to steer"' (Slocum-Bradley & Bradley, 2010, p. 32), governance is connected with the rules and procedures of how leadership decisions are made within organisations. The ethical governance of an organisation is dependent on who has been allocated governance responsibilities, and their 'personal integrity, attributes and skills, their understanding of and commitment to their role and their expertise and knowledge' of the organisational setting (Rytmeister & Marshall, 2007, p. 288). This explanation captures the moral and legal implications of why it is important to understand governance matters when running EC settings.

governance within EC organisations, governance refers to the overarching formal structures and accountability procedures that inform leadership decision-making when working with young children and their families.

Recently, Sharon Lynn Kagan, from the USA, collaborated with colleagues to produce the first book dedicated to governance matters in the EC sector (Kagan & Gomez, 2015). In the introduction, Kagan (2015a) laments that there is limited understanding or interest in pursuing governance matters in the EC sector and describes this as a situation where educators are 'flying the plane while building it' (p. 5). That is, trapped by the urgency of the moment, it is easy to ignore the broader context and the long-term implications of *not* stopping to think, and consider how, where and why you are 'flying somewhere'. Slowing down to reflect and making informed decisions today can be less risky in the long term.

to make sense of these comments further, read chapter 2 and reflect on how the continuous changes in government in Australia have impacted developments in the EC sector in this country.

Under the newly revised NQS (ACECQA, 2017, p. 174), Quality Area 7 has been renamed as 'Governance and Leadership'. This reflects the recognition of the importance of governance matters on quality provisioning and its link with leadership. The elements specified in this quality area highlight three aspects of governance that must be considered by all EC settings: service philosophy and purpose; management systems; and roles and responsibilities of those involved in decision-making and operation of the service (ACECQA, 2017, p. 174). The lack of substantive research on EC governance in Australian EC settings is, however, not helpful in assisting leaders and educators to get a better understanding of governance matters. We draw on governance literature published internationally to supplement our knowledge of leading EC settings in Australia to address relevant issues included in this chapter.

content covered in this chapter can be better understood when read in conjunction with chapter 2, which paints the relevant EC policy background in Australia; chapter 5 which provides guidance on strategic planning including developing a service philosophy; and chapter 8, which is helpful in understanding organisational change in times of significant policy change.

Governance matters describe the internal systems comprising the rules and processes that regulate decision-making within an organisation. These systems may be either formal or informal. Cobb, Danby and Farrell (2005) refer to the work of Foucault in explaining that governance matters reflect the distribution of power and control. As reflected in the two 'Leaders in practice' sections in this chapter, governance arrangements can enable leaders to monitor activities of their setting to ensure satisfactory achievement of compliance requirements, as well as guide future directions, by linking it to their long-term vision.

Global, national and local contexts of governance

Governance can be established at the global, national, and local levels. In Australia, for instance, governance of EC settings is influenced by policy directives from national, state/territory and local levels of **government**. Globally, having ratified the *Convention on the Rights of the Child* (UN, 1989), we are bound to uphold these Articles in all aspects of our work as EC teachers and leaders.

government
is the political system set up to run a country, state/territory or a local municipality.

At a national and global level, governance matters are also discussed in relation to how a country organises its systems of EC programs. Discussions about governance often refer to the distribution of political power in terms of how a country allocates its economic and social resources on behalf of its citizens (World Bank, 1992, cited in Slocum-Bradley & Bradley, 2010). Historically, in most countries governments have provided essential services such as education, health and welfare; and controlled the taxation, national laws and national security arrangements. Policies and procedures set up to manage these structures and systems describe how governments carry out their governance functions in an orderly way.

Accordingly, governance matters can be examined within the local context of an organisation, as well as more broadly, in relation to a particular sector, state or a country. Based on an analysis of data from 12 OECD countries, Neuman (2005, pp. 133–7) outlined three approaches to the governance of EC programs:

- *Administrative integration:* Establishment of national legislative frameworks enable governance matters to be managed under one authority. In countries such as Finland and Denmark, EC programs come under a single administrative system, which is today run by the Department of Education.
- *Decentralisation:* In this model, there is minimal control of EC settings by the government. As such, in countries such as Norway and the UK, the involvement of parents and other community members has emerged as an important feature of this type of decentralised governance situated within local communities.
- *Privatisation:* The presence of a high proportion of private operators in countries such as Australia and the USA reflects a market-oriented approach to EC program provision. The diversity of providers and the reliance on market forces necessitate the development of quality assurance mechanisms to reduce inequities in quality, affordability and access across private and public programs.

Countries such as Australia that have a federated system of policy making based on multiple levels of government illustrate a decentralised approach to governance. However, given the high proportion of private providers of EC settings in this country (ACECQA, 2016), the current context is more reflective of a privatisation model. The involvement of multiple management agencies also reflects fragmentation in governance and this can make information sharing and policy coordination challenging (Neuman, 2005; Vitiello & Kools, 2010). In Australia, the NQF is, however, intended to achieve consistency across the country through 'a jointly governed, uniform and integrated national approach to the regulation and quality assessment of education and care services' (ACECQA, 2011b). Reflecting the complexities of governance matters, note also that the NQF is administered at the state level and may be subject to state policy priorities and decision-making of local operatives, reflecting the complexities of governance matters in this country.

the federated system of government in Australia is discussed in chapter 2.

Pause–reflect–act 4.1

- Think about each of the three approaches to governance identified above in terms of the implementation of the NQS. To what extent has the establishment of ACECQA facilitated an integrated approach to quality assurance in EC settings in Australia?
- Interview someone with governance responsibilities in an EC organisation to discuss the advantages and disadvantages of integration, decentralisation and privatisation of governance arrangements.
- As an intentional leader, what systems will you put in place to ensure effective participation by staff from different disciplinary backgrounds, and those from diverse cultural backgrounds who are unfamiliar with EC programs and their governance arrangements?

Good governance

The notion of 'good governance' is something that is usually talked about when things go wrong! By simply having governance arrangements, it is assumed that an organisation has in place systems and procedures to govern ethically and efficiently to meet the objectives of the organisation. However, the 'proof is in the pudding', because implementation of governance can be messy, particularly when those responsible may not fully understand their governance responsibilities or the implications of what this could mean for the organisation. *In Leaders in practice 4.1, long-term child advocate Leanne Gibbs writes about her perceptions on the importance of why we need to better understand governance matters in the EC sector.*

LEADERS IN PRACTICE 4.1

Leanne Gibbs

Early Childhood Consultant and experienced Board Member, Sydney (NSW)

Visit Oxford Ascend to hear more from Leanne.

How would you describe the nature of governance in EC settings?

Governance is what holds the EC setting together and is the foundation for quality. If you are paying attention to regulations, and paying attention to your statutory responsibilities and the overarching management, then you can dedicate time and effort to strong leadership and sound practice. A high-quality educational program and practice is founded upon establishing a sound methodical approach to governance.

What are the key components of good governance?
The broad components of good governance include (but are not limited to) the management structure of the organisation; legal responsibilities; strategic and business planning; risk assessment and management of risks; compliance and monitoring of standards; staff performance monitoring and management; and ethical codes and practices. Together, these components influence how an organisation is run. They provide the foundation for quality provisioning in each centre and we need to first get these components set up right.

Why is it important for EC leaders to understand governance matters?
Of all the things that enable us to run an organisation well, the laws and legislation which set up the structural elements in relation to the management, and the style and type of management that is behind the individual service, are of critical importance. This is why whether it's a community committee, a larger auspicing body, or it's a private individual or a large corporation, it's essential that we understand the governance framework and the policy context in which we work as EC educators.

How can a leader contribute to improving governance of EC settings?
Leaders perform an important role in governance in ensuring the service is compliant in Quality Area 1. They must be an authority on the NQS and the EYLF. This ensures that leaders are a central point of interest, and information for management, and this means making themselves absolutely indispensable with their knowledge, and as an advocate for high standards in their service. Sometimes EC leaders might say, 'Oh, I don't have anything to do with the governance' but in actual fact they perform this absolutely key role in the governance of a service. Other areas of the NQS are more broadly understood by people who are driving the business, or who are managing the business or driving the strategy. Knowledge of the EYLF is critical professional knowledge and it must be present in order for every service to fulfil their mission in promoting children's learning.

What are some of the challenges of governance that you have encountered in EC settings?
I'll focus on challenges and opportunities within governance for community management. There are incredible benefits in community management and these contribute greatly to the EC landscape, but some say that is an outdated form of management because governance has become quite complex. I think that's a great shame because the value in having community management provides experience for peoples' civic contribution, for exercising influence, and for running and operating a community-based business. The challenges of complexity could be alleviated through professional development offered at an affordable fee, and offered by peak organisations or through funded government support in recognition of the largely un-costed contribution made by parent-led committees of management on a voluntary basis. It is also the responsibility of the managing committee to stay up to date on governance matters and take up every opportunity to explore resources and undertake professional development.

How are good governance and quality linked, and how does this impact on children and families?
When we have good governance we free ourselves to perform the important work that we do with children and with our team. Rather than being sidelined or side-tracked by governance matters, we can focus on the important work of relationships and of the programs and practices. Efficiency of governance allows people to have that time. Just as an example—if

you have good processes in a service, even around something like paying fees, and it's understood and managed well, that means a family, a parent or a carer may not come into the service and wonder how they could pay their fees, and divert someone to provide that information. Instead, that is clearly understood and actioned seamlessly, and everyone is satisfied.

Another example is a director who wants to think about developing their people really well within the service. Good governance will free up time and the funds, because good governance saves money. Well-managed budgets, well-administered services, can in turn ensure that services are on track and retain a strong focus on the core business of EC settings—the pedagogy and programs for children's learning. It frees up funds for professional development and allows the director more time to be in a mentoring and coaching role with staff. It also ensures that a service is operating legitimately with a legal framework. When they're doing that there's less stress, less crisis management, and services will be focused on the mission of achieving positive outcomes for children and families.

I believe good governance is absolutely essential. It is intricately linked with quality and you just cannot have equality without having really strong governance in the service.

Pause–reflect–act 4.2

- After reading this chapter, write two to three sentences of what you understand as the key components of governance matters in EC settings. Check your responses against the content covered in this chapter to see what aspects you captured well and areas that need further development.
- Reflect on Leanne's comments about the importance of good governance. To what extent were you aware of these issues based on your own experiences of EC settings?
- Arrange to have a discussion on governance matters with colleagues working with you at your EC settings. Assess the level of understanding and propose to have a follow-up discussion using content from this chapter. You could develop a short quiz of multiple choice answers or true/false questions using the contents of this chapter.

Go to oxfordascend *to hear Leanne's thoughts.*

Given the lack of research on governance within the EC sector we also present findings based on schools and communities more broadly; that is, of relevance to promote thinking and discussion. For example, in defining the concept of governance, educational leadership scholar Brian Caldwell (2013) explains that governance is 'the process whereby elements in a society wield power and authority, and influence and enact policies and decisions concerning public life, and economic and social development' (p. 5). Based on an analysis of governance systems around the world, Caldwell draws attention to questions about autonomy within a decentralised system. Within the EC sector, it is important to explore the different levels of decision-making—both within and externally to your EC setting—to understand where power and authority rest for different aspects such as staffing, budgets and program development.

In another example involving Indigenous organisations, Moran, Porter and Curth-Bibb (2014, p. 3) identified several aspects of good governance that are of relevance for EC leaders:

- Stable, ongoing funding (generally over a 3–5 year timeline) can lead to improved governance capabilities.
- Governance capabilities can be enhanced when discretion is devolved locally, including the powers to budget, plan and make operational decisions, allowing the organisation to respond to local priorities.
- Supporting culturally and contextually appropriate governing structures is likely to have a positive effect on governance capabilities.

These three aspects reflect the importance of stability in the funding arrangements, and the authority to identify priorities and make decisions that are in keeping with local community needs. This study also noted challenges of governance experienced by organisations operating within rural and remote communities in Australia: 'low population densities and mobile populations, combined with great distances to urban centres, create deficits in how people are represented politically, how services are administered, and how people access their due entitlements as citizens' (p. 10).

These findings reinforce the contextual nature of governance arrangements and the importance of governance as a strategy for inclusion and respectful cultural practice. It takes courageous leadership to explore alternative strategies to achieve good governance with limited local resources. This is where being connected to a range of networks and the use of technological skills can enable EC leaders to offer support, guidance or advice to assist others to progress and prosper, especially during a crisis such as recovering after a bush fire or floods. Having a good governance system already in place can facilitate early resolution and progress.

Pause–reflect–act 4.3

- How much time does your board spend looking at the educational programs being designed and delivered to children?
- How do these discussions influence decision-making about the business plans of your centre?
- Find out who is eligible to be a member of your board/committee—parents of children attending the centre; staff; and community members with specific expertise on finances, education, health and so on.
- In what ways is the leadership decision-making by the board/committee communicated to families and staff and how is their work evaluated?

By including parents and other community members when establishing the centre vision, philosophy and long-term strategic directions can facilitate public accountability. Based on findings from a study of schools in the UK, Young (2015, p. 14) raised concerns about the dominance of managerial expertise of school governance boards, and warns that this reflected 'deeper trends in wider society towards increasing managerialism and the marginalisation of non-managerial voices'. The voluntary nature of parent involvement in the management committees of community-based EC settings can sometimes make decision-making slow and difficult. To assist with setting organisational goals and decisions, parents can be offered 'training' on being more effective on governance matters.

Working collaboratively with parents can be mutually satisfying and it is likely that the educators themselves require training on how to participate in collecting data to support public accountability. Just like the board members, it is likely that staff also have no experience in program evaluation or governance. Being able to collate and analyse organisational data is different from teaching, and participation in program evaluation workshops can enhance skills and knowledge in actively contributing to this work and making better use of organisational developments over time.

Governance in practice

To understand how governance arrangements work within EC organisations, leaders must become familiar with the overarching **management structures**, policies and procedures that inform decision-making when working with young children and their families. This approach is also recognised in the NQS as reflected in Quality Area 7 standard 7.1 and its associated elements (ACECQA, 2017, p.174). Documents such as the constitution, minutes of meetings and annual reports can assist in learning about governance procedures of the organisation. Establishing formal systems of governance can provide clarity by outlining the lines of communication and authority as well as accountability responsibilities of specific individuals (such as the centre director) or a group (such as the management committee). To be effective, governance information needs to be made available and transparent in the way it is applied to decision-making in the organisation. In turn, a sense of security can be achieved through compliance with good governance practice. As Neuman (2005, p. 132) explains, governance is 'the "glue" that holds the pieces of the EC system together'.

management structures EC organisations are managed under diverse systems, ranging in size and structure from a single organisation to a group comprising two or more centres.

Broadly speaking, governance arrangements reflect the management structure of the organisation and the inherent distribution of power among the stakeholders who make decisions about the organisation's activities. Governance processes can involve a range of personnel who have a particular interest or role within the organisation. They include centre-based educators with senior executive roles (such as Sally Whitaker, Leaders in practice 4.2) or management staff who work at the council or municipal office (such as Karen Roberts, who was profiled in the first edition of this book—see pages 69–71), or the state branch office of a large company that owns and operates centres across the country. In community-managed EC organisations, governance responsibilities are shared with parents. They are typically unpaid volunteers with executive responsibilities as the president or chairperson of the management committee/board. In privately owned centres, governance responsibilities could be held by the owners or managers who run the day-to-day operations. In effect, governance underpins the work of everyone and can assist leaders in creating order, consistency and predictability in organisational decision-making. *In Leaders in practice 4.2, Sally Whitaker, an experienced centre director, describes her approach to governance.*

LEADERS IN PRACTICE 4.2

Sally Whitaker

Centre Director, Leederville Early Childhood Centre (WA)

Governance to me means the smooth running of the centre adhering to the laws and regulations that apply to us in the EC sector. We are a community-based service overseen by a management committee made up of parents. This committee is the centre's governing body and the assistant director and I are responsible for the day-to-day running of the centre. The management committee, including 11 parents, is responsible for the 'bigger decisions' such as employing the centre director. They sign off on the fee rate and accept the budget that the treasurer, bookkeeper and I have prepared. They approve large purchases such as a new oven, new guttering, internal painting—anything really over $5000. I circulate the quotes via email so that people can come prepared to discuss them at the meeting.

We are licensed for 64 children and are currently at 98 per cent utilisation. My role is to adhere to the national laws and regulations, including Occupational Health and Safety (OH&S) laws. I believe in honesty and transparency, and I believe this shines through in the way things are done at our centre. Committee meetings are held between 7 and 9 pm, which is after working all day, so it is a long day. Not everyone can make it to meetings every time and people do drop out for whatever reasons through the year too. We usually have about seven people there, with myself and the assistant director attending too. If the assistant director is away, the educational leader comes in her place (and if I am away, she accompanies the assistant director).

We have monthly staff meetings where things are discussed and the educational leader has team leader meetings where issues around curriculum are discussed. Any issues around governance are usually discussed at staff/committee meetings. To be honest, it depends on what the issue is as to when it is addressed. If it is really serious, it would be addressed immediately. The assistant director is heavily involved in the centre. She works full-time in the office, alongside me, managing enrolments. The educational leader is off the floor and leads the curriculum throughout the centre. She also assists in mentoring new educators and students within our centre. Both the assistant director and I manage the staff team of 28.

I have a good relationship with the committee. I can contact them via phone or email at any time. The chairperson comes in twice a week for a brief catch up about staff and any general matters. I also report on unusual big purchases, and have contact with the regulatory unit and any 'serious' matters that I feel need to be discussed in person rather than by email or phone. The treasurer and I meet once a week as she sights and signs all paid invoices

Figure 4.1 Centre governance structure

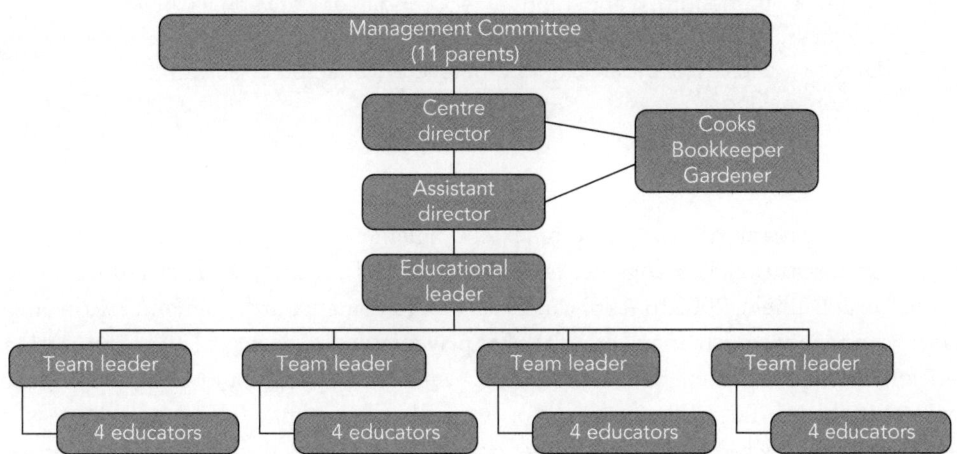

and this means we can discuss any budgetary issues. It is just good for them to know what is going on. I also work closely with my assistant director and sometimes it is useful to chat with someone else who is one step removed.

Committee meetings are held once a month and I distribute the agenda and my report one week beforehand. I feel I have a lot of autonomy regarding my role. I am responsible for all the employment of staff and their subsequent performance management. I deal with complaints and staffing issues, but if it becomes serious, I get the committee involved. So, for example, we have had a staff member involved in some conflict with other staff which resulted in that staff member walking off the job (casually employed gardener). Now, I dealt with that myself and then just reported to the committee that he had left. Parent complaints are also dealt with by myself and the assistant director. If anyone was unhappy with a decision, then I would refer them to the committee. Parents do complain to me, but it might be around little issues like shoes that are lost or that a parent didn't like the way someone spoke to their child.

Pause–reflect–act 4.4

- Reflect on the organisational flow chart of Sally's centre. Use this to think about the paid employment positions you have held and draw an organisational picture of one of the places where you have worked to show the various positions held by the people you worked with. Include yourself in this structure.
- Highlight people who had authority to make key decisions within this organisation. How did you contribute to decision-making in your organisation? Did you feel empowered or marginalised from the decision-making processes?

- Connect both the formal and informal reporting lines between various individuals. Reflect on the nature of leadership decision-making that took place in this organisation. What factors enabled effective decision-making?

Within EC organisations, 'the complex entanglement of key actors, power plays and structures, institutional arrangements, and intellectual property and related discourses' (Johnston & Duffield, 2002, p. 126) can impact on governance arrangements. Accordingly, leaders can benefit from being aware of the key players, what roles they play in organisational decision-making and their own relationships with these people and structures. Within community-based EC organisations, for example, there may be complexities when the same parents who are the customers or clients can also be members of the centre's management committee. These parents effectively hold the position of being the employers who can hire and fire staff. Likewise, when centres are part of a large private company or non-government organisation responsible for 10 or more centres, working out who is responsible for leadership decisions may not be easy. Regardless of the size or scale of the organisation, structures can promote ambiguity in the roles and responsibilities of governance allocated to employees and committee members, and if left unresolved, can create tensions.

EC management structures and governance

Leadership and governance responsibilities are interconnected with centre ownership and management responsibilities. Who owns the centre and the way they run the organisation may be reflected in their approach to leadership. Governance requirements also vary according to the way centres are established as a business. By adopting a structural or technical approach to governance, the legal obligations comprising what governance stakeholders are expected to do can be examined. The politicisation of governance practices has been raised in relation to the corporatisation of EC programs in Australia (Brennan, 2007). These discussions draw attention to philosophical or ideological perspectives on governance matters, which require exploration to ensure consistency in practice by all involved within a particular organisation.

mixed economy
there is diversity of ownership and management of organisations involved in delivering EC programs in Australia. The availability of this mix of private and community-based organisations within one country can be described as working within a mixed economy.

The existence of EC organisations that are funded privately and publicly reflects the notion that Australia is a **mixed economy**. This means that the ownership and management of organisations delivering EC programs can be private or community based. Traditionally, EC organisations have been categorised broadly as either 'for-profit' (FP) or 'not-for-profit' (NFP) on the basis of who benefits from the income generated in delivering EC programs. Although this may imply a polarisation between private (being FP) and public (being NFP) organisations, the reality is more complex because multiple variations in management structures that fall between these two models are possible.

Consider, for example, the following list of some organisations that may sponsor and manage EC programs in Australia:

- Universities and Technical and Further Education (TAFE) colleges that aim to support their students and staff with young children.
- Preschool centres funded by the state government that have a parent committee of management and are open only during the school term dates.
- Multifunctional Aboriginal Children's Services (MACS) run by Indigenous communities.
- Big companies, hospitals and banks that are large employers of parents with young children may manage or sponsor centres on-site or near the parents' place of employment.
- Faith-based organisations (such as churches) that may establish EC centres to support families with young children from disadvantaged backgrounds or as an outreach program for those who practise their faith.
- Schools that may establish EC centres on their school grounds to support staff and families with younger siblings and to act as a feeder program into the compulsory school years.

This is not an exhaustive list of sponsors, but it illustrates the diversity of stakeholders involved in managing EC organisations and their varied motivations for being involved in EC provision. The purpose and intent of the setting will influence their governance arrangements, including who has the authority and responsibility for making leadership decisions. Differences can also arise due to the beliefs and values that underpin the philosophical approach of the organisation and the level of management control exerted over day-to-day functions. For example, being part of a large national organisation can mean that centre-based policies are defined centrally and implemented through managers located at the head office or state/territory/regional branches of that organisation.

Given the kaleidoscope of management structures or models present within the EC sector, it is not possible to identify specific governance requirements that cover each system or structure. To be effective as an intentional leader, a sound awareness of the organisational structures, systems and lines of authority and responsibilities of leading the organisation is therefore central in understanding what governance involves. Governance work requires understanding both structural characteristics of an organisation—its size, management structure, history, rules and regulations governing its work—as well as the roles and responsibilities of those involved in governance matters. The subtleties and complexities of governance arrangements of each organisation are best learnt from the inside, as an employee. In essence, the leader's awareness and understanding of the particular characteristics of each workplace, including its history and future directions, hold the key to achieving good governance outcomes.

Pause–reflect–act 4.5

Taking into account the connectivity between governance arrangements, management structures and leadership, consider the following scenarios.

- You have started working as a director of a community-based preschool and soon notice that there has not been an annual general meeting (AGM) for two years; there are no minutes of committee meetings and the majority of parents you talk to do not know that there is a committee structure to govern the preschool. What steps will you take to raise these issues with the committee, given that you have very little knowledge of associations law and expected that this would already have been taken care of?
- As the owner of a stand-alone private centre who values input from families, how would you incorporate parents' perspectives in centre policies and strategic plans?

Governance roles and responsibilities in EC settings

Community-based EC organisations in countries such as Australia have a long history of being run by volunteer parents formally constituted as boards or management committees. Responsibilities of these boards/committees include monitoring and reviewing strategic goals and objectives as well as setting the organisation's vision, and clarifying the philosophy and approach to children's programs (Community Child Care New South Wales (CCCNSW), 2006). Roberts (2008) also acknowledges that members of boards or committees must have a sound understanding of their governance roles and responsibilities. This view is supported by CCCNSW (2006), which has designed a set of governance guidelines, including the following:

- Use of specific processes to appoint members and explain their roles and responsibilities.
- A clear identification of lines of authority in decision-making.
- The identification of conflict of interest and disclosure of relevant relationships between the boards/committees, staff and other individuals that can influence decision-making.
- Use of specific protocols to protect child and family privacy and confidentiality.
- Procedures used to make decisions, especially when urgent matters arise between meetings, are transparent and clearly specified.

These aspects may be typically incorporated into the constitution or rules of the organisation.

When an organisation is working well, it is an indication that good governance is in place. Although there is no agreement about the specific functions of governance in EC settings, the following principal functions are noted here:

- Allocation of human and fiscal resources
- Accountability in relation to compliance, consistency and data collation

- Collaboration within and external to the organisation
- Planning for both programming and fiscal aspects
- Regulation involving licensing and compliance
- Quality improvement of programs and the workforce and setting standards
- Outreach and engagement with families and communities.

Source: Adapted from Gomez, 2014, cited in Kagan, 2015b, p. 12.

Each of these functions can be acted upon as everyday operational matters in managing an EC organisation or a group of settings across a neighbourhood or a bigger region.

Thomas (2011) also concurs that good governance includes having 'evidence that the organisation is striving towards a sustainable business model, and effective and efficient business practices' (p. 118). Tensions arise when trying to balance the economic and social imperatives of the organisation. The extent to which key governance documents (such as the centre's vision and mission statements, business plans and philosophy) are aligned can also make a difference in the way leadership decisions are made.

As noted by Nicholson, Newton, McGregor-Lowndes and Sheldrake (2008), boards overseeing not-for-profit organisations have come under public scrutiny. Increasing demands placed on board members' competence and closer monitoring of their performance can make it difficult to attract and retain members. Within EC organisations, it is possible that the centre director may be more knowledgeable about governance requirements than the board. In their survey of more than 500 NFP organisations in Queensland, Nicholson et al. (2008) found that 'strategy and business planning emerges as the topic showing the largest gap between respondents' competence and the perceived importance for their Board' (p. 10). Anecdotal evidence suggests that in the EC sector difficulties also arise in identifying parents with appropriate expertise to join boards/committees to run EC settings. Accepting anyone who volunteers or reluctantly agrees may not be a sensible way to proceed in terms of establishing a board that is competent, capable and committed in running a viable, quality centre.

see chapter 13 for how key governance documents including business plans and philosophy can influence how leadership decisions are made within EC organisations.

Relationships between board/committee members and centre staff may also be complicated by the fact that the staff are responsible for educating the children of their employers, and they are hired/fired by the board comprising these parents. As such, the establishment of professional respect, trust and effective communication between the board/committee/owner as the employer, and the staff as employees may be awkward. Accordingly, a clear understanding of the lines of authority and maintaining professional relationships are essential from the beginning.

Pause–reflect–act 4.6

- Imagine your child is attending a long day care centre. You are interested in playing an active role in the way decisions are made at the centre. As a parent at the centre, what are the pros and cons of joining the management committee?

- Switch the roles now and imagine that you are centre director at an EC setting. What steps will you take to develop a good relationship with parents on the management committee?
- What does a new committee member need to know to carry out their governance responsibilities effectively?

Typically, governance structures and processes are enablers or factors that can ensure the effective functioning of an organisation. Those such as Kagan and Gomez (2015) are convincing in arguing that governance is the number-one element of an organisation or system that defines its success and sustainability. As such, they perceive governance as a strategy for organisational development as well as a systems transformation process. This means that EC leaders who want to introduce innovation and reform, and achieve significant change within their settings, must have a good understanding of governance matters as these mechanisms can be used to leverage modifications throughout the organisation/systems.

Kagan and Gomez (2015) present numerous examples of writers with first-hand experiences of governance changes within a variety of EC settings. Although these cases are contextualised to settings in the USA, the following five core goals of governance that must be addressed by the board/committee, invite discussion by EC leaders located anywhere:

- *Coordination*: What are the links between the different parts of the organisation/system and its programs?
- *Alignment*: To what extent is there coherence across and between the various elements of policy and practice within the organisation/system?
- *Sustainability*: How does the system/organisation respond to changes from within and externally?
- *Efficiency*: Are there any areas of overlap and duplication and how can these be removed or minimised to achieve better returns through maximum efficiency?
- *Accountability*: What strategies are in place to communicate and consult stakeholders of the organisation/system to demonstrate that the governance arrangements are effective in achieving the aims of the organisation/system? (adapted from Regenstein, 2015, pp. 36–7)

chapter 5 explores strategic planning and the application of ethical entrepreneurship.

Application of ethical governance can be seen when looking at the strategic organisational plans connected with the vision and long-term objectives of the organisation. In this regard, Kagan (2015b, p. 20) urges us to consider the 'three systemic outputs that are reasonable to expect from a well-functioning governance system' and these comprise:

- *Equity:* there is equitable distribution of funding for programs and services catering to young children and their families
- *Quality:* availability of services and programs of adequate standard for all children
- *Sustainability:* ensuring that there is stable provision of quality programs over time.

Pause–reflect–act 4.7

As an intentional leader, think about how you will go about addressing the following three issues:

- Responding to a parent who has made a complaint about a staff member.
- Identifying the need to change the way the outdoor playground is used.
- Dealing with the serious injury to a child at the centre.

Look at the governing documents covering policies and procedures at your centre in working out how you will respond to each issue.

Governance and human rights

There are global metrics that can be used to assess how well organisations satisfy their governance requirements (see, for example, Thomas, 2010). While these metrics have limited application to EC organisations, they do reflect a common concern about the importance of defining indicators of 'good' governance within principles of social justice and participatory democracy. This is achieved by aligning an organisation's governance arrangements with the Universal Declaration of Human Rights as this document stipulates the minimum standards that uphold human dignity during interactions between people (Office of the United Nations High Commissioner for Human Rights (UNHCHR), 2007), and this is explained as follows:

> When led by human rights values, good governance reforms of democratic institutions create avenues for the public to participate in policymaking either through formal institutions or informal consultations. They also establish mechanisms for the inclusion of multiple social groups in decision-making processes, especially locally. Finally, they may encourage civil society and local communities to formulate and express their positions on issues of importance to them. (UNHCHR, 2007, p. 2)

As can be seen, human rights principles can be used to inform governance arrangements such as when allocating responsibilities to staff and board/committee members. Accordingly, the application of five 'key attributes of good governance' as defined by the United Nations Resolution 2000/64 (UNHCHR, 2007, p. 4) comprise the following:

- *Transparency:* This explains the extent to which management processes are clear, unambiguous and easy to follow as well as information that is available and open to public scrutiny (that is, it is transparent). Transparency can empower service users (that is, children and parents) and staff, and is considered effective governance. However, some high level decisions may not be made public or discussed widely with staff and families for strategic or competitive reasons. Nevertheless, as Panousieris (2008) notes, it is important to keep everyone 'informed of changes in duties, policies and procedures' (p. 93). He adds that in relation to 'the empowerment of people from marginalised

balancing social/ethical responsibilities against economic imperatives is discussed in chapter 14.

groups'—as represented by those from culturally and linguistically diverse backgrounds, for instance—'the principles of participation, transparency and accountability are central to good governance' (p. 92).

duty of care reflects the fundamental obligation of all EC staff to ensure children within their organisation are safe from harm at all times while at the centre.

- *Responsibility:* Within EC organisations, all staff have a **duty of care** to ensure the safety and well-being of all children at the setting. Key personnel such as centre directors/ managers can have formal governance obligations in connection with their specific roles and identified in the Constitution of the organisation. Likewise, availability of position descriptions for board/committee members as well as having policy and procedures manuals, for example, reflect good governance (CCCNSW, 2006). Tensions can arise when balancing social/ethical responsibilities against economic imperatives.
- *Accountability:* The liabilities of organisations can be set according to various purposes such as staffing and budgeting. This requires legislative knowledge including taxation, employment and company laws. Within EC organisations, having specific procedures for things such as complaints management, and provision of professional learning to support staff, management and/or committee members reflects accountability and compliance with government legislation as well as consistency in responding ethically and equitably.
- *Participation:* By making explicit how children, families and staff can be involved in organisational decision-making everyone can feel they have the possibility of contributing to quality service provision. The centre's constitution or rules can indicate how decisions are made and who is involved. For example, all parents can have the opportunity to contribute to strategic decision-making at the centre, without this being limited to those who are board/committee representatives. Likewise, all parents can cast a vote to elect board/committee members, instead of recruiting specific individuals because of their expertise. These types of participatory processes are more likely 'to be perceived as legitimate' by those contributing to the organisational design, implementation and review processes (UNHCHR, 2007, p. 5).
- *Responsiveness:* The extent to which an organisation is aware, receptive and sensitive about both service users and employees can impact on effective governance. In particular, leaders must find ways to ensure the voice of marginalised groups or minorities can be heard in governance matters. 'Giving people time to consider options/ choices and make their own decisions' as well as providing induction and mentoring on management procedures are ways of reducing barriers to effective participation (Panousieris, 2008, pp. 92–3).

Overall, the application of these five elements in governance decision-making can vary according to who is the owner or the sponsor and how the organisation is constituted (as either a stand-alone centre or a group-based centre, for example). Some leaders may prioritise income generation while others may emphasise the importance of responding to children and families from disadvantaged backgrounds. Accordingly, leaders must have a sound understanding of the contextual dimensions and the constitutional requirements that underpin the organisation within which they work when implementing governance principles within a human rights ethos.

Pause–reflect–act 4.8

Consider the following scenario, which takes place within a city suburb with an ageing population. The parent management committee of a preschool is concerned with falling enrolments. What was once a well-established preschool can only identify 10 children for next year's enrolments. The EC teacher has been the director for 15 years and other staff have also been there for about the same period. There are few parents showing interest in being on the management committee and everyone is concerned about the future viability of the preschool. The long day centre nearby has offered to take over the management of the preschool. Some parents are happy with that offer and some are not.

- If you were on the management committee of the preschool how would you inform the parents of next year's children about the difficulties the centre is facing?
- If you were to recommend retaining the preschool as an independent centre, how would you justify it?
- What action would need to be taken if it was decided to take on the challenge of retaining the preschool as an independent centre? For example, how would you restructure the program and staff it within a set budget?
- What do you need to do to boost enrolments for next year?
- What are the competing ideologies that drive the management of EC services?

Reflecting on the key role EC leaders can play in addressing governance challenges, three suggestions made by Shawar and Shiffman (2016, p. 5) are presented here to stimulate collaborative conversations on how things can be improved in the future:

- *First, pursue small wins:* This acknowledges that it takes time to establish collaboration, and thereby 'deepen trust, commitment and shared understanding'.
- *Second, seek strategies that enable stability and flexibility:* While control of authority and accountability may be useful at the beginning, over time, as trust builds, promote local decision-making to address local issues.
- *Three, adopt an inclusive approach:* This is critical so that those whose needs are being served by the centre can have a direct role in the decisions that impact their lives.

Overall, one of the key messages of this chapter is that governance doesn't just happen—it takes time, thinking and planning. Kagan (2015b) believes that 'leadership is critical in the planning phase' (p. 23). Kagan (2015a, p. 5) also notes that there is a world-wide need for both theory-based conceptual work as well as empirical research on studying the impact of governance on children and families attending EC settings. Many questions surround the role of governance as a transformative process as opposed to the operationalising of policy and law and there is great benefit in this line of inquiry. EC leaders can also consolidate their skills and knowledge about governance matters by sharing experiences of good governance and stimulating further discussion on how to address the challenges encountered in leading governance decision-making.

Chapter summary

In this chapter, the concept of governance is explained broadly, and specifically in its application within EC organisations. The interconnections between governance, management structures and leadership are discussed in relation to stand-alone and group-based settings. The leader of an EC setting is directly impacted by the governance structure. It is essential for intentional leaders to understand the governance context within which they work and the lines of authority and communication that exist to make the organisation function successfully. From a social justice perspective, a human rights framework was adopted in exploring governance requirements in EC organisations. The nature of interactions between the people involved and their understanding of the governance arrangements will reflect their approach or style of governance being practised.

Key references

Caldwell, B. (2013). *Assessing the goodness of fit for Victoria of approaches to school governance in national and international jurisdictions.* Commissioned by the Strategy and Review Group. Department of Education and EC Development (DEECD). Final Report. Melbourne: DEECD.

This report looks at school governance in a variety of OECD countries, and defines governance as a process built on relationships between the school and the broader community. Lessons learnt can be considered by EC leaders as well.

Kagan, S.L. & Gomez, R.E. (2015). (Eds.). *Early childhood governance: Choices and consequences* (pp. 9–29). New York: Teachers College Press, Columbia University.

This book of edited chapters provides an introduction to governance from a systems development perspective. Affirming the inextricable link between governance and leadership, various authors present case studies of their experiences, highlighting the complexities of governance in EC settings in diverse locations in the USA.

Young, H. (2015). Knowledge, experts and accountability in school governing bodies. *Educational Management and Leadership*, 45(1), 1–17. doi: 10.1177/1741/143215595415

Based on a study of school governing bodies in the UK, this paper warns about dangers of focusing on managerialism, and these issues can apply to EC settings as well.

Online resources

Australian Childcare Alliance

This is a national organisation for childcare centre operators and has branches in several states.

www.australianchildcarealliance.org.au

Community Childcare Cooperative NSW

This organisation provides advice and professional learning resources to support both staff and boards/committees in EC organisations. It includes a handbook for committee members called 'So now you are on the committee' and a series of online resources that can be downloaded free of charge.

www.ccccnsw.org.au/resources/management

Office of the Registrar of Indigenous Corporations (ORIC)

This is an Australian government website, and homepage of ORIC, which is an independent statutory office that administers the *Corporations (Aboriginal and Torres Strait Islander) Act 2006*. ORIC provides training, support and publications including policies on running Indigenous corporations.

www.oric.gov.au

5 STRATEGIC PLANNING AND SOCIAL ENTREPRENEURSHIP

CHAPTER LEARNING OBJECTIVES

After studying this chapter you will understand that:

- Australian EC settings operate within an ethical business framework.
- EC teachers are often called upon to lead evaluation and planning processes.
- Collaboration with key stakeholders is an essential part of planning.
- An organisational vision that takes account of internal and external factors is critical to successful planning.
- There are different types of planning, including futures planning, strategic planning and operational planning.
- Marketing is an essential component of business viability.
- Social entrepreneurship is a framework that can guide leaders' marketing decisions and strategies.

Key concepts

marketing
rights of the child
social entrepreneurship
stakeholders
strategic organisational development
strategic planning
SWOT analysis
vision

Overview

Evaluation and planning are critical elements of high-quality, sustainable EC settings. Articulating the vision and purpose of the EC setting to current and future families is essential in ensuring the survival of the organisation in a highly competitive market place. Planning and marketing go hand in hand as organisations engage in social entrepreneurship by striving for a viable business where family and children's rights are at the forefront of decision-making. This chapter outlines approaches to planning and marketing that are reflective of intentional leadership. We begin by showing how evaluation of programs and the setting involves authentic collaborations with families, staff and children. This approach recognises the importance of the EC organisation within the community. Strategic planning is positioned as a process that builds on the evidence gathered through the evaluation process, and ensures that plans for the future take due account of both the external influences and the internal capacities of the EC setting.

This chapter highlights the essential consideration of balancing business principles with goals for high-quality outcomes for children that are guided by professional and ethical decision-making. Within this context, intentional EC leaders can embrace marketing and promotion of their service within a framework of ethical social entrepreneurship. It is necessary for both for-profit and not-for-profit organisations to market their organisation in terms of their core values and philosophy. Strategies that uphold children's rights are discussed in terms of guiding leaders' efforts to plan and market their organisation with integrity.

Context misconception

Through their relatively short history, many EC settings in Australia have operated somewhat under a mistaken belief that they were public provisions, exempted from the world of business and competition. Public funding was relatively stable and accountabilities were loose and sympathetic to the 'good works' ideology. Over the past 20 or so years the landscape of EC has changed dramatically and business ideas more closely associated with private enterprise and publicly listed corporations have become an everyday part of the operations of EC settings. Increasing calls for settings to be accountable for public funds and the establishment of quality assurance standards have amplified the demands on settings to be answerable to government, communities, families and children. No longer viewed as 'cottage industries', no matter their profit status, EC settings are now very much a part of the competitive business marketplace.

This shift is one of the reasons that **strategic organisational development** has become an integral part of the operations of EC settings. Whether it be a large corporation or a small stand-alone preschool, all settings need to think about the landscape in which they operate and, to remain relevant and viable, respond to societal and business expectations. Targeted evaluation and planning requires intentional leaders to think and act in strategic ways—not only to meet family and community expectations, but also to ensure the business is viable and has a strong strategic direction.

strategic organisational development an approach to organisational planning that takes account of the internal resources of the organisation and the external influences including the political, cultural and technical influences.

What is social entrepreneurship?

EC organisations may be described as social enterprises as they aim to benefit young children and their families during the preschool years. Mair and Marte (2006) define **social entrepreneurship** as 'a process involving the innovative use and combination of resources to pursue opportunities to catalyze social change and/or address social needs' (p. 37). These authors argue that the nature of the business in terms of being a for-profit or not-for-profit organisation is not relevant to being a social entrepreneur. It is more a case of how to balance social responsibility with sound business decisions. Likewise, when thinking of EC organisations as service providers, leaders will need to weigh up the impact of various factors from a social and/or ethical perspective. How an organisation contributes to the community will depend on its **vision** and how it positions itself within societal expectations for the delivery of human services. Leaders of social enterprises differ from those where there is less emphasis on societal outcomes. Social enterprises demand that senior executives and/or managers are conscious of the frequent need to straddle competing agendas. Dees, Haas and Hass (1998) argue that what distinguishes social entrepreneurs from other entrepreneurs is that they adopt 'a mission to create and sustain social values' (p. 5). Such a mission is pertinent to the EC sector—in particular, thinking about prioritising what adds value to or contributes to children's education and well-being in the community.

social entrepreneurship combines ethical business decisions that support the viability of the organisation, identify creative opportunities and contribute positively to the rights of children.

vision is a statement that reflects an aspirational future for an organisation. The vision captures concisely who the organisation is and what it hopes to achieve.

We contend that intentional leaders will situate business decisions within a social entrepreneurial framework. This involves basing decisions and directions for the organisation on what is best for young children while retaining a pragmatic approach to business viability. In Australia, guiding principles to such decisions can be found in the Code of **Ethics** (ECA, 2016), the Convention on the Rights of the Child (UN, 1989) and the National Quality Standard (NQS) (ACECQA, 2011c). Within a social entrepreneurship framework, intentional leaders can use these principles to guide the way they plan for and promote their EC service.

ethics
the principles and values that guide an EC leader's professional behaviour and practice.

The many faces of organisational planning

Much of the business and management literature describes planning using terms such as strategic, operational, business, long term or short term. This chapter gives focus to particular aspects of planning that suit the context of EC settings and acknowledge their diversity and uniqueness. Davies (2011) clarifies the various approaches to planning in the following way. He identifies *futures planning* as long term—looking up to 15 years ahead. This can be particularly useful in the development of a new setting or when introducing innovative approaches to education. ***Strategic planning*** is medium- to long-term planning—usually three to five years. As the name suggests, it is well suited for settings that know what they are about and what they would like to be achieving in the future. Strategic planning focuses on both the internal operations of a setting and external factors such as competition.

strategic planning
is a medium- to long-term planning strategy that takes account of the organisation's internal and external operating environment.

For this reason, strategic planning is often recommended for EC settings as they cannot ignore the external socio-political context in which they operate. *Operational planning* refers to short term and can be a smaller part of the larger strategic plan. Often focusing on specific operational issues rather than the total organisation, these plans can be from one to three years' duration. *Improvement planning* is usually shorter term and designed to address specific strengths or goals. The Quality Improvement Plan (QIP) required as part of the National Quality Framework (NQF) is one example of an improvement planning model where focused attention is given to specific targets and strategies. At different times and in differing circumstances, EC settings will probably call on a range of planning strategies and techniques. The remainder of this chapter looks at longer term organisational development and strategic planning, with a focus on the intentional leader's role in contributing to the future direction of the organisation.

The leader's role in organisational planning and development

Pisapia (2009) suggests that leaders of planning and change 'light the way' by creating a vision for all to see what is possible. They then 'run for the daylight' by recognising opportunities and gaps on which the organisation can capitalise (p. 99). Mintzberg (1994) says that they capture what they have learnt '... from all sources (both the soft insights from his or her personal experiences and the experiences of others throughout the organisation and the hard data from market research and the like) and then synthesize that learning into a vision for the direction that the business should pursue' (p. 107).

While speaking more directly to a designated leader such as a chief executive officer or the owner of a commercial business, these insights from leadership literature offer perspectives for intentional leaders in all ranges of EC settings to consider. The diversity of EC settings and their differing governance and leadership structures make it difficult to generalise about the specifics of the role of the leader. In many cases the EC leader will not have the final say or overall control to determine the vision and direction of the setting, but they will make a significant contribution to how the plan will be realised. In short, they will often act as the agent for the owner, committee or board in organising and operationalising the plan. Their talents for motivating, inspiring and reassuring key **stakeholders**, along with their in-depth knowledge of EC theory and pedagogy, can play a vital role in determining the success or otherwise of the planning process and realisation of the future direction. *Jane Bourne, the CEO of Gowrie (QLD) Inc. shares her career journey and outlines how she has influenced stakeholders within the various roles and positions she has worked in.*

stakeholders
people who have an interest in the decision-making and operations of the setting. They may be involved in various activities at the setting either directly (e.g. staff, families or investors) or indirectly (e.g. neighbours, community representatives or allied health and welfare professionals who visit the setting).

LEADERS IN PRACTICE 5.1

Visit Oxford Ascend to hear more from Jane.

Jane Bourne

Chief Executive Officer, Gowrie (QLD)

I have such a long history in EC and if I had enough time I would tell you all about it. It is very much a moment of 'are you sitting comfortably? Then I'll begin. Once upon a time …' Hopefully you as a reader will be able to do the same in 40 years' time!

I wrote an article for *Reflections* magazine in 2002 and stated then that I am still learning about management and EC—I will probably never stop. And I haven't. That was 15 years ago. Now I am the CEO of Lady Gowrie Queensland and it is one of the most amazing jobs one could have. If someone had told me 15 years ago I would be working with Lady Gowrie, I would have said 'I wish!'

My wish came true. The best thing about this position as I look back over the years is what I have accomplished to be here. To earn my place. My whole career has been an apprenticeship for this position. An apprenticeship for understanding strategic planning and social entrepreneurship.

Looking back, there was never any doubt that I would be a teacher and I worked hard to become one. I worked in England and learnt so much from four and a half year olds who lived in a low socio-economic area in Birmingham. I thought I could change the world with these children, all 42 of them; however, it takes a lot more than a 22-year-old first-year teacher. They taught me resilience, capture the moment, hard work and unconditional love. They taught me that every moment is precious if you want to know about learning, about life. They also taught me that I was not a saviour, I was in their moment. Good advice, which has never left me.

Thirty years ago I landed on Australian shores and went to work as a kindergarten director/teacher in Brisbane. I worked eight wonderful years teaching in this community sector, where staff, families and their children are all part of a very large community and as a teacher I worked tirelessly to earn the community respect and become a pivotal part of the daily lives.

I learnt something very personal in these years. I learnt that when I worked with the children, we became one team, one experience of many (if you understand). No one, not even families, fully understand the work we all do together to make everyone's day meaningful, joyful, inspirational, and full of trust and absolute learning. Learning about oneself, each other and the world around us, our environment and beyond. This is a pretty powerful statement to make; however, it was what I was blessed with. I am still blessed as I meet many of the same children now in their late twenties and early thirties. We laugh, we reminisce and we sing songs and recite old rhymes. This is what teaching is about. This is what we are about! There are friendships and networks made, opportunities for understanding better, what more can be done, what more I can do.

I had the opportunity in the next 15 years to work as a senior manager/leader in three management organisations. It was exciting and challenging and what was best was I could advocate for the right for children to learn at an early age—to be inspired—and I could do the same for the educators and teachers.

I worked hard to learn about the business of 'for-profit' childcare, the good and the not so good. I travelled all through Australia, to every major city, meeting people and making sure that all educators and teachers in the services knew me, were able to speak with me and had the opportunity to tell me their stories. I was a teacher just like them. I was also a leader who continued to test the social, cultural and environmental goals. I became an influencer (although I didn't realise this). So, for 15 years I learnt a new profession while wielding my lifelong goal to support children in their learning.

The one sure thing about my positions was that I never forgot who I was and my professional judgment and beliefs would never be compromised. A saying that has stayed with me is, 'you never know when you are entertaining an angel'. Everyone I met was and is important to me. They have been and are pivotal in my role then and now. Opportunities are far easier to make real if there are others by your side who listen, often speak the same language or who want to learn what EC is really all about. So then the position of CEO for Lady Gowrie Queensland was advertised.

It's a 'not-for-profit' organisation who believes without question or compromise in early learning and care, working in the community for 76 years. As the stars align, this organisation has grown rapidly throughout Queensland in the past six years. We work in many different sectors: family day care, long day care, an early year's centre and many community kindergartens. We work in the cities of Queensland and in remote areas such as Blackall, Eidsvold and Thursday Island.

Sustainability is of great importance to our success. People are important to our success, from our Board of Management, who has faith in what we do, to our employees and affiliated services, who trust our judgment and acknowledge that we work hard and advocate for social outcomes and the right of education of young children and families. What we get out of this is pride in our organisation and pride in one another. It would be a cliché to call Lady Gowrie Queensland a family affair; however, we gather community wherever it may be to believe in the rights of the family and the education of our children. This is now exactly where I want to be and where I will work to make a success out of a wonderful organisation, never forgetting that I have a role to play in influencing government and speaking up for our educators. Someone once said, 'Teaching is the greatest Act of Optimism'. What a truly wonderful sector to be a part of—no matter which part.

Pause–reflect–act 5.1

- What do you see as the core values of Jane's vision for her work in the EC sector?
- Jane talks about the importance of optimism. Why do you think optimism might be an important underpinning to the work of leaders?
- What is your dream job? Where do you want to be in 20, 30 and 40 years?

Go to oxfordascend *to hear Jane's thoughts.*

Strategic organisational development

Cummings and Worley (2005) define strategic organisational development as 'efforts to improve both the organisation's relationship to its environment and the fit between its technical, political and cultural systems' (p. 12). In EC contexts, this translates into organisations recognising both the internal and external factors that can enhance or weaken its success. This means taking into account social policy and legislative contexts within which EC settings operate and melding this with the organisational philosophy, ideals, visions and aspirations to develop thriving children's programs. A cycle of reflection, analysis and planning for the future is conducted in a way that resembles a planning process for children's learning. EC leaders can draw on the familiar process of planning and evaluation for children's learning and apply those principles to the broader context of organisational planning.

the social policy and legislative contexts within which children's services operate are discussed in chapters 2 and 3.

Strategic organisational development requires thoughtful and inspirational leadership that emphasises collaboration and shared decision-making. Depending on the size of the organisation it is often best to form a **planning team**. This team can take responsibility for coordinating the planning process, ensuring that all key stakeholders are consulted, and determining ways of eliciting and disseminating information throughout the process to keep all informed.

a **planning team**
a working group of ideally four to six people who represent the key stakeholders of the organisation and together coordinate the planning processes. The EC leader is a part of this team.

Getting started—guiding beliefs and values

Underpinning any future plans of an EC setting are the guiding beliefs and values that give the organisation a moral purpose (Nanus, 1992). Values represent the deepest expression of our ideals and principles. They articulate what is most important to us. Beliefs are what lead us to our values. They are our understandings drawn from knowledge, culture and experience.

Together, values and beliefs guide our moral purpose. They are the expression of why we do the things we do. In a business sense, values and beliefs enable us to organise our thoughts into actions and to determine what we want the business to achieve.

While values and beliefs are very personal and key stakeholders will have diverse and differing ideas, it is important for an organisation or business to agree on shared values and beliefs that reflect the foundations of its growth and development. Sorting out what are the core values and beliefs can take time and should involve in-depth discussions to ensure the sharing of different interpretations of key terms. A good place to start can be the development of a 'Values Data Bank'. This involves collating a list of words representing the key values and beliefs about working with young children held by the stakeholders of the EC setting.

Pause–reflect–act 5.2

What are your core values and beliefs about working with young children?

Brainstorm key words that articulate your core values and beliefs. Use the Early Years Learning Framework (DEEWR, 2009) as a starting point for building your data bank. Here are some ideas to get you started. Try to build a bank of at least 20 words that reflect the values of your organisation.

joy	empathy	respect
belonging	relationships	high expectations
reciprocity	agency	inclusion

In groups, try to decide which four or five values best represent the key ideas that guide your work with young children.

- To what extent were you able to agree?
- Which words were easy to agree on and which were difficult? Why?
- What valuable discussion took place during your attempts to reach agreement?

Developing an organisational vision

According to Nanus (1992), 'a vision is a realistic, credible, attractive future for your organisation' (p. 8). Drawing on the shared values and beliefs of the stakeholders, the vision creates a guiding light or direction for the organisation. The vision articulates where the organisation is headed and can assist everyone involved to understand the how, what and why of their daily work. Building on Nanus's ideas we can consider how to create a purposeful vision that will unite those involved to work towards an agreed future:

- *A vision is realistic.* This implies that the vision, while aspirational, also needs to be practical and possible. It is difficult for anyone to work towards a vision that is unrealistic or unattainable. People will lose focus and enthusiasm if they feel that they have been set up to fail.

- *A vision is credible.* It is important that stakeholders can see themselves as part of the vision, that it is not bigger than them, nor does it mislead or misrepresent. It needs to fit with existing legislation and government policies and all stakeholders need to be comfortable about explaining the vision and identifying with it in action.
- *A vision is attractive.* It needs to motivate and drive people to do their best. The vision should inspire and attract the best staff and encourage all involved to continue to strive for improved outcomes.

With a meaningful vision in place, the intentional leader ensures that it is visible and present in everyday practice and decision-making. While strategic placement of the vision in the foyer or staffroom can act as a reminder about the direction of the organisation, the leader ensures that it is alive and discernible. Taking the time to regularly reflect on the vision and encouraging staff to consider how it is enacted in daily practices and events can keep the vision in focus and motivate and inspire staff to think positively about the contribution that they personally make to building the setting's future directions.

Pause–reflect–act 5.3

Reflect on the vision statements of those centres you have worked in either as a student, staff member or director.

- Did any inspire you? Why/why not? Were you able to see any vision statements 'come alive' in your work at the organisation? Why/why not?
- Based on your four to five core beliefs about working with young children (see Pause–reflect–act 5.2), what might the vision be of a centre you would like to work in?

Evaluation

Gaining a sense of the current context and the relative strengths and weaknesses of an organisation are important considerations early in the planning process. This stage will involve a critical and in-depth consideration of all aspects of the business. In order for this evaluation to be thorough and extensive, reliable methods of evaluation must be determined and decisions made about who will be involved. Reflection is a good starting point for all involved: time for individuals to sit back and take a 'helicopter' view of the setting and its operations. In a sense, this reflection is capturing the 'where are we now?' question. One way of gaining the information needed to build a comprehensive picture of the current state of the organisation is through a **SWOT analysis**. Developed by Albert Humphrey from Stanford University, this process exposes the internal Strengths and Weaknesses, and the external Opportunities and Threats (SWOT) that currently characterise the organisation:

SWOT analysis developed by Albert Humphrey from Stanford University in the USA, this process exposes the internal Strengths and Weaknesses, and external Opportunities and Threats that characterise the organisation at a particular point in time.

- *Strengths*: those things within the organisation that are currently done well—these provide an advantage over other similar organisations.

- *Weaknesses*: those things within the organisation that need to be improved—they might disadvantage the organisation over other similar organisations.
- *Opportunities*: possibilities external to the organisation that exist and are not presently taken advantage of in the operations of the setting.
- *Threats*: external risks to the operations of the organisation due to factors such as increased competition, change in government policy or unstable economic conditions.

As individual stakeholders in the organisation contribute their perspectives of the SWOT, a picture of the organisation emerges and provides a platform from which to consider future directions and change.

Pause–reflect–act 5.4

Consider an EC setting that you know and brainstorm your views about its strengths, weaknesses, opportunities and threats. How might this information inform the planning for its future growth?

Gathering insights

Building on the information gained in the SWOT analysis, planning teams need to look for the data that will inform the planning process. Finding effective methods to gather data and make sense of it is essential and must suit the size and capacity of the organisation. Do not waste time and money on complex data collection strategies if there is no capacity to analyse the data collected. The planning team needs to consider the key participants and how they can best contribute their ideas. Surveys, questionnaires, focus group meetings or e-blogs are just some of the ways of effectively gathering together the views and opinions of all stakeholders. Finding strategies that appeal to people is not too time-consuming. It shows that there is benefit in participating, and is a key consideration in designing data collection strategies. Importantly, participants want to see that their contributions are valued, so the planning team must determine how they will communicate findings and follow up on issues that arise throughout the process.

In addition to the qualitative data gathered as stakeholders' views and opinions, planning teams should also consider the contribution that more quantitative or hard data can make in building a more comprehensive picture of the setting. Enrolment figures, waiting list statistics, staff turnover patterns, risk registers and the complaints register can also provide important insights into the internal workings of the setting. Intentional leaders will not try to hide the negative views or criticisms of the setting but rather bring this information to light in order to address the concerns that currently affect the operations of the setting.

External reports, census figures, localised data from the Australian Early Development Census (AEDC) and community demographic statistics can also offer insights into the local area, needs and desires of families, and trends in social and economic conditions. The planning team needs to consider all aspects of the organisation's internal operations and the various external influences to ensure that a comprehensive data set informs the planning process.

Including the voices of children

Strategic organisational development is usually thought of as a process involving adult stakeholders. Yet the context of EC settings requires input from children. Australia's acceptance of the Convention on the Rights of the Child (UN, 1989) and, in particular, Article 12, 'the child's right to express their own views about things that affect them', has prompted a growing awareness of the need to not only listen to what children are saying but to involve them in the design and conduct of research and projects that affect them (Pascal & Bertram, 2011). According to Lloyd-Smith and Tarr (2000), real experiences of children in educational settings cannot be fully understood by the inferences and assumptions of adults. Australian EC researchers such as Dockett and Perry in their 'Building a Child-Friendly City' (City of Wodonga, 2010) project, and the report by Harris and Manatakis (2013), provide strategies for including the voices of young children in decisions that affect them. Intentional leaders can look for ways to involve children in the planning process and enable their perspectives to form part of the data set that will inform planning decisions.

Pause–reflect–act 5.5

Gathering data to inform the organisational plan

Select one local government area and brainstorm the possible sources of data that might be collected to inform an organisational plan for an EC setting in that area. Develop a comprehensive list of possible data sources, being sure to cover the following aspects of the setting:

The *internal* operations:

- qualitative: views, opinions, reflections
- quantitative: reports, records, statistics.

The *external* environment:

- qualitative: general knowledge, views, predictions
- quantitative: statistics, trends, demographic changes.

Consider how this information might be presented in a way that can inform the planning process.

Collating and analysing data

The next step for the planning team is to organise and analyse the data to make sense of the views, opinions and statistics that have been gathered. Producing a brief but meaningful summary of each data set is a task that can be distributed among team members, but one person or a small team should be allocated the task of bringing it together into a coherent and useful report. Critical analysis of the data is needed to ensure that it leads the organisation to appropriate new directions. It also affords opportunities to take account of new thinking or current trends—for example, considering the organisational goals from a social justice perspective or reflecting on how the organisation has contributed to environmental sustainability. Some key questions at this stage might include:

- What is each piece of data telling us?
- What patterns are emerging across the whole community?
- Who is advantaged and disadvantaged by our current operations?
- Are there aspects of our operations that are excessive or wasteful?
- Where are the gaps in our provisions?
- What are others doing that we might want to think about?

Conversations addressing these and other questions will prompt thinking about ideas for the future. Looking for opportunities to exploit the strengths and opportunities of the organisation while looking for ways to reduce the risks of the weaknesses and threats can lead to a range of strategies to consider. Reflecting on the guiding beliefs and values and the vision of the organisation can act as a filter to think about each of these ideas and their fit with the organisation's strategic directions.

Identifying the goals, outcomes or key results areas

The leadership literature emphasises the importance of leaders having the personal qualities and skills to motivate and inspire others (Rodd, 2013). In relation to organisational development, the task of making sense of the data gathered and translating it into meaningful strategic goals requires intentional leaders to get others on board and feel a sense of excitement and enthusiasm about the future. Davies (2011) encourages the use of strategic conversations in this process. Such conversations can clarify the strategic directions and engage staff and families to see themselves as part of the organisation. Collaborative conversations integrate the individual perspectives of stakeholders into a shared and potentially powerful message. In this way, the intentional leader builds team cohesion and commitment to the strategic plans. Time to talk and listen to the ideas of others can also reduce stakeholders' anxiety about change.

chapter 8 deals with leading organisational change.

The leader plays a key role in engaging others in planning conversations and needs to model behaviour that encourages participation while disseminating information and listening to the ideas and anxieties of others. As a general guide, the stated goals and directions of the plan, adapted from Meyer (2003), need to be:

- *measurable:* able to be assessed for their effectiveness
- *acceptable:* agreed to by all who are committed to the organisation's vision, values and beliefs
- *flexible:* able to be adapted when circumstances change or to take advantage of innovation or new research
- *motivating:* inspirational for those involved to give their best and feel a part of the future

- *achievable:* able to be realised within the current constraints and resources of the organisation
- *consistent:* seen to match the vision and philosophy of the setting.

Taken together, these aspects address the findings of the SWOT analysis by making the most of the strengths and opportunities while minimising the impact of the weaknesses and threats.

Applying these criteria to all goals can assist in ensuring that the goals are relevant and realistic. It is all too easy in a planning process to be carried away with ideals and dreams. For the plan to be realised it needs to be attainable. For example, a goal for all four-year-old children to be 'ready for school' by December is not measurable unless we are able to define what 'ready for school' looks like for every child. Such a goal may not be consistent with a philosophy that emphasises individual difference and recognition of diverse abilities if we have a very tight definition of what 'ready for school' looks like. Applying the above criteria to each goal acts as a crosscheck to the goal's attainability.

Developing strategies—getting everyone on board

Once strategic development goals have been established, strategies to achieve them need to be developed. One approach to developing strategies is offered by the (formerly) NSW Department of Community Services (2007), which published the *Service Analysis and Business Development Resource Manual* to guide planning in children's services. The department recommended a series of questions to ask when designing strategies. These questions can assist in determining whether the proposed strategies will deliver the desired results or outcomes, as reflected in Table 5.1.

Table 5.1 Questions to guide the development of strategies

Who are we doing this for?	Identify the target group to which the strategy applies.
What do we specifically hope to achieve?	Clearly defined outcomes expressed as a measurable result. Key terms that indicate the level of quality, standard or numerical measure should be included.
What do we already do well in achieving this result?	Check the data collected for evidence of strengths. Draw on strategic conversations about what is working well. Consider how these strengths can be built on.
What more could we be doing?	Check the data collected for signs of gaps. Investigate current research and literature about this issue. Is there evidence from other settings that we might consider?
What changes do we need to make?	Based on research, brainstorm possibilities and sort through the pros and cons of each. Are there things we should consider stopping or adapting to achieve a better result?

Who are we doing this for?	**Identify the target group to which the strategy applies.**
How will we make the changes?	Exactly what needs to happen? What resources are required? Do we need professional development to increase our knowledge or skills? Establish a time frame for changes. Identify the lead person who will drive the change.
How will we know when we have achieved the result?	Design an evaluation strategy that fits with the outcome to be measured. Ensure that the measures—both qualitative and quantitative—are rigorous and reliable.

Note: Portfolio responsibilities for EC have changed since this document was released. The directorate of the former NSW Department of Community Services moved to the EC Directorate of the NSW Department of Education.

NSW Department of Community Services, 2007.

Keeping the plan alive

Another key task of the intentional leader is to see the plans through. While this sounds obvious, it is not always easy to remain focused when day-to-day events at an EC setting can easily consume the time and attention of the leader. To ensure that the plan is kept alive and moves the setting towards the long-term vision, it needs to be made an active document that is read and handled regularly rather than being quietly filed away until its term has expired. A good plan will articulate clearly the performance indicators that need to be reached as evidence of the success of the plan. Regular reporting against these performance indicators can keep the focus on the results, and encourages ongoing conversations about how the results are being realised. A schedule of reporting to management, staff, families and other stakeholders assists everyone concerned to see the results and recognise the impact of the changes being made.

Important in this phase is the need to acknowledge and reward success. This builds confidence, motivates staff and keeps the momentum of the plan growing in the right direction. A key question is what rewards can the organisation afford and what sorts of incentives are most appealing to the people you wish to motivate? Far from requiring grand gestures, most people are motivated if their efforts and contributions are acknowledged publicly in a newsletter or at a meeting. An occasional celebration to acknowledge reaching a target can also act to unite and inspire people to keep going. In short, the reward should in some way match the benefit of the achievement to the organisation. *This notion of recognition is something that Dennis Blythin discusses in his profile (see Leadership in action profile 5.2).* Recent research in Australia also found that EC teachers had higher job satisfaction and motivation when they were trusted or were given autonomy to do their work, and were respected and challenged professionally by the director and/or management (Jones, Hadley & Johnston, 2017).

Making mistakes and changing direction

The best of all plans for any number of reasons may not work or may need modifying to achieve a better result. Margy Whalley (2001) from the Pen Green Centre for Children and Families in the UK speaks of celebrating mistakes as she explains that making mistakes implies that an organisation has taken risks, and had the confidence to make decisions and live with the consequences. Likewise, Colmer (2008) writes about the importance of having doubt as a motivational strategy: 'If we do not have doubt we cannot be open to ask hard questions necessary for true reflection to occur' (p. 110). Mistakes also encourage reflection, thought and responsive change. Throughout the life of an organisational plan it is essential to reflect carefully on what is worth doing and what is not working. The best plans are those that can adapt and respond to changes in circumstances. Key to making changes along the way is careful consideration of the organisation's vision and philosophy. Together, these can guide decisions about change in line with what the organisation stands for and is keen to achieve.

Working in EC settings is rarely neat, tidy and predictable. Dynamic settings are drawn to innovative ideas and so do not want to be locked into a restrictive organisational plan that inhibits creativity. At the same time, staff want and need to have stability and not be exhausted by constant change and renewal. As Jordan (1987, cited in Whalley, 2001) observes, 'One needs to be prepared to work with contradictions and confusions. It is not a field for people who like to be clear cut; precise and polished ... it is a field of compromise, negotiation, flexibility, sharing and a balancing of conflicting interests' (p. 139). Finding the ideal space for complexity and tension that does not overwhelm or confuse people is the aim of all dynamic workplaces.

From planning to marketing

Once plans are agreed upon, the next logical step is to communicate the vision and future direction of the organisation to stakeholders, including potential clients. Using a social entrepreneurship frame, intentional EC leaders will ask critical questions drawn from the evaluation data that will inform their **marketing** and promotion strategies. Key questions EC leaders might consider are:

- How could we use the social entrepreneurial framework to guide our decisions about key messages?
- How will our public documents, policies and promotional material convey our key messages?
- Who can we test our ideas on—that is, someone who can provide critical feedback?
- In our messaging, how will we balance the **rights of the child** with the other competing demands of running a viable service?
- How will we ensure the decisions we make reflect integrity and do not disadvantage individuals?
- On what basis can we justify the business decisions we have made?

Central to 'branding' is communicating what the setting is all about and what it has to offer. Revisiting the setting's philosophy and vision will help guide branding decisions. Are there key ideas or approaches that the setting wants to promote? What are the most

marketing
involves working strategically to develop a presence in the community that promotes the organisation, its programs, and the value of EC and EC education.

rights of the child
the UN's Convention on the Rights of the Child (1989) requires countries to act in the 'best interests' of the child. The rights of the child are embedded in the Code of Ethics (ECA, 2016) used by EC educators.

see chapter 3 for a discussion on the rights of the child.

attractive features of the setting? Are there images the setting does not want to promote? Take a quick look at branding strategies used by EC organisations, especially centre logos. You will find a plethora of teddy bears, building blocks and stylised cartoon characters. Branding is concerned with the use of these images and words on the organisation's websites, name boards, letterheads and newsletters. Balancing the effectiveness of these images and text, from the perspective of being attractive and memorable, against a desire to promote a professional image of EC organisations as educational environments can present ethical challenges for intentional leaders. Negotiating branding concepts can therefore require an intentional leader to carefully consider and articulate their personal beliefs and values about the marketing and promotion of EC organisations.

Marketing—communicating vision to stakeholders

EC organisations operate in highly competitive and complex market conditions. Applying the thinking of pure market economics to the EC sector has increased the promotion of consumer choice where, ideally, parents select from a range of organisations that best suit their needs and desires (Davidoff, n.d.; Myers, 2005). Cleveland and Krashinsky (2005), however, argue that this competitive market does not necessarily equate to high-quality programs for children. The point of price sensitivity—the point at which the customer is prepared to pay for the service offered—is an important consideration when determining not only what is possible in a given market, but also what might be the priorities for families looking for EC services. It is important for EC leaders to understand the complexities of the economic landscape and the limitations these complexities can place on effective marketing strategies. Myers (2005) argues that in educational contexts it is important to understand that marketing is not about 'hard' selling. It is often more about building relationships and establishing a credible profile in the community.

Figure 5.1 illustrates how the marketing of EC organisations and making decisions within a social entrepreneurship framework is a balancing act. Tension is created by the push-down impact of global and national economic forces on the local organisation, which feel the

Figure 5.1 The balancing act of social entrepreneurship

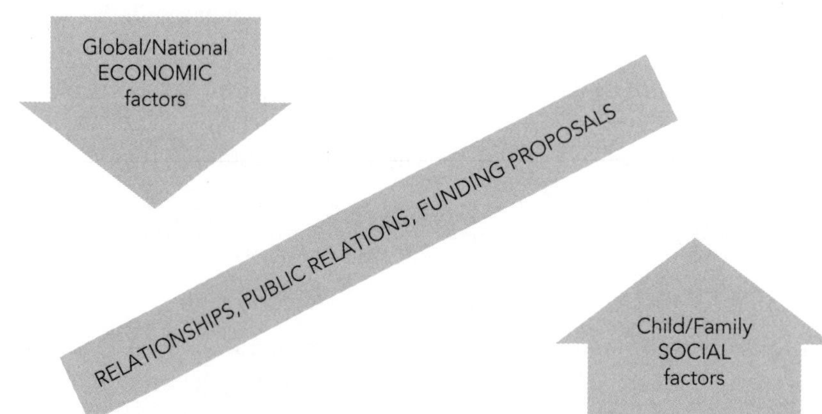

push-up of the social factors impacting on children and their families, who are themselves struggling to balance family economic and social needs. The challenge for EC leaders is to find a balance between meeting the needs of children as citizens, as well as their parents as paying customers, and the organisation as a viable business able to respond effectively and efficiently to community needs. Intentional leaders are conscious of these tensions and consistently strive to seek opportunities to minimise the discordance or disruption for the children at the setting. The social entrepreneurship framework can be a guide for intentional leaders who are trying to balance these competing forces.

Pause–reflect–act 5.6

Think about the types of marketing you are exposed to.

- What do you see as the key characteristics of marketing from a social entrepreneurial framework? (Think about EC centres or organisations you have worked in.)
- What examples of branding are you aware of?
- What images did this branding convey?
- How effective was it at communicating the centre's philosophy, vision and mission?
- In your view, did their marketing strategies sit within a social entrepreneurship framework? Why or why not?
- What ideas do you have about branding an EC organisation to promote it as an ethical business catering to young children and their families?

LEADERS IN PRACTICE 5.2

Dennis Blythin

Director, Primary OSHCare, Sydney (NSW)

I graduated from Leeds University with a BSc Hons in Mechanical Engineering in 1984 and knew pretty much then that I was never going to be a good engineer. It just didn't interest me enough. However, it did provide me with the opportunity to learn project management and business skills that would serve me well in later life. Twenty years later, in 2004 I found myself as general manager of an engineering construction company. I had all the trappings of corporate success, but I really wanted to run my own business rather than work for other people. My partner, Suzanne, had been working in the education sector for 20 years and she suggested we set up a consultancy to advise Outside School Hours Services on how to meet the newly instigated NCAC guidelines for the OSHC sector. I countered with the proposition that we could set up our own business to do that ourselves. Suzanne would handle the childcare aspects of the service and I would handle the business side of things. And so the concept of Primary OSHCare was born.

From the outset we were determined to change the way things were done in the sector. Our assessment at the time was that the sector was extremely fragmented. Many services were being operated by voluntary committees who tended to view OSH care as 'child minding' rather than a real opportunity to positively impact on the lives of children and their families. Also, the educators were drastically undervalued and underappreciated.

In July 2004 we opened our first service at Dulwich Hill Primary School. This was quickly followed by services in Bondi, Gordon and Ashfield. It was all a bit chaotic and, as we acquired more services, it became clear to me that we had to get the expertise residing in Suzanne's head down on paper. I'm a great believer in systems. In fact, I would go so far as to say that no organisation can successfully function without a clearly articulated and codified set of processes, along with an equally clearly written vision for what the organisation is about and why it exists. It never ceases to amaze me how many businesses fail to do this—and consequently fail! It wasn't easy, but we wrote down every aspect of operating an OSHC service. We also wrote a clear set of goals for the business and we precisely defined the values that underpin our whole reason for existence. This is a critical and powerful undertaking that allowed us to understand and deliver consistent highest quality care at every service we operated. And it's a never-ending task. We are constantly reviewing and revising how we do things as we gain more experience.

Having a set of written procedures and values is one thing, but they are of no use if nobody knows about them or adheres to them. Our job as leaders is to make these available to all our staff, train them in how to use them and constantly reinforce their implementation. We do this through a combination of cutting-edge IT systems, induction, training and, probably most importantly, leading by example. We have high expectations of people who choose to work with us. We have deliberately built a culture of excellence, which all our employees must buy into. The net result is that we are an OSHC provider in 36 schools and cater for 3500 children each week. In our most recent assessments by the regulatory authority we have been awarded 15 'Exceeding the Standards' ratings. We have raised the bar in the sector and significantly improved the experience of all stakeholders who come into contact with us—children, families, school communities, regulators and our staff.

There is a persistent idea among some people that there is something inherently wrong or immoral about running OSH care as a business: that it is exploiting the children and their families. I couldn't disagree more strongly. While there are, no doubt, some unscrupulous operators, I firmly believe that sound financial management has to underpin any operation if it is to be sustainable in the long term. It is possible to provide excellence without exploitation. We don't charge high fees to families and we don't skimp on resources or underpay any staff. We just constantly make sure everything we do is the best we can do. As a consequence, we now have a very successful business that is demonstrably exceeding all the standards. As we continue to grow, we are able to broaden our influence in ways we never dreamed of at the start. We are able to support local communities and charities. We are able to influence policy makers and regulators. We are able to provide children with opportunities and experiences that all too many simply do not get.

Suzanne and I sit at the top of a vibrant, dynamic organisation that genuinely improves people's lives and hopefully contributes to improving the sector as a whole. It's very exciting ... and we are only just getting going!

Pause–reflect–act 5.7

- What are the core values driving Dennis's vision for his organisation?
- Why do you think the OSHC (outside school hours care) services are seen as the 'poor cousin' in the EC sector?
- How has Dennis and Suzanne's intentional leadership shaped their organisation?

Recognition and image

Most communities have local business awards; this is a way of ensuring organisations are recognised for effective service provision to children and families. Leaders could nominate the setting for its innovative program or a staff member for excellence in teaching. These awards are usually advertised through the local business community or chamber of commerce and are given media coverage in local newspapers, radio, television or Twitter. There are also state and national teaching awards that are an opportunity to nominate qualified educators from the centre. For example, the Australian Scholarships Group (ASG) has the 'national excellence in teaching' awards (see www.asg.com.au/asg-neita).

These types of events can enhance a setting's professional image and are an excellent way of branding the unique aspects of the program and/or the exemplary staff working in the setting. These types of marketing strategies can also contribute to staff morale at the centre as staff feel valued and connected and this can impact on the quality of the program the children receive. Some staff may feel reticent about being nominated for an award as they see that what they are doing is their job. The leader may need to discuss with these staff why they are being nominated for an award and how they are seen to be working above and beyond the required expectations of their job in the way they work with the children on program matters.

see chapter 9 for a discussion on effective workplaces.

EC settings are now required to display the results of their most recent assessment and rating results. ACECQA has produced a range of ratings logos. These logos show clearly the standard met and can be used on promotional material by the setting. The logos are a quick and easy reference for families and help to build recognition of the professionalism of the work of EC educators. You can find out more about the rating logos on the ACECQA website www.acecqa.gov.au/how-to-promote-your-service-s-rating.

Pause–reflect–act 5.8

- Think of an organisation that nominates its staff or services for local community and business awards. If you were a leader in this organisation, what skills and knowledge would you need to complete the award nominations?
- If you were a leader of a centre, would you feel you have the skills to complete these award nominations?
- Why do you think some EC staff would be reticent to self-nominate themselves or the setting? Do you think it is linked to the 'tall poppy' syndrome? Why or why not?

Chapter summary

This chapter outlined approaches to evaluation, planning and marketing that are reflective of intentional leadership. It examined the various steps in a planning process from the perspective of intentional leaders. Acknowledging the influential socio-political context in which EC organisations operate, the chapter emphasised the leader's knowledge of the external environment. It also promoted the importance of authentic collaborations with community, families and staff and, importantly, recognised the importance of children's voices being part of planning processes. The chapter highlighted the essential consideration of ethical practice and decision-making guided by a strong vision balanced with the realities of operating in a business-oriented marketplace. Utilising a social entrepreneurial framework when examining planning and marketing decisions, intentional leaders can ensure that children's rights remain the focus of all that they do in their EC organisations. Situating planning and marketing of EC organisations within an ethics framework can guide EC leaders and balance the decisions and strategies they make to promote the viability of their organisations as well as provide high-quality EC programs.

Key references

Davies, B. (2011). *Leading the strategically focused school* (2nd ed.). London: Sage Publications.

This highly accessible book combines rigorous research with pragmatic commentary. It describes the nature of education settings and the complexity of working within strong political frameworks. Davies presents an insightful view of the leader's role, balancing strength of mind and wisdom of collaboration to achieve good outcomes.

Newman, L. & Pollnitz, L. (2005). *Working with children and families: Professional, legal and ethical issues*. Frenchs Forest, NSW: Pearson Education.

This book provides an ethical response cycle that could be used to examine whether the marketing and promotion strategies fit within an ethical framework. Using the cycle will enable you to consider planning issues including legal aspects, professional consideration, ethical principles, ethical theories, informed consent, judgment, action and documentation.

Whalley, M. (2001). Working as a team. In G. Pugh (Ed.), *Contemporary issues in the early years: Working collaboratively for children* (3rd ed.). London: Paul Chapman Publishing.

This chapter is an honest account of the struggles and commitment needed during the establishment phases of the Pen Green Centre. It emphasises the need for a strong, articulated vision to guide the decision-making and the importance of getting the community on board.

Online resources

Australian Early Development Census (AEDC)

The AEDC provides data on five key areas of children's development collected nationwide every three years. This information is used by policy makers, educators, parents and communities for planning (and research) that can improve children's development before starting school.

www.aedc.gov.au/

Community Child Care Cooperative NSW

This organisation supports those who are employed in the EC sector and has many resources that focus on managing and leading EC settings. This includes publications that cover marketing and setting up EC programs.

ccccnsw.org.au

Early Childhood Australia

Early Childhood Australia (ECA) is a national, not-for-profit peak organisation with a stated mission to ensure quality, social justice and equity in all issues relating to the education and care of children from birth to eight years. ECA has publications and other resources on ethical aspects of working in EC settings. The ECA Learning Hub has various resources that assist with understanding digital communications and copyright rules.

www.earlychildhoodaustralia.org.au

6 | PEDAGOGICAL LEADERSHIP

CHAPTER LEARNING OBJECTIVES

After studying this chapter you will understand that:

- EC curriculum and pedagogies are underpinned by philosophical and theoretical understandings and require strong leadership.
- Pedagogical leadership is central to influencing decision-making in contemporary EC contexts.
- The role of educational leaders under the National Quality Framework (NQF) is only one way of enacting the broader notion of pedagogical leadership.
- Curriculum decisions are grounded in understandings of local contexts and communities.
- Pedagogical leaders play a critical role in coaching and mentoring staff in EC settings.
- Pedagogical leaders contribute to community awareness of EC programs and children's learning.
- Pedagogical leaders need to be articulate about the value of EC pedagogy and take a leadership role with multidisciplinary teams.
- Pedagogical leaders inform and are responsive to policy documents impacting on curriculum decisions in the context of local communities.

Key concepts

coaching
curriculum
mentoring
networking
pedagogy
philosophies and theories

Overview

In the EC sector, pedagogical leadership is an emerging discipline area with a growing research base. While general educational literature on school leadership can be of some interest, the unique nature of EC settings and their workforce demands close attention to what it means to be a pedagogical leader within an EC context. In a landscape of multiple approaches to EC curriculum, it is crucial that a setting's philosophical approaches to EC education are clearly articulated and reflect contemporary theoretical understandings. A focus on pedagogical leadership can ensure that knowledge of how children learn and what is relevant learning for each child underpins the overall leadership approach within an EC setting. Pedagogical leadership involves sharing specialist knowledge about program planning and resourcing, and engaging with children and families. It recognises the diversity of experience that staff bring to each setting from a range of qualification backgrounds and often from multidisciplinary contexts. Pedagogical leadership can involve coaching, mentoring, initiating professional conversations and modelling ethical practice in order to build the capacity of the staff team as curriculum decision-makers. While the role of educational leader specified under the National Quality Framework (NQF) is one example of pedagogical leadership, this chapter extends the notion of pedagogical leadership beyond this specified role.

Building on the Early Years Learning Framework (DEEWR, 2009), this chapter suggests ways for leaders to engage staff, families and children in curriculum decisions that reflect local contexts. Pedagogical leaders can promote setting-based action research projects to extend understandings of curriculum issues. They can promote ongoing reflection and professional learning, which can lead to a culture of professionalism in the setting and can be effective in communicating to families and the broader community the importance of rich learning experiences for all children. In addition to enhancing the learning experiences in the local context, pedagogical leaders contribute to a greater understanding of the complexity and value of EC education in the broader community and social policy context.

Now is the time

National and international interest in early years development has increased in response to three significant factors:

- Growing awareness of the early years as critical to life outcomes, stemming from increasing scientific evidence, in particular brain research (Shonkoff & Phillips, 2000).
- Increased acknowledgment by governments that investment in the early years can be worthwhile in terms of later returns and savings (Garcia et al., 2016).
- The increased participation of young children in formal EC settings and consequent concerns about the quality of these settings (Barnett, 2010; Gammage, 2006; Press, 2006).

These three factors have contributed to a growing body of research about the impact of EC programs on children's development and later life outcomes. Moreover, increased attention has been given to the recommended experiences for children and therefore what sort of **curriculum** best supports children's learning and development. Within this context, what then is the role of an intentional leader in relation to curriculum and **pedagogy** in an EC setting?

curriculum is a program or course of study, or the content of a course of study. It usually suggests that learning outcomes are predetermined in order to fulfil the prescribed intentions of the program or course.

pedagogy is the art and science of education. In an EC context it gives a focus to educational theories, relationships, strategies and practices that educators can draw on when they make curriculum decisions and work with children in learning contexts to support and enhance their learning.

According to Nuttall and Edwards (2007), while the construct of curriculum is well understood in compulsory school settings, the notion of curriculum in EC settings is relatively recent. They suggest that it is only since the 1990s that terminology of curriculum and the development of EC curriculum documents have been commonplace in Australian EC contexts. Prior to this, terms such as 'program planning', 'observation' and 'evaluation' have historically been the more preferred terms.

Pause–reflect–act 6.1

- What do you understand to be the significant differences between curriculum in an EC setting and curriculum in a school context?
- During the consultations conducted in 2009 around Australia in relation to the Early Years Learning Framework draft, the terms 'assessment for learning' and 'outcomes' were hotly debated. Why do you think the EC profession may have reacted so strongly (often negatively) to these terms when they have existed in the formal school vernacular for many years?

While a number of Australia's states and territories produced early years curriculum frameworks and policy documents during the 1990s it has been the development of Australia's first national Early Years Learning Framework (EYLF) (DEEWR, 2009) that has consolidated a commitment to the formalising of young children's learning. Initiated under the Rudd government's 'productivity agenda' and central to the Council of Australian Government (COAG) EC reform agenda, the EYLF is seen as a key strategy for ensuring that children's experiences in EC settings are worthwhile and contribute to high-quality outcomes that set them up for life success. Significantly, the EYLF by definition is a 'framework' rather than a prescribed curriculum or syllabus. This requires educators to create more detailed curriculum using the principles, practices and learning outcomes as a guide. In contrast to perceptions of school curricular documents as content heavy and prescriptive in nature, the EYLF is described as providing

> ... broad direction for EC educators ... to facilitate children's learning. It guides educators in their curriculum decision-making and assists in planning, implementing and evaluating quality in EC settings. It also underpins the implementation of more specific curriculum relevant to each local community and EC setting. (DEEWR, 2009, p. 8)

The role for intentional leadership is significant here: guiding educators in the process of interpreting curriculum documents. This involves making thoughtful curriculum decisions that take account of local contexts, the setting's vision and philosophy, and children's interests and abilities, to create rich and meaningful learning environments. Curriculum in this sense can be seen as a lived experience where educators facilitate learning that is responsive to children, families and community contexts, while mindful of the importance of equity, social justice and outcomes for learning (Cheeseman, 2016).

This, then, is an important time for the EC sector. No longer on the periphery of broader education and social welfare policy, EC education is taking its place as an important component of government policy in its own right. This is a time for EC leaders to seize the opportunity to shape and influence what happens in the future—particularly in relation to curriculum for young children. In such times of reform and change staff can often feel anxious and uncertain and EC leaders have choices to make about how they will lead staff through these changes. Leaders with strongly articulated philosophies of education are known to be more effective in their pedagogical leadership because they are experts in the areas of teaching and learning of young children and guide change from a sound philosophical base (Siraj-Blatchford & Hallet, 2014).

Pause–reflect–act 6.2

Think about the EC settings you have visited or worked in.

- Was the curriculum visible to the staff, children and families?
- Why or why not?
- What language was used to describe the teaching pedagogy?
- How do you think the role of the EC leader impacted on the visibility and articulation of the curriculum?

The importance of philosophy in pedagogical leadership

An influential longitudinal study of EC provision—*The Effective Provision of Pre-school Education (EPPE) project* (Sylva et al., 2004a)—has been undertaken in the UK over the past two decades. This study has examined the key factors that contribute to effective outcomes for children from their formal EC experiences. One of the most significant findings in this study relates to the importance of leadership in contributing to positive outcomes for children. In the follow-up study, which focused specifically on leadership effectiveness, Siraj-Blatchford and Manni (2007) found that 'In the most effective settings better leadership was characterized by a clear vision, especially with regard to pedagogy and curriculum' (p. 13).

The implication of this finding is that leadership of EC settings must move beyond the day-to-day commitment to administrative and legal accountability and give a key focus to the discipline areas of curriculum and pedagogy. Sergiovanni (1998) recognised this when he said 'Schools with a strong and deep culture of teaching and learning know what they are about and communicate this ...' (p. 37). This is perhaps most important in EC settings where there are variously qualified staff and/or a high proportion of relatively inexperienced staff. Using school-based research, Marsh, Waniganayake and De Nobile (2016), for instance, assert that cultivating leadership conversations within their communities is a necessary first step to fostering shared understandings that can enhance school improvement including children's learning outcomes. Taking time for philosophical conversations and debates that generate a shared vision for learning is crucial if EC educator teams are to effectively live their vision and understand the implications of their pedagogical practices.

The role of the educational leader

One of the key features of the NQF was the introduction of the role of educational leader at each setting. Under the National Law and Regulations (ACECQA, 2011a), an approved service provider is required to appoint an educational leader to '... guide other educators in their planning and reflection, and mentor colleagues in their implementation practices' (p. 86). The NQF requires one person to be formally appointed to the position, but does not specify the qualifications or experience that person should hold. While this position is often taken up by the nominated supervisor of the setting, a number of EC settings now think more strategically about who is best placed to undertake this role. At the time of writing this book, the National Quality Standard was being revised and it was proposed that Quality Standard 7, element 7.2.2 be revised as follows to indicate that 'The educational leader is supported and leads the development and implementation of the educational program and assessment and planning cycle'. Readers are asked to verify the final words when available through the Australian Children's Education and Care Authority (ACECQA).

Considerations regarding knowledge, qualifications, interest in current research and capacity to lead have all been cited as factors in the decisions about who might take up the role of the educational leader (see Fleet et al., 2015). These researchers also report that in many settings there is a lack of clarity about the role and considerable variation in the ways that employers support educational leaders to carry out their roles. Other studies in this area (see Rouse & Spradbury, 2016) have identified a randomised approach to the appointment of educational leaders with varying emphasis put on the qualifications or knowledge of the leader. They concluded that it was important for educational leaders to have the expertise, confidence and authority necessary to enact their role to avoid the role becoming buried under a burden of extra responsibility that is not recognised, respected or credible to those they lead.

A number of localised practitioner inquiry projects have been undertaken to explore the role of the educational leader and better define how pedagogical leadership might be understood and enacted (see Botero-Lopez et al., 2014; Cheeseman, 2010; Green & Bickley, 2013). Each of these projects involved community of learner models of inquiry to examine how the role might be understood across a range of EC settings. In one of these studies, a small group of EC leaders based in Sydney met over a period of one year to discuss the role of pedagogical leaders in their settings (Cheeseman, 2010). One of the participants from this project, Karen Welch from Kids Campus Children's Centre (NSW), reflected on her role as the director in her childcare centre. She recognised that while her EC qualified staff were well placed to lead others in curriculum decisions, she had come to recognise the importance of her role in establishing the vision and ensuring that changes in curriculum were consistent with the centre's philosophy. She said:

> I recently realised that if I wanted to see curriculum change then I was going to have to lead it. I think that I thought that the qualified staff and room leaders would just 'do it' but have recently realised that such change needs guidance and direction—put simply, it is just not going to happen without me.

Karen's realisation is not all that uncommon. With so many pressing and competing demands on centre directors, she wanted to see the room leaders step up and take leadership for pedagogy. What was perhaps missing in this case was a clear vision of the end goal, the aim that all staff might be striving for.

In Leaders in practice 6.1, Rhonda Livingstone, the National Education Leader at ACECQA, shares her perspectives on the initiative of the Australian government to include the role of educational leader as part of the NQF. She reflects on her role at ACECQA and the important contribution that educational leaders bring to quality improvement in the EC sector.

Visit Oxford Ascend to hear more from Rhonda.

LEADERS IN PRACTICE 6.1

Rhonda Livingstone

National Education Leader, ACECQA

What was the background to the development of the position of national education leader at ACECQA?

The role of educational leader in an EC setting was first introduced in 2012 in the National Quality Standard (NQS) and underpinning the National Law and Regulations. We have long had positional leadership roles such as director and coordinator, but for the first time the important role of educational leader was recognised, acknowledged and embedded in the National Quality Framework (NQF). As a part of that commitment to educational leadership, the ACECQA board and CEO identified the need for someone to take on such a role nationally as national education leader at ACECQA.

I was appointed in early 2014 as the first national education leader. This role has evolved over time in response to changing needs of the sector and government agencies. The key emphasis of the role is building a shared understanding of the expectations and requirements of the educational leader role as outlined in the NQS and underpinning regulatory standards. There is a strong focus on supporting educational leaders in their important role.

More broadly, I work collaboratively with our colleagues in state and territory governments and the Australian government to build a shared understanding of the expectations of the NQS, underpinning regulatory standards and learning frameworks. The focus is on working collaboratively to support educators, service leaders, approved providers and others to meet or exceed the standards and continually improve quality for children and families.

I draw from my experiences in the education and care sector (now spanning more than 30 years), which have included a range of roles in preschool and long day care, including as a service director; being an assessor of programs and services for both the government and a community association; undertaking a range of funding, policy, program, training and leadership roles in government; and, for a short time, being a sessional academic with a university.

I feel very privileged to be part of the small group of skilled and knowledgeable officers from around Australia who worked on the development of the NQS and the related policy and assessment and rating tools, guides and resources as well as the training and testing program of authorised officers.

What is your vision for the role of educational leaders in EC settings?

I think an important part of the educational leader role (and indeed our collective responsibility) is to build confidence and empower educators to discuss their practice and think about how theory can inform their practice. I work collaboratively with colleagues in government and peak organisations to provide educators and leaders with access to information, resources and professional development opportunities. It is part of my vision that the EC profession proudly showcases and leads the way in terms of best practice in education and care.

Qualifications and knowledge of children's learning and development along with attitudes, dispositions and leadership attributes are all key qualities for educational leaders. I think it is important for educational leaders to:

- be inclusive
- identify and acknowledge strengths of educators and build on those strengths
- empower educators and identify opportunities for them to succeed as well as opportunities to build on these strengths and extend their thinking
- be open to learning and other ways of knowing and doing and keeping abreast of changes, research and best practice approaches
- drive continuous improvement by setting a positive example
- mentor, support, inspire, encourage, affirm and challenge pedagogy and practice in the role of a critical friend.

What are some of the key issues currently educational leaders are dealing with?
Importantly, effective educational leaders are skilful change managers. Change is inevitable if we want to move forward and learn from our experiences. I think one of the key challenges at the moment for educational leaders is supporting educators to meet the elements and standards in Quality Area 1—Educational Program and Practice. NQF Snapshot data suggests this is the most challenging area for services and educators to achieve, particularly the requirements related to critical reflection and the cycle of planning. Helping and empowering educators to identify strategies to document children's learning and development in a way that is meaningful and relevant, and importantly achievable, is imperative.

Recognising that documentation is just one part of the planning cycle, educational leaders can play a crucial role in supporting educators to develop skills and strategies to collect, analyse and interpret information and use it to reflect on their pedagogy and inform further learning opportunities for children. A key part of this process is supporting educators to understand the value of critical reflection—what it is, how to do it and how it contributes to quality outcomes for children and families. A great place for educational leaders and educators to begin is looking at the reflective questions in the approved learning frameworks. For example, in the EYLF, engaging in a discussion around 'Who is advantaged when I work in this way?' and 'Who is disadvantaged?' (DEEWR, 2009, p. 13).

While we caution about causal links, the latest NQF Snapshot data results indicate a correlation between educational leadership and Quality Area 1, which focuses on the educational program and practice. A high percentage of services that met the element relating to educational leadership (7.1.4) received a rating of 'Meeting' or 'Exceeding NQS' for educational program and practice (NQS Quality Area 1). I believe these assessment and rating results highlight the importance of the educational leader's role and the impact they can have on the educational program and practice as well as the value of their work within services and communities.

I would like to finish by congratulating all those who are leading educational programs, practice, research and reforms across Australia, whether they be working in education and care services, regulatory authorities, peak organisations, training institutions or universities; and whether they are professional development providers or myriad other individuals working to support the NQF vision: all children have the best start in life to create a better future for themselves and for the nation.

Pause–reflect–act 6.3

- Having read Rhonda's profile, how would you define what an EC educational leader is to someone who works in health services or another profession?
- What do you consider to be the essential criteria to be appointed as an educational leader in EC settings? Give your reasons.
- How prepared are you to become an educational leader in EC settings? Make a list of qualities and qualifications you have that would enable you to be an effective educational leader.

Go to oxfordascend *to hear Rhonda's thoughts.*

Creating a vision

philosophies and theories
curriculum models are underpinned by a range of theoretical and philosophical beliefs and assumptions that determine what will be included in a curriculum and what will be excluded or silenced.

chapter 5 contains more on ideas about philosophy and vision.

At all times, but particularly in times of change and reform, leaders must seek ways to motivate educators and keep the focus on an agreed vision. Developing an articulated vision for curriculum and pedagogy begins with an examination of the underlying **philosophies**, **theories** and principles that shape our professional beliefs about children's learning. It also requires critical reflection on the purposes we see for our EC settings and the goals we are aiming to achieve with children and families.

There are numerous contemporary approaches to EC curriculum that variously draw on theory, research and ideology. In many contemporary approaches to curriculum we can see evidence of attachment theory; child-development, socio-cultural and critical, postmodern and post-structuralist theoretical understandings. If leaders are to intentionally articulate a vision for curriculum and pedagogy they need to be able to identify the theoretical approaches that influence their beliefs and approaches to children's learning. This is the first step in creating a clear and coherent vision that can be embraced by staff with enthusiasm. All too often theory and philosophy are overlooked. In an environment that emphasises accountability it is easy to simply meet compliance rather than think about the underlying influences. Yet it is these underlying philosophies and theories that can enable a staff team to work together to create a culture of learning and professional growth.

Pause–reflect–act 6.4

Think deeply about how you make curriculum choices and decisions.

- What are the philosophical foundations of your beliefs about the purposes of EC settings?
- Which theories and approaches to curriculum are most influential in your plans and programs for children's learning? Why?
- Which theories and approaches are least influential to you? Is this because you have consciously dismissed the ideas or is it because you need to learn more about them?

How can I lead a team to facilitate better learning outcomes for children?

In any EC setting, qualified educators have a professional responsibility to model, **mentor** and open conversations that lead to the best educational outcomes for young children. Most contemporary EC curriculum documents, including the EYLF, require interpretation. They are not recipe books that can be followed like prescriptions. While all staff can play an important role in contributing to curriculum decisions, it is the qualified educators who should take lead responsibility for ensuring that learning is planned for. This means that curriculum will draw on the philosophical position of the setting and have a strong theoretical and evidence base.

mentoring
a process of supported learning involving two or more educators. Mentors can be provided under formal professional learning programs or can emerge informally through networking.

In addition to this, leaders need to be mindful that interpreting a curriculum document means taking account of local contexts and the desires and needs of each community and group of children. In order to do this well, educators need a thorough understanding of their surrounding community and the cultural influences that are important to the children and families at that EC setting. This requires educators to listen thoughtfully to the children, families and community.

Pause–reflect–act 6.5

How do we ensure we are responsive to the needs of children, families and the community as well as teach the EC pedagogy we value? Consider the following scenarios and reflect on what you would do and why.

- A child squashes a bug in the playground and says, 'All bugs are bad; my dad said so'.
- A parent has asked you to teach their three year old to read.
- The neighbours have complained about the noise the children make in the playground when they are playing outside.

Getting started

Making decisions about how to develop and document an educational program for young children will take considerable time and many conversations. Some points to consider are:

- Who will be involved?
- What roles should staff with varying qualifications play in the curriculum processes?
- How will staff meet to discuss and plan their programs?
- What types of records would we like to keep to show evidence of our curriculum?
- To what extent can we use technology to record our curriculum decisions and children's learning journey?
- How will we involve families?
- How will we group the children?
- How will we organise the environment?

Sufficient time must be given to enable educators to think, reflect on and document their curriculum or program. This requires leaders to advocate for and prioritise staff planning time, but also ensure this time is used effectively. There are a few key principles that should be considered from the outset:

- There is no one right or perfect way to document a curriculum or program. While there are accountability requirements under the National Quality Standard (ACECQA, 2011c), EC settings do not need to subscribe to a uniform approach.
- The best outcomes will be achieved if all staff contribute to the design of a centre approach to curriculum that is led by those with high levels of qualification. Curriculum decisions need to take account of both the philosophical influences of the setting and the broader accountability standards.
- Pedagogical leaders need to advocate for planning and programming methods that reflect sound EC principles and practices which are achievable for the staff in the setting. Overwhelming staff with unreasonable expectations for documentation can be very demotivating and detract staff from the important work of engaging in children's play and learning.

coaching usually, coaching involves explicitly modelling or directly instructing how to learn a new skill or knowledge. Coaching can also involve encouraging, practising and reviewing learning in an explicit way.

networking in EC education this involves establishing and maintaining professional relationships with others working in the EC sector as well as other professionals in school education, health and welfare (and so on) to better support children and families.

What else can I do?

There are many means of involving others in an educational program for children, such as modelling, mentoring and **coaching**; **networking**; and supporting the community. We will consider these now.

Modelling, mentoring and coaching

Pedagogical leaders find that they have greater success in creating positive change when they are actively involved in the change process and can show that what they are envisioning is actually possible. This can be achieved in a very hands-on way, by taking part in day-to-day decisions and actions involving curriculum, or it can be done by frequently meeting with staff to discuss and support their work. Modelling can be implicit—the act of modelling an action or decision can be observed by others and picked up unconsciously—or it can be explicit—the demonstration of a teaching practice or decision where the staff involved are aware that they are being coached. While staff may often learn quietly and unconsciously, intentional leaders need to be prepared to teach explicitly when needed. This does not need to be condescending or patronising, but can simply be an exchange of knowledge where the learning outcome is clearly identified. We do not learn everything purely by observation—at times it helps to be taught some basic principles to be successful.

In Leaders in practice 6.2, Christine Knox, Director of Coolamon Preschool, shares her experience of leading a small team in a relatively isolated stand-alone preschool in rural New South Wales. Her story highlights the importance of context and that the role of the educational leader is not a one-size-fits-all model.

LEADERS IN PRACTICE 6.2

Christine Knox

Director and Educational Leader, Coolamon Preschool (NSW)

I graduated as an EC teacher in 1979 and have been the director, nominated supervisor and educational leader at Coolamon Preschool for 37 years. My title has changed over the years and I have seen several changes to regulations and more recently the introduction of the National Quality Framework. While my role has changed over those years, I have essentially been a teacher of young children, manager of a community-based preschool reporting to a parent management committee and mentor to other staff for all that time. Although the NQF, for the first time named the position of educational leader, in reality I have always assumed that role as the only teacher in a preschool with only two to three staff at any one time.

Coolamon is 40 kilometres from Wagga Wagga, New South Wales, with a growing population of around two thousand people. The main employment is from agriculture (canola, wheat and sheep), Charles Sturt University and a growing tourism industry. It is a really mixed community and we have children attending the centre who travel sometimes up to 60 kilometres for a round trip for their preschool experience. Some of these children travel home from preschool on the local school buses. The preschool is a 25-place, single-unit centre and currently employs a qualified EC teacher, a Diploma of Education and Care educator and a Certificate III job-share educator along with a part-time administration officer. The Certificate III position varies from year to year according to the number of children identified as needing additional learning support and the preschool's budget. So essentially we have two staff that are permanently employed and a casual third educator each year according to our enrolments. In all, we have up to about 50 children each week. They are predominantly four year olds attending two to three days per week, but we also have a number of three year olds. The town has a central school (Kinder to year 12) and a Catholic primary school.

I have seen many changes in funding and regulatory requirements over the years, but probably the most significant has been the introduction of the NQF. Prior to the NQF, I was the only qualified person at the preschool, so I carried the full responsibility for the education program. The new requirement that all staff would hold at least a Certificate III was met with mixed feelings. At first, staff were resistant to gaining qualifications as they had many years of experience and felt they were not being recognised for what they had done so well for so long. So these staff sought to have some of their experience formally recognised (through Recognition of Prior Learning or RPL). In hindsight, I think it would have been more beneficial for all concerned to do the study and really learn about observations, planning and scaffolding children's learning.

The announcement of the role of educational leader was not a big change for me; it was something I had always done—it was embedded in my everyday practice of being the teacher. I guess the naming of the role made me think more about talking with the other staff and being more explicit in mentoring them. As time went on and they felt more comfortable with their new qualifications, they became more empowered and took on greater responsibilities, particularly for the things they enjoyed sharing.

In my role as the educational leader, I tend to be the one who raises issues for discussion and I find relevant journals and articles for everyone to read. We support the ongoing professional learning of staff and we encourage staff to attend any workshops that they are interested in. We hold staff meetings about twice each term but with such a small team it is often better to just have a daily catch-up after the children have gone home for the day. The good thing about a small team is that you do a lot of the small stuff in a fairly informal way. We put our energies into making meetings about some of the big things that need all of our attention. We made a significant change to the way we documented children's learning about six months ago so we have met several times over that period to give a concentrated effort to thinking that through. We are fortunate that within our small staff team, we have always worked well together and have respect for each other's strengths and opinions.

We found the expectations of the NQS and our first assessment and rating visit quite stressful. In hindsight, it was more about the unknown and we were happy to receive an overall meeting rating, with two 'exceeding' ratings in Educational Program and Practice and Staffing Arrangements. The process has given us things to focus on for the coming years. As we came to terms with the NQS, I found it really useful to be a part of our regional directors group. While I have always had good connections with teachers in other EC settings, in 2011 a group of nine preschools from this region (Adelong, Gundagai, Junee, Temora, Ariah Park, Ganmain, Leeton and Ardlethan—a region of about 200 kilometres) decided to formalise the network and meet once a month.

We were inspired by a similar group that had been operating for some time around Albury, so after talking with them we formed our own regional network group. We pooled some funds and employed a consultant to help us with policies and procedures. This was so valuable, as doing all of the policies on your own is really time consuming. In a small centre you have to do the same amount of policy development as larger centres but you have far fewer people to call on to help out. It made sense to get together and share our ideas. Then our consultant would go away and write up our thinking.

We have visited each other's centres and meet at our centre each term—usually in June, which is central for most of us. This has been a really important support for us to connect, tease out issues and problems and get advice from each other. We have become really close friends and colleagues. There is no defined leader of the group, but people just naturally take the lead on issues that are important for them. This network has been so important for us all. Working in small, stand-alone centres can be very isolating and you can go for long periods without really knowing what others are doing. Our centres are all very different, but we share a lot of issues that are common to rural EC settings.

I am about to retire from my position at the preschool and so I think about what advice I would give to the new teacher who takes over from me in the role of educational leader. I think the most important thing is to respect staff and listen to them. If you are coming into an established staff team, be mindful that the existing team have a lot of knowledge and experience to offer. They know the community so well and it is important in a small community to be sensitive to that community. It is also important to talk through your decisions and explain why you are doing things a particular way—people need to understand why you are doing the things you do—even if they seem like common sense to you. In a rural town it is also essential to get out into the community and build relationships. Getting to know the schools and library staff is essential but I have gained a lot from links with the aged care facility, the local council, the other EC settings (because children often attend more than one service), early intervention and community health staff. In a small community you can also have really good relationships with the police and the fire brigade and local businesses. These are the connections that really enrich the program. In a small town it is all about relationships.

Pause–reflect–act 6.6

- What do you think are some of the key differences between being an educational leader in a large long day care setting and that of a single unit preschool?
- The educational leader has an important role in initiating change and motivating other educators. What do you think are some of the important qualities for an educational leader to possess so that they provide a positive and inspirational role model for their team?
- In the context of this rural setting, what might you do to support yourself professionally if no network of educational leaders existed?

Leaders can model professional and ethical practice in relation to curriculum and pedagogy in a range of ways beyond modelling actions. They need to be up to date with current research and developments in the field and use this knowledge to inform discussion and provide staff with appropriate reading material and resources to invite conversations. This approach models and encourages a culture of continual growth and professional responsibility. Leaders can introduce critical and reflective conversations among staff that allow for different points of view and possibilities for others to challenge or suggest a change to the curriculum. A simple question of, 'I am interested in why you did it that way?' models a culture of openness and innovation and promotes distributed leadership as staff become more skilled, articulate and confident in their knowledge.

It is here that we can see how pedagogical leadership extends beyond the role of the educational leader. It is likely and perhaps desirable that a number of educators will become experts in particular areas of curriculum and pedagogy. Infant/toddler curriculum, learning in the outdoors, music or the arts are just some examples of the areas that individual educators may take responsibly to lead. Leaders of these specialties can draw attention to recent research and align this work to the setting's philosophy and policy framework, modelling philosophy in action. In this way staff are exposed to rich ideas and current thinking, which is less likely if the responsibility for being expert in all areas of curriculum and pedagogy fall to one specified person.

In bringing the team together, leaders can actively promote the use of the Code of Ethics (ECA, 2016) as a guide for pedagogical decisions. This brings to the fore the complexity of curriculum decisions and promotes an environment where critical reflection and questioning become a part of the everyday thinking of the staff team. The Code of Ethics can invite conversations about tricky curriculum issues and be a constructive way for teams with diverse backgrounds and beliefs to tease out the complexity of play and learning during early childhood.

Pause–reflect–act 6.7

- Think back to a professional experience placement or an EC setting you have worked in. Did you see modelling, mentoring and/or coaching examples being conducted by the leader of the program? Was it an effective way to support the staff and enact changes to the curriculum and pedagogy? How did the leader make time to support the staff?
- Think about your own learning style. How do you respond to feedback through mentoring and coaching? Do you feel comfortable mentoring and coaching others? Why or why not?

Networking and professional learning

Working within an EC setting can at times seem professionally isolating. This is perhaps more so in settings where there are fewer EC qualified staff. The generation of new ideas, the questioning of assumptions and the confidence to try something new is easier when we are in contact with other professionals who can act as sounding boards or help us to think through new ways of working. In recent years there have been numerous models of professional networks that have contributed to change and innovation. Some possibilities include:

- Hosting a meeting for staff at local settings to talk about an aspect of curriculum.
- Forming a practitioner inquiry group or professional learning community that meets regularly to discuss a specified topic and share practitioner research findings.
- Joining online discussion forums or establishing your own chat room to enable professional conversations when it is not easy for people to meet face-to-face.
- Making contact with state-based professional learning organisations and resource agencies to identify opportunities for networking meetings and workshops in your area.
- Organising a local pedagogical leaders group where those with lead responsibility for curriculum in a range of settings meet to share their experiences and questions.
- Making links with universities to develop partnerships where academic staff can work alongside centre based staff in a mentoring/shared learning experience.
- Arranging for groups of staff from your local community networks to attend conferences or professional learning workshops together to encourage ongoing conversations and collaborative work.
- Organising for network groups to present their work at conferences or workshops, further developing the skills and advocacy of staff involved.
- Getting together with local settings to request a professional learning session or organise a guest speaker.

Pause–reflect–act 6.8

- If you were asked to nominate the personal qualities and characteristics of a good educational leader in an EC setting, what would they be?
- Write a job description for an educational leader in an EC setting. Discuss with others how you would go about enabling the educational leader to undertake the tasks you have identified. Will time need to be allocated for the educational leader to undertake their role? How might the role be incorporated into the daily routines of the setting? Will the educational leader require space, time and resources beyond what is already available?
- The NQF requires only one person to be nominated as the educational leader. How do you see distributed models of leadership contributing to thinking about how this role might be considered, particularly in larger settings.
- Look at the Leaders in practice boxes in this chapter and reflect on what each leader states as being important aspects of their role.

See chapter 1 for information on distributed leadership.

Professional networking to promote pedagogical leadership

Professional networks have proven to be a valuable strategy for those seeking to better understand how the role of educational leader might be effectively understood and enacted across a range of EC settings. One such network was the subject of a six-month study funded by the then Department of Employment, Education and Workplace Relations (see Hadley et al, 2016). Three EC organisations (UTS Child Care Inc, Marrickville Council and Kuring-gai Council) supported the EC educators in examining their pedagogical practices, while reflecting on the EYLF. 'A key feature of the project was a recognition of the importance of pedagogical leadership in affecting long-term and sustained change for improvement' (Hadley et al, 2016).

This study began with a full-day staff seminar involving a partnership with Macquarie University EC academics where contemporary notions of teaching in EC settings were explored. Learning circles were established to follow up on this seminar and provide a facility for more in-depth conversations about participants' pedagogical practices. These learning circles were facilitated by an academic mentor whose role was to provide provocations and negotiate with participants in developing work-based practitioner inquiry projects. Participants in this project reported that they valued the regular meeting time, benefited from the opportunity to network with others across organisations and valued the involvement of academic mentors. One of the directors noted:

> It has been a great way for people to learn from each other. I have seen relationships form between my staff and colleagues from other services and I believe that these professional relationships will continue. It breaks down the isolation that some staff feel working in centres and opening up to new perspectives and that has to be a positive!

What resulted from this project was an increased confidence on the part of the participants to take a leadership role within their staff teams to initiate change and discuss with other team members possible improvements to their programs. The project work acted to make visible the educators' thinking and assisted them to articulate their practice to others in ways that inspired progress and change. In addition, the academics involved reported that their participation in this project assisted them to maintain currency with the complexity of regulatory reform (Hadley et al., 2016). Such partnerships benefit all involved and help to strengthen and broaden understandings of the work of EC educators.

Building partnerships and advocating in the community

The work of EC leaders is increasingly expanding into associated children and family settings. At the same time, we are seeing the growth of integrated settings that are employing multidisciplinary teams. It is increasingly important for EC leaders to develop positive working relationships with a range of people who will play a part in the lives of young children. This might include staff at local schools, community workers, allied health professionals and cultural and community leaders. It is critical that EC educators take leadership roles within these multidisciplinary teams so as to demonstrate and apply their unique knowledge and understanding of children's development and the best ways to support children's learning through play-based education programs.

One of the features of these emerging models of integrated services identified by Moore (2008b); Press, Sumsion and Wong (2010), as well as Nolan, Cartmel and Macfarlane (2012) is that multidisciplinary teams come from varying philosophical and theoretical backgrounds that influence their approaches to working with young children. Many approaches to learning and development that stem from health and welfare philosophies have been designed to resolve identified problems or overcome specific deficits. Such programs are often targeted at particular groups or individuals. More comprehensive EC pedagogical programs tend to promote more universal approaches that build on the possibilities and are not limited to specific deficits. While there is a place for a range of approaches within a comprehensive EC provision, pedagogical leaders have an important role to play in promoting education programs for young children that do not focus solely on needs and deficits. Where specific interventions are required, these can be sensitively included within a mainstream education program. Pedagogical leaders have expert knowledge that they can share with other professionals about inclusion strategies and the range of pedagogical practices that promote learning for all children.

A case study (Cheeseman, 2006b) that investigated the involvement of EC teachers in emerging community health and welfare programs for young children, found that EC teachers were not always able to easily contribute their expertise to these initiatives. Educators involved in these programs recognised the need to be articulate and to use data as evidence to build convincing arguments for pedagogical approaches to broader EC initiatives. The participants in this study found that being responsive and actively networking with health and welfare colleagues was the key to being included when new programs and local initiatives were being considered. It is necessary for EC leaders to be proactive and not sit back and take a 'wait to be invited approach'. Limited involvement of EC leaders in such initiatives runs the risk of fragmenting service delivery where families need to deal with multiple agencies often delivering conflicting or confusing messages. EC settings can be key players in integrating services for young children and families. Pedagogical leaders' expertise in children's learning and development is an essential element that can enhance and complement the approaches of health and welfare initiatives. Without pedagogical leadership, Macfarlane et al. (2010, cited in Nolan et al., 2012) argue that EC pedagogical knowledge can be marginalised and in turn can limit the possibility of early childhood staff being identified as leaders in such contexts.

The roles of educators in integrated settings can require high levels of skill in advocacy as educators work within teams of professionals to plan appropriate programs for children with specific support needs. Significant to this is the educator's ability to communicate clearly and convincingly the benefits of an inclusive and potentials-orientated approach to children's learning. The ability to clearly communicate the merits of particular approaches to children's learning requires leaders to be up to date in their knowledge of curriculum issues and research. When sharing perspectives of EC education against the hard research evidence of the health and welfare sector, it is essential that educators are clear and articulate with their evidence. One way of addressing this is for leaders to gather evidence of their pedagogical work with young children that they can speak knowledgeably and confidently about when communicating with professionals from other disciplines.

Pause–reflect–act 6.9

- How will you clearly articulate to other professionals what your approach to EC pedagogy is?
- Do you have clear evidence that would support your approach? What might be seen as valid evidence of the effectiveness of your approach to learning and teaching?
- What can you do to develop your ability to articulate your pedagogical work?

Chapter summary

Pedagogical leadership establishes a culture of professionalism in the setting and ensures that outcomes for children's learning and development are key drivers of the program's vision. The role of an educational leader is important to realising this vision, and a distributed model of pedagogical leadership may be more effective. Thinking beyond the immediate setting, pedagogical leaders communicate with families, other educators and the broader community about the importance of high-quality learning experiences for all children and contribute to a greater understanding of the complexity and value of EC education. Pedagogical leaders can make learning visible to others and challenge assumptions that working with young children is not babysitting. Their capacity to articulate key issues in curriculum and pedagogy promotes increased professionalism and improves the status and standing of all those who work with young children in EC settings.

Key references

Cheeseman, S. (2006b). Pedagogical silences in Australian early childhood social policy. *Contemporary Issues in Early Childhood*, 8(3), 244–54.

This article considers the literature relating to shifts in public policy bringing integration between education, welfare and health programs for young children and the role of EC leaders in this process.

Department of Education, Employment and Workplace Relations. (2009). *Belonging, being & becoming: The Early Years Learning Framework for Australia*. Retrieved from www.docs.education.gov.au/system/files/doc/other/belonging_being_and_becoming_the_early_years_learning_framework_for_australia.pdf

This is the national curriculum document for EC settings across Australia. This document is linked to the National Quality Standard and EC settings must demonstrate their use of the EYLF in the development of the philosophy, policy and curriculum of each setting.

Early Childhood Australia (2016), Code of ethics. Retrieved from www.google.com.au/#q=eca+code+of+ethics+2016+pdf

The Code of Ethics was developed by the EC profession to articulate the agreed principles and values that underpin the complex work and decision-making of EC professionals. The code provides a framework for reflection about the ethical responsibilities of those who work with young children.

Taguchi, H.L. (2010). *Going beyond the theory/practice divide in early childhood education. Introducing an intra-active pedagogy*. London: Routledge.

This book unpacks both theory and practice and challenges dominant discourses about learning. Case studies include childcare, preschool and university students, related to pedagogical documentation, and how new approaches to learning can be made visible.

Online resources

Early Childhood Australia National Quality Standard Professional Learning Program

This website houses many resources that support EC leaders working in the sector in terms of implementing the National Quality Framework.

http://www.ecrh.edu.au

Educational leadership

Watch Sandra Cheeseman (one of the authors of this book) speak with two EC educators about their role as educational leaders.

www.earlychildhoodaustralia.org.au/nqsplp/e-learning-videos/talking-about-practice/the-role-of-the-educational-leader/

Roscommon County Childcare Committee

This committee was established in 2002 and is a partnership of the statutory, voluntary, community, and private sectors, including parents and families working together for the enhancement of EC care and education in County Roscommon, Ireland. Its website has many podcasts on leadership.

www.roscommonchildcare.ie/videos-podcasts/

Watch 'How can we model pedagogical leadership in the early childhood care and educational setting' and compare the information in this video to the content of this chapter. What are the similarities that can be draw between Ireland and Australia in terms of pedagogical leadership? Are there things we could learn from other countries in terms of this role?

www.youtube.com/watch?v=xYvEk6nj0DI

7 LEADING INTENTIONALLY THROUGH ADVOCACY AND ACTIVISM

CHAPTER LEARNING OBJECTIVES

After studying this chapter you will understand that:

- Advocacy and activism are professional and ethical responsibilities of EC.
- There are key differences between advocacy and activism.
- Because politics influences EC education, intentional leaders need to influence politics.
- Critically reading policy and practice opens up possibilities for advocacy and activism.
- Intentional leaders adopt deficit and strengths-based approaches to advocacy and activism.
- Leaders can practise advocacy and activism at a personal, centre, community and systems level.
- Advocacy and activism are integral to intentional leadership and the provision of quality EC education.

Key concepts

activism
advocacy
critically reading social policy

Overview

Leading quality EC programs necessitates advocacy and activism within the EC setting and more broadly in the public sphere. To this end, this chapter aims to build leaders' capacity and commitment to being effective advocates and activists for children and the early childhood profession in ways that are grounded in children's rights and social justice agendas.

The case for advocacy and activism

advocacy
advancing the values, needs and interests of an individual or group within existing frames of reference.

Advocacy and **activism** may, at first glance, seem out of place when talking about leading an EC setting. While for many EC leaders the decision to practise as an educator stems from a desire to work with young children and to make a difference to their lives, this desire is often confined to ensuring that the learning experiences they provide support children's learning, well-being and development. Advocacy and activism, therefore, may be regarded as practices more suited to peak bodies and community workers.

Pause–reflect–act 7.1

Most people who seek employment in EC settings say that they were driven by their passion or interest in working with young children and their families. Reflect back on your own decision to enrol in EC studies and/or work in an EC setting.

- As an EC leader, how do you anticipate making a difference in the lives of young children?
- In what ways do you anticipate your practice would involve advocacy and activism?

activism
the questions, assumptions and discourses on which policy and practice are based and promoting through action how these might be implemented outside existing frames of reference.

This chapter is in itself an exercise in advocacy and activism, as it seeks to make a claim for advocacy and activism as being fundamental to an intentional leader's practice. First, and concurring with Kieff (2009) and Gibbs (2003), we suggest that advocacy and activism are the professional and ethical responsibilities of all educators, and particularly of intentional leaders. EC leaders are well placed to recognise and address any barriers to the optimal learning, development and well-being of children attending an EC setting, and of children more broadly. Examples of such barriers include a parent without family support suffering from postnatal depression; the play of some children that marginalises or excludes others; suspected child abuse or neglect; a staff member not able to afford to upgrade their qualification; a local council announcing that their EC centres will no longer take enrolments for children under two years of age; inequitable access to quality EC education programs for Indigenous children; and proposed government policy that threatens to lower quality standards. In each of these examples, EC leaders can take action in ways that can benefit the child or children affected.

These ideas are fundamental to the Code of Ethics (ECA, 2016). While not a legal requirement, this ethical code makes it incumbent on leaders to work in the best interests of children's safety, well-being and development. The Code of Ethics also makes explicit that educators' professional responsibilities entail advocating for the provision of quality education and care, and laws and policies that promote the rights and best interests of children and families.

Given that children do not vote in government elections, EC leaders are, first, well placed to identify and take action on issues that affect children's rights, well-being and development. Second, advocacy and activism are critical to the practice of an intentional leader because, as discussed in Chapter 2, EC education is inherently political. Although 'teaching' and 'education' might seem like neutral concepts, how each is understood and applied is shaped by political agendas. Politics impact on:

- *curriculum*: curriculum documents and dominant discourses influence what young children are and are not taught.
- *types of EC settings*: while prior to the 1990s most educators in Australia, would have taught in a community-based setting, today market-based provisioning means that many will practise in a for-profit setting.

- *who attends EC settings*: enrolments are impacted by various government policies including those pertaining to women's workforce participation, school starting ages and others such as the 15 hours' provision for four year olds, which affect access to EC education programs.
- *the quality of education programs*: quality can be both supported and hampered by government regulatory requirements.
- *the status of EC education*: whether the education of young children, including babies and toddlers, is valued. In turn, this status can impact on educators' pay and what EC settings are like as workplaces.

Thus, EC education is far from value free. The more that intentional leaders engage in advocacy and activism, the more the provision of EC education can be underpinned by the rights and interests of children and the values espoused in the Code of Ethics.

Intentional leaders have a vision for the sort of world they want children to grow up in and the sort of EC settings they want young children to access. This vision serves as a starting point for advocacy and activism. Seeing your vision at work can lead to action where you showcase that good work as a model to others. Conversely, seeing instances where your vision falls short can lead to action where you seek change for the better. *In Leaders in practice 7.1, Alicia Flack-Konè—an EC teacher with more than 25 years' experience working in the sector—outlines what drives her to advocate for young children.*

Visit Oxford Ascend to hear more from Alicia.

LEADERS IN PRACTICE 7.1

Alicia Flack-Konè

Early Childhood Teacher, Northside Community Services, Yurauna Centre, Canberra Institute of Technology (ACT)

I have been in the EC profession since 1990 as a volunteer, untrained assistant, diploma-qualified educator, and EC teacher. Currently I work in an EC environment at Northside Community Services, through Yurauna Centre, Canberra Institute of Technology, ACT in a mixed age group with Aboriginal and Torres Strait Islander children.

I don't remember when I first engaged in EC advocacy as it is something that has evolved over time. I do remember experiencing first hand gender discrimination when I was a child, then in my teens and on into my adult life. At first, as an educator my vision was 'to show girls they can too!' In my practice I would remind girls they were strong and could do anything they wanted. I would share visuals of women leaders around the world from various countries, and this was all with infants and toddlers. I would translate songs to empower girls or at least include them in songs.

Over time I noticed that inequities were much bigger than just gender-based, and addressing them wasn't as simple as having conversations in the classroom. A broader context and engagement with children about religion, 'race', class, abilities, sexuality and culture was needed. I wanted to empower children to think critically and have the tools to stand up to what is unfair. I continued to read and found *Anti-bias curriculum: Tools for empowering young children* by Louise Derman-Sparks (Derman-Sparks, Staff, A.T.F., & the A B C Task Force, 1989) helped develop my thinking and give advocacy-based teaching practices 'a go'. I also talked to my colleagues to try to find ways to share and honour the voices of children and people not heard, who were marginalised within the community at local, national and international level.

Through these resources and conversations I started to 'take risks' by introducing conversations, visuals and literature into my practice that aimed to challenge stereotypes, biases and injustice. I became intentional about what books I read to children. For example, I began to use books like *The Rabbits* by John Marsden and Shaun Tan (Marsden & Tan, 2010), *This is Our House* by Michael Rosen (Rosen, 2007), *The Smallest Samurai* by Fiona French (French, 2008) and *The Rainbow Cubby House* by Brenna and Vicki Harding (Harding & Harding, 2006) in my curriculum. Books like these encouraged children to think differently about the world. I also used annual events to introduce or continue on conversations. For example, Sorry Day gave me permission to talk about children who were taken from their parents, while Easter provided an opportunity to talk about other religious celebrations. Another strategy I developed was to sing social justice songs to children at rest time, such as *Streets of London* by Ralph McTell (McTell, 1969) and *She's got Her Ticket* by Tracey Chapman (Chapman, 1988). Two parents and grandparents asked me about *Streets of London* and later looked up the song on YouTube at home. They were so appreciative that I was 'teaching' their son about social justice.

During this time I realised that I needed to actively engage with EC peers who critically examined their practice or similarly grappled with addressing inequity and injustice in their practice. I couldn't do this work in isolation. I joined the Social Justice In Early Childhood group where I heard first hand stories of lived experiences. This gave me further insight into the injustices that occurred in our community and an opportunity to come together with other educators in solidarity. It was a great forum to hear and see how EC teachers were grappling with issues of social injustice.

What drives me to do this advocacy work? It is important to me that children feel proud of who they are and comfortable with their identity. I also want children to be able to stand up for what is fair and just, and to have the words to be able to communicate this. I have believed this for a long time and continue to practise this every day, within the classroom, the curriculum, the community and internationally. I remember in the late 1990s when I was a team leader in a preschool room in the inner city of Sydney and autism was not yet well known as a common diagnosis in the community. I was informed by the director that we would be having a family with a child who had autism. I didn't know anything about it so one lunchtime and after work I sat at the computer and researched what I could to find out about autism. I wanted to ensure that the child starting at our centre would be supported for who they are, and would know that we welcomed them into the space and would accommodate and be flexible where needed.

I believe it is my responsibility, our responsibility, to do what we can to ensure that children feel empowered and positive about themselves; for children to belong and care about others no matter who they are or where they are from; and to have the skills to act with others or alone against injustices. My vision for a fair and just classroom, community, and world continues every day and has never stopped.

Pause–reflect–act 7.2

- When reading Alicia's profile, what values and beliefs did you identify in terms of her advocacy work?
- Are these the values and beliefs that might drive your practice? Why/why not?
- Read the children's books that Alicia refers to and develop appropriate questions to use with young children to discuss the benefits of family diversity based on these stories.
- Reflect on whether you could use the same children's books to stimulate discussions about social justice matters with your EC colleagues.

Go to oxfordascend *to hear Alicia's thoughts.*

The remainder of this chapter discusses the concepts 'advocacy' and 'activism' and how they can be put into action by leaders. Findings from an Australian study (Harrison et al., 2008), which explored elements that support and sustain the provision of high-quality EC education and care in long day care centres, are used to illustrate advocacy and activism in action. Phase two of this project involved identifying case study centres in New South Wales that had consistently rated as high quality on external measures which included the national Quality Improvement and Accreditation System (National Childcare Accreditation Council, 2005) and exploring educators' and parents' perspectives about which structures and processes contributed to their respective centre's high ratings. Notably, to varying degrees all directors of these six centres (three urban, three rural) practised as advocates, and three as activists for children, their staff and quality EC education.

Exploring advocacy and activism: two types of influence

The terms 'advocacy' and 'activism' are sometimes used interchangeably, or 'activism' may be described as advocacy that is political or radical, where direct action, such as a rally, is used to influence policy or legislation. In the EC context, both advocacy and activism are actions that intentionally seek to influence outcomes which are in the best interests of children, families and educators, and which promote children's rights and social justice. Both advocates and activists act on behalf of and/or with others to promote or bring about change that is consistent with their vision for children and quality EC education.

Pause–reflect–act 7.3

- When you think about the terms 'advocacy' and 'activism', which words, images and people come to mind?
- Reflecting on the definition and meaning of advocacy and activism, how would you position yourself as an EC advocate and activist for children and their families?

Table 7.1 Key differences between advocacy and activism

	Advocacy	**Activism**
Focus	An issue	The political in an issue (power relations)
Premise for action	Within existing frames of reference. These are commonly accepted, taken as given.	Outside existing frames of reference. The legitimacy of these frames is questioned.
Broad strategy	Create spaces and opportunities for improvements to be made within existing discourses.	Challenge dominant discourses and offer alternatives.
Tactics utilised	Multiple, including working with the media, networking with key stakeholders, raising public awareness, meeting politicians, fundraising, writing a submission and collecting signatures for a petition.	As per advocacy, developed from a critical reading of the issue.

Source: Sumsion, 2006.

More specifically, there are important and distinct differences between the two forms of action. Drawing on Sumsion (2006), these differences are summarised in Table 7.1 and then further explained. These differences can be explained further by considering possibilities for advocacy and activism within Australia in response to the National Quality Standard (ACECQA, 2011c). The discussion that follows focuses specifically on Standard 6.1, 'Supportive relationships with families'.

Advocacy involves an acceptance of established ways of thinking about a problem and seeks to make changes within existing frames of reference. With respect to Standard 6.1, advocacy would stem from an acceptance of the premise that it is a responsibility of educators to develop and maintain respectful, supportive relationships with parents and other family members. Consequently, the focus of any ensuing advocacy work would be to promote and effectively implement this premise and/or address any barriers to its implementation. The broad advocacy strategy utilised would require consideration of how to best effect positive change that would enhance staff support of and respect for families. Specific tactics utilised could entail developing a budget plan that supports a request to management for above NQS ratios which would give staff time to develop more meaningful relationships with parents.

In contrast, activism requires a questioning of the legitimacy of accepted dominant perspective(s) or thinking about an issue. To do this, activists focus on the politics or power relations embedded in a problem; that is, the agendas, interests and discourses that shape how it is presented. Bacchi (2009) presents a useful six-step process intended to be used to **critically read social policy**, but which can also be applied more broadly to any issue. The six steps are:

critically reading social policy involves an understanding that policy is political and value laden, not neutral, and therefore requires an understanding of the values, interests, agendas and discourses that shape policy.

1 What's the problem?
2 What assumptions underlie this representation of the problem?
3 How has this representation of the problem come about?

4 What is left unproblematic in this problem representation? Where are the silences? Can the problem be thought about differently?
5 What effects are produced by this representation of the problem?
6 How has this representation of the problem been produced, disseminated and defended? How could it be questioned, disrupted and replaced?

Applying these ideas to the NQS Standard 6.1 can generate questions such as:

- In whose interests are staff–family relationships framed?
- Who stands to lose or gain from such a framing?
- Which dominant discourses or ways of thinking and speaking about EC education does this framing come from?

Inserting the political into ordinary, seemingly neutral issues such as staff–parent relationships allows for underlying assumptions to be challenged in ways that advocacy does not as easily lead to. In one case study centre in the Investigating Quality study (Harrison et al., 2008), an activist reading of Standard 6.1 questioned the assumed one-sided responsibility of educators to establish and sustain respectful and supportive relationships with families. Such an assumption was regarded as consistent with a positioning of EC settings as 'services' and parents as 'consumers' or 'customers' (Fenech et al., 2010b). Having reflected upon and debated the accepted premises, activism next involves proposing alternative frames of reference. Again drawing on the activism of leaders at the case study centre, activists could develop a 'mutual rights and responsibilities' approach to staff–parent relationships. In this alternative framing, parents would be regarded as partners with staff, with a shared responsibility for the well-being of children and the centre community (not service).

Starting points for advocacy and activism

EC texts often talk about advocates and advocacy (and implicitly, activists and activism) in a particular way—for example:

> Advocates are people who stand up for, speak for, and work to enhance the lives of others who are not able—or yet able—to speak for themselves. (Kieff, 2009, p. 9)
>
> Advocates ... advance a particular case or cause, usually on behalf of a powerless constituency. (Ebbeck & Waniganayake, 2004, p. 163)
>
> Advocacy is about speaking out, acting, and writing to promote and defend the rights, needs and interests of people who are in some way disadvantaged. (Gibbs, 2003, p. 6)

As the above definitions illustrate, advocacy and activism are often framed in a *deficit* way, where action is taken *in response to* a perceived problem, such as funding cuts or limited available support services for children with speech delays, and *on behalf of* an individual or group unable to advance their own cause.

While this framing of advocacy and activism reflects much of the important work advocates and activists do, it is also important to consider that action and advocacy can be *strengths-based*, where action is undertaken *proactively* to promote a cause that is good and important.

In a recent small-scale investigation into centre directors' promotion of early learning and early child development to their current and prospective parent users (Fenech et al., 2016), one of the five director-participants undertook intentional, strengths-based advocacy work in her everyday practice. Strategies she utilised included:

- taking parents on centre tours and explaining to them why the centre environments are set up as they are, what learning is expected to ensue and what development opportunities the children will have. Discussion on these tours also involved highlighting staff qualifications and why these are important, and promoting the centre as a place of learning.
- redirecting parent conversations. For example, going beyond enquiries about fees and opening hours to asking parents about the learning and development hopes and expectations they have for their child.
- providing parents with opportunities to sit in on play-based learning sessions, with the educator explaining to them how learning and development are being supported.
- using language such as 'teachers' (not 'staff' or 'carers') and 'learning' (not just 'care') that showcased her long day care centre as a place of learning, not 'child care'.

These practices are illustrative of how strengths-based advocacy work can be authentically and proactively incorporated into a leader's day-to-day practices.

Pause–reflect–act 7.4

Visit the websites of the following organisations and groups:

- Australian Community Children's Services: http://ausccs.org.au/
- Australian Research Alliance for Children and Youth (ARACY): www.aracy.org.au
- Community Child Care Co-operative NSW: www.ccccnsw.org.au
- Early Childhood Australia: www.earlychildhoodaustralia.org.au
- Secretariat of National Aboriginal and Islander Child Care: www.snaicc.org.au/
- Social Justice in Early Childhood group: www.sjiec.org/

Now consider the following questions:

- What examples of advocacy and activism can you find?
- Does each organisation/group have a deficit or strengths-based approach to advocacy and activism?

Intended impact of advocacy and activism

When seeking to influence or make a positive difference for young children, intentional leaders need to consider the level of impact at which they wish to effect change. As Figure 7.1 illustrates, advocacy and activism can target four levels of impact, ranging from the micro to the macro.

At the micro base is the *personal* level of impact, where leaders aim to make a positive difference to the life of a child or family attending their setting. Next, leaders can make an impact at the *centre* level, for themselves, the families at their centre community and/or their staff. The benefits of action here will be confined to the centre. Moving to a more macro impact, advocacy and activism in a *community* context seek to bring about change at the local level. Here, leaders work alone or in collaboration with other individuals, services and groups in the local area to bring about change intended to benefit children, families and educators in the local community. Finally, advocacy and activism at the *systems* level seeks to secure government policies, provisions (funding and programs) and legislation that meet the rights and interests of young children. Change here is 'big picture' and can be targeted to local, state, territory and national politicians and government agencies as appropriate:

Figure 7.1 Levels of impact of advocacy and activism

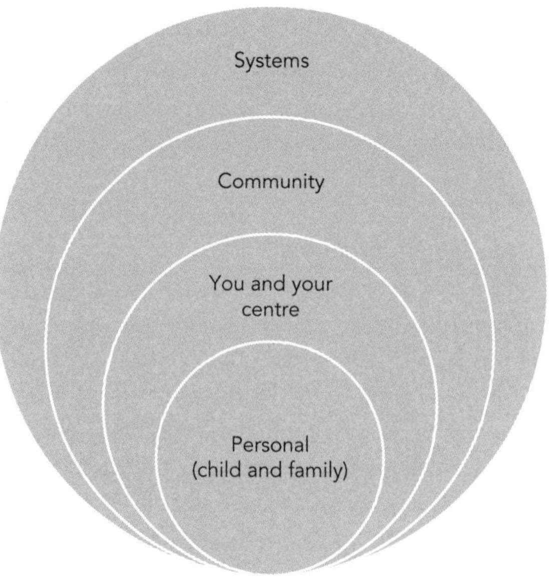

- *Personal advocacy/activism*: action aimed at influencing outcomes for an individual child or family.
- *Centre advocacy/activism*: action aimed at influencing outcomes for centre staff or the centre itself.
- *Community advocacy/activism*: action undertaken at the local level aimed at influencing outcomes within a community context.
- *Systems advocacy/activism*: action aimed at big-picture change. Action is directed to social policy, government provisions and legislation in ways that will influence outcomes for children.

Pause–reflect–act 7.5

Think of an issue you feel passionately about that affects the lives of young children and their families. List possible advocacy and activist strategies that EC leaders could utilise at the personal, centre, community and systems level of impact, and from a strengths and deficit-based perspective.

- Which of these strategies would you feel comfortable acting on? Why or why not?

Leading intentionally through advocacy and activism

This chapter has highlighted advocacy and activism as ethical and professional responsibilities of intentional leaders who can play a critical role in advancing children's rights and a social justice agenda. There are key differences between advocacy and activism, noting, however, that both can be deficit and strengths-based and have an impact at personal, centre, community and systems levels. These key ideas are now brought together in Table 7.2, which provides examples from the Investigating Quality study (Harrison et al., 2008) of what advocacy and activism might look like in practice from a deficit and strengths-based starting point, and at varying levels of impact.

To illustrate these ideas further, Leaders in practice 7.2 focuses on Brigitte Mitchell, an EC teacher with nearly 20 years' experience in EC education. In her profile, Brigitte talks about the advocacy and activism work she has undertaken and continues to undertake in her professional practice.

Table 7.2 Examples of advocacy and activism applied from a deficit- and strengths-based approach at different levels of impact

	ADVOCACY		ACTIVISM	
	Deficit-based	**Strengths-based**	**Deficit-based**	**Strengths-based**
Personal	You organise a fundraising event to raise money for specialist equipment that will enable a child with additional needs to attend your centre.	You attend and take a leading role in the local children's interagency monthly meetings. You see these meetings as an opportunity to network and build respectful working relationships with health and welfare professionals to whom you can confidently refer parents and children as needed.	A parent questions you about why your centre does not have formal reading, writing and numeracy activities to help prepare her four-year-old child for school. In addition to demonstrating how her child is developing these skills through play-based activities (advocacy) you take the opportunity to discuss the centre's philosophy of helping to prepare children for life.	You use the curriculum to explore issues of equity and social justice so as to provide a foundation for children to develop as active citizens concerned with the needs of others.

	ADVOCACY		ACTIVISM	
	Deficit-based	**Strengths-based**	**Deficit-based**	**Strengths-based**
You and your centre	Concerned that stipulated regulatory standards fall short of those recommended by Early Childhood Australia, you educate centre parents/management/owners about the critical role robust staff:child ratios play in the optimising of children's learning and development, as well as in the job satisfaction and retention of staff, and seek for above regulatory ratio standards to be implemented.	Mindful of the importance of staff retention for the provision of stable, secure relationships for children you present management/centre owners with an action plan of initiatives designed to enhance job satisfaction and staff retention.	You invite your new local member of parliament to visit your centre so you can promote quality EC education as encompassing practices and learning opportunities that support children's rights and social inclusion.	You critically read your centre philosophy and all policy documents and rewrite them, using language that promotes the centre as a learning community, not a service.
Community	You liaise with local councillors and the Chamber of Commerce to build support for the need for additional EC services in your area.	You promote your centre and the good work you do by being visible and involved in the local community, e.g. having a stall at the community family fun day; arranging coverage of the centre's annual open day in the local paper.	You attend community events and use the local media to counter community perceptions that childcare is glorified babysitting.	You hold monthly orientation sessions for prospective parents and use these as opportunities to showcase why you employ university qualified teachers in the babies' room.

	ADVOCACY		ACTIVISM	
	Deficit-based	**Strengths-based**	**Deficit-based**	**Strengths-based**
Systems	You write or contribute to a submission in response to a government draft policy in EC education.	You are a member of a number of EC advocacy organisations. This membership enables you to keep abreast of developments in the field, about which you actively inform parents and management.	You participate in a rally that seeks to highlight the lack of pay parity between EC teachers employed in primary schools and those employed in an EC setting. In doing so you wish to bring attention to the fact that university qualified teachers are integral to staffing in EC settings.	You apply for 'Excellent' status as per the NQS. In your application you draw attention to the advocacy and activism work you do and how this contributes to a notion of 'quality' that encompasses early learning and development but, equally important, social justice and children's rights.

LEADERS IN PRACTICE 7.2

Brigitte Mitchell
Early Childhood Teacher, Baya Gawiy Buga yani Jandu yani yu Early Learning Unit, Fitzroy Crossing (WA)

I am an EC teacher with a four-year Bachelor of Education (Early Childhood) from Western Sydney University. I completed this degree while working casually in the sector after completing a Diploma of Children's Services and Certificate III in Children's Services traineeship. I have 18 years' experience in the sector working with children aged birth to eight years and have been a qualified teacher for 12 years. In this time I have worked for local government and community-based centres, as well as NSW Health and NSW Department of Education and Communities settings. I have been a union delegate, branch councillor and activist for the United Voice Big Steps and Quality Matters Campaigns since 2011. I am also a member of the Social Justice in Early Childhood group and have been a member of its annual conference organising committee since 2015. At the 2015 conference I presented part of a tribute to the late Elizabeth Dau, the editor of the first and second editions of *The Anti-Bias Approach in Early Childhood*. I am currently working as a teacher of two and three year olds in a WA child and family centre early learning unit for Aboriginal and Torres Strait Islander children.

Promoting ECE to parents

I promote the importance of ECE to parents through my everyday conversations with them or through my documentation of children's learning. I do this by sharing my philosophy and research and theory in relation to their children's specific context. In documentation, as in conversation, I try to simply state in words and pictures what learning is occurring and why it's significant. I have also spoken to families regarding ECE industrial issues and/or asked them to be involved in actions such as petitions, rally days and media statements or writing.

Families are a very important and powerful part of children's early education and care. Therefore, issues affecting their educators and their education cannot be separated, so working collaboratively to share images and knowledge with families is embedded in my practice for today and tomorrow. Families can be strong advocates for their children alongside their teachers.

Promoting ECE to politicians

I promote the importance of ECE to politicians by writing them letters, sending them Tweets on Twitter or commenting on their Facebook posts, inviting them to visit my centre, visiting their offices, signing petitions to be delivered to them, speaking at party conferences, doing media comments and stories for print and television media on industrial issues and participating with questions and comments on the Q&A program, writing submissions and encouraging colleagues, education networks, families and friends to do so too. I refer to ECE policy, curriculum frameworks, research, theory, the UNCROC and the ECA Code of

Ethics and read what politicians may value or have stated prior to actions. I have found telling 'my story' on why an issue is important to me is a powerful way to enact change too.

Being a teacher is political. Politicians can shape future laws and policy as our local members of parliament with their positions and portfolios. We also have a responsibility to hold them to account as part of big picture change for the ECE sector as advocates for young children as per the ECA Code of Ethics.

Promoting ECE to the general public

I promote the importance of ECE to the general public by meeting or tweeting celebrities or other journalists and activists to have as public supporters of ECE issues, attending rallies and public actions by wearing promotional T-shirts, and speaking to the media in regard to contemporary issues at hand for ECE. This also includes print and TV stories or comments organised by our union. I find that talking or letting my networks know about this work provokes conversations with family and friends, which promotes awareness about ECE. I also find that general conversation about exactly what an ECE is and what its benefits are to children in the here and now and in a bigger picture way for society is also a way to promote its importance.

The general public is not embedded in the ECE profession and they vote and may have/had young children or wish to do so. They are voters participating in a democracy and they may support measures taken relating to their future that is in ECE now. So making them aware of messages in regard to changes we as teachers want to see is vital.

Pause–reflect–act 7.6

Having read Brigitte's profile, how would you now define the following actions?

- advocacy and activism in action
- deficit- and strengths-based
- seeking to have an impact at the personal, centre, community and/or systems level.

Which values and beliefs have underpinned Brigitte's advocacy and activism?

Overcoming barriers to practising advocacy and activism at the systems level

Despite the importance of advocacy and activism in EC contexts, Australian research (Hayden, 1997; Mevawalla, 2009; Mevawalla & Hadley, 2012; Nupponen, 2006a) and academic commentary (Macfarlane & Lewis, 2012; Woodrow & Busch, 2008) suggests that educators, including those in leadership positions, do not easily affiliate with advocacy and activism at the community and systems levels. Identified barriers include a lack of time to undertake what is perceived to be 'extra' work; a lack of confidence and/or perceived required experience; a prioritising of centre-based work (teaching) over work considered to be non-core (systems advocacy); a sense of powerlessness to effect 'big picture' change; ambivalence about using power; and limited or no affinity with systems advocacy. That advocacy and activism are not required elements of practice in Quality Area 7 of the National Quality Standard (Commonwealth of Australia, 2010b), which focuses on leadership and management, also presents as a further potential barrier.

Given these identified barriers, what might motivate educators, particularly those in leadership positions, to be systems advocates? A recent Australian study (Fenech & Lotz, 2016) reported on interviews with four EC teachers who practise systems advocacy in their everyday work. Findings showed that these teachers were ethically driven to advocate at the systems level. More specifically, their systems advocacy generally stemmed from a mix of deontology, utilitarianism and virtue ethics. *Deontological* or *duty-based ethics* concerns a sense of obligation or duty: a sense of what one 'ought' to do. Having been taught in their teacher training that advocacy needed to be part of their professional teaching practice drove two participants to advocate. For a third male participant, being in a formal leadership position that afforded monetary and other benefits obligated him to advocate for improved wages for lower paid educators. *Utility-based ethics is concerned with the maximisation of good and the minimisation of harm.* All participants in the study had a concern for improving outcomes for children and families—particularly those from disadvantaged backgrounds—and educators in the sector. This concern stemmed from a strong understanding about and belief in the early years as a critical period of development and the benefits quality EC education can bring to children, families and society more broadly.

Finally, *virtue-based ethics* is concerned with the development of specific attributes deemed to be the basis of a 'good' life, such as justice, courage and fortitude. This character-based ethics was most dominant in participants' transcripts, with a sense of social justice emerging as the strongest driver of their systems advocacy. Participants all had a deep commitment to equity and fairness, and the elimination of inequality. For them, making a difference as a teacher extended beyond the classroom to the public sphere as they sought a change in policy and legislation that they believed would address children's inequitable access to EC education. In particular, they were committed to addressing the rights of those from disadvantaged backgrounds; teachers' and educators' low wages and professional status; children's perspectives, rights and interests being disregarded in the political arena and in the media; and the lack of universal quality EC education.

Another way to overcome barriers to systems advocacy practice is to form collaborations with other educators so that advocacy work—and systems advocacy in particular—is not done in isolation. Such collaborations could be with colleagues and broader networks, as Alicia and Brigitte referred to in their 'Leaders in practice' profiles. Or, it could be with peers working in centres in your local area or region, as the following example illustrates.

In Northern New South Wales five directors from community-based preschools first came together in 2003 to network and provide collaborative support. Over time, membership of this small, informal group grew to comprise of directors from 25 preschools in the area. Realising that meetings often involved sharing frustrations and concerns about preschool access and viability, the group expanded its focus to advocate for preschools in the region. In 2012 the group formally became an incorporated association—the Northern Rivers Preschool Alliance—and today has members representing 42 community-based preschools. The group's vision, 'for every child in Northern New South Wales to have access to high-quality, affordable, well-managed ECEC, and for the Northern Rivers Preschool Alliance to be the peak body representing community preschools in Northern New South Wales' reflects its advocacy mission. While now a formal legal entity, the group is still very 'grass roots' in its advocacy work, with all members consulted on key issues and policies, such as the NSW Preschool Funding Model and the NSW Education Department's recent Start Strong funding policy. Each member preschool contributes an annual membership fee from which funds are used to employ a director from the alliance for 10 hours a term to lead the alliance's advocacy work. This role includes setting up meetings with relevant government department officials, politicians and peak EC groups; and writing template letters that members can use in their own advocacy work. This advocacy role is important not only in leading and co-ordinating advocacy activities, but also in empowering individual members to undertake systems advocacy themselves.

Systems advocacy work that the group has undertaken includes meeting with the New South Wales Minister for Early Childhood Education and the New South Wales Education Departments' Executive Director for Early Childhood Education to discuss funding concerns; and raising preschool access and viability issues through the local media. The group's Facebook page, www.facebook.com/northernriverspreschoolalliance, also provides its followers with information and resources about preschool access and funding, thereby enabling the impact of its advocacy work to extend well beyond its member base in Northern New South Wales. The longevity and effectiveness of this advocacy group can be attributed to a number of factors: the establishing of the advocacy-leadership role; the passion and commitment of individual director-members to children and preschool education; members' desire to voice concerns specific to the Northern Rivers region; the added collective advocacy power that the group has from its 42 members; and the use of social media to connect and resource members, to highlight issues affecting the group, and to promote its advocacy work.

Being a member of EC peak bodies also provides opportunities for educators to be supported in systems advocacy work. For example, in 2016 Early Childhood Australia launched the 'Early Learning, Everyone Benefits' campaign, designed to increase public knowledge of the benefits of investment in early learning. The campaign website includes useful resources for educators to use with families and others in their local community to build their understandings of the importance of the early years and quality EC education (see www.everyonebenefits.org.au/educators).

Pause–reflect–act 7.7

Having read this final section, reflect on the barriers that prevent you from being a systems advocate for children, families and your profession.

Now consider what might support your leadership practice as an advocate or activist:

- Which rule, utility or virtue-based ethical drivers could you draw on?
- With whom could you join forces to support or undertake systems advocacy work?
- Which campaigns of existing advocacy groups or peak organisations could you support?
- Look up the 'Everyone Benefits' website (www.everyonebenefits.org.au) and join the campaign's Facebook page. Commit to sharing one of the campaign's resources with staff at your centre and using the resource with a particular target group such as families, your local member of parliament or your local newspaper.

Chapter summary

Advocacy and activism are often unacknowledged but critical components of an intentional leader's practice. Advocates seek change within existing frames of reference, while activists' work stems from critiquing the political in practice and policy. Advocacy and activism can make both simple and marked positive changes in the lives of children, families and educators. Intentional leaders with a commitment to children's rights and social justice can engage in advocacy and activism from a deficit- and strengths-based perspective, and at personal, centre, community and systems levels.

Key references

Bacchi, C. (2009). Introduction. In *Analysing policy: What's the problem represented to be?* (pp. ix–xxii). Frenchs Forest: Pearson Australia.

This chapter provides an accessible and practical guide to critically reading social policy and can also be used to critically analyse practice.

Fenech, M. & Lotz, M. (2016, online first). Systems advocacy in the professional practice of early childhood teachers: From the antithetical to the ethical. *Early Years: An International Research Journal,* 1–16. doi: 10.1080/09575146.2016.1209739.

This article reports on the ethical influences that motivate four EC teachers in Australia to undertake systems advocacy in their everyday practice.

Gibbs, L. (2003). *Action, advocacy and activism: Standing up for children.* Marrickville, Sydney: Community Child Care Co-operative (NSW).

A 'how to' advocacy text specific to EC educators. Includes chapters on skills, strategies and tactics.

Sumsion, J. (2006). From Whitlam to economic rationalism and beyond: A conceptual framework for political activism in children's services. *Australian Journal of Early Childhood,* 31(1), 1–9.

This article promotes political activism as a viable way forward for educators to work towards universal high-quality EC education in the face of challenges posed by the political context in which educators practice.

Online resources

Centre on the Developing Child at Harvard University, USA

This centre offers a cutting-edge research and development platform aimed at transforming policy and practice connected with young children and their families. It has many online resources of relevance to educational leaders on a variety of topics.

www.developingchild.harvard.edu/resources/
building-adult-capabilities-to-improve-child-outcomes-a-theory-of-change

Early Education Show Podcast

Produced by Leanne Gibbs (former CEO of Community Child Care Cooperative NSW), Lisa Bryant (freelance journalist) and Liam McNicholas (experienced EC teacher) these are weekly podcasts exploring topics connected with professionalism and advocacy, including interviews with guest speakers.

www.earlyeducationshow.podbean.com

8 LEADING ORGANISATIONAL CHANGE

CHAPTER LEARNING OBJECTIVES

After studying this chapter you will understand that:

- Change is constant and is a great force for renewal and innovation in EC settings.
- There are different types of change within EC settings.
- EC leaders can assess change by adopting an ecological perspective.
- Change can be challenging and therefore resisted.
- Change can be seen as a collaborative and shared experience that builds capacity.
- Interpersonal relationships and ethics are important in driving organisational change.
- Reflective action on change can enable leaders to effect sustainable change.

Key concepts

critical reflection
innovation
reflection
reflective action
reflexivity

Overview

Change can be described as an abstract concept reflecting both complexity and diversity. This makes it difficult to quantify or measure change and it can be rather daunting finding reliable ways of demonstrating the nature and extent of change that has occurred as a result of a planned intervention. Popular sayings about change such as 'a change is as good as a rest' and 'if it isn't broken, why fix it?' reflect the challenges of explaining the meaning and purpose of implementing change within EC settings. Organisational change has often been perceived as negative and, previously, scholars (see Fullan, 2016; Rodd, 2013; 2016) have tended to focus attention on how leaders can deal with the resistors. Today there is better understanding that change is not always bad or negative, and that it could also bring about positive changes and new opportunities for all.

Given the constancy and inevitability of change, there is also general agreement that leading and managing organisational change is one of the key responsibilities of today's EC leaders. Aligned with the implementation of the National Quality Framework (ACECQA, 2011b), a person appointed to the position of an educational leader in Australia is perceived as a 'change agent'. It is also possible that leadership work is distributed and shared among several key staff and the presence of teacher leaders attached to particular groups of children is an emerging trend that works well in Finland (see Heikka et al., 2016). Research by Fleet et al. (2015) and Grarock and Morrissey (2013) clearly indicates the potential for confusion within centres where there are multiple leadership positions comprising the centre director, the second in-charge (or deputy director), and room leaders. If the title as well as the responsibilities of being the designated educational leader are included *within* one of these positions, when pursuing organisational change, it is imperative that the lines of authority are clarified and communicated to all involved at the centre.

The word 'innovation' signifies that something revolutionary or a major advancement has occurred within an organisation. This shift in practice, processes or even the products that are produced as a result of the changes being introduced could indicate progress. It is possible that some people within the organisation may see the innovation through a pessimistic lens or as a retrograde step, while others may be welcoming of the new achievement. When there are conflicting views or feelings of ambiguity and insecurity following a major change or innovation, those in leadership positions are expected to bring harmony back to the workplace. Intentional leaders, however, plan ahead to bring everyone along, with the changes being implemented in an orderly way. Their aim is to create a sense of ownership in developing a new organisational culture where everyone feels they were kept informed about innovations being implemented. In being consulted about various aspects, staff are also made to feel they contributed in some way to bringing about the modifications to practices and thereby have a sense of ownership about the whole experience of participating in the change processes.

Pause–reflect–act 8.1

Many of us join the EC profession with a desire to make a difference in young children's lives. Given below are three quotations by international leaders about change. There is no denying that these three women have effected change by making a difference in people's lives in their countries of birth.

> Angela Merkel: 'The question is not whether we are able to change but whether we are changing fast enough.'
>
> Aung San Suu Kyi: 'We will not change in matters of policy until such time as dialogue has begun.'
>
> Marian Wright Edelman: 'You really can change the world if you care enough.'

Source: www.brainyquote.com

- Reflect on the above quotations to see how you could apply these insights when seeking organisational change in your setting.
- Construct a statement that reflects your personal approach to leading change as an EC educator.

Types of change

A look at the types of change, as described by Rodd (2015, pp. 186–7), provides a useful way of making sense of the directionality of the forces of change that impact EC settings. In brief, these are:

- *Routine changes* occur when regular schedules (such as the fee collection day) or activities (for example, story time before nap time) are modified or varied.
- *Induced changes* are generated, caused or come about because of a variation somewhere within the organisation's environment—either internally or externally—and are usually planned to encourage adjustments.
- *Crisis changes* are typically unplanned occurrences, appear unexpectedly and may create a calamity or chaos because of the suddenness and intensity of their impact.
- *Innovative changes* reflect creativity, originality and advancements in current practice. The anticipated improvements may emerge from solving an ongoing problem within the centre, or as a creative suggestion arising through participation in a research study.
- *Transformational changes* are also sometimes described as revolutionary changes. The implementation of transformational changes represents a radical variation in the systems, structures and processes of the organisation as well as the attitudes, actions and interactions among the people connected with the organisation.

These brief descriptions do not explain the extent of the impact such changes can have on an organisation—its people, plans, processes and policies. Some may never feel the impact of the changes directly or concretely. Others may experience the full force of the changes immediately, incrementally and/or long after the initial implementation period has passed. How big or small the changes were, the drivers of the change, or the purpose, goals and timelines for implementing planned changes are all best understood by examining each situation within its own context.

Framing change through an ecological perspective

Imagine the way a pebble, when thrown, creates ripples as it touches the water. Likewise, the impact of change can be felt throughout an organisation and its surroundings. Some of this impact may be obvious, even predictable, easy to see and felt immediately. Some consequences may not be visible at all, but are felt deeply by some individuals or systems. In other cases, the impact may not surface and become visible for several years, and although it may be predictable, it could be felt in different ways by different individuals or groups. Herein lies the complexity of answering questions such as, 'How big is this change?' or 'We are doing fine, so why is this change necessary?' and 'Who really benefits from this change?' Above all, what most people want is an answer to questions such as, 'Why should I bother or care about this change?' or, put simply, 'What's in it for me?'

Preparing to respond to such questions is an essential part of leading change. Anticipating questions, as well as thinking through the potential answers ahead of making any official announcements about change initiatives, can also assist in reassuring staff that the leader has a plan and is thoughtful, caring and considerate by taking into account equity and inclusivity when making decisions. This also suggests that leaders are empathic (and compassionate) in being able to see the potential impact of major changes from the perspective of others. In this way, the demonstration of leadership that combines strategic planning and emotional intelligence can provide an effective foundation for initiating, implementing and achieving successful outcomes from a change initiative.

In assisting leaders to consider change initiatives systematically, we recommend framing this work from an ecological perspective (Bronfenbrenner, 1979; 1994). This approach was used successfully, as reported by Hadley et al. (2016) in their project on pedagogical leadership with a group of 10 EC centres in Sydney, New South Wales. Their model has been slightly modified by placing the educator at the centre of the change initiative, as indicated in Figure 8.1, and each layer is described briefly as follows:

- *Microsystem* is represented by the educator or the leader who is at the heart of this ecological system, and therefore can both influence the direction of change and be influenced by the changes that occur.
- *Mesosystem* stands for the EC organisation employing the educator or leader. The boundaries of the organisation are represented by the centre's vision, mission and philosophy, as well as the policies and practices that guide the work of the staff and the organisation's users—that is, the children and families who are the primary focus of the EC programs provided by the centre.
- *Exosystem* embodies the local neighbourhood or region where the EC centre is located. The demographic characteristics of the local population and the economic and social resources available can influence what happens within the organisation.

Figure 8.1 Framing change through an ecological perspective

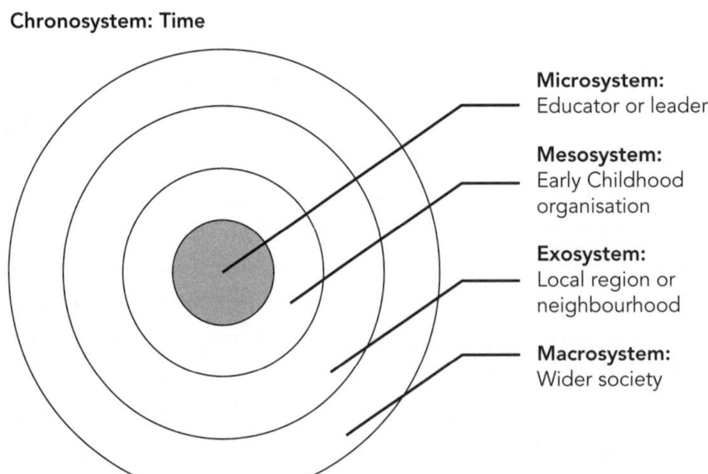

Source: Adapted from Hadley et al., 2016, p. 110.

- *Macrosystem* takes into account a broader view of society and includes the national laws, regulations and policy on EC centres of the country.
- *Chronosystem* reflects the overlays of time across and between each layer identified within this model.

In describing each layer of this ecological systems framework, we began by positioning an individual educator or leader at the heart of the system. It is also possible to place all the staff, not just one of the educators or the leader within an organisation, at this central positioning. In this way, this framework embraces the collective nature of learning, and the notion of 'communities of practice' (Wenger, 2010) that can be established within EC settings.

Moreover, this framework can be extended to include more than one centre in one locality as it is up to those involved to define the 'borders' of their learning community. In this sense, this model is flexible and can be adapted according to the context of where the change initiative is being implemented. An ecological framework is therefore a resource or a tool that can assist leaders to plan, implement and evaluate initiatives of change and **innovation** in an orderly way. It can be used to identify the stakeholders, governance structures and policy documents of relevance to the educators involved as a starting point. In this way, both internal organisational elements and external factors, which can either support or hinder the progression of change, can be captured in mapping the plans as well as in monitoring ongoing work and reflecting on achievements and influences over time.

innovation signifies that something revolutionary or a major advancement has occurred within an organisation.

In Leaders in practice 8.1, the team at Gowrie, Victoria tells of a rapid change brought about by an opportunity to take on the operation of an existing service. Their careful consideration and respect for the contextual factors that were new to them are an example of how change was considered in the context of an EC setting reflecting Bronfenbrenner's (1979) ecological systems model.

LEADERS IN PRACTICE 8.1

The team at Gowrie, Victoria

Jodie Knox
Manager, Early Learning, Gowrie (Victoria)

Michelle Gujer
Manager, Children's Programs, Broadmeadows Valley (Victoria)

Andrew Hume
CEO, Gowrie (Victoria)

Visit Oxford Ascend to hear more from Michelle and Andrew.

Acknowledgement: This profile is dedicated to Jodie Knox, who sadly passed away just days before the interview for this profile was recorded. We have done our very best to include Jodie's perspectives and contribution to the project and trust that she knows what a lasting impact her contribution to EC will have.

This is a profile of a practitioner team who in late 2015 led a change process to take on the management of an existing 128-place EC setting in Broadmeadows, Victoria, that is co-located with Broadmeadows Valley Primary School. The team at Gowrie Victoria, led by CEO Andrew Hume, took on the service as part of their strategic direction to demonstrate high quality provision in contexts that were different from those we had previously operated in. We were keen to share our learning experience with others in the sector. Gowrie's two existing services were located in relatively high socio-economic communities in close proximity of the CBD. Broadmeadows was a very different community. This experience of change highlights the significance of the context of each community—an important factor in any change process. Along with Jodie Knox, Manager, Early Learning, and Michelle Gujer, Manager, Children's Programs, Broadmeadows Valley, the team took on the operations of the service in an eight-week period (over the year-end holidays)—from signing the contract to opening the doors for the children. Their story is one of intense teamwork, change and rapid learning. Michelle says, 'We knew that we could not just replicate what was happening in our other services. This needed to be unique and we needed to learn about this community and how we would fit.'

Andrew shared that when the opportunity to take on the operations of the Broadmeadows site came up, everyone in the organisation, including the Board, was enthusiastic and could see that it was a good fit with Gowrie's strategic direction. The strategy, partner selection and site selection criteria had all been pre-agreed with the Board, which helped tremendously with the pace of decision-making. The site gave them the opportunity to 'Champion Good EC' (their purpose) by demonstrating high quality practice in a complex community at a reasonable price; and to make transition to school invisible by working in partnership with the school and families.

Of course, nothing is ever simple and they needed to look beyond the idealised dream to the pragmatics and viability. Before anything else, the school and Gowrie Victoria needed to assure each other that they were aligned in terms of aspirations, values and learning philosophies. They each spent a day in each other's services to assess the quality of each other's practice, to meet team members and to see the philosophies in action. It was essential that this was a high quality and sustainable service if Gowrie was going to put its name to it. Passion about the project was necessary, but it took a lot of business and implementation planning, negotiating and willingness to take on considerable risk by both Gowrie and the school to make it a reality. Team members brought different skills to this—they each have respect for what each other brings. It has been important to realise that they don't all have to be experts at everything. Andrew says, 'If we trust each other and are clear on what we are trying to achieve we can draw on each other's strengths and leave each person to get on with what they are good at'.

Michelle says she came on board when Jodie asked her to move from her position as Manager, Children's Programs at Gowrie Docklands. 'I had made similar moves earlier in my career. Leaving a centre I loved and had put a lot of energy into to move to the great unknown. Did I really want to move on and take on something new? Absolutely!' Michelle had worked in this community before and had good relationships with many key people in the community. 'I know of the importance of relationships and that is what makes all of this possible.'

Jodie also had an unrelenting enthusiasm and energy for this project. They really needed each other, because there were some very tough times and at times it was difficult to see how they could realise this vision. In times of big change they needed high levels of support and understanding. They realised how important it was for the organisation to have a can-do attitude and many people from across the organisation had a role to play, even if that was just carrying a greater load in the other services while people were pulled into the Broadmeadows work. Michelle says, 'We never underestimated how much we had to rely on each other. We worked really hard—really long hours, but we all really wanted it! It was bigger than all of us, but together we were determined to give it our all'.

It was a very systematic change. Jodie led the implementation. In the early weeks, the team met every week. Jodie had the experience and a clear vision for what would be needed to make this smooth. Michelle says, 'Jodie's knowledge and willingness to listen to what I was asking for was so valuable. I didn't feel like I had to relentlessly advocate—she trusted me. Jodie was very solution focused—she didn't get bogged down by what was not possible but had a real "let's fix it and move on" approach. Her positivity was a real driver for us all'.

Probably one of the best decisions they made was around recruitment. They deliberately looked for a combination of educators from the service: both existing Gowrie educators and educators from the sector more generally. This was designed to have both content and context expertise and to make sure that the Gowrie experience from other contexts did not dominate. In all, they were looking at recruiting 16 new people in about three weeks. They invited applicants to a group interview and information day. This worked really well because it gave them the opportunity to be really clear about their expectations and carefully select teams that they felt would work well together. They recruited based on values and expertise and the group setting was useful to see how people's values played out. This proved a very successful strategy as they have had very little turnover of staff since the centre opened.

The melding of familiar and unfamiliar educators was also a successful strategy. While they wanted the foundations to be the purpose and values of Gowrie Victoria, they also needed to listen and learn about this context. The varied backgrounds of staff, while always a challenge, helped them to achieve this. Throughout this change process they learnt that the 'Gowrie Way' is not one way. Their approach is certainly built on common values, but the programs look very different at each Gowrie centre. For us, change was not about just replicating what they were already comfortable with.

Michelle feels strongly that one of the keys to successful change management is empowering leaders to lead. 'I drive the communication through the room leaders. We were forced to talk with each other because a lot of systems were still being put in place. We set up regular meeting times fortnightly with room leaders and one-on-one meetings in between. Lots of daily catch up and just an open door to keep talking policy. I know the staff well, but I leave room for leaders to deal with the day-to-day issues that arise and provide support where needed.

'I also feel that another key driver to building an effective team is to build a culture of trust, honesty and being part of a learning community where an organisation views mistakes as learning opportunities and this being genuinely practised at every level. It is tempting to micro-manage in times of significant change, but I have had to learn over the years to let go of my fear of making mistakes. I base my leadership on what I have experienced both good and bad and the way I want to be treated, listened to and consulted. We have to empower people to be decision-makers because the task is too big for one person'.

One of the great learnings from this process has been that change takes a long time. They have to regularly check in and recall what it was like a year ago—how far they have come. Andrew says, 'While starting the service was an intense piece of work, we were always acutely aware that this opportunity provided the potential to make a contribution to the community in Broadmeadows. Good work takes time and requires the collective efforts of children, families, community and service providers. It is pleasing a year on to see the huge progress that the children have made and to watch the first group of children moving through to the school. Because of the shared values and vision between the centre and the school, these children already have established relationships, are familiar with the rooms and will find a curriculum including a play-based approach'.

The constant presence and the pervasiveness of the impacts of change are universal characteristics of EC settings. Some indicators of these changes are easily visible, especially when observing children's growth and development during their early years. Visible indicators, such as those related to how the play areas are organised, may not be changed every day or may be reorganised monthly. The nature of how the staff roster is organised, if managed well, and how staff come and go before and after their shifts, may appear seamless, thereby creating a sense of security for both children and their parents. Not every change can be intentionally led and planned with particular aims and goals defined in order to complete a project for instance. Some changes emerge suddenly, without any prior notice, and others could have been predicted but the signs could be ignored or dismissed as an impossibility.

Pause–reflect–act 8.2

Having read the Leaders in practice above, consider the following questions:

- Who or what was critical in getting staff on board to commit to making the changes?
- How can leaders build staff's capacity to embrace change? That is, how can leaders enable staff not to fear change, but to embrace change as an exciting opportunity to do something different?
- What skills do you need to learn for driving organisational change?

Go to oxfordascend *to hear Michelle's and Andrew's thoughts.*

Leading complex organisational change systematically

Having examined a variety of frameworks, Rodd (2016, p. 55) presents a model that can be used by EC leaders to keep track of leading complex organisational change in an organised way. It is based on seven elements: vision, consensus, skills, incentives, resources, action plans and evaluation. The meaning of each of these elements is discussed in detail in various other chapters in this book, such as Chapter 5, which examines the importance of the organisational vision and ethical practice. Within this context, we also recommend that EC leaders take a look at what Fullan (2016) describes as 'right' and 'wrong' drivers that influence the direction of organisational change, as outlined in Table 8.1.

chapter 5 covers strategic planning and social entrepreneurship.

Table 8.1 Right versus wrong drivers

Right drivers	Capacity building for results	Collaborative work	Pedagogy	Systemness
Wrong drivers	External accountability	Individual teacher & leadership quality	Technology	Fragmented strategies

Source: Adapted from Fullan, 2016, p. 42.

Emerging from research conducted in Canada, Fullan explains that the 'right' drivers reflect the way leaders bring the various elements of the organisation together to effect change. In contrast, the 'wrong' drivers cast a shadow of pessimism or negativity. Some may question the reason for placing technology as a wrong driver. Noting that technology is becoming 'more and more powerful, cheaper, and more available', Fullan recommends that we 'make pedagogy the driver and technology the accelerator' (p. 45). Fullan (2016) is also convincing when he declares that accountability measures imposed by external agencies never work in achieving complex organisational change successfully:

> Accountability measures plus sticks and carrots do not and cannot, ever, accomplish this feat. Higher, clearer standards, combined with correlated assessments are essential along the way, but they will not drive the system forward. (p. 43)

Fullan (2016) is equally adamant in stating that 'no nation has improved by focusing on individual teachers as the drivers' (p. 43), and the ineffectiveness of hiring 'high performing principals' to rescue dysfunctional schools (p. 44). The challenge is to focus more attention on the paired 'right' drivers that are coupled with the wrong ones as listed on Table 8.1. The right drivers, reflecting collegiality, trust and mutuality, as well as respect, offer better prospects of realising equity, justice and inclusivity, and thereby achieving organisational change in ethically satisfying ways.

Given the context-specific nature of organisational reform, leaders seeking changes in EC settings must also be mindful about local impact factors that can hinder or support their efforts. Accordingly, Fullan (2016) notes the importance of internal accountabilities that reflect collective responsibility for everyday work, including the collection, analysis and preparation of evaluation data. He suggests that successful collaboration and effective pedagogy can be powerful motivators or become the right drivers of sustainable organisational change. Referring to research evidence, Fullan (2016, p. 52) also states that with success comes 'a deep shift from "my" to "our"' when referring to a classroom, school, district or country. Encapsulating this holistic sense of belonging or ownership when advancing change within an organisation, Fullan (2016, p. 53) coined the concept of '***systemness***—the new recognition that each of us must contribute to the betterment of the bigger system, *and* benefit from it. We *are* the system! This is what the new meaning of change is all about'. (italics in the original)

systemness provides a framework for understanding organisational change in a structured and coordinated way.

Looking at organisational change through an ecological perspective as described at the beginning of this chapter represents systemness in both theory and practice. That is, Figure 8.1 presents a conceptual model of how we can study organisational change in an orderly way. Its application will vary depending on the particular contexts of the EC settings you are studying or working at. Therefore, the practical issues of relevance will differ from one setting to the next, but as a framework you can apply the same key concepts represented by the different layers shown in Figure 8.1.

Fullan (2016) also reminds us that 'behaviours and emotions often change before beliefs' (p. 39). As such, keep in mind the possibility that personal feelings connected with friendships can confuse or conflict with relationships between colleagues at the workplace. Wider reading of research-based evidence is also necessary in probing further to ascertain deeper understandings about the nature of interactions within EC settings. For instance, Colmer (2016) discusses the notion of an 'ethic of care' (p. 294) being established by centre directors when implementing complex change within their organisations:

> Leader influence offers a powerful enactment of an ethic of care, with individual well-being nurtured through opportunities to participate in meaningful, collective professional practices involving intellectual challenges, rather than focusing on individuals' personal needs and interests. (p. 294)

These research-based insights provoke thinking 'beyond simplistic ideas of educator relationships as friendships' (Colmer, 2016, p. 318). This includes leaders shifting their thinking from daily operational matters to focus on long-range strategic plans for developing the organisation holistically.

Leading change effectively in EC settings

Simply put, although there are plenty of books on leading educational change, there are no easy recipes or templates to structure this work on how to lead organisational change effectively. In writing a book dedicated to achieving change through practitioner inquiry, Fleet et al. (2016, p. 12) refer to 'a visionary on-site leader as a change thinker'. The promotion of change may begin by identifying an appropriate question 'of significance, of outcomes and practices, of plural ways of knowing and questions of relational practices' (Fleet et al., 2016, p. 12). The question(s) provide(s) the stimulus for discussion, debate and deep **reflection**. The ultimate goal is to shift thinking away from compliance and conformity to generating new knowledge and demonstrating agency and professional autonomy as EC educators and leaders. Implementing change under practitioner inquiry methods, for instance, can include scaffolding learning by an external expert. However, Fleet et al. emphasise that 'employer-supported change agents have the potential to shape sustainability in ways not possible to outside facilitators' (p. 13).

reflection in EC contexts demonstrates an educator/leader thinking about their own work, as well as work done with others, to improve their skills and knowledge in purposeful ways.

Research-based evidence that provide some insights about aspects which contribute to leading change within EC settings include the following:

- *EC expertise:* the knowledge and skills necessary for leading organisational change in EC settings can be acquired through formal studies at a university, or informally through workplace experience, as well as through professional networking and mentoring.
- *Personal qualities:* leading change in sustainable ways calls for qualities such as creativity, courage, personal commitment, mindfulness and flexibility. Leadership capacity also reflects abilities and interests, as well as the values, beliefs and attitudes of those enacting the role of a leader.

- *Time and resources:* allocation of an appropriate budget to assist with carrying out the necessary tasks to achieve change as planned is essential. Funding to purchase publications and other materials, consultancy fees for an external mentor, hospitality and back-filling staff are relevant budget items.
- *Authority:* the ability to influence decision-making about innovations or reviewing and amending current practice depends on how the leader's authority is perceived by others, including staff, parents and the local community. However, authority is not always tied up with a job title or a position; it has more to do with who you are as a leader, and what you do in working with others to effect change.
- *Support:* given the collective nature of leading organisational change, leaders need management endorsement as well as collaborative assistance—or at least a willingness to try—from colleagues within the EC setting.

By way of examining change from the perspective of an individual at the heart of an ecological framework, we present the trajectory of career changes that Andrew Bagnall has actively pursued since becoming an EC graduate more than 10 years ago. His story captures how intentional leadership can drive personal professional change.

LEADERS IN PRACTICE 8.2

Andrew Bagnall

Principal, Buxton Primary School (VIC)

As I embark on yet another geographical and professional shift, it has been timely for me to reflect on what changes I have made professionally and how these changes have impacted on my professional and personal life. In short, I left the safety of family and friends when I completed my EC degree to find solitude in the mid north coast of New South Wales (NSW), becoming the director of a small preschool for eight years. I then moved to a remote Indigenous community in the Northern Territory (NT) as a primary school teacher for two years. Returning home to start life with my wife as a family in rural Victoria, I was employed as a primary school teacher for four years. I wrote this profile, surrounded by boxes, awaiting the next shift to another rural region to lead Buxton Primary School, located in a small community ravaged by the bushfires on 7 February 2009. This school has been through a difficult period, including several changes of principal. When I think about each of my big moves, there are some consistencies that appear and remind me of three pivotal factors that surface each time I face a new challenge.

Professional capacity

I have always been drawn to extremely challenging professional opportunities. Importantly, I take these on only when I have felt my skill set would at least enable me to have some level of success! Stepping straight into a leadership role as a preschool director straight out of university definitely threw up many challenges. Here, I quickly built a safety net of like-minded colleagues who could support me. Consultation has always been key for me. When I have a sense of the perspectives of all stakeholders, decision-making is more transparent. Difficult decisions still have to be made. When you can consider how decisions impact on others, however, I find much greater confidence in collaboration and the paths our decisions have created.

My experience and love for EC education led me to question how adapting an EC lens to primary education might look. The natural direction for me was to find a place where I could have some autonomy over curriculum design and implementation, and this led me to the NT. This was an extremely challenging environment, and it reaffirmed for me that learning occurs everywhere, and is embraced when communities have an understanding of its greater purpose and are provided with opportunities to be involved. The relationships I developed with the families, children and community were reflective of the EC ethos of inclusivity and social and emotional understanding.

Returning to rural Victoria to be closer to my family was a significant factor underpinning my return home. I was fortunate to find a role in a school that was transitioning from traditional curriculum design to the International Baccalaureate, which was built around inquiry based teaching and learning. Any small teaching successes I had in the NT were about to be developed further in a larger school setting. Reflecting on this decision professionally, it was a practical evolution from my previous 10 years in education: I gained great understanding of the complexity around curriculum planning, play based learning, and working within a large organisation.

My latest challenge is to move with my wife and baby daughter as the teaching principal in a very small school in another community that's new to me. I will, again, draw on my previous experiences in this new role. The opportunity to have autonomy over decisions that impact learning, the experience of working with a small community and the possibilities of learning alongside children for a number of years is incredibly exciting. This new move is also very daunting, much like the ones before it. However, the opportunity to apply what I know, and to have confidence in my expertise and experience, can alleviate these concerns. I draw confidence in returning to something familiar in leadership—that is, being a director of a small preschool has many similarities to becoming a principal of a small school. I have come full circle!

Personal stimulation and work–life balance

In each move, a significant factor in embracing change has been the opportunities to enjoy experiences outside my professional work. Moving from Melbourne to the mid north coast was a bit of a no-brainer really! Spending time in a warmer, more consistent climate was incredibly enticing for someone who is active and needs to be outdoors to de-stress. Similarly, in the NT, living in a remote community with people who still embrace a very traditional lifestyle was a unique opportunity and incredibly motivating. My most recent move will see our family living in a small town, with access to beautiful mountains for walking, riding, hiking and skiing. Creating balance in the work–life relationship can be incredibly difficult, but, in seeking to make positive influences over communities, this balance has been critical for me. Therefore, finding a community and environment that we connect with is vital for balancing out the sometimes difficult or challenging work environments. Of course, at times this balance tips too far one way, and I have been fortunate to have people around me who can gently steer me in the right direction when this has occurred.

Purpose

Finally, understanding the greater purpose behind the change has been a conclusion I have only recently come to realise, but one that has been significantly and perhaps subconsciously driving change for me anyway. At different points over the past 12 years I have been motivated to make change based on a professional challenge and opportunities to achieve the work–life balance. Beneath that sits a greater driver, and that has been to embark on a personal journey that tells me something about who I am.

My shift away from Melbourne to the mid north coast was also a chance to prove that what I thought I knew and believed in about learning in EC and working with young children could be applied. My philosophy and understanding around this grew exponentially because of the eight years that followed the shift; however, I was seeking experiences to be part of the decisions that led to learning. When moving to remote NT, I was driven by a need to understand more about myself—something that had been prompted in the Aspiring Leaders Forum sponsored by Children's Services Central in NSW, and implemented by Macquarie University and Semann & Slattery. I was fortunate to be part of this year-long professional development experience as it proved pivotal for me in reflecting on the question of self-identity and leadership. I returned to Ballarat to be with family and loved ones and to reconnect with my parents, siblings and grandmother. The move I am embarking on now has a greater purpose of bringing up my little girl in the countryside with opportunities to build connections with the world around her in a beautiful region in Australia.

Each professional change has been carefully calculated with the three drivers sometimes outweighing each other. However, elements of each remain the same. My greatest moments have come about because I have remained true to the purpose behind the change. The challenges I have faced and the experiences I have had could not have been predicted, nor would these have deterred me had I known them. I am a better person for taking a leap. I would encourage anyone to do their research, but to also listen carefully to the heart and head talking to each other about the greater purpose you are seeking! I do feel that I have a strong philosophy around my role as a teacher, a facilitator of learning. No doubt it will continue to evolve, and when I feel that professionally and/or personally I am no longer being challenged, or I am not seeking challenge, then it is time to reconnect with my purpose again.

Pause–reflect–act 8.3

In beginning his first appointment as a primary school principal, Andrew articulated his reflections on three key themes that have sustained him during the various periods of transition from one job to another.

- Use Andrew's story to reflect on the importance of the organisational context in understanding change, for both a leader and other staff as individuals, and also when working as a team.
- Reflect on what Andrew needs to consider as principal of a school that has undergone significant challenges in a rural community ravaged by bushfires.
- Consider how your professional and personal lives can merge when seeking professional change as an EC educator.

Reflective action on change

'Reflective practice' is a catch-cry or buzz phrase found in the fields of education, health and social welfare that produce graduates who complete professional practice experiences during their degree towards becoming a practitioner such as a teacher, nurse, social worker or doctor. Although reflective practice embodies the integration of theory and practice in each of these disciplines, more care is needed in unpacking the meaning and use of each of these concepts, especially if seeking transformational change. Although there is insufficient space to do justice to this discussion in this chapter, a brief definition of three key concepts is offered as a starting point:

- *Reflection:* defined previously in this chapter, this is a process of thinking about our work.
- ***Reflexivity***: builds on the concept of reflection by referring to our ability to recognise our influence on our work.
- ***Critical reflection***: extends on the two previous concepts by getting us to question the assumptions, values, beliefs and ideology underpinning our work.

reflexivity is our ability to recognise our influence on our work.

critical reflection questions the assumptions, values, beliefs and ideology underpinning our work.

reflective action brings together the two components of thinking and doing, and thereby reflects the theory and practice connections.

The concept of **reflective action** was coined by Michael Fullan (2016, p. 39), a world authority on leading change in educational settings, to emphasise the importance of thinking and doing when learning about new things. He believes that one of the powerful motivators for changing as an individual 'comes from new experiences that give us something new to think and learn about' (p. 39). Consider these comments in terms of planned organisational change that arises through restructuring the governance arrangements, implementing required government policy reforms, or when redesigning the building and grounds of an EC centre. Sharing such experiences offers numerous opportunities for collaborative reflection and learning. Within these contexts, EC leaders can play a key role in developing educators' capacities for reflection and critical thinking by establishing an organisational culture that advocates learning together, and from each other.

Having the space and opportunities to engage collaboratively as a group in reflecting about current practices, critical incidents, ethical dilemmas, alternative strategies to improve practice and new ideas to innovate programs or design new play spaces may not be a priority in EC settings. Chapter 5 aims to draw attention to this gap in strategic planning as well as everyday practice. Chapter 14 looks at how to establish spaces for educators to think and learn during their everyday work schedules. Using this space on a regular basis for reflective discussions, and thereby making it recurrent or a 'normal' part of everyday work, can make adopting change seem more doable.

refer to chapter 5 for advice on strategic planning.

Based on insights gleaned from research on educational settings, Fullan (2016, p. 41) also encapsulates the mutuality of learning together to develop a shared vision by asserting that '*effective change processes shape and reshape good ideas, as they build capacity and ownership among participants*' (emphasis in the original). The two-way nature of learning means that both ideas and processes are integral to achieving change successfully. Fullan (2016) also affirms the establishment of a shared vision for an organisation as 'unquestionably necessary for success' (p. 39). This claim has been previously confirmed by other leadership scholars such as Harris (2004); Leithwood (2004) and Robertson (2011).

More specifically, based on findings in an Australian study, Marsh, Waniganayake and De Nobile (2016), for example, have reported that school leaders can foster shared understandings about student learning among staff, students and their parents by 'cultivating conversations within their communities' (p. 580). They add that establishing a common language that can enable various stakeholders to discuss issues in ways that they can understand each other is an essential first step to developing a shared vision for school improvement and defining aims and actions to achieve this goal.

Hattie (2012, p.14) has also reinforced the importance of being intentional by calling on teachers to 'see themselves as evaluators of their effects on students'. Building on this body of knowledge, the series of questions and prompts presented for consideration by Marsh, Waniganayake and De Nobile (2016) within schools pursuing organisational improvements is reproduced in Table 8.2 to assist EC educators and leaders to begin such conversations within their own organisations.

Table 8.2 Exploring beliefs about learning and teaching: questions for school communities

Questions	Prompts
1 How do people learn?	Identify theories of how people learn
2 Who owns the learning in our school?	Students, teachers, parents, external?
3 What beliefs inform your practice as a classroom teacher?	Is passion a pre-requisite of effective teaching?
4 How do you assess your effectiveness as a teacher?	How should the school assess the effectiveness of teaching and learning? Why?
5 What do positive relationships between students and teachers look like?	How do we best cultivate positive relationships between students and teachers?
6 What goals and expectations are important for our community?	Who is our community?
7 How should we assess the effectiveness of our community?	How will we know we are successful? What should we measure?
8 To what extent has the school invested in building relationships so that trust is established and teachers are able to be vulnerable with their colleagues?	Are we intentional in creating purposeful time for rich conversations and collaboration between staff?
9 How do we encourage leadership to emerge at the school?	Are most tasks led by those in formal leadership positions?
10 What beliefs about learning and teaching are held by our students and parents?	What do we currently do to find out about our students' and parents' expectations?

Source: reproduced from Marsh, Waniganayake & De Nobile, 2016, p. 590.

To engage in these conversations wholeheartedly, each of the above 10 questions require time for reflection at a deep level, both as individuals and together as a community. There will also be other questions and prompts that are more relevant for each setting and therefore Table 8.2 stimulates planning as well as ongoing considerations over time. It is also suggested that these conversations may be enhanced with the involvement of an external expert, particularly during the initial stages and/or when challenges arise in shifting to new ground (Fleet, De Gioia & Patterson, 2016; Raban et al., 2007).

Pause–reflect–act 8.4

- Think about conversations at your organisation. What have you learnt about learning and leadership during these conversations?
- Is there a shared understanding about the philosophy guiding the programs you deliver? In what ways do staff agree or disagree with the assumptions underpinning this philosophy?
- Use the questions in Table 8.2 to make an action plan on how to develop a shared language about a centre's philosophical approach to EC education.

Leading change ethically

According to Rodd (2016), when leading change, EC leaders encounter ethics in two ways: on the one hand, Rodd explains that most educators consider they have 'an ethical obligation to improve the quality of early years experiences and provision' (p. 38). These moral underpinnings are today integral in shaping the professional identity and workforce responsibilities of EC educators. On the other hand, 'competent and authentic change leaders at every level within the sector' are expected to have 'drive, intuition, empathy and a strong moral compass' (p. 43). As can be seen, consideration of ethics is both a professional role and a personal quality of educators in general, and leaders more specifically.

more information about professional communication and ethical practice is given in chapter 9.

Hughes (2015, p. 460) writes that there is a general silence on matters of power and politics 'within typical explanations of leading change' presented in academic literature. There is a perception among some scholars that although 'critical scholars foreground ethical approaches towards leading change' (Hughes, 2015, p. 459), others writing about change 'give the impression that it is somehow unworldly or naïve even to mention ethical considerations' (as cited in By, Burns & Oswick, 2012, p. 4). Positions of leadership nevertheless provide leaders with power and authority over others, and if left unchecked, can be harmful. In their analysis of success and failure of organisational change,

> Burns and Jackson (2011) argue that all approaches to leadership and change are underpinned by a set of ethical values that influence the actions of leaders and the outcomes/consequences of change initiatives for good or ill. (cited in By, Burns & Oswick, 2012, p. 2)

In driving change, concern has also been expressed by By, Burns and Oswick (2012) that when those occupying senior executive positions place their egos and self-interests first, they sacrifice the collective well-being of others. When appointing leaders, it is necessary to assess their capacity to achieve transparency in decision-making, accountability and adherence to ethical values. To leverage learning as a way of promoting commitment, Alavi and Gill (2016) recommend increasing 'dialogue for continuous development and encouraging others to share their ideas' (p. 12). The importance of continuing professional conversations informally and during planning meetings is very clear in the Gowrie Victoria story of change included in this chapter. By, Burns and Oswick (2012) also suggest that there is an ongoing responsibility on followers or stakeholders 'not to be passive observers' by ensuring that leaders are ethically accountable by 'identifying and ending unethical practices' (p. 4).

Research also shows that leaders can play one or more of the roles of framing changes, shaping behaviours and creating capacity within their organisations (Lawrence, 2015). Demands to satisfy public expectations within an unpredictable economic and political landscape places continuing pressures on educational leaders to effect changes within centres. This includes being open to new ideas, and being flexible in accommodating changes that could emerge suddenly or incrementally. When acting mindfully 'to make ethical judgements', Sinclair (2016, p. 183) suggests that:

> Leaders may need to be able to set to one side their usual habits such as diligent preparation, and instead substitute close attention to noticing what is emerging moment by moment. This new data may be of a different kind to what they are used to giving attention to, and it may require them to let go of some of their usual sense-making responses.

While breaking away from what you are comfortable with may not be easy, intentional leaders who value learning ought to take a risk in shifting their own behaviour.

Chapter summary

In this chapter, leading change has been explained as being contextual, complex and challenging. To do it effectively, leaders must act with forethought, and be prepared and flexible in being open to potential changes that emerge unexpectedly. Adopting an ecological framework to assess, plan, implement and review complex organisational change can enable leaders oversight of leading change ethically in systematic ways. Reflective action on change within EC settings, including asking critical questions, opens up spaces for learning and innovation and establishes a shared language for communicating with various stakeholders. This is a necessary first step in achieving organisational change.

Key references

Derman-Sparks, L., LeeKeenan, D. & Nimmo, J. (2015). *Leading anti-bias early childhood programs: A guide for change.* Washington, DC: National Association for the Education of Young Children.

Louise Derman-Sparks, the American who pioneered the work on developing anti-bias, collaborates with two others to write about how EC leaders can be strategically intentional in implementing change to achieve social justice.

Fleet, A., De Gioia, K. & Patterson, C. (Eds.). (2016). *Engaging with educational change: Voices of practitioner inquiry.* London: Bloomsbury Academic.

This book provides numerous examples of change initiatives within EC settings in Australia using the method of practitioner inquiry. These stories reflect the power of individual agency of educators as well as the importance of employer support in achieving sustainable change.

Rodd, J. (2015). *Leading change in the early years: Principles and practice.* Maidenhead, Berkshire: Open University Press.

Rodd is among the first EC scholars to recognise the importance of EC educators learning to lead change. This book is a ready reference for understanding both the principles underpinning change processes and the leadership skills needed to guide change within EC settings.

Sinclair, A. (2016). *Leading mindfully.* Sydney: Allen & Unwin.

This book presents courageous possibilities for leaders seeking alternative ways to facilitate sustainable change both as individual professionals and in leading organisational change. It calls for a focus on the here and now, as well as doing less and being more. Based on Sinclair's personal journey of discovering and experiencing mindfulness, it provides a sound introduction to leading effectively with body and heart.

Online resources

Early Childhood Research Hub

This website is a central repository of Australian EC resources, quality standards, support and forums. It has many online resources/publications of relevance to leaders advocating for quality EC programs.

www.ecrh.edu.au/home

Quality Area 7

Watch the following clip, which outlines how Quality Area 7 relates to the importance of managing change in EC and the importance of including all stakeholders in the process.

www.ecrh.edu.au/national-quality-standard/quality-area-7-leadership-and-service-management

TED Talk on leadership

Jim Hemerling talks about five ways to lead in an era of constant change. Listen to his talk and see what similarities you can find between the TED Talk and the discussion in this chapter on leading change.

www.ted.com/talks/jim_hemerling_5_ways_to_lead_in_an_era_of_constant_change -t-172458

PART TWO

LEADERSHIP IN CONTEXT

9 INTERPERSONAL AND WORKPLACE COMMUNICATION

CHAPTER LEARNING OBJECTIVES

After studying this chapter you will understand that:

- Inspiring and influencing others requires effective interpersonal and workplace communication skills.
- Active listening, emotional intelligence and conflict management are fundamental to an intentional leader's repertoire of communication skills.
- A responsibility of an intentional leader is to develop this skill set in themselves and their team.
- Communication skills need to be exercised within a 'power with' rather than a 'power over' framework.
- Exercising effective communication while working ethically is critical to the building of relationships that support quality.

Key concepts

active listening
communication
conflict management
discourse
emotional intelligence
ethical practice
power

Overview

To inspire and influence, leaders need to be effective communicators. Jillian Rodd, renowned EC leadership author, has gone so far as to suggest that 'successful leadership in EC is a matter of communication more than anything else' (Rodd, 2013, p. 63). Effective communication is integral to a quality EC centre because it promotes strong relationships with children, families, colleagues, and professional and community stakeholders. Fundamental to the building and maintaining of such relationships is effective interpersonal and workplace communication. Communicating with a diversity of individuals and groups within and external to the EC setting—verbally (using spoken and/or written words, including signs) or non-verbally (body language in face-to-face contact, including posture, facial expressions and tone of voice)—requires proficiency in skills that include active listening, showing empathy, practising emotional intelligence, managing conflict, managing change and working in teams.

Communicating effectively in the context of an EC setting, however, can be challenging. Potential barriers to effective communication include parents and staff having different values, beliefs and expectations regarding a child's learning and care; competing demands on educators' time; changing staff rosters and work hours; the unpredictability and busyness of an EC centre; varying levels of staff qualifications and experience; and a preoccupation with one's own needs and interests. A role of the leader as an intentional communicator is to limit, identify and address any barriers that may be impeding effective communication processes while also supporting the development of communication skills in themselves and their staff, and developing strategies to share and build mutually respectful expectations with families.

power
the influencing of someone else's values, thoughts and actions. Power can be a positive force (e.g. when exercised within a social justice framework) or a negative force that is unethical.

To assist the intentional leader to be an effective communicator, and facilitate communication within their EC centre, this chapter begins with an introduction to effective communication. It then provides an overview of three key communication skills: active listening, emotional intelligence and managing conflict (noting that Chapter 8 focuses on managing change), before situating an application of these skills within a framework of **power** and ethics. The chapter closes with a focus on the use of social media as an effective but potentially fraught medium of contemporary communication within the EC sector.

Introduction

What is communication? While at face value this may seem a simplistic question it is an important one for intentional leaders to consider. How communication is understood will inform how a leader seeks to develop their own communication skills and influence positive interpersonal and workplace communication within EC centres.

communication
is the process of verbally and/ or non-verbally conveying and perceiving messages, which may or may not involve the use of power.

Consider these definitions of and ideas about **communication**:

- 'The means by which we represent our thoughts and feelings to others, transmit knowledge, solve problems and build relationships.' (Rodd, 2013, p. 68)
- A transmission of a message from a source to a receiver. (Miller, 2015)
- 'Any behaviour—verbal, nonverbal or graphic—that is perceived by another' (Dwyer, 2016, p. 3)
- The constitution of meaning. (Miller, 2015)
- A form of power. (Harms, 2007)

These definitions and ideas conceptualise communication in multiple ways that have different implications for an intentional leader. For example:

- Communication is purposeful; as such, a leader can consider how communication may be utilised to inspire and influence.
- Communication is more complex than a linear transfer of information. The intended message may not be comprehended in the way intended, and may require ongoing communication until a shared understanding and acknowledgment of that message is established.
- Communication thus may require multiple modes to reinforce the intended meaning, as well as opportunities for collaborative dialogue.
- Communication can be an exercise of power, but it may also be an opportunity where power is shared or distributed. How power is used will in part depend on the model of leadership exercised.

Pause–reflect–act 9.1

- Reflect on a recent communication you have had that you considered was effective. What communication skills did you and the person(s) you were communicating with demonstrate to make this communication 'work'?
- How did the method of communication used—a face-to-face conversation, telephone call, email or Skype chat, for example—influence the effectiveness of getting the message through?

Interpersonal and workplace communication skills

This section introduces the intentional leader to three fundamental interpersonal and workplace communication skills: active listening, **emotional intelligence** and conflict management.

emotional intelligence is the ability to perceive feelings in ourselves and others, to effectively control one's emotions, to be socially aware, and to communicate effectively and influentially.

Communicating effectively through active listening

According to Rodd (2013), the most common criticism of leaders in EC centres is that they do not listen. This criticism is perhaps indicative of the multiple barriers to effective communication that are particular to EC centres. In addition, while effective communication requires a strong skill set, EC leaders and educators are generally not provided with such training in their pre-service teacher education courses. Notably, a small-scale study that provided **active listening** instruction to a group of pre-service teachers found that parents rated these students' listening skills higher than for a control group of students who received no instruction (McNaughton et al., 2008).

active listening is hearing and understanding what another is saying, and communicating this under-standing back so that the receiver of your communication believes they have been heard.

Active listening involves hearing and understanding what someone else is saying, and communicating this understanding back in such a way that the receiver of your communication believes that they have been heard (Dwyer, 2016; McNaughton et al., 2008). Importantly, listening actively means attending to both verbal and non-verbal communication. Exercising this skill and ensuring authenticity has flow-on benefits for an intentional leader. Active listening enables children, parents and staff to feel valued and respected, and in turn, in understanding the perspectives of others, can provide a leader with opportunities for new ways of thinking about how to move an EC centre forward and improve its provision of EC programs.

Strategies that support active listening and enable listening for understanding include (McNaughton et al., 2008; Rodd, 2013):

- *Paraphrasing*: restating the message in your own words to demonstrate understanding.
- *Questioning*: asking questions for elaboration or clarification purposes. Open questions that require more than just a 'yes' or 'no' response are particularly useful for these purposes.
- *Summarising*: recapping the communicated message.

- *Attending*: using non-verbal communication and words such as eye contact (pending cultural background) to convey interest and attention, open posture, nodding of the head, or saying 'Uh ha' or 'I see'.

Pause–reflect–act 9.2

As a team, watch the following videos on active listening and take notes:

- www.youtube.com/watch?v=7PFX23Ynkfs (Gary Tomlinson, 2012)
- www.youtube.com/watch?v=ESujTCel6lM (gordontrainingint, 2010).

The first video provides an overview of active listening skills, while the second demonstrates active listening in practice.

- Which active listening skills were used in the second video? Discuss the potential of using these skills in your work as an EC educator and/or leader.
- As a team, develop a scenario or use an interaction that occurred at the centre as the basis of a short role play. In the role play, one staff member is to play the role of the main speaker while a second staff member plays the role of the active listener. Video record the role play.
- Again as a team, debrief the role play, focusing particularly on the active listening skills that were demonstrated and how they could have perhaps been exercised more strongly. Ensure that feedback is constructive and supportive.

Communicating effectively through emotional intelligence

The concept of emotional intelligence was developed by psychologist Daniel Goleman (1995; 1998; 2000) and encapsulates the belief that effective decision-making, relationships and leadership require emotional, and not just rational or cognitive, intelligence. According to Goleman (1998, p. 317) emotional intelligence is 'a capacity for recognising our own and others' feelings, for motivating ourselves, and for managing our emotions, both within ourselves and in our relationships'. Emotional intelligence involves the following four key capabilities (Goleman, 2000):

1 *Self-awareness*: This awareness is two-fold. First is being aware of or tuning in to how you are feeling and why. Second is being aware of the impact of these feelings, for example, on your productivity and on those around you. Here, feeling self-confident and being able to make accurate self-assessments is important.
2 *Self-management*: This capability concerns the control of your own feelings, as well as a consistent demonstration of character traits such as conscientiousness, initiative, adaptability and trustworthiness.
3 *Social awareness*: This is about being aware of others, and their feelings and needs. It involves having empathy for others, or put simply, being able to put yourself into

someone else's shoes. Here, having an understanding of the message a person is conveying and demonstrating that understanding to them is key. In other words, being able to actively listen is critical. For the intentional leader this awareness extends to an awareness of the needs of the organisation and its stakeholders.

4 *Social skill*: This is about channelling these skills into effective communications that are visionary, and collegial; that will inspire and influence others, and build individual and team capabilities. Social skills are also necessary for managing conflict, which is discussed in the following section.

An intentional leader's exercising of emotional intelligence is said to benefit the well-being of staff and the well-being of the organisation overall (Barron, 2012). This is because emotional intelligence has both intrapersonal and an interpersonal dimensions. As such, this competency is of particular benefit in times of change when emotions can be volatile and stress levels high (see Chapter 8 for an in-depth discussion on leading and managing change).

Pause–reflect–act 9.3

The following video provides a short overview of emotional intelligence: www.youtube.com/watch?v=OoLVo3snNA0.

- As you watch the video, write down where you believe your strengths lie, and in which areas you think you could develop further.
- Find a trusted colleague or mentor and seek feedback on your reflections.

Communicating effectively through conflict management

As much as an intentional leader may exercise active listening and emotional intelligence, it is unrealistic to expect that an EC centre will be devoid of conflict. In a cautionary reminder, Rodd (2013, pp. 85–6) points out that 'conflict is an inevitable part of living and working with other people and, because the EC profession is essentially about working with people, the potential for conflict is high'. The inevitability of conflict is why it is important to acknowledge that from time to time situations arise and there is a need to address the issues before a small problem snowballs into an insurmountable problem between staff.

In practice, this means that there needs to be a staff grievance and a family grievance policy at each centre. It also means that on induction, a new staff member will know what the strategies are for dealing with conflict in various situations. Leaders must be able to take into account and understand the diverse perspectives (including differing values and beliefs) that can underpin conflict. Staff and families need to be heard and to feel valued throughout the conflict-management process, as well as feeling they are part of the solution.

In any EC centre power can manifest in destructive ways between the leader and staff, as well as among staff (Bruno, 2007; Hard, 2006, 2009; Rodd, 2006; 2013). Power struggles can manifest in bullying, gossip, intimidation, passive aggression and 'horizontal violence' or psychological violence, which is targeted at staff perceived to be practising in ways contrary to the norms of the centre (Hard, 2006). Because such power struggles negatively impact on staff morale, job satisfaction and collegiality, the provision of quality education and care for children also suffers. This is particularly important to avoid as children are sensitive to and insightful about the feelings of the adults who are responsible for their sense of well-being.

The intentional leader's task is not to avoid or quickly put an end to conflict, but to understand it and seek a productive outcome for all involved (Owings & Kaplan, 2012). We use the term '**conflict management**' deliberately to reflect the leader's goal of resolving conflict constructively in ways that can improve and strengthen relationships and move the centre forward in its mission and vision.

conflict management the process of productively working through content- or relationship-based communication issues, such that the conflict becomes an opportunity for learning and enhanced team effectiveness.

Conflict arises from an interplay of the 'content' or 'relationship' components of communication (Northouse, 2015). 'Content' relates to the message being communicated, such as a discussion about when staff meetings are to be held. Disagreements can arise over beliefs and values (such as whether staff meetings are important and/or attendance should be compulsory) or about defining goals and strategies (such as the frequency and day/time of meetings). 'Relationship' relates to the process of communication and stems from three broad issues (Northouse, 2015): esteem (staff not feeling valued); control (staff feeling views are not noted); and affiliation (staff not respecting the centre director and dismissing or mistrusting the director's motives). It is critical that the intentional leader builds respectful, collegial working relationships with and between staff. In this way, strong relational foundations can be established that provide the basis of a healthy and productive conflict-management process.

Given how complex and volatile conflict can be, it is beyond the scope of this chapter to detail effective ways to manage a conflict situation. Following is an introduction to two commonly used conflict-resolution strategies—assertiveness and mediation. These are particularly productive when exercised in conjunction with active listening and emotional intelligence. The intentional leader is encouraged to consider how their EC centre as a workplace may mitigate conflict; for example, through centre policies and procedures. Ruth Knight's video resource, 'Managing conflict in your workplace' further explores conflict in the workplace (see the online resources list at the end of this chapter).

Assertiveness

In contrast to being submissive or aggressive in a conflict situation, expressing your needs and interests assertively—that is, clearly and confidently while showing respect for the other person (Dwyer, 2016; Rodd, 2013)—can open up dialogue that allows issues of concern to be raised and heard. Using 'I' statements is a useful strategy for communicating assertively. 'I' statements comprise of four messages: how you are feeling; the context or behaviour of the other person that triggers what you are feeling; the impact of the other person's behaviour on you; and a request for alternative behaviour or action considered to be reasonable.

For example, 'I feel frustrated and confused at our team meetings when you turn up not having read the article that we agreed as a team we would all read. This means we have to spend time informing you about the article, which I don't think is fair or a good use of everyone's time. What I would find helpful is you letting me know if there is some reason why reading the articles is difficult for you, because you seemed keen about the idea when we first discussed it'. It would also be useful to enlist the reluctant reader into developing a solution to the problem by asking questions such as, 'How might you be able to manage reading an article done before the next staff meeting?'. This affords the staff member the opportunity to think and reflect and to understand that their input is required and valued.

Eleanor Shakiba's video, 'How to speak assertively with I statements' (Shakiba, 2014), provides more clear examples of effective assertive communication, including the use of 'I' statements. See www.youtube.com/watch?v=sswGv9iH-4o.

Pause–reflect–act 9.4

- Over the course of one week, keep a journal in which you reflect on your communication with your colleagues and parents. Focus particularly on occasions where being assertive appeared necessary. On these occasions, note whether you considered your communication to be submissive, aggressive or assertive.
- Commit to using 'I' statements in your interactions as needed and note the response received.

Mediation

When conflict cannot be resolved by means of assertiveness and negotiation, mediation may be necessary. In this process, the parties voluntarily agree to come together to discuss their concerns under the guidance of an independent mediator. The mediator is an impartial facilitator whose role is to provide a forum where each party can raise their concerns while also being expected to hear and acknowledge the concerns of the other. The mediator is also responsible for facilitating the exploration of ways forward for those involved in the mediation.

The intentional leader should give careful consideration to mediating a conflict between centre employees. Usually mediation is utilised when a conflict has escalated, and communication between the parties involved has deteriorated. Successful mediation requires high-level communication skills as well as time to devote to a number of meetings so that agreed outcomes can be reached.

Should the conflict be between the centre employer and an employee, the Fair Work Ombudsman offers a free mediation service to assist both parties. For further information, see www.youtube.com/watch?v=zxrjO_cGQAo, (FairWorkGovAu, 2015), or go to www.fairwork.gov.au/how-we-will-help/how-we-help-you/help-resolving-workplace-issues/working-with-you-to-resolve-workplace-issues.

Conflict and the workplace setting

In addition to these strategies, the intentional leader can also reflect on aspects specific to the centre and to their leadership that may limit the generation of conflict and help the management of conflict when it does arise. For example:

- *Employment of staff*. Is the professional philosophy of potential staff explored in the job interview, to ascertain whether it aligns with the centre's philosophy?
- *Working conditions*. To what extent is the health and well-being of staff supported through provisions such as staff:child ratios, time for program planning, above award wages, and support for professional development?
- *Centre policies*. Are these clear, regularly reviewed and updated, and reflective of best practice that supports the centre's vision, mission and philosophy?
- *Centre budget and professional development*. Are any funds allocated for the development of communication skills of the leader and other centre staff?

In the chapter so far we have considered three fundamental interpersonal and workplace communication skills: active listening, emotional intelligence and conflict management. We now consider how an effective application of these skills is in part dependent upon an appreciation of power dynamics and the exercising of ethical leadership.

Effective communication as 'power with', not 'power over'

As alluded to earlier, EC centres can at times be seething hotbeds of power relationships and conflict (Rodd, 2013). Power is quite palpable in all of its guises, whether covert or overt. Power appears and can thrive on a continuum from passive resistance to horizontal violence (Hard, 2006). To ensure that workplace culture and communication reflects social justice and equity in all relationships with and between management, staff, children, families and regulatory bodies, it is important that intentional leaders are aware of the dynamics of power: how it is used and also how to promote a more positive and wise approach to identifying and dealing with power-related problems as they emerge and become embedded daily.

Drawing on the work of social theorists of power (French & Raven, 1986; Raven, 1993) and leadership texts (see, for example, Dwyer, 2016; Owings & Kaplan, 2012; Robbins et al., 2009) we identify five sources of power that a leader can have at their disposal:

- *legitimate power:* the power that comes from being in a position of authority (such as centre director, room leader, nominated supervisor)
- *coercive power:* a leader's capacity to control or punish
- *reward power:* the power a leader can use to influence others through the offering or withholding of material and/or financial benefits
- *expert power:* power that is derived from a leader's specialist knowledge, skills and expertise
- *referent power:* a leader's capacity to influence others because of their personal characteristics (for example, charisma) and resources (for example, status).

Pause–reflect–act 9.5

Think about the sources of power described above.

- Identify examples of how leaders you have worked with have exercised power.
- What impact did the exercising of each of these forms of power have on staff, children and families?
- If you are in a leadership role, which of these forms of power do you exercise? How does your communication with others in the centre reflect this exercise of power?

Implicit in these perspectives is the idea that power is something that a leader owns and can exercise over others. Situating power as control over others, power is conceptualised as a repressive and negative force. In contrast is a *power with* approach, which seeks to authentically involve others in decision-making processes (Fuqua, Payne & Cangemi, n.d.). The emphasis here is on caring for others rather than dominating others.

The work of French philosopher Michel Foucault (1977, 1978, 1980) broadens this traditional view of power. For Foucault, power is bound in and exercised through **discourse**. Put simply, a discourse comprises statements that define how something ought to be talked or thought about. Discourses create truths that shape how we think and what we believe about something. For example, established 'childcare' discourses circulated in the media convey certain truths, such as 'long day care is primarily for working women', 'affordability is more important than quality', and 'education for young children takes place in preschools for four year olds rather than for all children birth to five years in long day care centres'. In turn, these truths have the capacity to shape how leaders and educators in long day care think, and what they do and do not do. For example, the truth that education is for preschoolers may explain why, in long day care centres, EC teachers generally work with three to five year olds, not babies and infants. Importantly, Foucault asserts that in any power relationship there is always room for freedom to be exercised. This means that intentional leaders and other members of an EC centre have scope to voice their own perspective about prevailing discourses. Implicit in the concept of discourse, therefore, is communication because communication can be used to promote and question particular discourses.

discourse involves messages that define how something (e.g. EC education) is talked about. Discourses shape values, beliefs and attitudes.

The discourses that prevail in an EC centre will influence centre approaches and practices. It is incumbent on intentional leaders to consider the dominant discourses that operate at their centre. For example, which discourses shape your:

- centre's provision of quality: The rights and best interests of the child? Getting children ready for school? The EC centre as a community?
- relationships with families: Family are the child's primary teacher? Staff are experts in child development and therefore know what is best for the child? Partnerships with parents enable strong child and family connections to the centre?
- budgeting: The EC centre as a business? The EC centre as affordable means that it enables women to work? The provision of high-quality education for young children?

- employment of staff: Working with children is women's work? Teaching is what happens in schools, not EC centres? An EC centre is a microcosm of its local community and cultural context?
- pedagogical practices: Children learn from birth? Children are innocent? University qualified teachers enhance children's development? Learning happens in play? Indigenous perspectives are relevant in centres where Indigenous children are enrolled?
- relationship with regulatory authorities and compliance to requirements: Meeting the National Quality Standard (NQS) ensures quality for children: The NQF supports educators in their provision of quality education and care for young children? The NQF standardises quality to prescriptive, technical practices?

In thinking about these questions, the intentional leader can also consider questions such as:

- how are these discourses explicitly and implicitly communicated?
- are the discourses 'owned' by some centre community members and not others?
- is there consensus or conflict about the discourses?

see chapter 3 for a full discussion of the NQF and NQS.

In Leaders in practice 9.1, Associate Professor June Wangmann considers power in the context of the various leadership positions she has held. June has had a long-standing involvement in the provision of services for children and their families in Australia. She has played a significant role in the development and analysis of EC policy, and served on many Commonwealth and state advisory committees, having played a major role in the development of the national accreditation system for children's services. In recognition of her contribution to services for children and families in Australia, June received a Commonwealth Government Centenary Medal in 2001, a NSW Children's Week Award in 2002 and the Macquarie University Alumni Award for Distinguished Service in 2007.

LEADERS IN PRACTICE 9.1

June Wangmann

Early Childhood Consultant, Sydney (NSW)

In the period 1993 to 2005 I held three newly created and rather challenging leadership positions. The first of these was the position as Head of School for the Institute of Early Childhood (IEC), Macquarie University. The IEC had just moved from a College of Advanced Education into a university environment. From this position I later moved on to set up two offices for the New South Wales government: the NSW Office of Child Care and then the NSW Parenting and Research Centre.

Each leadership position takes place within a unique context and while an understanding of this context provides an essential framework for one's work, I have found there have been certain similar elements that have underpinned my general approach to leadership. In each of these positions I first needed to understand the use of power within each organisation and use that understanding to inform and strengthen my own leadership strategies. All leadership positions involved elements of power at various levels within the organisational structures.

Within this context I have always seen power existing as a reciprocal relationship between myself and the people and organisations I worked with. I have always tried to share power through being consultative, listening, communicating and creating opportunities for individuals to build on their own strengths. The core element that has formed the framework for all my work has been an understanding of the political context. In Australia, EC services have been and continue to be developed within an intensely political environment. This has meant my focus has been on the 'big picture' of EC provision rather than single issues. Taking account of where things will probably move in the future means that people can create change and shape the future, rather than have the future created for them and policies thrust upon them.

From the big picture I have had a vision of what I wanted to achieve and put in place processes whereby others get to share and have input into this vision. All strategies/ initiatives, to be successful, need to involve the team in all aspects of the process. The relationships that then develop are the glue that holds an organisation together and provide the platform for the distribution of power.

It is important to emphasise that with initiatives that create change, the process is not always easy. I learnt very early on in my work that there are times when things did not happen as I had planned or expected—some things just don't work. It has always been important to be able to reflect/analyse on what went wrong, get feedback from staff/colleagues on what could be done differently, then pick myself up and go on to put in place some new strategies.

Pause–reflect–act 9.6

- Which leadership traits does June consider important when negotiating the use of power?
- Which connections does June make between her communication and her exercising of power?
- Which character traits do you think enable leaders to operate from a 'power with' rather than a 'power over' perspective?
- Which leadership character traits do you feel you have and which ones would you like to develop?

ethical practice involves continually working and making decisions through explicit, thoughtful consideration of legal and professional requirements, ethical principles and the organisation's philosophy.

Effective communication as ethical practice

For the intentional leader, effective communication needs to be ethical *and* practised in the context of ethical leadership (**ethical practice**). As discussed in Chapter 3, EC leaders and educators can be actively guided by the ethical standards outlined in the Code of Ethics (ECA, 2016). In addition to the values espoused in this professional code, intentional leaders can turn to widely accepted ethical principles and theories to inform their decision-making the Code of Ethics (ECA, 2016) is discussed further in chapter 3.

and interactions with others (Newman & Pollnitz, 2005; Owings & Kaplan, 2012). These principles and theories are:

- *autonomy:* upholding an individual's right to freedom and choice, with an obligation to respect that of others
- *beneficence:* contributing to the health and well-being of others
- *non-maleficence:* not causing harm or risk of harm to others
- *justice:* promoting equality and social justice
- *fidelity:* demonstrating faith and loyalty through honesty and maintaining confidentiality
- *utilitarianism:* bringing about the greatest good for the greatest number. According to this theory, decisions and interactions are 'ends-based' (Newman & Pollnitz, 2005)
- *Kant's categorical imperative:* seeking to uphold duties or principles that are considered to be right (such as telling the truth), irrespective of the consequences. According to this theory, decisions and interactions are 'rule-based' (Newman & Pollnitz, 2005)
- *altruism:* supporting the well-being of others and maintaining healthy relationships. According to this theory, decisions and interactions are 'care-based' (Newman & Pollnitz, 2005).

In an EC centre, power struggles can arise over ethical dilemmas and communication can be fraught. Unlike legal issues, where there is a clear 'right' and 'wrong' position, ethical dilemmas are more complex because they involve competing values and beliefs (Newman & Pollnitz, 2005). An intentional leader can drive a *power with* approach, utilising effective communication skills, to work through such dilemmas by utilising Newman and Pollnitz's (2002) ethical response cycle. This cycle involves consideration of the dilemma with regard to any relevant legal requirements; professional standards such as the Code of Ethics (ECA, 2016); ethical principles and theories; and informed inclination, where professional judgment is exercised in light of knowledge of the context (for example, the organisation's philosophy) and the specific circumstances of the dilemma. Working through ethical dilemmas requires the intentional leader to exercise, model and encourage the effective use of communication skills such as active listening, emotional intelligence and conflict management.

Pause–reflect–act 9.7

Consider the scenario below. Work through Newman and Pollnitz's (2002) ethical response cycle to consider how an intentional leader could seek to resolve the dilemma in an ethical manner.

> Monica has been an educator at an early learning centre for 25 years. She loves the children and is regarded by long-standing families as 'part of the furniture' at Greenwood. Recently, Monica's husband passed away. Rather than take leave, Monica has continued to come to work. Staying at home on her own was too difficult and she prefers to be around the children.

A relatively new parent, Jackie, complains to you about Monica's level of competence. Jackie is concerned that Monica seems distracted and not focused enough on the children. Yesterday when she came to pick up her son, Jackie noticed that Monica was spending a lot of time wiping down a table that appeared clean. Monica also gave vague responses to Jackie's enquiry about her son's day. This behaviour has been happening for the past week and Jackie is worried about the level of education and care her son is receiving.

Now imagine that you are the director of this centre. How might you exercise active listening, emotional intelligence and conflict resolution in this situation?

The remainder of this chapter focuses on how effective communication within power and ethical frameworks might be practised in relationships and interactions with and between children and staff. The intentional leader must utilise ethical principles and theories, the Code of Ethics, and their professional philosophy and knowledge base to strive for 'power with' rather than 'power over' communications.

see chapter 11 for a discussion of relationships with families.

Communicating with children through 'power with' and ethical approaches

The importance of professional decision-making using 'power with' and ethical approaches in relation to communicating with children cannot be emphasised enough.

Meeting the child and the family

On meeting the child with their family for the first time, the relationship begins—a relationship that has the potential for many meaningful encounters in the future. Most often children are only thought about in the here and now, but an intentional leader will think about the person they are to become: What will we be providing for this child? Will we see the child as a citizen of our community? Will we be able to create the culture of social justice for this child and facilitate the development of their empathic habit of mind (Costa & Kallick, 2000)? The leader will set the tone for the relationship through their communication. Engaging with the child warmly and respectfully is as important as it is to engage respectfully with the adults involved with the child's upbringing. The relationship with the child should be inclusive, democratic and built on trust, not a powerful teacher–child relationship.

In formal situations such as the enrolment interview, adults (educators and parents) sometimes ignore the child, perhaps only consulting them at the end of the interview to ask whether they like the centre. Power is with the adults—the child is powerless because they are unlikely to know whether or not they like it. An intentional leader will not overlook the child, but will include them in the conversation, regardless of age, as children have the right to be acknowledged during this process. Contemporary approaches to research with young children (such as Clark & Moss, 2011; and Harris & Manatakis, 2013) provide strategies for involving children by listening carefully to the many ways that they communicate their ideas and feelings. As Rinaldi (in Clark et al., 2005) explains, this broad concept of listening is '... not just about listening with our ears, but with all our senses—sight, touch, smell, taste, orientation' (p. 20).

Including children in the planning of the curriculum and program

Long before it became a regulatory requirement it was a professional responsibility and sound EC practice to include children in discussions as well as the decisions about curriculum and their work and play (Jones & Nimmo, 1994; Katz, 1995). EC practitioners in Australia now have the EYLF and the NQS to guide practice. In Quality Area 1 Educational programs and practice, the standard 1.1.2 is, 'Each child's current knowledge, ideas, culture, abilities and interests are the foundation of the program' (ACECQA, 2017). Engaging with children requires a trusting relationship built on mutual respect, with an understanding that children live in diverse cultural communities and have different dispositions for learning, different abilities and different learning styles. Therefore, when children are not included in the decision-making processes, they are not free to contribute to the decisions that will ultimately shape their experiences and educational outcomes.

Guiding children's behaviour

When guiding children's behaviour, children need time to develop an understanding of what is acceptable in a shared space. The objective is for the child to gain control of the internal impulses that lead to inappropriate actions or behaviour (Porter, 2008). Adults need to be aware and respectful of the diversity in child-rearing practices. They should communicate and work collaboratively with the parent(s) and the child in negotiating appropriate behaviour and conversations within the learning community. The EYLF Outcome 2, 'Children are connected with and contribute to their world', provides clear statements about the way educators can enable children to 'develop a sense of belonging to groups and communities and an understanding of the reciprocal rights and responsibilities necessary for active [and respectful] community participation' (DEEWR, 2009, p. 26). As advocates for the child, adults must model democracy and fairness and create a culture that reflects a socially just approach to behaviour guidance practices.

Negotiating conflict

Children need support in negotiating conflict in their play and in their relationships with their peers as well as with the adults in the centre (including their families). The adults must be aware of the play or conversations as they unfold, observe the changing dynamics and be ready to step in to model a way of managing the conflict fairly, ensuring the rights of other are respected. The adult's role is to support children in understanding each other's perspective and to consider the options for resolving the conflict. In this model, the adult is a mediator or mentor—not the person with the power to resolve the issue. While it takes more time to ensure power is distributed equitably between conflicting parties, it results in the diffusion of power struggles and in lessons in democracy and respectful negotiation.

Social justice and young children

Children are very aware of the beliefs and values of their families and of those adults who are responsible for them in EC centres. Children hear adults' family discussions and conversations and begin to try to make sense of the world through these interactive relationships while their knowledge is being socially constructed (Newman & Pollnitz, 2005). This is described by Cannella as a 'silent knowing' (1997, p. 3). As a result of being within earshot of their families' comments and debates, children absorb biases about gender, race and ability; the issues around refugees and war; and catastrophes such as drought, fire and flood, and body image. Their perspectives may or may not be in accordance with the values of the centre; however, much can be gained by reflecting with children and engaging in challenging biases through meaningful discussions, experiences and resources that afford multiple perspectives and ways of living life within a family and a community.

Within their EC centres, leaders can instil a culture where educators pay attention to the everyday conversations of children, as biases and power surface when a child tells another child they cannot come to their party; there cannot be two mothers or two fathers; you can be the baby or be the dog; you can bring me that block; girls cannot play this game; only boys like transformers; your skin is dirty; this baby doll is the prettiest; Barbie is beautiful; blind people cannot play this game ... and other such typical comments. Leaders can enable children to think critically and to raise their concerns about world events respectfully, ethically and without making a judgment about the child's family or cultural context. Indeed, in light of the current social problems of family violence these skills and understandings are important in developing future relationships based on a more equitable sharing of power.

Pause–reflect–act 9.8

- How does power flow in relationships with and between children at your centre?
- In addition to the aspects considered above, you may also like to consider structural arrangements that can impact on staff relationships with the children as well as their families. Consider, for instance, enrolment patterns (for example, minimum two-day enrolments), consecutive or non-consecutive day attendance, and the entering and exiting of families after the orientation period (for example, is this staggered?).
- How might staff support children in managing their relationships with others in a more respectful and socially just way?

Communicating with staff through 'power with' and ethical approaches

As with children, there is scope for intentional leaders to exercise effective communication and ethical practices to mitigate destructive power dynamics with and between staff. These can be exercised proactively and responsively in various aspects pertaining to the employment and management of staff. In the Investigating Quality study, which explored the practices that supported high-quality care in six case study centres (Fenech et al., 2010a), such practices included:

- *Recruitment of staff*: establish from the outset a culture of freedom and respect, for example, promote your core values in the job advertisement and your centre philosophy in the job description; ask applicants about themselves, including their passions, skills and interests and how they might like to use these in their practice; clearly establish description roles and responsibilities in the job, including those pertaining to staff relationships; be strategically selective about who you employ, and only employ someone you think aligns with the centre's philosophy, will add to the mix of the existing team and can uniquely contribute to the centre's ethos.
- *Orientation of staff*: budget for your new staff member to shadow a pedagogical leader for at least one day and ideally for one week; provide time-out periods where new staff can read the centre's philosophy and staff handbook, ask questions and be supported in their transition.
- *Development of staff*: provide a meaningful annual performance review where you collaboratively identify strengths and areas for further development; budget for professional development, not just technical training; budget for weekly curriculum and monthly staff meetings; and establish mentoring partnerships for all staff.
- *Inclusion of staff in curriculum development*: involve staff in curriculum development by utilising the diverse skills, backgrounds and interests of staff and mentoring staff in curriculum planning.
- *Development of staff morale and job satisfaction*: provide opportunities for staff to contribute to centre practices and curriculum; budget for programming time and staff professional development days; provide space for staff to rest and relax; celebrate achievements and special occasions.

chapter 10 looks at employment and management of staff.

Pause–reflect–act 9.9

- How does power flow in relationships with and between staff at your centre?
- Think about your own experience working with staff in EC centres. What do you consider to be your strengths for fostering collaborative, ethical relationships?
- Evaluate how well your communication skills foster 'power with', ethical relationships with staff. In which areas might you improve?

Using social media

Social media is an avenue where interpersonal and workplace communication come together, and where power differentials and ethical considerations come into play. Social media has been defined as consisting of 'websites that build on Web 2.0 technologies to provide space for content creation, networking, dialogue, collaboration, social interaction, media sharing, bookmarking and community formation' (Dwyer, 2016, p. 25). Web platforms such as Facebook, blogs, YouTube and Twitter provide leaders in EC centres with multiple means—other than traditional means such as telephone calls, emails and newsletters—of communicating with parents and other stakeholders. Social media offers exciting opportunities for leaders to engage parents, communicate about their child's learning and development, invite feedback on the service, and promote their service vision and philosophy. Similarly, leaders can also use social media to build team relationships, market their service, provide professional development, and share resources and information with staff.

As with any communication, social media must be exercised judiciously by taking into account power relations and ethical considerations. Inappropriate postings, blogs, tweets and so on risk damage to the reputation of an EC centre and its staff. Misuse of social media includes sharing information without permission, disclosing others' private details, disclosing too much and/or inappropriate personal information; posting of derogatory remarks, cyber bullying, breaching professional–personal boundaries, and making false or misleading claims (Dwyer, 2016).

With a social media policy in place, the intentional leader will strive to ensure that social media is used in ways that move the EC centre forward, living out its mission and philosophy and towards its vision and strategic goals. Neville Dwyer from the Dorothy Waide Centre for Early Learning and Griffith Central Preschool provides some examples of how social media is used ethically at his centre (Dwyer & Highfield 2015). Strategies include a policy on social media that includes guidelines on what can and cannot be shared, including images of children; the use of password protected software that limits the sharing of videos with families; and a Facebook page that is open only to current and former staff. In these ways, social media is used cautiously and wisely. EC programs are spaces for collaboration and relationships; for building respectful learning communities; and, most importantly, for children's learning and meaningful experiences. Social media should support our pedagogy, not define it.

In Leaders in practice 9.2, EC consultant Jennifer Ribarovski outlines what she has experienced to be the strengths and potential pitfalls of social media—in particular, Facebook.

LEADERS IN PRACTICE 9.2

Jennifer Ribarovski

Early Childhood Consultant (NSW)

Can you share a little about your qualifications, experience and current work in the EC sector?

I am an EC teacher with over 35 years of experience in the sector. I completed a childcare certificate straight out of high school, and in subsequent years completed my Bachelor of Teaching (EC) and a Masters of Educational Leadership and Management. I've worked in preschools, long day care centres, health, disability and support services, public schools, universities, regulatory authorities and with the national authority. Throughout my early career, I had three sons, and am very recently a proud grandmother. Currently I teach at Sydney University and I have my own EC consulting business. My career has been diverse and has stretched me professionally and personally at every turn, but there are some fundamental principles that underpin my work and the professional decisions that I make every day. They are that children must be at the forefront of both operational and pedagogical decisions, and that children are innately skilled learners with rights as active social citizens. I believe that EC education is the perfect platform to create a just and fair society, and that children have the capacity to enact the change that is so necessary in today's complex world.

How do you use social media in your work to inspire and empower educators to reflect on and work towards quality EC education for young children?

Over the years, and particularly in more recent times, social media has become a powerful communication tool that has brought with it many advantages. The moment my granddaughter was born in Paris, I could see her on FaceTime and congratulate her parents! Social media has the power to strengthen relationships, to shrink vast geographical distances and to advocate for fairness and justice. But conversely, it is equally capable of doing exactly the opposite. Facebook forums, for instance, can be a source of support for EC educators as they share practice and reflect on their work. Mentoring relationships can be established online that can build the confidence of educators and hone their expertise, and contribute to longstanding relationships being formed. But equally, differences in philosophical perspectives can lead to division, questioning educators' practices and undermining their confidence, contributing to a sense of professional isolation and uncertainty.

In my current consulting work, I use a range of social media tools to both advocate for the rights of children and families, and to support educators to grow and develop as confident and capable practitioners. This hasn't come easily to me though. I'm not from a generation that is technologically literate, and so using social media tools is a skill that I've had to work hard to develop. Initially, I saw this as necessary to be current in the market, and something that I had to do, but certainly didn't want to! But in a relatively short space of time, I've come to see social media as a powerful and valuable communication tool that can bring about effective and positive change. An example of this is a project that I recently led with three remote services in Western Australia. Because I couldn't physically be at their centres on a regular basis, and they were located around 600 kilometres apart, social media proved to be an effective way to overcome their geographic isolation, and their lack of face-to-face networking opportunities. This project centred around educators and teachers reflecting on their routines and practices to think about opportunities for children's agency. As they modified their practices, they reflected both in images and writing, and then uploaded their reflections to a closed Facebook group established for this purpose. I then provided feedback and further ideas for them to think about and implement as they went about the process of change. Once a week, we met by Skype and educators shared their practice, reflections and further ideas for improvement. This built their ability to reflect on practice, their collaboration skills as they worked together, and the development of a positive and supportive culture leading to a professional learning community. As their skills developed throughout the project, I was able to withdraw my support, knowing that the group would continue and that the learning and development would be sustained.

Can you share some insights about how an awareness of power and ethical considerations can assist an intentional leader's effective use of social media in their everyday practice?

While this proved to be a successful project, there were some important ethical considerations and agreements that needed to be established prior to its implementation, such as ensuring that:

- the approved provider understood the project and endorsed it in writing, including the use of Facebook as a learning and development tool
- ground rules about acceptable communication are established; for example, always using respectful and professional language
- permission from children and families was given to share images and reflections with the group
- images would not be shared beyond the closed Facebook group by using appropriate privacy settings
- a single moderator would be responsible for approving posts, providing a source of accountability
- personal Facebook accounts, required to join the group, were adjusted to protect the personal information and privacy of participants
- no additional participants would be added to the group without the permission of existing members, and that information would not be shared beyond the membership of the group.

With these agreements in place, the group was confident to fully participate, adding to the project's ongoing success.

Pause–reflect–act 9.10

- Consider the tools you use to communicate with families. Do they reflect a reliance on traditional communication mediums, or are you making effective use of available social media?
- Write down any barriers that are preventing you from communicating through social media. How might you go about addressing these barriers?
- In her profile, Jennifer discusses the potential of using social media to support professional development. How might you use social media to support the professional development of yourself and the staff at your centre?

Chapter summary

Rather than relying on a formal title of authority, an intentional leader will exercise effective communication skills, and seek to build staff communication capacity. Active listening, emotional intelligence and conflict management are key to effective communication. In EC centres, power operates through discourses and in relationships with and between children, families and staff. Through their communication and ethical practices, intentional leaders strive to promote relationships that are empowering, collaborative and respectful. Conflict and ethical dilemmas are inevitable in any organisation, yet communicating effectively and working ethically can enable 'power with' rather than 'power over' relationships, which can enhance a sense of belonging in the organisation and a commitment from all members of the EC centre to the provision of quality education and care for young children.

Key references

Newman, L. & Pollnitz, L. (2002). *Ethics in action: Introducing the ethical response cycle*. Watson, ACT: Australian EC Association.

This definitive publication details how leaders and educators can adopt an ethical response cycle to work through power struggles in an ethical way.

Rodd, J. (2013). *Leadership in early childhood: The pathway to professionalism* (4th ed.). Crows Nest, NSW: Allen & Unwin.

Chapters 4, 5 and 6 explore key facets of effective communication for leaders of EC centres, including emotional intelligence, assertiveness and conflict resolution.

Online resources

Managing conflict in the workplace

After brainstorming the impact of conflict on the workplace, Ruth Knight facilitates a one-hour seminar that explores constructive vs destructive conflict; why conflict happens; preventing conflict; and managing conflict. In *Managing conflict in your workplace* consideration is also given to the impact of communication styles on triggering and managing conflict.

www.youtube.com/watch?v=ILUkGb4sZ0s

Listening, speaking and understanding

Active listening, Gordon Training International. (2010)

www.youtube.com/watch?v=ESujTCel6lM

Active listening skills, Tomlinson, G. (2012)

www.youtube.com/watch?v=7PFX23Ynkfs

How the communication process works, Alanis, M. (2012)

www.youtube.com/watch?v=q6u0AVn-NUM

How to speak assertively with I statements, Shakiba, E. (2014)
www.youtube.com/watch?v=sswGv9iH-4o

Leading with emotional intelligence in the workplace, Talks, C. (2014)
www.youtube.com/watch?v=OoLVo3snNA0

10 | CREATING A COMMUNITY OF LEARNERS

CHAPTER LEARNING OBJECTIVES

After studying this chapter you will understand that:

- Building a team of skilled and qualified educators can contribute to quality outcomes for children and families.
- Effective recruitment, retention and professional learning are necessary to build sound morale within EC settings.
- Effective communication contributes to developing a culture of collaboration.
- Mentoring and coaching strategies can support leadership growth and development.
- Intentional leaders create the ethos or tone of the workplace environment.
- Sound human resource policies and procedures are an essential feature of ethical workplaces.

Key concepts

ethical workplaces
recruitment
retention
workplace culture
workplace ethos

Overview

Educators are the foundation of high-quality program delivery and they can work well when supported and mentored by effective leaders. Crucial to this support is the creation of workplace security, stability and job satisfaction for all employed within each organisation. By providing transparent human resources policies and procedures, consistency can be achieved and assist educators to feel valued as professionals. Contemporary EC leaders face numerous challenges in recruiting, retaining and promoting staff within their settings. Intentional leaders can make a difference in developing an organisational culture and ethos at the workplace that is respectful of all employees. This chapter guides leaders through the complexities of their human resources responsibilities in ethical and strategic ways. It examines the use of mentoring and coaching as strategies to nurture leadership. The discussion covers the topics of recruitment, conditions of employment, staff support and human resources policies.

Creating an ethical workplace

Intentional leaders aim to create effective workplaces that are ethically sound and set high standards for staffing that go beyond the minimum regulations stipulated in the National Law and National Regulations (see www.acecqa.gov.au). Safe Work Australia (see www.safeworkaustralia.gov.au/Legislation/PublicComment/Pages/Model-WHS-CoP-Public-Comment.aspx) has also drafted a model for 'Work Health and Safety Codes of Practice' and an issues paper, which includes 'Preventing and responding to workplace bullying'. These policies and laws can support the intentional leader in creating **ethical workplaces**.

ethical workplaces are EC organisations that provide socially just human resource policies and procedures for all staff.

What are the characteristics of an ethical workplace? An ethical workplace ensures that all staff are:

- remunerated according to their professional qualifications and experience
- provided with employment conditions that include at least the basic leave entitlements (such as annual leave, sick leave and family leave), superannuation and workers' compensation
- able to contribute to decisions concerning themselves (as well as the children and families)
- provided with support for ongoing professional learning and development
- respected and valued regardless of differences in background characteristics including age, ethnicity, experience, gender, language, marital status, qualifications, religion, sexuality and social class.

see also chapter 15, which explores in depth the concept of professional learning and development, and the development of a professional learning community.

These ethical aspects are embraced in the Code of Ethics (ECA, 2016) and reflect collegiality and professionalism among educators. Leaders are responsible for working with management to ensure that ethical values are reflected in the organisation's human resources policies and procedures. This also means that there is a commitment to collaboration, equity, inclusion and transparency in decision-making on staffing matters.

The notion of an 'ethical workplace' is not a new concept. About two decades ago, Sergiovanni (1994) articulated a leadership model that represented the 'head', 'heart' and 'hand'. The 'head' represents how the leader looks at the world of work, the 'heart' represents the beliefs and values of the leader, and the 'hand' depicts the decisions, actions and behaviours of the leader. According to Sergiovanni (1994) these three aspects intertwine and affect the decisions made by intentional leaders. To establish an ethical workplace the leader engages with all of these aspects. The 'head' in the EC setting includes the regulatory frameworks that the leader is accountable to. These accountabilities (such as a shortage of university qualified educators), in turn, can impact on the 'heart' or what the organisation values and rewards at times such as when recruiting educators. Finally, the 'hand' relates to the decisions that are made and how the leader interacts with management, staff, families and children. When taken together, these aspects can inform and influence the nature of the **workplace ethos** in EC settings.

workplace ethos is one aspect of the organisational culture, reflecting its tone or broad characteristics as reflected in the philosophy underpinning the organisation's vision and mission.

Pause–reflect–act 10.1

Use Sergiovanni's model to think about how your head, heart and hand might influence the way you would like to work with your staff team.

- To what extent does your current organisational structure (the 'head') fit with your own personal philosophy and values (your 'heart')?

- How can you make sure your behaviour as a leader (your 'hand') can fit the organisation's vision?
- What factors influence your decision-making (your 'head') as a leader within your organisation?

Every organisation requires a sound vision to provide high-quality outcomes for children and families as well as a space where staff are respected and valued as knowledgeable and skilful professionals. Having a vision based on commonly agreed values and goals can enable decision-making in a consistently ethical manner. This supports our focus on intentionality—that is, leaders play a key role in thinking through and articulating to staff the way decisions were made to align with the commonly agreed vision. There is no one right way to create an ethical workplace and it may take time to build a collegial and inclusive environment where all staff feel comfortable to contribute actively.

Pause–reflect–act 10.2

Think about the different approaches taken by leaders in EC settings in the way regular staff meetings are conducted. In relation to these examples, reflect on the following questions.

- What approaches do you think showed more intentionality in the way that the leader guided staff to relate the decision to the centre vision?
- In doing this, to what extent did the leader dominate the discussion or enable staff to contribute freely?
- To what extent was this approach successful or not successful in enabling staff to participate in the discussion?

Approaches to working with staff

Staff matters are typically described as 'human resource management' (HRM). With increasing appreciation of nurturing staff in every way, large organisations employ people with HRM expertise to oversee this work. Publications specialising in this topic are easily found and in this chapter we provide a broad overview to raise awareness of HRM in relation to the EC sector. According to Oldroyd (2005), HRM may be conceptualised as two dimensions—'HARD' or 'SOFT'—to enable the framing of staffing issues analytically and strategically. 'Hard' approaches typically focus on the tasks performed by staff and the rules provide accountability through the implementation of organisational policies and procedures in linear ways. 'Soft' approaches to working with staff reflect an emphasis on the people or the staff, and can be more flexible in the ways policies and procedures are implemented.

An intentional leader will be conscious of approaching HRM decisions in a way that is compatible with the ethical characteristics of the workplace. There is no single right approach, and contextual features of each setting as well as qualities of leadership can influence which approach is more compatible with local conditions. The duality of leadership and management functions as described by Oldroyd (2005) can be seen in EC settings. That is, these tasks are often performed by one person, and typically this can be, for example, the centre's director. An outline of the key characteristics of the two dimensions of HRM as adapted for EC settings is presented in Table 10.1.

The 'hard' side of HRM emphasises the tasks or structural elements including the centre's policies and procedures. In contrast, as Oldroyd (2005) explains, the 'soft' side of HRM focuses on the people or the social and psychological aspects. Leaders also explore different components of the organisation when implementing either approach to HRM. If following a hard approach, leaders are expected to ensure that systems are in place to hire the 'right' staff to satisfy the organisation's objectives. This begins with having job specification statements, protocols for advertising positions, interviewing, selecting and appointing the person to a job. Once employed, the staff member will be made aware of internal staffing policies and procedures to ensure that they do their work efficiently.

In contrast, leaders with a preference for the 'soft' elements of HRM work with staff through empowerment and efficacy, and focus on the individual and their role within the organisation. Efficacy is concerned with an individual's 'competence, confidence and capacity for success' (Oldroyd, 2005, p. 196). These personal qualities are often associated with 'emotional intelligence' (EI), a term coined by Goleman (1998). According to Oldroyd (2005), creating a healthy organisation requires recruiting staff with emotional intelligence and creating a learning culture within the organisation that includes professional learning and feedback. The intentional leader will adopt a mix of both 'hard' and 'soft' approaches.

Table 10.1 Two dimensions of human resource management (HRM)

	'HARD' HRM (instrumental/ rational)	**'SOFT' HRM (expressive/ developmental)**
Focus	on tasks	on people
Purpose	get tasks done; achieve desired outcomes	motivate and nurture staff
Scope	structures, policies and procedures	individual and team relationships, and organisational culture
Leadership	transactional—promotes efficiency and high standards	transformational—values driven, interested in feelings and beliefs
Key words	competition, professional accountability, quality, strategic planning	commitment, efficacy, empowerment, professional autonomy, teamwork

Source: Adapted from Oldroyd, 2005, p. 188.

Another approach gaining momentum in EC settings when working with staff is the 'strengths-based approach' (McCashen, 2005). As leaders have to work effectively with a range of professionals from various backgrounds, including diverse disciplines, professional experiences and cultural backgrounds, this approach has become popularised. The strengths approach focuses on the existing strengths of the person (their capacity and competency) and then empowers the person to build on these strengths (Maton et al., 2004; McCashen, 2005). Creating a strengths-based **workplace culture** requires open and honest communication whereby expectations about all aspects of work are transparent and clear, and ongoing feedback is provided to staff (McCashen, 2005). The strengths perspective asks:

workplace culture is a shared understanding of the beliefs and values that influence the work arrangements within an organisation.

- 'What is working?' rather than 'What is the problem?'
- 'How do you want things to be?' rather than 'What do we need to change?'

Leaders who use a strengths approach seek to develop confidence in each staff member as they work and reflect on their strengths and identify ways of improving practice. Leaders also find that this approach can assist staff to take responsibility for the issues they face or the changes they need to make to work effectively within the team and organisation. A strengths-based research project jointly run by the Benevolent Society and Lady Gowrie NSW, conducted in Sydney that aimed to support EC settings in working with multidisciplinary teams utilised a strengths approach with a group of EC directors in long day care and preschool settings (n=45). The participants received several training sessions and met monthly for discussion in reflective learning circles (RLC). The RLC focused on working with colleagues from a strengths-based approach; working with families—implementing family centred practice; and working with children. In terms of working with their colleagues, participants noted that focusing on strengths changed the way they supervised and managed their staff (Antcliff et al, 2007), as indicated in the following statement:

> I found it hard as I was recognising what staff weren't doing. This was a good learning [experience] for me as it made me look at things differently. (Inner East Learning Circle, 8/2/07)

In most EC settings, working with staff relates to how the hierarchy of authority and responsibility for decision-making is organised. Some settings operate with a more 'top down' approach whereby the decisions are generally made by management and include a Board and/or staff who occupy the position of centre director or chief executive officer. In this type of setting, it is possible that only those in senior management positions may be allowed to have discussions with the families about a child or select what types of resources are purchased and how they are used. In settings that adopt a flatter structure, leadership roles and responsibilities may or may not be as distinct.

retention strategies are used to support staff, both individually and collectively as a team, by building on their strengths and by addressing weaknesses.

Job satisfaction is also a hot topic in the sector. There is growing concern as recent studies are reporting high staff turnover. For instance, figures of between 20 and 50 per cent turnover rates annually have been recorded for long day care centres (Department of Education, 2014; Huntsman, 2008; Irvine et al., 2016) and the recent Productivity Commission report also noted **retention** difficulties of EC teachers (Productivity Commission, 2014). Research conducted by the Social Research Centre (2014) argue that high levels of stress and low job satisfaction are often attributed to high turnover rates in the EC sector. Job satisfaction and retention is an area that requires more research in terms of what it is that makes staff stay in the sector. An interesting study has been conducted by Jones (2016). For this research she surveyed 229 participants from long day care centres throughout Australia in regard to current job satisfaction; overall satisfaction with the profession; intention to turn over; and whether the setting was meeting the three basic psychological needs of autonomy, relatedness and competence as outlined by Deci and Ryan's (2014) theory of self-determination. She then interviewed 10 EC teachers who scored high in job satisfaction to understand what it was about their workplaces that made them highly satisfied and unlikely to leave. Her quantitative and qualitative results showed that these teachers stayed and were highly satisfied because they: (i) felt autonomous in their role (were trusted to do their job); (ii) related strongly to the centre (including other staff, children, families and the leader of the program); and (iii) felt competent in terms of feeling effective and challenged in their workplace (Jones et al., 2017).

Pause–reflect–act 10.3

- What do you see as the advantages and disadvantages of implementing the various approaches to working with staff discussed above?
- Do you think autonomy, relatedness and competence are important components for ensuring staff have higher job satisfaction? Why or why not?
- What other approaches to staffing have you observed being used in EC settings? Identify aspects that you consider promote retention.

Building a centre team

The National Quality Standard (NQS) promotes respectful and ethical interactions and relationships among staff working in an EC setting (ACECQA, 2011c). In particular, this is discussed in Quality Area 4 on staffing arrangements. There is now sufficient research-based evidence to support the notion that well-qualified EC teachers are critical to quality program delivery (Fenech et al., 2010; Sylva et al., 2004b). In Australia, government policy reforms and the introduction of the NQS have resulted in all educators working in the EC sector to have a minimum qualification of a Certificate III in Children's Services. This standard also requires EC settings to have a university qualified EC teacher. It has been shown that the attainment of high-quality outcomes for children and families in EC settings is also related to three key structural elements consisting of staff:child ratios, the size of children's groups and opportunities for professional learning (OECD, 2011). It is no surprise that small ratios and groups with well-qualified educators can yield better outcomes for children. An intentional leader understands these key components of a quality program and uses research evidence to support planning discussions with management as well as to attract high-quality educators to build a team with appropriate knowledge and skills.

regulatory frameworks underpinning the work of EC educators are explored in chapter 3.

It has also been shown that 'a higher level of specialisation and professionalism among staff would permit greater workforce autonomy and the ability to exercise professional judgment' (Bretherton, 2010, p. 34). However, staff ability to demonstrate independence and creativity in their professional decision-making can be curbed by simple compliance with licensing regulations, with little or no critical engagement in what these requirements mean (Fenech & Sumsion, 2007a; Osgood, 2004; Woodrow & Press, 2007). Leaders can address this dilemma in various ways at the local level of their organisation by creating opportunities to discuss regulatory or compliance matters. Periodic assessment of qualifications and experience among the staff team and allocation of funding to systematically upskill staff can enhance professional autonomy in decision-making, especially by those in leadership roles. It is also vital that educators have the opportunity to meet regularly to discuss curriculum and procedural issues and to reflect critically on theory and practice.

see chapter 9 for more discussion on power and resistance.

Pause–reflect–act 10.4

Think about when you have worked with staff in EC settings.

- What types of ethical work practices, including staffing arrangements, have you witnessed as required in the NQS?
- What are your views about working in settings that have hierarchical management structures?
- Would you feel more comfortable working in settings that implement a flat structure of decision-making? Why or why not?
- Make a list of key characteristics of your ideal workplace and explain their importance in setting the tone of the workplace.
- In explaining your preferences, reflect on the advantages and disadvantages of the different approaches to working with staff discussed in this chapter.

Go to oxfordascend *to hear Angela's thoughts.*

Mentoring as a leadership strategy

Mentoring is frequently highlighted as a way of learning how to become a leader, as well as a way of surviving as a leader (Ebbeck & Waniganayake, 2004; John, 2008; Rodd, 2006b; Wong & Waniganayake, 2013). Regardless of the length of time or experience in a leadership role, a mentor can be an effective sounding board or a critical friend who provides confidential advice, support and guidance to novice or experienced leaders. Possibilities of working with a mentor or coach are depicted in Figure 15.1 within the Guided Learning sphere. This is one of the many strategies that can be used for continuous professional learning as educators.

see chapter 15 for a further discussion of professional development and learning strategies.

The classical origins of mentoring reflect a top-down, unequal power hierarchy where a more experienced, high-status mentor assumes responsibility for guiding a less experienced novice (Ebbeck & Waniganayake, 2004). In more recent literature, there has been recognition of the constructivist nature of mentoring, and this is based on an appreciation of the mutuality of benefits from the teaching and learning that occurs between the mentor and the protégé or mentee (Bollinger, 2009; Mullen, 2008; Orland-Barak & Hasin, 2010). Wong and Waniganayake (2013) have also conceptualised mentoring as the integration of three dimensions, comprising roles and responsibilities; skills and knowledge; and the qualities and dispositions of those involved in the mentoring partnership.

This shift away from looking at mentoring as being one-directional—from the expert to the novice—is an important development that requires closer examination when implementing mentoring processes within the EC sector as it questions traditional beliefs about mentors being senior staff who are older and experienced. Instead of focusing on factors such as age, experience in the sector and qualifications in isolation, educators are encouraged to consider the interplay of personal and professional attributes of the mentor and mentee as well as organisational factors such as the size of the centre, number of qualified and experienced educators, their expertise, interests and gaps in learning and resources available in the local community. As these relationships can be shaped by a range of factors, careful thought and planning needs to go into establishing mentoring and coaching programs within organisations.

EC centre directors are often expected to mentor in order to provide guidance and direction to novice educators or aspiring leaders (Slattery, 2009a). It is also possible that mentoring colleagues within an EC setting is an expectation of those employed as educational leaders. Despite the popularity and use of mentoring as a leadership development strategy, the absence of substantive research studies that follow participants involved in mentoring beyond a 12-month period makes it difficult to critique its long-term sustainability, effectiveness or influence.

Care must also be taken by management or the centre director to ensure that everyone understands the difference between staff supervision and mentoring. Staff supervision or management of staff is not the same as mentoring. Challenges can arise when mentoring is tied to employment accountabilities of a particular position. It is proposed that those involved in a mentoring relationship can benefit best from having flexibility, freedom and mutuality of support from each other. When the mentor is the centre director/manager who is responsible for staff supervision, inevitably they can be expected to adopt a managerial stance over the mentee. This relationship reflects a power imbalance because the director/manager, by virtue of their higher position in the organisation, has more authority over other staff. In large organisations employing 10 or more staff, it can be difficult also to assess the extent to which a centre director/manager can effectively mentor a full team of staff while being seen to be impartial. Appointment of an external mentor or finding mentors outside the setting is one way of overcoming these challenges. If mentoring staff is built into staff job descriptions, clear guidelines outlining the expectations of both mentors and mentees can assist in maintaining professional relationships underpinned by ethical values such as trust, integrity, equity, impartiality and compassion. These values are linked with the Code of Ethics (ECA, 2016), and can be used as a guiding framework when participating in mentoring activities.

In the literature, the concepts of mentoring and coaching have been used simultaneously. To reduce confusion between these two concepts, Figure 10.1 considers the key aspects of each concept.

Figure 10.1 Comparison of mentoring and coaching

MENTOR
- Understands teaching and learning processes.
- Does not need specific technical expertise.

MENTORING is a process where skills and knowledge are shared

COACH
- Provides directive instructions to learn a particular set of skills.
- Has expertise in a specific skill set that others want to learn.

COACHING focuses on developing a specific skill set

Both mentors and coaches...
- Are good listeners
- Provide guided learning experiences
- Promote self-development
- Provide independent and correctional advice
- Challenge and inspire

As can be seen in Figure 10.1, there are similarities and differences between mentoring and coaching. However, as noted by Hayes (2004, p. 10), 'coaching is not mentoring but mentoring requires coaching skills'.

Mentors and mentees can work collaboratively, and this approach can be incorporated into organisational policy. Mentors and mentees can, in turn, work out specific methods that are appropriate for their local context.

Pause–reflect–act 10.5

- Reflect on your professional experiences of working in EC settings. To what extent do they reflect mentoring and/or coaching relationships?
- What factors may constrain and/or assist the development of a mentoring relationship between staff and supervision of staff in EC settings?

Mentoring programs can also be found online, and these are described as either e-mentoring or web-based mentoring. These programs are structured typically to follow a set course, and can be found embedded within university coursework studies (see, for example, Packard, 2003; Sinclair, 2003). Additionally, as noted by Wong (2010, p. 22), there are business or public websites that 'offer to help you find a suitable mentor that can share their skills, experiences, and networks (for example, the Australian Women's Mentoring Network)'. Again, the absence of research on the use of these types of online resources makes it difficult to critique the usefulness or effectiveness of technologically-based mentoring approaches.

Consequently, the potential for cloning or reproducing a copy of the mentor is high. In the long term it is also possible that instead of liberating the mentee, this type of top-down transmission model of transferring knowledge from the expert to the novice will lead to dependence, not independence. This lack of professional autonomy does not augur well in terms of developing a strong, competent educator. Therefore, before embarking on mentoring and coaching activities, all participants are urged to examine each other's roles and responsibilities openly and honestly. These discussions can set the foundation for the future in terms of the benefits realised through this type of professional learning used by educators, especially to nurture future leaders for the sector.

Staff policies and procedures

Intentional leaders approach staffing matters systematically and strategically. This is reinforced in the NQS through Quality Areas 4 and 7, which require settings to have appropriate arrangements for staffing as well as governance and leadership respectively, to enable effective management of a quality service (ACECQA, 2017). This means leaders are required to develop a staffing framework reflective of the organisational philosophy and incorporating the long-term goals and current objectives outlined in the vision and mission statements respectively. As Bretherton (2010) found in her research, employers have reported that the setting's philosophy statement can be used effectively 'to clarify the principles underpinning **recruitment**, workload management and skill composition' as well as dialogue and negotiation with parents, especially when difficulties emerge (p. 30). Policy documents can also outline for each staff member expectations about the job, and the roles and responsibilities they are each hired to perform.

recruitment refers to the employment of appropriately qualified EC staff, in keeping with the organisation's vision, philosophy and strategic plans.

In an ethical workplace it is also assumed that the organisation complies with legal obligations connected with staffing including laws on child protection (such as the completion of working with children checks), anti-discrimination, equal employment, occupational health and safety and workers compensation. Likewise, it is essential that there are sufficient finances to pay wages and conditions. Importantly, research shows that payment of wages above the recommended award rates as well as offering permanency (in contrast to casual appointments) are effective strategies for retaining skilled staff (Bretherton, 2010). This is particularly important in recognising and rewarding educators who achieve postgraduate qualifications and in promoting staff who demonstrate sound leadership potential.

chapter 13 looks at the importance of money matters.

Pause–reflect–act 10.6

Government regulations can require that each organisation has a set of policy documents covering staffing matters.

- Look at the NQS and make a list of staffing policies required. Look at a setting you know and examine their staffing policies.
- Discuss with staff working under these policies their strengths and weaknesses, and document what you have learnt from these discussions for future reference.

In Leaders in practice 10.1, Karen Palmer discusses her approach to creating a community of learners. She emphasises the importance of relationships and trusting staff as individuals.

LEADERS IN PRACTICE 10.1

Karen Palmer

Executive Director, Unicare EC Education, Perth (WA)

I have worked in the EC sector for over 30 years and it has taken me quite some time to learn how to create a community of learners within my workplace. I have discovered that I am not the 'be all and end all' of everything! That it takes a team of very different people with very different skill sets to create something magical. Creating a community of learners requires a dedication to creating relationships with people and understanding what they bring to the table. It requires not only an understanding of their talents, special abilities, likes and dislikes, but the ability to place trust and value in each individual. When educators can truly feel this, they really fly and feel that they can be creative in their thoughts and ideas. The challenge is to allow them to fly and not be tempted to 'clip their wings'.

I currently work in a large service with 52 educators, and I know that if we are to achieve an effective workplace, then we all need to learn together, even if the area of learning is somewhat unfamiliar. An example of this occurred one afternoon at a pedagogical leaders meeting when we were brainstorming future goals, ideas and 'where to next' topics. Two educators began a passionate discussion about a TV documentary about the effects young children had on dementia patients and comments were made around how this could happen at our service. Other educators were enthused by the topic and so began the amazing journey with our 'Treasuring Life' program (bringing children and people living with dementia together). Educators were encouraged to research, document and put in place a plan which would work for our particular service.

Educators researched the topic of dementia and how contact with the elderly could have an amazing reciprocal outcome for them and our children. While educators had a great idea, we had to work and learn together and I found that my role was that of encourager, cheer leader and scaffolder of their existing knowledge as we all learnt together about the world of a person living with dementia. We currently attend a small centre for people with dementia every week with a group of six children. The results have been staggering and I wouldn't have believed the change in the clients or the beautiful empathy and compassion demonstrated by our children if I had not listened, encouraged and supported the educators in this project. The end result has seen real transformation in some educators as they have witnessed their own idea, research and project work come to life.

So why create a community of learners? Because 'The people who are crazy enough to think they can change the world are the ones that do'. (Steve Jobs)

Pause–reflect–act 10.7

- After reading Leaders in practice 10.1, consider whether Karen's perspective fits within a 'hard' or 'soft' HRM approach.
- Think about your personal qualities and document how you would like to work with staff.
- Make a list of your current skills by reflecting on your strengths and identify aspects that require further development.

Recruitment and retention of staff

Effective recruitment and retention of staff requires due consideration by the leader, and is influenced by a variety of factors, which include:

- *The organisational framework including the philosophy, vision and mission will impact on who is recruited to 'fit' the organisation.* For example, if the philosophy of the setting emphasises working closely with families and including them in the decision-making processes of the setting, staff employed will need to feel comfortable with having families present in the setting as well as having the interpersonal skills to effectively engage with families. If the vision is to have a diverse staff team (consisting of a mix of work experience, gender and ethnicity, for example) these background characteristics can also influence who is considered for a position.
- *The strategic plan and budget have a direct impact on staff employment conditions.* For example, having an extra EC qualified teacher—or a first year graduate or a teacher with many years of experience—has to be budgeted for because each category of teacher carries different rates of pay. The statement of duties and expectations for the position can impact on the appropriate fit of an individual within the setting. For example, if the duties include the person working a particular shift, the person recruited would need to be able to meet this expectation.

employment of staff is a key consideration in the business plan and the budget as discussed in chapter 13.

- *The qualities and strengths preferred for the team.* For example, if the aim is to build the leadership of the educators working with infants, a person who is interested in babies and is passionate about learning during infancy, and also has experience of working with a dedicated team of staff needs to be recruited.
- *The qualifications required for the position.* This will be linked to the regulatory requirements as well as the strategic plan for staffing. Intentional leaders are also aware of the importance of addressing staff's professional growth systematically, including the acquisition of initial qualifications and motivating continual learning for all staff.

Leadership is also necessary to employ and retain staff with qualities or dispositions that reflect the community context of each setting. It is possible that staff dispositions may be influenced by innate factors (such as a person's temperament) as well as values and beliefs connected with the individual's cultural, linguistic and religious backgrounds. Importantly, one of the critical findings of the *Starting strong II Report* (Organisation for Economic

Co-operation and Development, 2006), which looked at the provision of EC education of young children in some 20 OECD countries, was 'the failure of pedagogical teams to reflect the diversity of the neighbourhoods they serve' (p. 17). This analysis of workforce diversity at the local level is hampered due to the absence of sound data 'on the cultural and linguistic diversity of the EC development workforce itself', as recognised by the Australian government in one of its issues papers (Productivity Commission, 2010, p. 23).

Pause–reflect–act 10.8

During a conversation, when asked why she was not keen to use childcare for her baby, a mother, originally from an African country, replied, 'Why would I leave my baby with someone who doesn't look like me, can't talk like me, can't cook food like me, doesn't smell like me or can't sing like me?'

- What is this mother actually trying to tell us?
- How would you reassure parents from diverse ethnic or cultural backgrounds that their children's interests and needs would be met by staff at your centre?

Reflect on your own cultural background and consider to what extent it may influence your leadership style.

- What steps will you take to increase your ability to support children and families from diverse family backgrounds?

The above reflection indicates the importance of employing diverse staff in leadership roles. Lumby and Morrison (2010) have written passionately about the absence of sophisticated theorising or engagement in the practice of leadership diversity as performed by those who are from visibly different minorities living and working in affluent Western societies, as reflected in the following comments:

> The significance of Whiteness and gender is largely absent in mainstream writing on leadership theory, both in relation to its impact on staff and on learners. The dance of individuals who move in and out of particular identities related to their visible characteristics is rarely discernible in generic work about leadership. (p. 5)

Intentional leaders can be fully aware of the linguistic, cultural and religious backgrounds of their staff and work towards actively making use of their diverse experiences and expertise. This includes creating opportunities to enable staff from diverse ethnic or cultural backgrounds to demonstrate their leadership capacities and learning from them alternative ways of exercising leadership roles and functions. In this way, everyone can contribute to knowledge construction and improved practice.

Another aspect of staffing that is sometimes overlooked is the gender composition of your team. According to Rohrmann and Emilsen (2015), the gender imbalance in the EC workforce has been recognised as a policy consideration since the 1990s. In Australia, in the last National ECEC Workforce Census, published in 2014, males represented approximately 6 per cent, with the majority of these staff (that is, 17 per cent) being employed in vacation care services and outside school hours care settings (16 per cent). It was further noted that the median age was 26 years for men, in comparison to 36 years for women (Department of Education, 2014, p. 2). While the trend in Australia is smaller than in Norway, where males account for 10 per cent of the EC workforce, men represent less than 3 per cent of the EC workforce worldwide (Warin & Adriany, 2015). However, in stark contrast to these patterns, Neuman, Josephson, and Chua (2015, p. 30) have reported:

> men make up more than half of the pre-primary teachers in Liberia and Tanzania (ILO, 2012), and about 45 per cent in the Gambia (EI, 2010). In Namibia, only one-third of pre-primary teachers were female in 2004, but the percentage of trained female teachers (33 per cent) far exceeded the percentage of trained male teachers (12 per cent) (UNESCO IBE, 2006f). Other countries outside Sub-Saharan Africa with significant proportions of male teachers include Brunei (22 per cent) and Timor-Leste (17 per cent) (SEAMEO, 2015).

Concern about the absence or limited availability of male teachers in EC settings has led to numerous government initiatives in various OECD countries to provide incentives to attract male teachers. Due to the absence of longitudinal research or systematic evaluations, the extent to which these initiatives have been successful in recruiting and retaining male EC teachers is difficult to know. Likewise, the actual increases anticipated by governments have also not been fully realised. Interestingly, Rohrmann and Emilsen (2015, p. 3) report that Turkey achieved more than 5 per cent of male pre-school teachers with 'neither public nor political debate on gender issues in that country'.

In presenting findings of recent research involving EC teachers in Sweden and Indonesia, Warin and Adriany (2015, p. 2) stated that reproduction of the traditional gender binary between women and men was being reinforced with little or no discussion about gender identities. They also noted that religious and political influences can reinforce the construction of masculinity and femininity as well as traditional male and female roles in a society. A small minority of participants in their study, however, stood out as 'living examples of a transformation from gender blindness to gender consciousness' and this transformation was made possible 'through their critical engagement with academic gender studies and also through their participation in gender focused research' (p. 10).

Findings such as these, while reinforcing the social construction of gender identities, also provoke EC leaders to consider the importance of opening up safe spaces to discuss issues about the implications of gender when employing staff, and the centre's approach to children's gender socialisation. It is also recommended that leaders take steps to explore the views of parents about their perceptions about employing male teachers, particularly for the babies' room. The example highlighted by Carrie Rose in Leaders in practice 11.1 is an important reminder of how gender identity can impact children as well as adults. As a group of staff, critical analysis of their beliefs and assumptions about gender socialisation is necessary in achieving a shared approach that is respectful of personal choice for both children and adults.

Pause–reflect–act 10.9

- Is it essential to have male teachers to teach children about masculine identities?
- How can you explain the different rates of employment of men in EC settings between OECD countries and Asian and African countries noted in the UNESCO report in this chapter?
- What differences, if any, do you anticipate between male and female educators performing leadership roles in an EC setting?
- Survey parents and staff to ascertain their perceptions about employing male teachers at your centre. Collate, analyse and discuss the findings in setting new directions for the centre.

staff professional learning is considered in depth in chapter 15.

Finding the right staff who will fit the organisation is only the first step to successfully recruiting and retaining them. Organisations with the support of their intentional leaders can also make a difference by contributing to staff professional learning from a long-term perspective. EC staff teams are diverse in terms of training and experience. This means there is no one right way to support staff, and intentional leaders need to use their knowledge and skills as well as their intuition to appropriately support staff.

Building the organisational culture

All organisations have an internal culture, which may be observable in its building design, name, logos, rituals and history of establishment. The founder or leader can influence the organisational culture (Dubrin et al., 2006). Consider, for example, Mohamed Yunus, the founder of the Grameen Bank in Bangladesh, or Bill Gates, founder of the Microsoft empire; these individuals are inseparable from their businesses. Within EC settings, the culture and ethos of the organisation can ensure stability and continuity for staff, families and children. Organisational culture reflects the values, beliefs and philosophy that underpin the work of the EC setting. Depending on the age of the organisation, certain practices may be considered rituals or traditions of the organisation. For example, each Friday a mobile coffee cart came to serve 'free' coffee (or hot chocolate) as a regular ritual at one centre, and this was one strategy that centre management used to provide a special treat for their staff each week (Waniganayake et al., 2008).

At another centre, calling out to the centre's cook, 'Morning Thelma', was something that all children, parents and staff did upon arrival at the centre every day. It symbolised how much everyone loved the cook and her centrality in creating a sense of family or community at the centre. The kitchen at this centre was located near the entrance and the open plan design made it easy for Thelma to be seen as she went about her cooking every day. Being cheerful, kind and generous, she talked freely to adults and children and knew every child by name. This kind of 'presence' of a leader within their organisational setting can influence the tone or atmosphere that is felt when visiting a school or an EC setting. Research by Marsh, Waniganayake and De Nobile (2014, p. 23) suggests that by being present, educational leaders can 'develop supportive relationships and have a positive influence upon the school's climate and culture' and ultimately, these aspects influence children's learning outcomes.

While there will be pros and cons about the nature or the perceived 'value' of such practices, take into account the aims and objectives of planned strategies and the impact they have in promoting social engagement and creating a sense of belonging within the organisation. Analysing the findings of her research led McFarlane (2015) to conclude as follows:

> When examining organisational cultures, it is important to examine not only how tasks are shared amongst educators, but more so, how tasks are 'completed together' (Hujala & Eskelinen, 2013, p. 229), which evolves out of a 'culture of collective responsibility' (Rodd, 2013a, p. 48). Examination of educators' relationships in this study revealed the multi-directional nature of relationships amongst educators employed within the same centre and between centres, as well as between the educators and the Head Office, and how these relationships contributed to the development of positive organisational cultures. (p. 56)

It is also recommended that readers reflect on the how the organisational culture influences the initiation and implementation of changes within the EC setting—this could involve changes in personnel, routines, building design, program development and accreditation status. Building trust through making small changes to policies, procedure or basic routines can contribute to strengthening relationships among staff as well as with children and their families. McFarlane's study also demonstrated the importance of effective communication strategies between different layers of the organisation in creating a sense of belonging and that 'the sense of attachment to the centres, and the development of inclusive and team oriented organisational cultures can influence the delivery of quality services to children and families' (McFarlane, 2015, p. 68).

chapter 8 looks more specifically at organisational change.

LEADERS IN PRACTICE 10.2

Angela Chng

Early Childhood Teacher and Team Leader, Mia Mia Child and Family Study Centre, Sydney (NSW)

Visit Oxford Ascend to hear more from Angela.

I completed my diploma in EC in Singapore and came to Sydney to complete my undergraduate studies as an international student. In order to gain a better understanding of the cultural shift I had to make in becoming a teacher here, I worked as a casual staff at various centres while completing my studies. I came to realise each centre had its own culture and pedagogy and can differ greatly between contexts. I was employed as an EC teacher room leader with the three to fives upon graduation at the community-based centre. During that time, I was given space to explore the responsibilities of my role as a teacher and how I would shape the curriculum. As a new teacher, I was mentored in developing principles around working with families and staff and learnt how to articulate my thinking and pedagogy. I also began my professional journey as a supervising teacher to students who were undertaking their EC degrees and diplomas. These first few years as a full-time EC teacher laid the foundations of my future work with children, families, staff, students, volunteers and community.

I decided to take on part-time postgraduate studies after a few years, completing a Master of EC while working full-time. I saw upgrading my knowledge as an important aspect of being a teacher—an opportunity to consolidate some of my learning and to extend my pedagogical thinking and values. It was an opportunity to re-engage with theoretical understandings and because of my practical experiences and encounters I was able to make connections between theory and practice. After a semester of my postgraduate studies, I began working at Mia Mia Child and Family Study Centre at Macquarie University, Sydney as the EC teacher team leader of the three to fives room.

Mia Mia has a threefold vision; teaching, research and community. Carrying out my responsibilities and being accountable to this vision is part and parcel of my everyday work. I was challenged with my perspectives and beliefs not only about teaching but the EC sector in general. We believe in investing in qualifications of staff as a factor that contributes to quality education. Hence, every classroom has a degree-qualified (or higher) EC teacher as the team leader, leading each classroom. Our centre director, Wendy Shepherd, has a vision for Mia Mia to work towards a teaching team of teachers. Hence, staff are encouraged to upgrade themselves with the assurance there is a career pathway, where their employment will continue with their new qualifications. We are now seeing through our fourth staff member upgrading from a diploma to a teaching degree.

I was the first team leader who had to rethink how the room will work and look like with two degree-qualified teachers in the same classroom. With my knowledge and understanding of responsibilities of an EC teacher, I was able to create a framework that envisioned how team teaching and leadership would happen in our room. I took on the role of a mentor, supporting the neophyte teacher in her new role, setting goals with her and pacing the responsibilities she had to undertake as an EC teacher. During this time of team teaching, it was clear maintaining the role of the team leader held by the more experienced teacher is still an essential part of what makes it successful. I have always believed in the importance of investing in people: colleagues, volunteers and students. My vision and philosophy in establishing team teaching in my room is not about one teacher now having to 'step down' or where 'responsibility is now less for each teacher'; rather, it means 'our plate has become bigger' as the neophyte teacher now has to 'step up' and the quality of our work with children and families should also grow. Our team teaching experience should signify double the joy, double the thinking, double the perspectives—bringing more depth to the curriculum and working towards a seamless flow in our accountability and challenges to the school's vision.

Being just as observant as I am with children, to understand what the neophyte teacher's strengths and areas to work on are, to learn about their pedagogical goals and then developing shared goals towards the room's vision to support them in their achievements and progress helps them to know what is expected and what to work towards. Knowing when to do some hand-holding (coaching) and when to let go is important—mentoring should develop from a coaching relationship to a peer mentoring one. This includes evaluating a situation after it has occurred; at times playing the devil's advocate; and knowing and understanding how the other person would like to be supported. Being generous with my time, knowledge and experiences, unpacking decision-making processes, and explaining why and how things are handled and evaluated will enable the neophyte teacher to understand better.

Growing in leadership must be supported with opportunities for professional development. Our annual staff retreats—attending conferences, workshops and presentations—have contributed in extending my pedagogical thinking and perspectives. Sharing my work at our annual Pedagogical Dialogues day (also known as Open Day) with the EC sector; during visits from local, national and international visitors to our school; through in-house and sector-specific publications and professional presentations; and opportunities to give lectures and tutorials to teacher education students have extended my skills and wealth of knowledge. A willingness to learn, to be thrown into the deep end, to take critical feedback with humility and grace, to stand up for my opinions and values, and to be open to differing opinions, feedback and perspectives are dispositions I continue to work on.

Pause–reflect–act 10.10

Read Angela Chng's profile in Leaders in practice 10.2. Angela is the ECT team leader at Mia Mia Child and Family Study Centre. In her profile, she discusses how she has grown and developed as a teacher and how she was supported and mentored along the way. Why do you think she has remained committed to the sector? In terms of Angela's own career and her work with other neophyte teachers, reflect on the following:

- What strategies is she using that are effective in increasing her own job satisfaction level as well as that of the staff she works with?
- How has the vision and philosophy at Mia Mia supported this job satisfaction?
- What types of professional learning would you use to support Angela if you were the leader of the program?

Go to oxfordascend *to hear Angela's thoughts.*

Creating an ethical workplace and organisational culture can support staff in their work with children, families and the community. The intentional leader is pivotal in creating this ethos where staff feel valued, wanted and happy to come to work every day.

Chapter summary

It is essential to quality human resource management to create a culture within the EC organisation that respects diversity and understands the importance of recruitment, retention and professional learning, which includes mentoring and coaching. Sound human resource policies ensure transparency and situate all decisions within an ethical frame that meets the philosophical beliefs of the organisation. Creating an effective workplace will have a positive impact on quality outcomes for children and families utilising the setting. Intentional leaders play a pivotal role in creating these effective workplaces for EC staff.

Key references

Bretherton, T. (2010). *Developing the childcare workforce. Understanding 'fight' or 'flight' amongst workers*. Workplace Research Centre, Sydney: University of Sydney.

This report reinforces the importance of developing a well-qualified staff in EC settings. It provides a thorough examination of workforce development and productivity strategies being used by innovative employers in Australia who are committed to recruiting highly skilled staff.

Bryant, L & Gibbs, L. (2013). *A director's manual: Managing an early education and care service in NSW.* Sydney (NSW): Community Childcare Ltd.

Although primarily aimed at settings in New South Wales, this resource outlines key aspects of being a director of an early education and care service, including managing staff.

Jones, C., Hadley, F. & Johnstone, M. (2017). Retaining early childhood teachers: What factors contribute to high job satisfaction in early childhood settings in Australia? *New Zealand International Research in Early Childhood Education*, 20(2), 1–18.

This article outlines Catherine Jones's research on the job satisfaction of EC educators completed as a Masters of Research thesis. There are key findings/strategies that are worth considering for leaders who want to nurture and retain their staff.

Rohrmann, T. & Emilsen, K. (2015). Editorial for the special edition on men in early childhood. *European Early Childhood Education Research Journal*, 23(3), 295–301, doi:10.1080/1350293X.2015.1043804.

This is a special edition dedicated to research on men in EC and is of interest to those wanting to know more about the challenges of hiring men in EC settings as a global issue.

Online resources

Children's Services Central

This has excellent resources to support leaders in EC. It is also a training agency.

www.cscentral.org.au

St Luke's Innovative Resources

Visit this website for strengths-based resources that can be used with staff in EC settings.

www.innovativeresources.org

11 RELATIONSHIPS WITH FAMILIES

CHAPTER LEARNING OBJECTIVES

After studying this chapter you will understand that:

- Educators have a responsibility to develop authentic relationships with families, and to do this professionally and sensitively.
- Educators and families share the responsibility of educating and nurturing children's sense of identity and well-being, and fostering their learning and development.
- Facing challenges in relationship building can create opportunities to forge meaningful relationships.
- Families are diverse culturally, as well as in structure, level of engagement and desire to communicate.
- Intentional leaders establish a culture of building relationships between educators and families.
- Intentional leaders ensure policies and processes allow for educators to build relationships with families.
- Respectful and meaningful relationships between families, children and educators are integral to EC programs and benefit children's sense of belonging.

Key concepts

collaboration
decision-making
professional boundary
respectful relationships

Overview

Families are integral to an EC program and building relationships with families is vital to the education and nurturing of children. The development of authentic relationships between staff and families leads to enrichment of the program with positive outcomes for children. In some settings there can be a 'them' and 'us' culture as staff and families attempt to forge respectful and productive relationships. The intentional leader needs to be aware of, actively promote, and value the multiplicity of ways that relationships with families and staff can grow and evolve. This requires the intentional leader to develop authentic and professional approaches to working with families. How the intentional leader welcomes families into the EC 'learning community' has an impact on the tenor of the relationships built.

Introduction

Contemporary families in Australia experience life very differently from the way families did just 50 years ago. Families face pressures from relatives, friends, neighbours, professionals and the media (print and digital) about how to raise their children. Added to this are the diverse structures of contemporary families, comprising different mixes of men, women and children beyond the traditional nuclear heterosexual family of Mum, Dad and children. Likewise, societal trends that impact on family lifestyle and well-being—for example, women's increasing participation in the paid workforce, the transient nature of families as they move from place to place for work, and less access to support from extended family—are factors that can have a bearing on the relationships educators build with families. Each relationship will be different based on the circumstances of the family. The nature and type of support and resources families require can vary at different points in time. Building relationships with families provides an opportunity to create a learning community, and requires the consideration of diverse viewpoints of staff, families and children.

Building effective, collaborative partnerships with families is the sixth quality area of the National Quality Standard (NQS) (ACECQA, 2017). In the Early Years Learning Framework (DEEWR, 2009), families are regarded as a critical resource for educators. As 'the primary influence in their children's lives' (DEEWR, 2009, p. 103) families can enhance the quality of the EC programs their children attend through their participation in the setting and through information they can share with educators about their children.

refer to chapter 3 for a discussion on the National Quality Standard.

Ensuring families' voices are heard and listened to requires staff to listen and work with families in their settings. For instance, Hadley and Rouse (in press) investigated staff and family perceptions and the practice of staff in establishing family partnerships as described in the NQS and EYLF. They identified a lack of alignment between the educators' practice and beliefs with the families' expectations for the relationship. The study took place in four community-based long day settings in New South Wales and Victoria over a period of time spanning eight years. Hadley and Rouse assert that the relationship (partnership) was one of 'help-giver–help-seeker' with little capacity for reciprocity to be built.

Families come in many diverse forms that vary according to culture, sexuality (gay, lesbian, bisexual, transgender and intersex families), economic status, and nuclear and non-nuclear makeup (single parents, blended families, or adoptive, surrogate or extended families) so there is a lot to be learnt in creating a space for sharing expectations and developing reciprocity. Research shows that many of these diverse family structures do not see their family represented in the resources and discussions used in EC settings and may therefore not feel welcome to 'regular' events (see Cloughessy & Waniganayake, 2014; Robinson, 2002; Skattebol & Ferfolja, 2007). For instance, in their research, Cloughessy and Waniganayake (2015), found that EC centre 'directors felt that they were being inclusive of lesbian-parented families' by not distinguishing families according to their preferred identities (p. 5).

Research, however, suggests that educators need to rethink this approach to family diversity in their settings by encouraging visibility and recognition more explicitly. In this context, it is the responsibility of the intentional leader to influence the organisational culture where staff develop relationships with all families by respecting their preferred identities. Intentional leaders promote a philosophy that situates families within the setting, not outside of it. In a research project conducted with Indigenous families in New South Wales, as a part of the larger Child Care Choices study, families noted they often did not feel like they belonged, felt judged and were concerned about inadequate communication and consultation in terms of management and curriculum decisions (see Bowes et al., 2011). Intentional leaders will develop clear policies in **collaboration** with families, so that there is equity and justice for all, regardless of their differences.

collaboration between staff and families brings different skills, knowledge and experience to a setting. Collaborating with families is essential for children to feel a sense of belonging.

An enabling strategy is to have regular family information sessions for new families. In these sessions the philosophy, policies, pedagogy and expectations for children's education and the shared responsibilities between staff and families and children can be discussed in an authentic and open way. Families have the opportunity to ask questions and talk about their expectations. They will then be able to make a considered choice about the alignment of staff and family expectations and practice before placing their name on the wait list, or not. The opportunity to make a choice promotes mutual respect for each other's expectations and creates a space for more meaningful dialogue: '[F]families state the capacity to form trusting relationships is of key importance, and unlike in other relationships, trust needs to be immediate' (McGrath, 2007, cited in Hadley & Rouse, in press, p. 7.) The relationship between educators and families should be about understanding the shared responsibilities of educating and nurturing children.

chapter 5 has more detail on philosophy and policy development.

Intentional leaders are also committed to employing educators from diverse backgrounds to reflect the families and the community where the EC setting is located. Intentional leaders ensure that program information, forms, policies and resources reflect the diversity of family types. This is done by, for example, using enrolment forms that refer to Parent/Guardian 1, Parent/Guardian 2, Parent/Guardian 2 and so on—rather than only 'mother' and 'father'—to reflect respect for children who live with lesbian or gay parents (Cloughessey & Waniganayake, 2011) or who may be fostered, adopted, living with grandparents or in an extended or blended family. When working with families, educators can form relationships not only with parents but also with the extended circle of family and friends, including grandparents and other key persons such as neighbours who may serve as emergency contacts for the child. It is imperative that the intentional leader supports educators to be inclusive in their interactions with those identified as important people by a child's family. Such diversity should be valued and can provide a rich mosaic of relationships and the ability to work closely and respectfully together. Welcoming and making Aboriginal and Torres Strait Islander (ATSI) families comfortable is another important consideration.

chapter 9 has more discussion on employing educators from diverse backgrounds.

Families with complex experiences

Families today increasingly look to the EC setting to provide:

- a place for their child to be cared for while they work or study. Families rely on EC settings as women increasingly participate in the paid workforce (see Brennan, 1998; Pocock, 2003)
- a place for their child to be educated. Brain research has highlighted the importance of the child's environment in the early years. These findings support the notion that EC development is critical and shapes a child for life (see Linke, 2000; McCain et al., 2007; Shonkoff & Phillips, 2000; Shore, 2001).

- parenting support due to the increased isolation of families from other family members/community networks. Traditional supports once available to parents of young children through grandparents, for example, are increasingly scarce or non-existent (see Brennan, 1998; Penn, 2005; Pocock, 2003).

The complex lives and experiences of today's families were highlighted in Hadley's (2007a) PhD study, which investigated the level of shared perspectives and meaningful participation between families in diverse situations and their EC setting. In Phase One of this research study, Hadley studied in depth three families who each had a three-year-old child attending an urban EC setting in Australia. These families comprised an Aboriginal and Torres Strait Islander family; a culturally and linguistically diverse family; and a family wherein the father had a physical illness. The study found that all three families felt an immense sense of responsibility for the care and education of their child. This felt responsibility related to the financial and emotional pressures of providing for their child and was exacerbated by the high expectations the families placed on themselves to be the best providers they could. The families all discussed how work and/or study commitments were perceived as essential in providing now and/or in the future for their child. The families outlined how their work and study commitments affected their ability to maintain a balance because the parenting role impacted on their capacity to mix and socialise regularly, develop their own self-identity and have time away from the commitments of parenting.

This issue of striking a balance in parenting has magnified with the increase in media coverage of the importance of the early years. The pressures families feel in being 'good parents' have been captured by multimillion dollar businesses in the market for parenting resources (Mead, 2007). There has been a proliferation of parenting books and various 'child smart' resources, toys, websites, blogs, classes and even reality television shows (for example, *Supernanny* and *The House of the Little Tiny Tearaways*) in the past 15 years. This focus on parenting raises the question of the role of the EC setting in addressing the needs of families, and subsequently promoting community support channels that will assist parents in dealing with the stresses and issues of bringing up children today. A more recent study conducted by Hadley (2014) in four EC settings in Sydney, involving culturally and linguistically diverse families and EC-degree qualified teachers found that parents with a child in an EC setting still face struggles. For instance, in Hadley's study the parents and teachers 'valued different experiences ... and also disagreed about the level of communication that occurred between' them (p. 91). Intentional EC leaders need to be familiar with this type of research and think about how differences in values and beliefs about children's learning experiences can be addressed better so families can feel supported and valued at the EC setting.

Pause–reflect–act 11.1

- Reflect on your family, the roles and responsibilities of family members and the experiences you had as a child. Do you see differences in your experiences from those of children today?

- Think back to when you decided to be an educator—did you think that supporting and working with families was an integral part of your role? Why or why not?
- Think about the increased pressures on parents to be the best parents they can be. How do you think this impacts on what they want/need from the EC setting? How can the educator appropriately support families while educating and caring for the children?

What does building relationships with families mean?

How does the intentional leader provide a space for relationships to be built with families? Families, as we know, have different stresses, different needs and different opinions on what they want from their EC setting for their child/ren. Families also have their own beliefs and practices as to what they consider is best for their child. These varied experiences and beliefs influence the way a family interacts with the educators in the setting. Also, because of their own beliefs and experiences, educators will relate differently to different families. For example, one may feel an instant rapport with some families (perhaps the ones that think/act/look like them), while feeling unsure or uncomfortable with others (perhaps the ones that do not think/act/look like them).

Moss (2010) speaks about creating 'places of encounter'. He explains this as not 'othering' difference, nor trying to understand or make it the same for all families. When leaders try to make things the same (understand or situate the difference in their world view) they do not open themselves up to other possibilities or other ways of being. To begin to build relationships with families the intentional leader must first value the importance of diversity and alternative ways of thinking. The leader needs to feel confident and be able to articulate the setting's philosophy and the policies that reflect these values, and provide space and time for relationships to be created and nurtured. Moss (2009) discusses the need for EC settings to experiment, which requires educators to be 'open-ended (avoiding closure), open-minded (welcoming the unexpected) and open-hearted (valuing difference)' (p. viii). When leaders open themselves up to this way of building relationships there are many possibilities and opportunities for the families and educators of the setting to be connected.

During the family information session (mentioned above) there is an opportunity to advocate for children and women in regards to the setting's policy of building respectful ethical relationships. Along with advising families of the child protection policy and the related responsibilities of staff being mandatory reporters there is the opportunity to discuss the setting's policy about preventing domestic and family violence with the aim for children to develop respectful, non-biased and ethical relationships with each other, staff and families for now and for the future through critical reflection on behaviour and attitudes. This is a good opportunity to share with families the beliefs and values about EC education and the importance of the EC years as a critical time in a child's life. As children are beginning to explore the complex processes of building ethical **respectful relationships** in different

respectful relationships require the intentional leader to listen, to ask questions and to be open to a variety of ways of working with families.

social contexts, and observe different values and attitudes this is the opportunity to share understandings about this process at home and in the EC setting.

The most important element of relationship building is being aware of gender bias or gender inequity. Robinson (2013), in her research about children's knowledge of the relationships they live with and are witness to, posits that 'parents can underestimate their children's capacity to understand information about sexuality and relationships' (p. 131). Therefore it is valid to consider that 'building a society that is more critically reflective about gendered and sexual relationships, and that contributes to new cultural norms of non-violence and ethical relationships, needs to begin in EC' (p. 131). To support staff in EC settings to understand the issues that impact on children's relationship building, and to assist them in working with children to critically reflect on the processes, Early Childhood Australia (ECA) developed three online learning modules for staff in EC settings to complete at their own pace (see the links to online resources at the end of the chapter).

While this policy and strategy at first glance may appear not relevant to an EC setting, important insights can be gained from stopping to listen and reflect on the language children use in their relationships with their families and peers. Gender bias is evident in everyday conversations and play scenarios. The lack of respect for family members can also be evident in certain situations, including drop-off and pick-up times. For instance, families may tolerate the way their child interacts with them at these times, but the EC staff may feel awkward if they see the child's interaction as being disrespectful to the family member(s). This raises the question of who is responsible in this situation. Should the staff say something or intervene? Does the family recognise the interaction as disrespectful but are worried how to respond when the EC staff are present? Hadley and Rouse (in press, p. 4) argue that interpreting the EYLF and NQS guidelines about relationships with families is 'potentially problematic' as much depends on how the guidelines are interpreted. Moving beyond the definition of partnership, the leader should be invested in promoting that family relationship in the setting and outside of the setting are ethical and mutually respectful.

It is the leader's responsibility to ensure there is a mutual understanding about the importance of working with families. It may seem a small step to intervene when a child acts disrespectfully towards their family member, or when a child says to another, 'you can't play here'. It is never too soon to begin the process of sharing the understanding of developing ethical and respectful relationships with young children. Consider Robinson's (2016) research with young children and her proposal to start in EC, in partnership with families, to look more critically at the way children are learning about building relationships. This shared responsibility consolidates a meaningful relationship when tackling difficult issues together, with the common goal of building respectful community relationships, now and into the future. This also moves forward the understanding that relationships with parents should include the children and staff in an authentic and meaningful way to transcend the notion of 'help-seeker and help-giver' (Hadley & Rouse in press, p. 5). *These complexities are referred to by Carrie Rose, who discusses in Leaders in practice 11.1 how they build authentic relationships with the diverse families and children that attend her centre.*

LEADERS IN PRACTICE 11.1

Carrie Rose

Owner and Pedagogical Leader, Rosie's Early Learning Centre, Logan (QLD)

As we are a small centre, each educator develops relationships with all children from all the rooms. We believe that this creates a community feeling in the centre and gives children and families opportunities to have a relationship with each team member. The children's primary educators generally develop the strongest relationships. However, over the years we have observed how children and families develop strong relationships with educators from previous years and these continue to evolve throughout their stay at Rosie's.

Children with diverse learning needs, complex situations (including significant court order requirements) and diverse cultural requirements enter our service. Our philosophy recognises that children's sense of agency is promoted when children feel a sense of belonging and this is evident throughout the centre where family photos adorn walls and family members are welcomed and strongly encouraged into the program.

The 'Emerging image of the Child' form* is used to document when children require this individualised thinking and planning. Examples of this are how to best support a child if the child's parents have significant court orders; or the child is suffering from a heightened separation anxiety; or the child's self-regulation skills are not yet fully developed. This individualised planning system has been developed to provide children with the support needed and as a tool for communication with families and other educators. The plans may be ongoing or they may just be short term and we see this as an important factor in supporting the skills for lifelong learning. Secondly, we also provide support for the parents. For example, when a child begins at the centre after the family has moved into a women's domestic violence shelter. These children and women flee from their homes with not much other than the clothes they are wearing. On starting at the centre, we organise a collection for the family in confidence. This could be clothing, books and toys for the children and something like toiletries for the mother. We donate these to the families to help them regain some control over their lives.

A sense of belonging is facilitated through a range of experiences including rituals or routines at the centre and others that are spontaneous. Collaboration occurs in small and large group projects to allow children and families to develop shared knowledge and pleasure in learning. Many projects initiated individually lead to collaborative play, research and investigation by larger groups of children. The research that educators complete when developing the Statement of Intent* reflects the emotional well-being of children at all times. As this is shared with family feedback and input, the approach of holistic lifelong learning becomes more apparent and understood.

Educators also engage the children in relaxation techniques such as yoga, meditation and reflective walks to further share with children strategies that can help our bodies relax. The children are encouraged to communicate their feelings, share their ideas verbally and listen to and acknowledge the feelings and ideas of others. This enables children particularly from non–English-speaking backgrounds to communicate and find 'their way' to develop a sense of belonging in the community at Rosie's.

Building children's capacity to reflect on issues of equity is also important. Engaging children in a framework of thinking about their actions and responses around fairness, kindness and safety is embedded into the centre's practice. Children's assumptions about gender, ability and cultural norms are gently challenged and scaffolded to enable children to view situations from a variety of points of view. Equity and fairness is discussed, explored and developed in conjunction with the children to ensure all children are treated respectfully. For example, a child who was biologically a girl was beginning to make decisions to be a boy. It was evident that these feelings were very strong and we began working with the child and the family by acknowledging this, and providing emotional support and relevant information to the mother, to enable her to better support her child. The child developed a very strong sense of self-worth and has transitioned into school seamlessly with the support of her family, Rosie's and the school. Follow-up with the family was made once the child started school to enquire if we could offer any other assistance in adapting to school.

At Rosie's, we foster a loving and caring environment in which each child is valued and respected as an individual. This environment builds the trusting relationships on which all further interactions are based. Vygotsky's theory of how children find the 'More Knowledgeable Other' (MKO) to learn new information drives our thinking of collaborative learning and how we can continue to assist the children to find their 'MKO'. This will look different for each child and we understand that we are not always going to be this 'MKO' in their lives.

(*Note: for anyone wanting more information about these documents please contact the centre through its website: www.rosiesel.com.au).

Pause–reflect–act 11.2

Think about EC settings you have worked in.

- What indicators were there to demonstrate the centre's philosophy on respecting family diversity?
- How were families of different backgrounds, religions, structures (for example, gay and lesbian, blended, adoptive, extended) welcomed and honoured in these settings?
- Were all families heard or were some silenced? Why?
- What proactive role did the staff in leadership roles take in developing these relationships and connections with families?

Respectful, authentic and professional relationships

Creating respectful and authentic relationships requires a leader to rethink the parent partnership paradigm. Historically, partnerships with families were defined by the level of involvement a family had with the EC setting. Rethinking the parent partnership paradigm, however, requires a shift from focusing on participation or educating families in ways that may not be authentic (for example, preparing food or handing out parent pamphlets without discussion) to building genuine connections and creating space to nurture a sense of belonging and reciprocity. For example, consider what it might mean to have centre policies that state:

- We have an open door policy.
- All families are welcome.
- We respect diversity.
- We implement an anti-bias curriculum.

Do these statements necessarily create a space for meaningful dialogue, authentic relationships, a sense of belonging and reciprocity? Or do these types of statements create a space to inform families about what is done (see Crowburn, 1986; Giovacco-Johnson, 2009; Hadley, 2012; Hadley & Rouse, in press)? How might you open up the setting (through your philosophy/policies and actions) to families to create new possibilities or relationships? For ideas or suggestions on how to achieve the requirements of the NQS, Quality Area 6, 'collaborative partnerships with families and communities' (ACECQA, 2011c), refer to Hadley and De Gioia (2010).

Authors such as Hughes and MacNaughton (2001) argue that building relationships with families is complex and often problematic for EC staff. For example, in one of their research studies Hughes and MacNaughton (2002) highlighted the tension that occurred between staff and families when they were communicating with parents. The different viewpoints on particular practices can contribute to these tensions. For example, there could be a diversity of opinions on the implementation of a play-based curriculum or educational activities; how to manage children's behaviour; or approaches to toilet training, feeding and sleeping practices (De Gioia, 2009; Gonzalez-Mena, 2001; Hand & Wise, 2006; MacNaughton & Hughes, 2011). However, if staff value these differences and want to move beyond an 'us versus them' perspective when working with families, there needs to be a place for open, honest, non-judgmental dialogue that can help build these connections, examine tensions and promote discussion about differences of beliefs and values.

Creating a sense of belonging in the program requires commitment from leaders and time for educators to explore their own values and beliefs and how these impact on their interactions with families. An 18-month research project conducted for Families First NSW by Gowrie NSW (Families First NSW, 2007) involved collaborations with parents (both users and non-users of EC programs), children and staff in 16 children's services (long day care, preschool, occasional care and family day care), as well as staff from eight community agencies. This study found that educators working with families of cultural and linguistic diversity required training in cultural competency (Hadley, 2007c). The EYLF (DEEWR, 2009) emphasises the importance of staff understanding diversity. For example, one of the practices includes cultural competence. This is described as educators who are culturally competent respecting multiple cultural ways of knowing, seeing and living, celebrating the benefits of diversity and having an ability to understand and honour differences (DEEWR, 2009, p. 16).

Pause–reflect–act 11.3

Think about the examples of practices below—where do you think you fit on the continuum and why? What has influenced your beliefs and values: family, experience, workplace and/or study? Think about the families you may work with. Where do you think they may fit on the continuum and why?

Play-based learning .... vs .... formal structured learning

Should children have choices within a play-based focus or should the educator program and plan experiences that focus on academic learning taught by rote and with stencils?

Expressive emotions .... vs .... controlled emotions

Should children be encouraged to express their emotions and talk about their feelings or should children learn to control their feelings and try to fit into the group?

Future oriented ....vs .... present oriented

Should you program for the long-term goals of the children you teach (what you want them to achieve) or should your program reflect the short-term wants, needs and interests of the children and/or families?

Scheduled planning ....vs .... flexible planning

Should your program have a formal routine that is based solely on pre-planned experiences or should your program be more flexible and based on activities that meet children's needs?

Source: Adapted from Hadley, 2007c.

Research has also highlighted the importance of providing informal get-togethers for families and educators (Hayden et al., 2005). These informal meetings have been found to break down the barriers to families and create spaces for families to chat to the educators in a less formal manner. In a New South Wales families research project (Hadley, 2007a), 80 per cent of the families interviewed indicated they wanted to attend social events offered by the EC setting as they saw it as an avenue to make connections with other families as well as see their child in an environment with other children. Worryingly, in this same study 12 per cent of educators said they had no opportunity to talk with other families who used the same setting. Hayden et al. (2005) found that the centre directors had a crucial role to play in facilitating informal get-togethers, and when families were involved in the **decision-making** processes at the settings their participation rates increased.

decision-making intentional leaders make decisions after listening to families and considering the philosophy underpinning the EC programs at each setting.

Pause–reflect–act 11.4

- Thinking about your setting, what sorts of opportunities have you seen being provided to families to meet informally?
- Why do you think this is an important way of breaking down the barriers to open up communication channels for families (especially those from diverse backgrounds and family structures)?
- What do you think the leader can do to create a culture where families feel welcomed and want to contribute to their setting?

Creating a partnership with a family begins before they enrol their child in the setting. It includes how the family is treated on the phone when they make that first call asking about any vacancies at your setting for their child; how they are then welcomed on their first visit; how they and their child are oriented to the program; how the staff communicate with the family from day one about their child; how the staff check in with the family once they have started; how the staff invite families to participate; how the staff deal with tensions and conflicts of practices; and how the staff support the family in times of crisis or need. Creating connections with families is an evolving process and requires the leader to develop these skills with the staff. As Tobin, Arzubiaga and Figueroa Fuentes (2007) state:

> For ECEC programmes to promote diversity and social inclusion, they need greater understanding of the cultural backgrounds and social worlds of the families of the children they serve, and greater communication between practitioners and parents. (p. 34)

Diversity within relationships

There is no one way to create partnerships with families. Some families will be very involved and engaged with the setting and educators, and other families will seem more distant or disengaged. Leaders need to build a culture within their settings where it is accepted that families can participate in different ways. This requires leaders to instil in the educators that participation in itself is not a partnership and that families have a right to choose how they are involved in the setting. It also requires leaders to allow educators to understand that it is acceptable to give more attention to some families at different times (Hadley & De Gioia, 2008). Hadley (2010) argues that this requires leaders to position building partnerships as an equity issue where each family is treated individually. This requires leaders to be proactive and aware of any critical issues families are facing and provide the opportunity to discuss these issues in ways that are participatory, non-judgmental and mutually respectful for all parties.

A New South Wales Families First project (Benevolent Society, 2008) conducted by the Benevolent Society and Gowrie NSW worked with 45 educators (comprising centre directors and teachers) in three regions of Sydney. As part of the project the participants were asked to rethink how they built partnerships with the families that they were not so connected with. Some examples of what these educators did included the following:

> In one long day care centre they had a recently separated family. Mum always did the drop off/pick up so they had a good relationship with her. Mum was trying to bad mouth Dad to staff but the staff stayed neutral, steering conversations away from this by using active listening techniques, cutting off etc. The director contacted Dad by phone and asked if he wanted to be added to the email list regarding his children. Next time he came in he smiled, took his time instead of rushing away and really appreciated being included.
>
> In one occasional care centre they were not seeing Mum very often, as the child's grandmother usually did the drop off. The child had intense special needs and the service was struggling with ways to provide support to complement other support Mum was receiving. Staff were concerned that Mum was very down about all the negative feedback she was receiving from specialists. To show her some positives the service took a photo of the child doing 'rock a bye bear' and made it into a photo board of the child's achievement. The teacher dropped it off on her way home (as Mum works in the shopping mall where the centre is located). She was very appreciative of the effort the service had gone to, as well as getting some positive feedback about her child. The mum is now sharing the specialist information with them and feels as though she is 'getting somewhere' with her child. (Benevolent Society & Lady Gowrie Child Centre NSW, 2007)

Most families dread receiving a phone call from the EC setting as it usually means something is wrong or their child is sick or has been hurt. Imagine changing this paradigm by providing other avenues for families and staff to connect with each other. Other ways of building connections with families could include phoning the family or sending them an email/note to share a positive story of what their child did that day. Increasing the frequency of sharing 'positive' news with parents about how their child spent the day at the setting can assist in strengthening partnerships with families. By opening up to these possibilities we are making sure that every child in the program is being provided the best care and education.

Pause–reflect–act 11.5

Think about your workplace. How does the intentional leader ensure that educators:

- treat families on an individual basis, with particular needs, interests and capabilities?
- balance the time it takes to build relationships with all families and give extra support to those families as and when they need it?
- are supported to determine which families need extra support?

Have you seen other ways intentional leaders have established a culture of building connections with families?

Collaboration and decision-making processes

Creating a trusting space so that families feel comfortable to share and discuss their needs and issues is important to building close connections with families. Creating spaces for collaboration and decision-making processes are complicated aspects of relationship building with families. The type of management structure of the setting (such as community-based, corporate, private, cooperative or faith-based) means there will be different expectations of families in terms of being involved in the decision-making processes. For example, owners of a privately owned setting will not necessarily have a parent management committee that makes decisions about staffing (recruitment, hiring and firing), whereas in a community-based setting the parent management committee would be involved in these processes.

The philosophy of the setting will impact on how decisions are made and shared with families. Families can contribute to the program and offer insightful ways of thinking about aspects of the curriculum or responsibilities of managing the setting. Families can be strong advocates when seeking improved funding and regulations for EC services. For instance parents can become involved in campaigns that lobby governments. See, for instance, the 'Parenthood' website, which is a place where families and educators can work together on improving EC access and equity (www.theparenthood.org.au/about). Aspects to consider in involving families in these broader conversations and directions of the setting are which families have a voice and why; and how can intentional leaders ensure that all families are included and can contribute to these decisions?

see chapter 6 for more discussion about pedagogically based curriculum.

Resolving how decisions are made about individual children because of requests from a family can create connections and/or tensions. It is imperative that educators are able to articulate the pedagogically based curriculum decisions they make, in accordance with the centre's philosophy. Educators need to first listen carefully and hear what the family is saying/raising. Second, educators must feel confident enough and supported by their leaders to disagree if a family's request does not align with the philosophy and pedagogy of the setting. For example, research with diverse families (Adair & Tobin, 2008; De Gioia, 2003, 2009; Hadley, 2007a, 2007b, 2007c) illustrates that many immigrant families are focused on their child succeeding in the country where they are now living and do not see the importance of reflecting the child's home language or culture in the EC setting (Hadley, 2007b). This means that some families from diverse backgrounds want the setting to 'teach and reflect' the dominant cultural ways of knowing and learning so that their children can succeed without feeling constrained by their family cultural backgrounds. For example, one father stated that what he wanted was 'a figure of a teacher who says yes/no and tells them what they can and can't do. Teach him for school' (Hadley, 2007a, p. 148). In comparison, in the same research study, staff were focused on providing choices (co-constructing knowledge with children), building relationships and encouraging children to initiate their own learning (Hadley, 2007a). Examining these differing perspectives of the curriculum highlights some of the tensions that can arise between some families and the setting.

Pause–reflect–act 11.6

Read the following scenarios and reflect on what you would do and why.

- You ask a family to write down some key words in their child's home language and, one month later, you still have not received a reply.
- A family asks the educators for a school readiness program (including writing their name, cutting with scissors and completing maths and literacy worksheets) to be implemented for their four-year-old child.
- A family asks you not to allow their son to dress up in the princess outfit or play in the dress-up area.
- A family asks that their three-year-old son not sleep at the centre during the day. The staff have tried to meet the family's request but often struggle keeping him awake.

Professional boundaries

EC educators can struggle with balancing the line between being professional and developing connections, relationships and partnerships with families. This tension arises in scenarios such as attending birthday parties, meeting families on weekends, exchanging phone contacts, dropping children home and babysitting. Leaders establish expectations about these issues; for example, some settings do not allow staff to do babysitting, whereas others do, but may ask the family to sign a confidentiality contract. The arrangement the setting develops will be strongly influenced by the context and community they are situated in. For example, in a small rural setting where there is only one EC setting the staff will be highly visible in the community and more than likely mixing with families at social events. A setting in a large city may mean the staff live outside of the local community and are unlikely to mix with families at social events; or the setting provides transport and this may mean a staff member drives or is on the bus that collects the children from their home.

Other professionals, such as social workers, build debriefing into their work to ensure that the social worker can maintain a **professional boundary** and discuss issues with their workplace supervisor. What can EC leaders do to ensure the line between staff personal/private lives and workplace relations is not blurred? Leaders may be called on to support staff who may have families disclosing personal issues such as:

— a marriage break-up
— the family business going into bankruptcy
— the family home being repossessed
— domestic violence in the family
— wanting to have their child assessed for learning difficulties.

This is where it is important that a leader has established links with appropriate agencies that can support families facing complex family issues. It is important that leaders support staff by debriefing as needed and also by helping staff to understand their role is not to solve family problems but to empower families to seek support from appropriate community agencies.

professional boundary
intentional leaders need to create a culture that supports staff to build respectful relationships with families that have clear boundaries and expectations of each other.

the role of working with the community is discussed further in chapter 12.

As an experienced EC teacher who has worked in three states—Queensland, New South Wales and the Northern Territory—**Benjamin Walker** has encountered children from diverse family backgrounds. *In Leaders in practice 11.2, Ben reflects on these experiences and shares his thoughts about what is important when working with culturally diverse families.*

LEADERS IN PRACTICE 11.2

Benjamin Walker

Early Childhood Consultant and Teacher, Cairns (QLD)

My experiences of working with children and families from diverse cultural backgrounds stem from directing EC services in Sydney, Darwin and Cairns as well as years of experience in various roles working with Indigenous EC services. Some immigrant and refugee families come from countries that don't have formal EC services like we have in Australia. Generally, when families are not familiar with EC settings it may mean they are less likely to engage with educators about their child's learning. For example, language barriers may prevent some parents from seeking the information and supports they need. Things get more complicated when vulnerable families present with complex issues and require special supports both within and outside the EC setting.

Another issue, while not exclusive to culturally diverse families, is that of engaging fathers. In many cultures it is still women who are seen in that traditional role of looking after children. Getting dads more involved in their child's learning is often best tackled by letting mums know that dad is welcome and his role is equally valid and valued by the service. It is good for dads to see representations of men in the service, so I always encourage families to bring in photos of fathers and their children engaged at home and put them up. It's good to try and make fathers feel more comfortable participating in the service by asking them how they would like to be better involved with their children's learning and education.

Working well with culturally diverse families also has benefits for everyone. If you run a service that is capable of encouraging all children to be tolerant and develop positive attitudes towards people of any origin or background, then that in itself is a very good thing long-term. After all, today's children in EC settings will grow up to live, go to school and work with people from diverse cultures; respecting each other's identities is the foundation of a harmonious multicultural society.

EC leaders wanting to work better with culturally diverse families may like to consider the following:

- *Train all staff to be culturally competent.* Children and families will have a better experience if all educators are equipped with appropriate knowledge and understanding of how to work in respectful and culturally inclusive ways.
- *Address families' language barriers.* The strategies you choose are context dependent. In some settings, I've found employing bilingual staff to be hugely beneficial. Making resources available to families in their language is also something parents truly appreciate. In Indigenous settings, I simply could not get by without the contribution of the community's cultural support workers.

- *Place a high value on creating a sense of belonging.* When you go out of your way to ensure that a child's culture is respected and celebrated, the service's relationship with the family will grow. There's a lot you can do to make sure children and families feel welcome and that they belong at your service. For example, make sure the program is flexible in meeting a family's unique needs. Ensure the links are there to community services and agencies that can assist families and make things easier, and ensure the child's culture is encouraged and represented within the service.

Pause–reflect–act 11.7

Think about both of the 'Leaders in practice' profiles in this chapter.

- Can you identify their philosophies in building relationships with families?
- What are the similarities and differences?
- What is your approach to building relationships with families?
- What skills and strategies do you need to enact your approach?

Online communication

Another area that contemporary EC leaders have to consider is the use of electronic media and online technology to communicate with families and among colleagues. This includes the use of a variety of applications that can be accessed through mobile phones, tablets and computers. In discussing the pros and cons of online communication, Rodd (2013) expresses that caution is essential, for instance, when using email:

> As with verbal communication, good email communication is about sending messages in the most appropriate manner at the most appropriate time. Email is a tool for improving communication, but it also can be used as a weapon if the message shows lack of concern for the recipient. Inappropriate use of email can cause pressure on people that produces stress, overload and resentment. (p. 99)

Access to and use of electronic communication strategies requires thorough investigation within each setting so that clear expectations are worked out to support staff and families. Issues regarding privacy and confidentiality in terms of who has access to the mailing lists and the content covered—as well as when, why and who sends out emails from a particular workplace setting—are important points for discussion by educators and parents.

Likewise, with the increasing popularity of Facebook and other social networking sites, questions are being asked about how these sites should be used and interacted with. However, as this is an emerging issue the empirical research is limited. Interestingly, the Facebook discussion in the school sector is related to relationships between teachers and students. For example, the Queensland government's Department of Education and Training has mandated that teachers are not to associate with their students on social network sites (as cited in Weaver, 2010, p. 26; www.education.qld.gov.au/corporate/codeofconduct/pdfs/

refer to Chapter 9 for more information on using social media in EC settings.

det-code-of-conduct-standard-of-practice.pdf). Other issues relate to how teachers manage a professional and personal presence on these sites (see Robards, 2010). The discussion about families and teachers 'befriending' each other does not seem to be emphasised in the EC sector. Questions to ponder further include whether it is appropriate for families and educators to be 'friends' on Facebook; and what the implications are of these friendships outside of the setting? These need to be thought about carefully by EC leaders. Many of these electronic programs have the ability to communicate with families about their child's day. As this is an emerging area, again, there is limited research. Anecdotally we do know that many EC settings are using these programs and are working through ethical questions such as:

- Where is the children's information stored (for example, on a setting's server or in the cloud)?
- What aspects of these records are visible to other educators in the setting and why?
- What records are shared with families?
- How can the sharing of information/records encourage communication between educators and families—for example, what are the expectations?

EC educators must act as responsible digital citizens in the way they collect and disseminate information about children's play to their own families, as well as others, in respectful ways. Given the complexities and unforeseen aspects of dealing with online communication, educators are strongly encouraged to actively seek opportunities, learn relevant skills and knowledge, and keep up-to-date with technology integration in EC settings. The Office of the Children's e-Safety Commissioner, for instance, provides useful resources for both parents and educators on the prevention and protection of children and young people from cyber bullying (www.esafety.gov.au/education-resources). In this way, leaders can play a key role in raising issues about online communication with staff and families, as well as children. Establishing appropriate protocols and policies can help promote online safety and enable everyone involved in the EC setting to make better use of social media communication resources for professional work in ethical ways.

Pause–reflect–act 11.8

Thinking about technologies and ways of harnessing these to build relationships with families will require leaders to think outside the square. In terms of managing these social media sites, reflect on the following:

- What have you experienced personally or professionally?
- How have you seen computer documenting programs work in relationship to building partnerships?
- Collect policies that help define the professional boundaries for staff and families using Facebook. Analyse these critically in terms of developing an online communication policy for use in your own EC setting.
- Do you think it is okay to be friends with families on sites such as Facebook? Why or why not?
- How does the community where you live or work in (for example, rural and remote versus metropolitan) impact on the professional boundaries that exist and why?

Chapter summary

Intentional leaders are fundamental to establishing a program that enables educators to work with children and their families collaboratively as partners. When an organisational culture is created and nurtured that provides opportunities for families and educators to work in partnership and to build mutually respectful and ethical relationships, the children benefit. Creating these partnerships is not always easy and requires intentional leaders to support educators to feel competent to work with families in diverse ways and establish reciprocity. This requires educators to reflect on their practices, open themselves up to other possibilities and feel confident about the pedagogical decisions they make as EC educators as well as avoid a 'them and us' attitude. Educators can become more confident in engaging authentically with families about the real issues that emerge, and to ensure views and expectations are shared and strategies developed collaboratively. Also, as new technologies enter the sector, the issue of how we build and maintain partnerships with families will need to be constantly rethought.

Key references

Bowes, J., Kitson, R., Simpson, T., Reid, J., Smith, M., Downey, B. et al. (2011). *Child care choices of Indigenous families. Research report to the NSW Department of Human Services (Community Services)*. Retrieved from www.iec.mq.edu.au/research/cfrc/research_approaches/vulnerable_and_at-risk_families/child_care_choices_of_indigenous_families.

This report outlines findings from a study conducted with Aboriginal and Torres Strait Islander families in New South Wales. These families were from urban, rural and remote communities and shared their perspectives on EC and school experiences. This report would be useful for educators in EC settings who are passionate about ensuring their setting is inclusive of all families, including Aboriginal and Torres Strait Islander families.

MacNaughton, G. & Hughes, P. (2011). *Parents and professionals in EC settings*. Maidenhead, Berkshire: Open University Press.

This book unpacks much of the authors' research and work with families and staff in EC settings in Australia. It provides ways of thinking and working with families that can challenge norms and help settings implement fair and just policies and practices in terms of building relationships with families.

Robinson, K. (2013). *Innocence, knowledge and the construction of childhood: The contradictory nature of sexuality and censorship in children's contemporary lives*. Routledge: UK.

Kerry Robinson provides an important aspect of children's lives that is usually not acknowledged or is simply taboo and too difficult to talk about, which is that young children really do know more about relationships than we give them credit for. This book would be an excellent resource for staff to assist them in critically reflecting with children about behaviour and attitudes that are discriminatory and not appropriate in building respectful relationships.

Special Taskforce on Domestic and Family Violence in Queensland. (2015). *Not Now Not Ever Report: Putting an end to domestic and family violence in Queensland*. Brisbane.

Chaired by the Honourable Quentin Bryce AD CVO, former governor-general of Australia, the 140 recommendations identified in this report set the vision and direction for Queensland's strategy to end domestic and family violence and ensure those affected have access to safety and support. www.communities.qld.gov.au/gateway/end-domestic-family-violence/about/not-now-not-ever-report

Online resources

Office of the eSafety Commissioner

Influenced by the rising rates of cyberbullying, this Commissioner was established to oversee the online safety of children and young people in Australia. They offer various educational resources and programs for children as well as educators and parents so that these new technologies can be used responsibly to ensure safety for all.

www.esafety.gov.au/about-the-office/role-of-the-office

Preventing family and domestic violence

There are numerous resources and campaigns promoting the prevention of family and domestic violence in Australia. These include 'White Ribbon Day' and 'It Stops Here'. Each state/territory also has information available through various government and non-government agencies and some examples include the following:

Canberra: www.communityservices.act.gov.au/search?query=domestic+and+family+violence

New South Wales: www.domesticviolence.nsw.gov.au

Northern Territory: www.domesticviolence.nt.gov.au

Queensland: www.qld.gov.au/gov/domestic-and-family-violence

South Australia: www.1800respect.org.au/service-support/south-australian-domestic-family-violence-and-sexual-assault-service

Tasmania: www.dhhs.tas.gov.au/site_search?query=violence+counselling+and+support&collection=dhhs-meta

Victoria: www.dvrcv.org.au

Western Australia: https://www.wa.gov.au/search-results.html?cx=013143409236470047600%3Aw3rlsolxaty&q=community+safety+domestic+violence&sa=Search&cof=FORID%3A11

Secretariat of National Aboriginal and Islander Child Care (SNAICC)

On this website you will find the resource *Growing up our way: Aboriginal and Torres Strait Islander child rearing practices matrix* and other supporting documents. These could provide a catalyst for discussion with staff about various approaches to child rearing.

www.snaicc.org.au

Start Early package, from Early Childhood Australia

This professional development package comprises three modules: Respectful Relationships; Gender, Respect and Identity; and Father Inclusive Practice, aimed at preventing domestic and family violence from a long-term perspective. It recognises that behaviours and attitudes established during EC can be carried throughout life, and that EC educators can play a key role in shaping the formation of non-violent, respectful relationships.

http://www.earlychildhoodaustralia.org.au

12 COMMUNITY ENGAGEMENT

CHAPTER LEARNING OBJECTIVES

After studying this chapter you will understand that:

- An intentional leader's role has the potential for building useful connections and coalitions within local and broader communities.
- Intentional EC leaders collaborate effectively with professionals from a range of disciplinary backgrounds and create dynamic groups for various reasons or purposes.
- Leaders need to develop skills and strategies to connect with other professionals, agencies and community members, and build social capital within the community.
- Multidisciplinary programs and teams can promote community connections and successful coalitions.
- There are many ways to develop and build connections both inside and outside of the EC setting.

Key concepts

community
community coalition
connections
multidisciplinary teams
social capital

Overview

EC organisations can be a meeting place for developing effective, supportive and connected communities for children and families. Such places enable community engagement to flourish—to be a two-way process whereby the community is invited in and the setting reaches out to the community. By engaging with local communities, a leader is building knowledge about an understanding of EC education within their community. Building community relationships also enables the organisation to connect with appropriate agencies and others within the wider community. These connections can provide important insights into local contexts and customs and forge relationships between otherwise loosely connected or unconnected people, groups and organisations. The leader's role in creating opportunities for sharing information and resources can provide natural intersections with other community services and support agencies. Research shows that leaders cite building relationships with the community as difficult, primarily due to time pressures and limited resources. This chapter provides strategies that intentional leaders can implement to build and develop sound community relationships. These strategies include community outreach, networking, public forums, advisory committees and media engagement.

What is community engagement?

The EC **community** transcends geography and includes relationships and values in regions, cities, towns, suburbs, neighbourhoods or virtual communities. The area of a community, its size, its location (within a metropolitan or rural region), its natural resources (rivers, flora and fauna) as well as its people and their cultures, histories, languages, religions, and family size and structures, can all influence the nature of interactions and relationships that exist within a community. Community engagement is about building ongoing relationships between people, places, groups and organisations. In this chapter, community engagement is considered to be the **connections** EC leaders form with families, professionals, local groups and organisations for the purpose of achieving better outcomes for children and families. In this way, educators can contribute to the **social capital** of a community in sustainable ways.

community includes all individuals, organisations and groups who connect because of a common purpose.

connections refers to the links and relationships developed within a community, an organisation or a network.

social capital incorporates the trust, reciprocity and networks that contribute to the social wealth and societal well-being created through community engagement.

Robert Putnam, an American political scientist, coined the term 'social capital' (Putnam, 1995). Social capital refers to the social wealth or societal well-being created through community engagement. The social prosperity of a community is reflected in the sense of common identity and sense of belonging perceived by its citizens. The coming together of three key ingredients—namely, trust, reciprocity and networks—enables the creation of social capital (see Figure 12.1). As people meet and get to know each other, relationships and trust can develop and be nurtured over time. Reciprocity, or mutuality, is nurtured when people realise the benefits of the relationship for everyone involved. The existence of networks—both informal (such as book clubs, neighbourhood safety and environmental groups) and formal (such as football/netball clubs, the Country Women's Association and cultural or faith-based organisations)—is symbolic of people coming together because of shared interests, abilities or needs.

Social capital is the 'social fabric' or 'glue' (Putnam, 1995, p. 51) that connects people, creating a sense of community. These interconnections between people enable networking,

Figure 12.1 Key ingredients of social capital

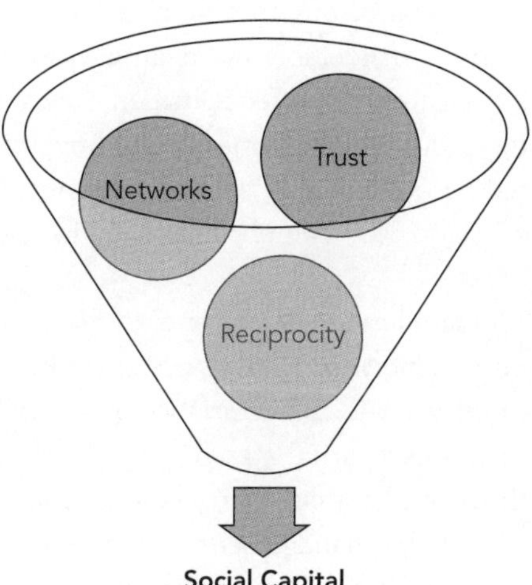

sharing of resources, and feelings of belonging, trust and mutual benefit (Onyx & Bullen, 1998; Putnam, 1995). This focus on mutual benefit can be a catalyst for people to come together to work collaboratively and thereby contribute to a healthier lifestyle for all families and individuals in that community. Pence and Benner (2000) situate this focus within EC settings as 'engagement of the entire community in a dialogue about quality childcare and more generally, about what we as a society want for our children' (p. 365). Moss (2009) sees this type of engagement as enabling an EC setting to be a democratic site where collective choices that are ethical are made possible.

For EC leaders, community engagement involves:

- working with families, staff and the community to establish and continually develop quality EC programs
- working with a range of professionals who also work with young children and their families
- networking with agencies and organisations that support families
- building alliances with key community groups within and beyond the EC sector.

On the one hand, EC settings are ideally placed to facilitate community engagement as they are places of encounter (Moss, 2009) for staff, children, families and community. On the other hand, the extent to which EC settings can be open and accessible to the community that support families to manage or balance their family or workplace responsibilities can, at times, be limited (Tayler et al., 2002). This requires that intentional leaders rethink how they respond to staffing arrangements and regulatory licensing requirements for operating particular program types. Bowes, Hayes and Grace (2009) discuss the positive outcomes for children and families when their needs are equitably included, supported and respected within EC programs. There are benefits also for children's development, health and well-being, which is one of the five outcomes for children described in the Early Years Learning Framework (DEEWR, 2009). We argue that accessing EC settings by children and families is a crucial building block to true community engagement.

see chapters 10 and 11 for more discussion on how to create workplaces that are centred on a 'community of learners' approach and that foster relationships with families.

EC leaders also need to consider the community they are working in. For instance, we know there are vulnerable members of our communities and EC leaders may be working in communities that experience considerable disadvantage. Research has shown that EC programs for vulnerable children are more effective when they are community driven, have qualified educators delivering programs, have meaningful involvement of families, and are integrated with or supported by other family services and health professionals, especially allied health services (Engle et al, 2007; Campbell et al., 2014; Heckman et al., 2010; Siraj-Blatchford & Woodhead 2009).

We know that children and families also experience difficulties in gaining access to high-quality EC settings. Barriers that prevent gaining access to EC settings can be related to the beliefs and attitudes about various characteristics of a family's background including their socio-economic circumstances, marital status, gender or sexual identities, cultural or religious background, health issues, language barriers and disabilities. These attitudes may be reflected both ways—not only by management and staff at the centre, but also by the families themselves, who may not fully understand the importance of EC settings in terms of the learning and development for their children (Ahmad, 2011; Penn, 2005; Streuli et al., 2011). Thus, it is a key role of the EC leader to know their community, and to connect with the agencies and organisations in their community to ensure all children have access to a high-quality EC program. *In Leaders in practice 12.2 we profile Angela Thompson, who is working with diverse stakeholders in her community to develop and sustain access to all its children.* In this way, EC leaders can lead a community coalition to uphold the best interests of all children anywhere.

Involving families, staff and the community

With some forward planning, EC organisations are well placed to become the keystone of a **community coalition** and an effective community resource. In support of reconceptualising the role of the EC organisation, Moss (2009, p. 1) believes there is a need to 're-think, reform and re-position EC education and care' for the benefit of children and families. Grace, Cashmore, Scott and Hayes (2016, p. 359) state 'there is an education silo, a health silo, a social welfare silo, a criminal justice silo, a housing silo, etc'. It is time for these silos to be demolished once and for all. If EC settings and professionals from other disciplinary heritages actively pursue collaboration we will be far more effective in responding effectively to the children and families in our communities. To this end, EC leaders have an important role to play in breaking down the professional disciplinary silos that stop us from sharing our skills, resources and expertise with the same children and families we all seek to serve in our communities.

community coalition
a relationship developed with other like-minded people and organisations for the purpose of achieving an agreed common goal.

Involving staff, families and the community is a way of ensuring that your EC setting becomes an essential organisation within your community. An easy place to begin is for staff, families and community representatives to review the centre's philosophy and aims of its programs. In the development of these statements and manifestos it is essential that the leader's and other staff members' beliefs and values are tabled for discussions with families and community representatives. Such encounters will contribute to the equitable and democratic processes that can underpin the implementation of meaningful programs for children and their families (Moss, 2009). Mutual respect, sensitivity and understanding generated during these encounters contribute to the development of social capital in and around EC settings.

Pause–reflect–act 12.1

- In building relationships among children, their families and centre staff, how can an intentional leader demonstrate the importance of respecting the rights of everyone?
- What steps or strategies can a leader take to ensure that the voice of children, families, staff and community representatives are fairly represented in a centre's policy decisions?

- Have you seen centres involve staff, families and community representatives in developing and revising their philosophy? What made these centres successful?
- Arrange a visit to a centre that has a good reputation for community engagement. Reflect on the strategies they used and identify ways you could use these in your own work.

Working with families and agencies in integrated ways

Under the National Quality Standard (ACECQA, 2011b), development of 'collaborative partnerships with families and communities' (p. 145) is recognised as Quality Area 6. Previously, research (see Hayden et al., 2002) has indicated that developing community connections may not have been seen as a high priority or key role of EC educators and leaders. However, seeking to develop connections with agencies and organisations in their community that support children and families must be a priority for today's EC leaders. By establishing these links, a leader can be ready to connect families to appropriate agencies when the need arises. By maintaining these relationships, leaders can also ensure that families can be referred to the most relevant agency that can support them.

Another way of creating links with families and agencies is to provide an integrated approach where education, health and social services collaborate in the provision of services to children and their families (Tayler et al., 2002; Grace et al., 2016). In such a context, the building of social capital that enhances community life becomes possible through supportive coalitions provided for all families, regardless of their personal circumstances. Since the late 1990s governments in countries such as Australia and the UK have pursued integrated service models that cater for both child and family needs from one site or as a hub of services. These services may include a mix of the following:

- EC education programs for children birth to five years as well as holiday care for school age children.
- Early intervention services for children with additional needs including play therapy, audiology, speech and physiotherapy.
- Other health services including screening programs, maternal and child health nursing, immunisation and dental checks.
- Programs for parents, such as adult education classes to learn English, computer skills, financial advice and income maintenance.
- Family support programs such as supported playgroups, parenting skills, nutrition, respite care, family counselling, specialist groups for teen-parents or fathers, jobs network, cooperatives and housing support.

Provision of these services requires a mix of professionals usually drawn from education, health and social services backgrounds. Within integrated child and family services, the aim is to find ways for these professionals to work together as a team so that services are delivered in a seamless way. Extensive discussions of the complexities of integrated models and the challenges encountered in leading integrated services are well documented (see Aubrey, 2007; Moore, 2008a; Press et al., 2010; Siraj-Blatchford & Siraj-Blatchford, 2009) and include the following:

- capacity to govern across a range of organisational structures and systems
- establishment of a collaborative ethos across **multidisciplinary teams** and professional heritages
- enactment of leadership in inclusive ways by building on the strengths of multi-agency teams
- efficient distribution of resources, both financial and material, to deliver high-quality services throughout
- priorities collectively set when responding to complex child and family needs
- multidisciplinary teams.

multidisciplinary teams comprise of a range of professionals from diverse backgrounds (such as teachers, nurses and social workers) working together to deliver various programs and services to children and their families.

According to researchers such as Aubrey (2007) and Whalley (2006), the establishment and enactment of a shared philosophy and vision hold the key to successful integration. This is never easy, even if the staff share a common professional orientation. Individual staff members' personal beliefs, values and attitudes can influence how they interact and develop relationships. This situation can be exacerbated when a mix of professionals from different disciplines such as education, health and welfare come together to work with the same children and families in one location. Other important elements for the successful integration of services identified by Atkinson, Doherty and Kinder (2005) are for professionals to be strategic and committed; have a clear understanding of roles; share a common purpose; share information in terms of funding and resources; and be tenacious and visionary in order to achieve change or appeal to a wider cross-section of the community. As noted by Siraj-Blatchford and Siraj-Blatchford (2009), staffing of integrated settings requires good management to ensure various professional groups can work cohesively together. For most educators, integrated services represent new ways of working with other professionals (Press et al., 2010). Therefore, intentional leadership is critical in identifying shared values and goals as a way of binding everyone to a common purpose, regardless of disciplinary boundaries or ideologies.

see chapter 15 for strategies that can be used to create a shared language among staff, parents and community members.

There is a need for EC programs to be more responsive to the diverse needs of children and families, and integrated services are one way of achieving this. There are also other ways, including the provision of auxiliary programs through your EC setting on a regular basis. Consider, for example, the provision of family support in parenting skills; counselling; problems with housing or early intervention programs for children (such as screening for auditory and vision problems); behaviour guidance; and speech therapy or physiotherapy. Support may also be needed with regard to nutrition and food allergies or intolerances. There are other community needs, such as cooperatives for gardening, transport, maintenance, shopping or babysitting, and children's clothing exchanges. Such program inclusions must reflect the needs, skills and strengths of the families within the organisation's community members. The EC leader can find out who offers these programs in their local community, and if none exist, they could advocate for the establishment of these by leading a community coalition for action involving children, families and other professionals.

The leader will need to make decisions about how the EC program can meet the needs of children and families in the community. One approach could include creating an advisory group or a community coalition that includes the diverse voices of the community. This group or coalition could then actively pursue programs and avenues to create community connections. This provides opportunities for the EC program to become a hub, a place where the community feels safe and secure, and want to be there to learn, work or share resources and have their needs and interests met. For example, in their research involving children and families from disadvantaged communities, Grace, Bowes and Elcombe (2014, p. 271) reported that 'Child enrolment in an early childhood service and higher levels of family engagement with the service were significantly more likely when families perceived childcare to be safe, when there were high levels of family connectedness, and when families were involved in other professionals (e.g. social welfare)'. Building trusting relationships with families begins with the EC leader. It may also be possible to allocate the role of building and maintaining connections with relevant agencies to become a part of a staff member's duty statement and budget time to develop these connections.

Pause–reflect–act 12.2

Creating a hub is one way of working collaboratively with other agencies and organisations to support children and families in a community. For some centres this may not be possible due to factors such as geographical isolation (such as being the only EC setting available in a remote rural community) or lack of resources (for example, lack of qualified and experienced staff). As the leader of your EC setting consider:

- What types of networks are needed or could be useful for the children and families in your local community or region? Explain your decisions as you will have to justify this to your management and staff team to obtain their support and willing participation in this venture.
- How will you go about establishing professional networks in your locality?
- What resources do you need to create and maintain this hub or network?

Networking within the sector

Networking both within and outside the sector contributes to positive outcomes for children and families and creates opportunities for those within the community to become involved and engaged with the EC program (Hadley, 2000; Hayden et al., 2002). Rodd (2013, p. 234) advises, however, that 'successful networking—that is, engaging the cooperation of others—takes time, communication skills and good interpersonal relationships'. In a study conducted as part of an honours degree it was found that educators prioritised internal networking (advocacy actions with parents, staff and colleagues) in their everyday work over external networking (advocacy actions with external stakeholders) (Mevawalla & Hadley, 2012). Rodd

(2013, p. 239) also highlights the importance of EC leaders becoming politically aware and active so that they may 'work proactively to inform and influence governments about the needs and requirements of children and families'.

Fenech and Sumsion (2007a) argue that practitioners who are isolated in their own settings can feel a sense of powerlessness and frustration with regulatory and legislated requirements. However, forming supportive networks—and subscribing to or joining advocacy groups to share beliefs, values and understandings about the requirements—has the effect of lessening feelings of isolation and powerlessness. As a member of a coalition of practitioners such as Social Justice in EC (www.socialjusticeinearlychildhood.org) or the support of peak EC organisations such as ECA (www.earlychildhoodaustralia.org.au) educators and leaders can become empowered to engage in consultations and forums about legislative changes and to contribute to the development of the processes and documentation required for future accreditation, compliance and policy development. Formation of support and advocacy groups on curriculum, accreditation and quality has the potential for further improving practice and advancing EC knowledge through professional development and mentoring with the best interests of children at the heart of action.

see chapter 7 for strategies for becoming better at advocacy and activism.

In Leaders in practice 12.1, Marina Papic's story demonstrates her tenacity as a leader as she has moved out of the academia back into direct service provision. Her profile demonstrates how she has used her skills and knowledge about research-based evidence to enhance professional practice and thereby directly influenced EC program provision in the community in which she now works.

LEADERS IN PRACTICE 12.1

Dr Marina Papic

Manager Kids' Early Learning, Blacktown City Council (NSW)

My vision for high-quality EC education is based on several factors. First, I bring to this role as the Manager of Kids' Early Learning at Blacktown City Council over 30 years of practical and leadership experience including researching and working with communities. I use this expertise for raising the quality and pedagogy of our EC services. I believe whatever we do must be evidence based, research informed and evident in all of our documentation about children's learning. This is quite a different focus for the local government context and has required a rethinking about incorporating research evidence in our programs, and engaging with research is new for many staff. For example, the staff developing our 'Ready for School and Ready for Life Programs' are considering current research and are investigating innovative practices so that the program we deliver will be of the highest quality.

Second, I believe that engagement with the community—linking with, for example, allied health, education, other children and community services—is essential. I believe this is a more effective way for us as a council to operate. For instance, we are engaging with varied community and health services in a project that will see a speech pathologist employed to come into a number of services as a member of staff to work with the children, families and educators. Another example of working closely with the community has been a project funded by Family and Community Services (FACS) looking at how we can engage families from low socio-economic and diverse cultural backgrounds. By working with many stakeholder agencies including the NSW Department of Education, BOSTES, parenting support services, university representatives and other EC organisations and providers we can start to think about what is best for the children in this community and how we can make our services more accessible and appropriate for all children and families in our community. For instance, I know EC qualifications do matter in EC settings; my research background informs me of this. So I want the best and most qualified EC teachers working in our services. So it is about planning for this: what are our current levels of qualifications, who in the organisation wants to upskill and complete further studies and how can we attract high-quality EC teachers and educators into our services? This requires us to engage with universities and TAFEs for professional experience placements and traineeships. We want to support their work as well as give students a good experience while they are studying EC.

Third, staff need to be provided with opportunities to be in positions of leadership. This could be working on projects with the community, sitting on committees that engage with our community partners, and also having a voice and say about our organisation. By providing staff with professional development they can become the advocates and leaders for EC and our sector. For example, at the moment staff are involved in developing a practitioner inquiry project with some external academics with the plan for staff to present at a conference later this year. This means they can share what they are doing, what they learnt, and strive for best practice in their work with young children. Our commitment to research-informed practice and to leadership is evident in our successful educator conference 'Leading the Way', where 10 internationally renowned EC researchers and experts presented current research and approaches to innovative practice.

Family engagement is also linked to high-quality EC settings and the research again provides evidence for us on this. We are currently looking at what services families engage in within the community to see if we can tap into them that way. We found that some families take their children to library sessions such as the interactive, early literacy program Baby Rhyme Time for children from birth to two years of age. This program is designed to support parents and carers to enhance their child's early literacy. We are working with library staff to look for opportunities for our EC staff to attend and support those sessions to build our connections with these harder to reach families so they can feel more comfortable coming into our services.

Engaging with families is a big goal and we are working with other services within the council and across the community to engage more effectively with our diverse families. So, in many different ways we are trying to engage with the community to ensure we have the best services for the children and families in our community. We are one organisation, one team, and we have a shared vision and mission. Our staff are reporting they do feel like they 'belong' and this is critical—it's not just about children and families belonging, but the staff need this too. Rebranding to Kids' Early Learning has been successful in supporting this sense of belonging. Working with many stakeholders and even ones traditionally viewed as competitors is making a difference for our community. We have relationships with health organisations, the Department of Early Childhood, FACS, other local children's services, universities, TAFE and national organisations such as Goodstart. This ensures a united and integrated approach to meeting the needs of the children and families in our local government area.

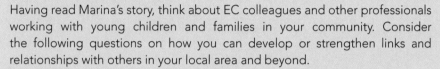

Pause–reflect–act 12.3

Having read Marina's story, think about EC colleagues and other professionals working with young children and families in your community. Consider the following questions on how you can develop or strengthen links and relationships with others in your local area and beyond.

- What skills and attributes do you have that can enable you to connect with diverse professionals? Are you a connector, maven or salesperson (see the following section)? Or are you all of these?
- What skills and attributes do you think you will need to develop or work on to improve your ability to connect with others in the community?
- What would you do if you encountered resistance in prioritising EC perspectives?
- Think about the potential outcomes for children, families and the community by developing closer connections with other EC colleagues. Identify two to three specific goals to achieve by working with other professionals in your community. Develop an action plan to operationalise these goals and activate it within a specified timeline such as six to 12 months or one to two years as appropriate.

There are lessons to be learnt from Marina's story. Within the competitive environments we work in today, some people may be wary about sharing and be protective of their program operations and their knowledge. Sharing ideas, hardships and achievements does not disadvantage any program or organisation. Rather, professional collegiality can support the improvement of professional practice and relationships within a local community. Most importantly, sharing knowledge and understanding can create a win-win situation for everyone involved.

Networking beyond the sector

Just as networking within the sector and your EC setting is important, it is also crucial to develop connections within the wider community. EC leaders need to develop the skills to be 'connectors, mavens and salesmen [salespeople]' (Gladwell, 2000, p. 30). Connectors are those people who have that ability to connect, to develop a bond easily and with many people, not limiting their connections to their workplace or profession. Rather, connectors see the opportunities in engaging or connecting with others from many walks of life and professions.

Leaders need to develop skills for engaging with others and a key to this is to be a good listener. Gladwell (2000) describes a maven as a person who has particular knowledge and ideas but also the ability to connect with others to draw them into pursuing the ideas. The salesperson has the ability to sell the idea to others. A maven thinks strategically about extending their networks through the personal connections they, their employees and clients have in the community. Developing relationships can include taking children on regular informal excursions in the local area so that children are visible in the community. Using images of children visiting local shops, parks and the library, EC leaders can communicate the joys that children bring and the importance of learning during EC. Open days and hosting fundraising events for public campaigns (such as breast cancer or SIDS prevention) can also present good opportunities to promote the importance of EC programs and bring the community into the EC setting. Staff being visible in advocating for young children within local communities can also build a positive image of the professionalism of the setting.

Networking outside of the EC arena creates opportunities for the EC professional to discuss the issues of young children and their families with the influential leaders within their community. Networking is about giving as well as receiving, having a clear understanding of the needs of the EC professional and their EC setting, as well as how others can be supported and empowered. Listening to the other person's story promotes the flow of communication about the other person's roles and responsibilities or vision for change. This information can create the platform for seeing possibilities and sharing EC knowledge and roles and responsibilities as well as the goals of the program. This is where being a maven, or expert, is critical so that one can effectively promote the value of EC education and the benefits to children, their families and society.

read chapter 9 for information about the value of ethical communication.

To promote the benefits of EC education within the community a leader needs the information to filter into the broader community in ever-widening circles. EC leaders can create a tidal wave or an epidemic that is irresistible and will spread beyond the little corner of the world that is the EC setting. In order for the EC program to benefit from such connections with the community, leaders and educators must be prepared to give back just as much to the community. Relationships with the broader community can also build local support and recognition for the work being done by the EC setting. Connecting with other services and local businesses that support families is one way of directing marketing strategies to those who have contact with young families most often. Such connections are mutually beneficial to both professionals and parents. Building relationships with local maternal and child health services, for example, can mean that these professionals are more likely to recommend your organisation to families who are their clients. It also means you can refer families that are using your organisation to the most appropriate agencies when they have a particular need relating to their children (for example, dental care or speech difficulties) or the family (for example unemployment and need for financial advice).

In addition to these professional connections, intentional leaders can invest in building relationships with local retailers and businesses that may gain mutual advantage from working together. Reciprocal arrangements whereby EC organisations display images of children's learning (such as pedagogical documentation or artworks) in the local shopping centre can help to attract families to consider your organisation for their children. Agreeing to promote local businesses in your newsletter can also consolidate good relationships that work and benefit both the EC setting and the business. Placing brochures in the local medical centre and in turn including publicity or promotional brochures about these facilities in the foyer of the EC setting can also be mutually beneficial in establishing networks, as can capitalising on local businesses that have regular contact with families. Local real estate agents, for example, are usually among the first to be in contact with families moving into the area. Asking them to include a brochure or even a promotional fridge magnet about the EC settings in a welcome pack may be helpful to families getting to know their new area.

Pause–reflect–act 12.4

In considering the above strategies for networking, intentional leaders must be mindful of the professional and ethical considerations in partnering with other agencies. A few key questions to ask are:

- What aspects of the publicity material or campaign are mutually beneficial for the EC setting and the sponsoring agency or families at your setting?
- How are children's images represented in the promotional material of your setting?
- To what extent does your current public profile put the centre in a positive light and appeal to children and families who may not be currently accessing your service?

Angela Thompson, who is profiled in Leaders in practice 12.2, exemplifies an intentional leader who is also a significant connecter, maven and salesperson creating an inclusive community with far-reaching benefits for the wider community. Angela values being intentional about building a network within and beyond the local community to bring about change benefiting children and families.

LEADERS IN PRACTICE 12.2

Angela Thompson

Senior Associate, Semann & Slattery

The Mining Minds Education Partnership is a program funded by BHP Billiton in partnership with education consultants Semann and Slattery, local education leaders and community members. It partners with communities in Roxby Downs, Woomera, Andamooka and Marree in remote South Australia. It aims to build an authentic collaboration to promote the development of the towns as the community of choice for education.

It was crucial to the project's success that it built on existing community strengths and was driven by the community. Having a whole of community approach required the engagement of various stakeholders in the early stages of this project. As a local resident and educator for 12 years it was my role to identify the stakeholders and bring them together. I found it was the relationships and strengths-based approach that I had built over time that allowed us to develop trust. We met formally and informally, often over a cup of tea in the local café, with community members, schools, educators, children, students and families. We collated and analysed relevant local and international data, considered past initiatives and recommendations and liaised with BHP Billiton and a forum of local education leaders.

The information collected from these consultations was shared with the wider community via a number of avenues including posters with key ideas, sharing data at forums and dissemination through the projects newsletter. Three key ideas emerged in relation to families:

- It is critical to the success of children that teachers, parents and the community hold and convey high and positive expectations for children's learning.
- Partnerships with parents that raise the awareness of their crucial role in their children's education and provide them with the skills to do so would make a significant difference in outcomes for children.
- There is a recognised strength in our community and building on this strength by working in partnership with families, educators and children will improve outcomes for children and the community. Involvement in learning was seen as a whole of community role.

So, in partnership with parents, we set up a local learning community that built on local strengths and ideas. A group of local mothers is undertaking further study in education. Several educators have been supported to be involved in practitioner inquiry projects where they have developed successful partnerships with parents, particularly in the areas of transitions and sharing curriculum. Local parents who run businesses have contributed to curriculum delivery at a high school level by jointly teaching economics units.

As the project moves into its third year, we are seeing the establishment of a community hub, a child-friendly venue in a shop in the main street. Recently, BHP Billiton announced $4 million partnership with the state government to place an integrated children's centre in Roxby Downs that has a dedicated parent engagement program. So, like local parents and educators, we have high expectations for the future of family engagement in our community.

Pause–reflect–act 12.5

Having read the two Leaders in practice profiles in this chapter, ask yourself:

- What do you see are the similarities and differences between them in terms of building connections within their community?
- What skills did Marina and Angela use to build their community connections?
- Find out exactly where the two communities of Blacktown and Roxby Downs—the two locations where Marina and Angela work respectively—are located within Australia. Obtain some of the basic demographic or population information from the Australian Bureau of Statistics for these two communities. Reflect on the potential challenges each community presents in the delivery of EC programs.

Working with the media

Public media is both a commodity and a strategy that EC educators often overlook. The intentional leader can be strategic in developing connections with the media and building relationships with local newspapers and other media outlets to enhance connections with others in the community. Offering to write a regular column on EC matters or joining in a local community radio program can not only bring attention to EC issues but can also enhance the presence of children in the community through the high profile or visibility of your setting and the people who work there. For example, a participant of the Aspiring Leaders Forum (which was a year-long professional learning program in New South Wales for educators and established under the auspices of Macquarie University, Semann and Slattery, and Children Services Central) developed a connection with the local newspaper in her region and wrote a regular column about her EC program. By taking the lead in engaging with the media, the intentional leader can have a say over the information that is being published in the local community newspaper. This strategy also provides an opportunity to promote a positive view of EC programs to counteract the typical 'bad news' or 'just cute' messages about EC programs that appear regularly in popular media.

Issuing occasional press releases celebrating special events or community-wide festivals can be of interest to local newspapers keen to capture life in the local area. Taking the initiative to create a press release and capture appropriate photographic images can make it easy for journalists to prepare the story (there are many websites that provide media and press release templates). Over time this can lead to a relationship where they may contact the EC setting for photo shoots or stories relating to young children. Some years ago, Stephens (1998) urged EC leaders to develop closer working relationships with the media. She argued that as experts in EC, leaders can play an important role in the development of newsworthy items that appeal to media outlets and thereby raise awareness of EC matters in the community and reinforce the importance of EC for lifelong learning and democratic citizenship.

Other ways of engaging the media can be inviting journalists to cover open days, special celebrations or community events that are held at the setting. Inviting local politicians and dignitaries to these events also provides the leader with opportunities to advocate more broadly about EC and can also attract media coverage. Building on established relationships with the local media can be useful in garnering assistance and support in times of need. For example, local media coverage of the damage to EC organisations caused by bushfires and floods across Australia over the years has yielded widespread community support and donations to assist in rebuilding and resourcing these organisations. The human interest nature of these stories and the desire of those not directly affected by the disasters to play a part in the restoration of services for children and families have touched people far and wide. The media's capacity to capture such events and communicate the stories broadly was effective in drawing attention to the importance of EC organisations in the life of communities devastated by natural disasters. In other instances, the local community has housed EC organisations in alternative spaces until they were rebuilt. For example, in 2016, educators in Victoria walked off the job to protest about the need for equal pay for educators working in EC settings (see www.facebook.com/UnitedVoiceECEC/videos/1447928258575211).

This demonstration led to many media outlets reporting on the story and helped raise awareness of some of the issues currently faced by educators working in EC settings.

If contacted by the media for a story or comment, be sure to check the right to review and sign off on what has been written before it is published. Prior to answering any questions, sharing information or providing access to the program for photographs or filming, it is best to negotiate ways of ensuring the accuracy and privacy of those involved in a story that is being published or broadcast on radio or television. Remember that at times the media requires sensational stories to sell newspapers or media programs. How often has there been a positive story about EC programs in the media? How many times have the images portrayed in newspapers or current affairs programs highlighted negative messages? Ask for the assurance that the images (once they have been authorised for use) will only be used for the particular report and not archived to be used over and over for different stories and contexts.

Permission for media access must also be sought from the organisation and the staff. Likewise, parents need to give their permission for their child to be photographed and filmed and children also need to be consulted. The media need to be made aware of the ethical process and standards that underpin EC programs and if the leader makes the guidelines clear about accessing the program by the media, then perhaps they will respect EC programs and the children and families. EC leaders need to examine any relationship with the media within a social entrepreneurship framework. By using this framework, leaders can assess the relationship to ensure if it will contribute to promoting the rights of children and ensure high-quality EC programs are advocated for and promoted in their community.

The leader's role in building connections with the community

Marina's and Angela's experiences in their community outreach work reflect Chaskin's (2001) argument that community capacity is created when there is engagement and participation of various community members. Chaskin (2001) also advises that to engage effectively with the community there needs to be:

- skills of the individuals
- strengths of organisations to access financial capital
- networks of relationships
- leadership and support.

Given the multi-ethnic nature of many communities comprising children and families from diverse cultures, countries and heritages, Rodd's (2013) advice on becoming culturally competent is also an important consideration for both educators and leaders of EC settings. Being culturally competent involves being respectful, responsive and responsible in acknowledging diversity and demonstrating professionalism in all aspects of communication with children and families as well as staff. Rodd (2013, p. 76) asserts that 'culture and language are critical to learning and play a key role not only in the way people communicate but also in how they think about and understand the world'. As such, recognising that learning from children and families about what they know about their own cultures and heritages is important in supporting staff to be open to new understandings about becoming culturally competent.

Devoting time to forging and building relationships at the local, community and political levels does pay dividends. Outreach work undertaken with generosity and inclusiveness builds the capacity of the community in forming coalitions and achieving goals. By doing this, the intentional leader is building a community resource. Developing and building connections both inside and outside of the organisation does indeed build social capital that has far-reaching benefits for the whole community and beyond. Marina and Angela have shown how powerful intentional leadership is in forming community connections and coalitions for change.

Pause–reflect–act 12.6

Reflect on the following list (adapted from Hadley, 2000) and think about what you as an EC leader may need to consider in developing connections in your community:

- Your setting has a philosophy and set of goals that have been collectively agreed upon.
- You are allocated time to consult with the community and to attend important meetings in the community.
- You have a clear vision of what is to be achieved.
- You are familiar with the local community.
- You have developed networks with local council, referral agencies, local schools, health practitioners, local businesses and other relevant agencies/organisations or groups of interest.
- You utilise staff and parents as a resource.
- You share information about your setting with the community.
- Your setting reflects the needs of the community.
- You share resources with other community organisations and encourage two-way communication.
- You consult with people in the community, such as health practitioners, police and local organisations, on what their needs are.
- You invite key players in the community into the EC setting.
- You are articulate about EC and the research that supports its importance.
- You are confident to discuss EC issues at community meetings and with the public.
- You are recognised as an expert on EC within the community.
- You utilise resources such as the local media to support the causes for children and families.
- You are involved with local committees that are related to children and families.
- You are involved in community meetings and/or groups about young children and families.

Establishing and nurturing connections with the community takes time, commitment, resources and skills. EC leaders who do this successfully often operate out of their comfort zone and take risks to build these relationships. It also requires the intentional leader to be confident in their knowledge and expertise but to balance this with a willingness to listen to the community and provide a centre that understands and reflects the needs, strengths and interests of the community.

Chapter summary

This chapter has discussed the potential within a community for the intentional leader of an EC program to build connections and relationships, and to develop coalitions to effect change or to pursue a goal in building community engagement. There is also the opportunity for the EC program to become the focus of and a resource for its community for the benefit of the children and families. The ripple-on effect of embracing the rich diversity of cultures, programs and agencies that operate within a community can provide benefits reaching out into the community. The EC program can become a space or a site for education and relationships to flourish, enhancing community life and child and family health and well-being. It does require the leader to develop communication skills and the ability to set goals and prioritise community connections to promote the positive elements of EC education and the relationships that build social capital.

Key references

Grace, R., Bowes, J. & Elcombe, E. (2014). Child participation and family engagement with early childhood education and care services in disadvantaged Australian communities. *International Journal of Early Childhood*, 46(2), 271–98, doi 10.1007/s13158-014-0112-y.

This paper reports on a research study involving 101 disadvantaged families about family engagement in EC settings. The authors use their findings to reaffirm the importance of adopting a community and family focused approach to early years provisioning.

Grace, R., Hodge, K. & McMahon, C. (Eds.). (2016). *Children, families and communities. Contexts and consequences.* (5th Ed.). Melbourne, Australia: Oxford University Press.

This book presents insights on a diversity of contexts children and families may experience and the influences that these can have on children's development, health and well-being and the connections that are made.

Press, F., Sumsion, J. & Wong, S. (2010). *Integrated early years provision in Australia. A research project for the Professional Support Coordinators Alliance (PSCA)*. Bathurst: Charles Sturt University. Retrieved from www.cscentral.org.au/Resources/Publications/FinalCSUreport.pdf.

This is a report of a national research project that looked at service integration by focusing on government policy, governance, leadership, organisational culture and ethos as well as front-line professional practice and teamwork. Case studies and examples of effective leadership strategies used in a variety of contexts offer useful lessons for those interested in community engagement.

Online resources

Centre for Youth Wellness

This website outlines a national effort in the USA to revolutionise paediatric medicine to potentially transform the way society responds to kids exposed to significant adverse childhood experiences and toxic stress. The organisation is led by founder and CEO

Dr Nadine Burke Harris and its mission is to respond to the real threat of 'toxic stress' or as she calls it 'childhood trauma' and how this is potentially life altering. She talks about this being an urgent public health issue. There are messages on this website that you could use to garner support in your community for assisting vulnerable children and families.

www.centerforyouthwellness.org

Dropping off the edge

This research was originally undertaken by Tony Vinson in 1999 when he mapped communities in terms of disadvantage. The Dropping off the Edge follow-up study in 2015 sadly found that not much had changed in terms of communities who experienced the most disadvantage even though governments had targeted these communities and invested money for programs. The report argues that 'strengthening the most disadvantaged communities with a tailored, targeted and sustained approach is the most efficient use of resources, and will deliver benefits for the entire community'. The need for community-driven programs (a grassroots approach) is needed if a real difference is to be made. You can assess your community and access the resources and reports that can help you work with your community stakeholders to make a difference.

www.dote.org.au/about

Nadine Burke Harris: How childhood trauma affects health across a lifetime

Listen to Nadine's excellent TED talk about how she became involved as a paediatrician.

www.ted.com/talks/nadine_burke_harris_how_childhood_trauma_affects_health_across_a_lifetime

Ounce of Prevention Fund

Since 1982, the Ounce of Prevention Fund has persistently pursued a single goal: that all children living in the USA—particularly those born into poverty—have quality EC experiences in the crucial first five years of life. This website has excellent resources (both printed and video clips) that can arm you with information to help develop your pitch to a community about the importance of EC programs.

www.theounce.org/who-we-are/about-us

Watch this clip about the first five years of life. How could you use the messages in the video to advocate for all young children and effect change in your community?

www.youtube.com/watch?v=GbSp88PBe9E

13 MONEY MATTERS

CHAPTER LEARNING OBJECTIVES

After studying this chapter you will understand that:

- Basic accounting language, principles and processes can assist in monitoring money matters of EC organisations.
- 'Integrated reporting' presents a holistic approach to business planning and highlights the relationship between business, society and the environment.
- Legislative requirements; social ethics; sustainability; and operational, pedagogical and financial matters are interrelated.
- Monitoring the utilisation of places against budgeted income and expenditure is essential to maintaining a healthy financial, ethical and sustainable bottom line.
- Familiarisation with regular income and expenditure cycles is the key to understanding the pattern of cash flow in and out of the organisation and, so, to financial stability.
- Reading financial statements can inform strategic planning, provide an analysis of an integrated reporting and outcomes model and highlight risks in running EC centres.
- EC Leaders can incorporate opportunities to strengthen a centre's finances and contribution to the community and society when preparing a business plan.
- Responding strategically to current and anticipated changes within the local community and political arena is important for long-term financial stability of an EC organisation.

Key concepts

business plan
checking financial statements
financial planning
healthy (financial) bottom line
Integrated Reporting Model
small business enterprise

Overview

This chapter aims to equip EC leaders with the competence and confidence to participate fully in the business life of their organisation. An EC leader's engagement in 'money matters' is an important factor in the financial viability and stability of an EC centre and, consequently, in the organisation's capacity to realise the vision, mission and strategic goals of a high-quality EC program. EC leaders who can readily recognise and respond to the many and varied factors that impact on their organisation's financial health, and the centre's value within the wider community, make a contribution well beyond the financial bottom line. A high-quality, well-run EC centre enhances the social capital of its own community and the wider society.

Leaders are encouraged to consider socially responsible and sustainable approaches to business to ensure the services they provide are delivered in an ethical, just and equitable way. At the same time, EC leaders must balance their attention to, and investment in, high-quality educational pedagogy with the need for efficient financial management. EC leaders cannot be expected to have a full understanding of accounting language, principles and processes. However, some understanding of financial matters can enable leaders to participate in the centre's budget preparation; to evaluate the organisation's capacity to meet its goals and objectives; and 'to converse with accountant(s)' to 'tell them what they can do for you' (Godbee, 2007, p. 1). Often, non-accountants are put off by the financial jargon used by accountants. Familiarity with accounting terminology and concepts can give leaders more control over how their organisations function and perform both financially as sustainable businesses and as quality education providers that make an ethical contribution to society.

EC centres as small business enterprises

a **small business enterprise** typically employs fewer than 20 staff. This is the definition used by the Australian Bureau of Statistics (ABS) and has been applied in this book. Note that various regulators such as Fair Work Australia and the Australian Taxation Office adopt other criteria and these definitions may change according to government policy.

It is useful to consider an EC centre as a **small business enterprise** (Morgan & Emanuel, 2010). The leader's involvement can ensure that the decisions about income and expenditure will more likely reflect the centre's philosophy and vision, prioritising the best interests of children. In this way, it is also important to understand that 'companies cannot think of themselves apart from society—they are part of it. And that needs to come through in their communication on value' (Druckman, cited in Adams, 2013, p. 27). Understanding this nexus between the internal and external environments of the centre holds the key to effective business planning.

The types of providers of EC settings vary in Australia, and include both for-profit and not-for-profit businesses. The 2014 report of the Inquiry by the Productivity Commission into Childcare and EC Learning states that 'around 50 per cent of approved services are provided on a for profit basis' (p. 81) and the ACECQA NQF 'Snapshot' in November 2016 indicated a continuation of this pattern. About half of all EC settings are managed by single operators, and the remainder by large businesses, groups or networks. This range of business models means expectations of EC leaders, and their roles and responsibilities in financial matters, also vary. Relevant factors include the Productivity Commission's findings that profitability within the EC sector differs across providers and from one year to another. While, on average, the majority of centres make a profit, around one-third may operate at a loss in any one year. The type of centre, therefore, can have a significant impact on how income and expenditure must be balanced, and any profit generated, throughout the year.

However, both profit and not-for-profit businesses have something very important in common when it comes to financial health. High occupancy levels underpin the profitability of centre-based care, regardless of its business model (Productivity Commission, 2014, pp. 81–2). This means the many interrelated factors that influence occupancy levels—such as local demand, affordability (not simply price, but the capacity of local families to pay), program quality and design, and competition from other providers—are vital in maintaining the financial stability of the business. Given this complexity, EC leaders are encouraged to consider the value of working within an 'integrated model of financial reporting', which is explained in the next section.

The Integrated Reporting Model

The **Integrated Reporting Model** is based on the work of the International Integrated Reporting Committee, led by Carol Adams (2014) and Gleeson-White (2014), which identified six economic and social capitals. It recognises that 'companies are part of society and their strategy and business models must consider the context of their activities' (Druckman, cited in Adams, 2013, p. 23) within their communities. (See www.drcaroladams.net/the-international-integrated-reporting-council-a-call-to-action/)

the **Integrated Reporting Model** is an approach to financial reporting that tells a story of the organisation's ethical contribution to society and effective disclosure of the six capitals (financial, manufactured, intellectual, human, social and relationships, and natural).

The 'capitals' as they relate to an EC organisation are:

- *Financial*: income (for example, fees and subsidies) and expenditure (e.g. staffing, food and utilities) as well as investments, loans and leases
- *Manufactured*: buildings, fixtures, office and kitchen equipment, landscaping, access roads and educational resources
- *Intellectual*: output of the teaching and support staff, documentation of programs, observations, developmental records, emails, newsletters, policies and processes
- *Human*: staff induction or on-boarding, professional development, longevity and continuity of staffing, staff meetings and staff's loyalty, and contribution to the organisational culture as a learning community
- *Social and relationships*: fair trading within the community and sustainable practices; contribution to the local community and wider Australian society; the reputation and relationships within and externally with other professionals, policy makers, banks and schools
- *Natural*: use of both renewable and non-renewable resources, including water, and provision for heating, cooling and lighting; and the organisation's impact on the natural environment in the use of materials and resources.

Using these elements to analyse the business processes, leaders can be more ethically aware and intentional in the way they influence the business life of the organisation. These ideals are reflected in Gleeson-White's (2014) proposal that it is not sufficient for accountants alone to consider the financial capitals of an organisation without addressing the impact of this on society and the environment of an organisation's activities. Such a holistic approach is especially important in EC education, as a service provider relies heavily on reputation and community goodwill to achieve full utilisation.

The Integrated Reporting Model can be easily aligned with an educational organisation such as an EC centre. Importantly, 'the capitals draw attention to the role of non-financial resources, which are often insufficiently recognised and acknowledged' (Adams, 2013, p. 47). It is valid to consider, for example, that pedagogy is closely linked to 'manufactured' assets through the purchase of manufactured goods and services. Are these goods and services produced ethically, using sustainable resources? Are the intellectual capabilities of the staff valued and used equitably? Think about each of the six capitals in terms of how they impact on the overall functioning of the organisation as a system or a small business enterprise.

EC leaders' roles and responsibilities in financial matters

chapter 5 looks in depth at strategic planning. The business plan must be aligned with the strategic directions or the bigger picture of how the organisation aims to grow and prosper.

a **business plan** for an organisation outlines the financial basics, including the resources available, goals—prioritising items to be achieved—and a market analysis. It reflects the management's capacity to run a viable business.

see chapters 2 and 3 for a discussion on EC policy and legislation.

Today's EC leaders are expected to be responsible for quite sizable amounts of money (see Table 13.1 for some examples). They need to budget for day-to-day operations and for long-term costs including staffing, educational resources, special projects and other goals that may affect spending decisions, such as environmental sustainability. Of necessity, strategic planning in EC settings requires keeping abreast of government reforms, relevant research and educational theories. Likewise, in dealing with the money matters of the organisation, it is essential to develop a **business plan** to indicate 'how the organisation will achieve the goals within the strategic plan' during the period specified (Bryant & Gibbs, 2013, p. 234). The business plan has the business goals, objectives, target market information and financial forecasts that you are aiming to achieve over a given time period. It is important to prepare a business plan when starting or growing your organisation and reviewing its progress.

External factors may include changes in government regulations and polices that affect the sector, research findings indicating the desirability of change, or educational theories, curriculum modifications or additions. Leaders are expected to advise and support management's decision-making by anticipating the flow-on effects of government policy reforms on the centre's internal operations. For instance, funding policy changes affect the centre's quality improvement processes. These policies are therefore directly connected to the centre's immediate and long-term operations and are nearly always related to financial costs and time constraints set externally by government, the bank or another organisation.

In turn, these requirements may have pedagogical implications related to teaching practice, ratios, resources, routines and record keeping, all of which are linked to a centre's finances. For example, at the time when the NQS was being established when a change in staffing for babies was legislated through government policy one staff member was required for every four babies, instead of the previous ratio of 1:5. As this is a mandated change, and if the centre's staffing was not already at 1:4, the impact on fees must be taken into account in future budgets. Most government reforms have a period of grace or time granted to become compliant. Leaders can use this time to revise the business plan and involve families in budget discussions.

Internal factors include the social, relational and ethical elements of the organisation. For example, an educational leader may need to advocate for release time for educators to meet with families, and to plan, document and introduce innovations. Leaders must be able to make the case that such working arrangements are essential expenditure as they represent both an investment in children's learning as well as in the centre's public reputation as a high-quality, and therefore desirable, service provider. Likewise, staff may want or need to attend public forums or relevant conferences or industry events. Consequently, budgets may have to allow for relief staff, for example, to ensure programs are delivered consistently.

Pause–reflect–act 13.1

A group of parents comprising four families has come to you requesting the centre provide only organic food. As organic food is more expensive, this potential additional cost needs to be considered when making any decision to change.

- What would your ethical response be to these families?
- What will you need to take into account when making your decision?
- If you decide to purchase the organic food, how would you present this information to the centre's management and families in order to explain the proposed fee increase at the centre?

Leaders can play a key role in developing a business plan to incorporate policy changes or to adjust to other internal or external environmental impacts on the centre's programs. In keeping with a social justice approach, involvement with both staff and families in designing a business plan should begin early. Families, as well as management and staff, need to be included in the strategic planning of the organisation. Collaboration is key as this provides the motivation for staff and families to invest in the centre in multiple ways. For example, embracing research-based evidence on the use of qualified staff or participating in centre management may enhance the working environment at the centre. Likewise, organising an organic vegetable cooperative, for example, can strengthen relationships with families.

It is difficult to single out any one factor, or set of factors, as the key to a centre's financial success. However, by combining 'financial stability' and 'social responsibility' an organisation is more likely to achieve sustainable growth. Financial stability may, for example, be reflected by employing of the majority of the staff on a permanent basis, rather than as casuals. Importantly, stability of staffing arrangements also provides consistency for children and families and is considered a hallmark of high-quality organisations (Layzer & Goodson, 2006, p. 560). For the same reasons, if forced to use casual staff, it is appropriate to establish a pool of casual staff who can become more familiar with your setting over time.

'A good reason for investing in your human capital is that your workforce becomes more productive and more likely to meet your strategic goals' (Woods, cited in Adams, 2013, p. 38). As leaders play a key role in what information is made available to staff and families, and how and when it is distributed and discussed, they must also understand the opportunities effective communication provides to foster positive relationships with staff, families and the community to advance strategic goals. The flow-on effect is that children, families, staff, the community and the economy benefit. 'Essentially, children's services operate like any other small business, and prudent financial management leads to well-resourced centres, which contributes to positive outcomes for children' (Community Child Care Co-operative NSW, 2009a, p. 100).

Understanding financial planning and legislative accountabilities

Leaders must intentionally expand their business acumen—or their ability to make good judgments about the financial matters of the organisation. This includes familiarity with basic accounting language, principles and processes. A sound starting point is to build a positive working relationship with the qualified financial manager responsible for bookkeeping and/or managing the centre's accounts and to demonstrate a willingness to participate in financial matters. It is also recommended that leaders identify their current areas of strength and skills, as well as any other skills they may need to develop to enable them to participate in and contribute confidently to managing a centre's finances.

There are training organisations in each Australian state and territory that provide advisory support and financial management workshops or presentations on request. There are also primers and books about basic accounting principles, many short courses or online study programs, and information sites (see the list at the end of this chapter). As Wagner (2006, p. viii) advises:

> With just a little effort on your part, you can become financially literate. You may not be able to speak the language of finance fluently, but you can learn it well enough to manage your way around. The secret to success is that you don't have to learn everything there is to know about finance and accounting. You only need to learn enough to know the right questions to ask.

checking financial statements involves regularly monitoring the financial activities of the EC organisation against the set budget and business plans to ensure business viability and to identify financial trends over time.

financial planning involves identifying and managing the financial risks of operating a centre as a small business enterprise to ensure financial stability.

Wagner (2006) also suggests the 'ILE strategy' for **checking financial statements**: '*I*dentify key numbers; *L*ook deeper and ask why; and *E*xamine the entire statement' (p. 12). Seeking assistance in checking financial statements can also enhance the leader's awareness and knowledge of monitoring the organisation's financial activities in keeping with the set budget and the business plans of the centre.

Just as accounting is a specialised field, pedagogy is also a specialised body of knowledge. A leader's pedagogical expertise needs to be shared to ensure management aligns a centre's financial goals with its pedagogical and quality values. The role of the leader is to balance the attention and focus on educational pedagogy with efficient financial management. The Integrated Reporting Model provides a sound approach. A brief overview of some of the terminology, principles and processes related to financial management is provided below.

Key **financial planning** concepts relevant to an EC setting include *assets* (manufactured) and *liabilities*. Assets include 'fixed' aspects (for example the land, building, equipment and furniture) and 'current' items (for example, monies owed to the organisation). *Liabilities* include mortgage payments or rent, monies owed to outside organisations and management fees. The EC leader needs to be aware that the value of items purchased decreases or depreciates over time. Information about the centre's assets should be listed in an *inventory*: a record of all equipment, resources, furniture and appliances used in the centre, including the outdoor equipment. The *inventory* also documents the original cost, date of purchase and expected time frame within which the equipment will need to be replaced.

Referring to the inventory helps in planning ahead and making *provision* (setting aside funding) for replacements in future budgets. However, the *book value* (original cost) of assets does not equal to the *market value* (current value if it were to be sold) so provision should always reflect the actual cost of replacing an item. For example, while the cost of microwaves and printers has come down, the cost of some larger appliances (such as refrigerators) has increased over the years. This means it is wise to keep abreast of the cost of items needed in the future by checking websites or retail catalogues. When developing the centre's business plan and budget, this information will assist in factoring in realistic costs, as well as enabling leaders to identify goods manufactured to meet fair trade and environmental standards.

Pause–reflect–act 13.2

Make a list of the basic items that are 'assets' in each playroom and estimate what you think the current value of each item might be. Next, list the equipment in the office, kitchen and laundry. Make a cursory estimate of the cost of each item. Then, check websites and catalogues to find current prices.

- Were you surprised at the amount of money tied up in kitchen equipment and play resources?
- Which items are you most likely to replace and how often will this be necessary?
- How did the task of compiling an inventory enhance your understanding of the cost of equipment and other resources at your centre?
- Were you able to identify the origins of the resources? Are they locally and/or sustainably produced?
- Make a list of efficiency measures you can use to reduce costs and increase the financial viability of your centre.

An inventory does not include the *intangible assets* of the centre—for example, the *goodwill* and community spirit generated as a result of quality staff, good ratios, teamwork and collaborative practices that characterise a high-quality EC program. Such intangible assets are built up over time. When selling a business—from a doctor's surgery to a newsagency—goodwill and reputation can make a difference to the sale price. In the case of an EC centre, such intangible assets can include a healthy waiting list and full occupancy, and would likewise boost the market value of the business. Aligning pedagogical aims and financial goals enables centres to achieve a **healthy (financial) bottom line** and this is in keeping with the six capitals of the small business enterprise.

healthy (financial) bottom line

typically refers to the financial viability of an organisation as a business, and reflects a good fit between income and expenditure.

see chapter 6 on pedagogical leadership.

In financial terms, accountability goes hand in hand with *liabilities and compliance*. *Liabilities* are typically monies owed that must be paid within set terms—for example, within 30 days of the purchase of an item or service/s). *Compliance* refers to an organisation's responsibility to abide by or satisfy various laws, regulations and conditions related to financial matters—for example, an EC centre may receive a grant or a sponsorship for a specific project from a particular government department or a private company. This means centres must keep certain documents that enable them to demonstrate that the funds received were used for the purpose specified in a funding contract or agreement. Failure to meet these conditions (that is, to comply with the agreement) may result in some type of penalty (such as a fine or the withdrawal of funds or funding for families). Accountability requirements range from detailed, formal, written documents to more informal arrangements and may include expectations that are not easy to understand. If this is the case, a leader with financial responsibilities for the centre must seek support from a qualified professional to clarify expectations before signing an agreement.

The costs relating to other compliance matters, such as *licensing* and *registration fees* are often 'hidden' within expenditure as operating costs. However, it is valuable for educators to understand that the conditions of licencing and registration often mean a centre will incur related costs. Some related costs include staff attending workshops to update their skills and knowledge in mandated areas such as first-aid, health and safety, and child protection. A leader also needs to advocate and budget for staff professional development (that is, intellectual capital) so that educators are abreast of current research and knowledge related to curriculum. These less-visible operating costs should be discussed with families (social relationships capital) so they can appreciate the real costs of delivering quality children's programs—and understand they are an integral part of a quality program—and that this will have a flow-on effect on fees. *These considerations are reflected in Leaders in practice 13.1, which features Daniela Kavoukas, the director of a community-managed EC centre in suburban Melbourne.*

LEADERS IN PRACTICE 13.1

Daniela Kavoukas

Centre Director, Flemington Childcare Co-operative, Flemington (VIC)

As the director, what are your key responsibilities in terms of the 'money matters' of running a community-managed EC centre?

The financial management of Co-op (where I work now) is always floating around in my head somewhere, even in my dreams, I'm sure. Some days it's like a game of chess—I can't move one thing until the other piece falls into place, and the money must come in before it goes out.

Coming to the Co-op taught me a new appreciation for the financial aspects of operating a not-for-profit community-managed centre. Of course, there are the everyday monetary tasks required to keep any business afloat—like paying wages, bills, invoicing families, comparison quotes from utility companies … the list goes on. However, entering an organisation that was struggling financially opened my eyes to the importance of having a solid comprehension of the financial aspects of Co-op. I completed a financial management course for not-for-profit organisations to understand how to read profit and loss reports and balance sheets. Budgets became serious, down-to-the dollar detail and every possible expense and income was documented.

Knowledge of the financial aspects meant that I could also support the board of management in their role, whether it be through conversation, examples or organising committee training. Collaboration with the board has been critical in ensuring that the forecast expenses and business plan for Co-op are not just my thoughts. The goal for the Co-op is to remain viable long into the future—this means we must find the balance between financial viability and affordability for families without cutting quality. To do this I start with a budget template that is only my staffing expenses, outlining what isn't negotiable. Food is our second biggest expense, and another item where I refuse to negotiate quality. Items such as craft materials, consumables, and excess Lego, puzzles and toys are things I try to reduce. We seldom order from teaching catalogues when households have so many items that we can use. Second-hand coffee tables make great child-size tables and look much more homely.

Good relationships with families are paramount in all aspects of the service being sustainable. We explain to families from the beginning that we have low ratios and well-qualified staff, which makes our fees a little higher than some in the area. Conversely, these good relationships support communication with families when times get tough—if families need to come and talk to you about financial strain, or if you need to approach a family regarding late payment of fees, established rapport with families reduces the stress of these difficult conversations.

How does your EC pedagogical knowledge inform your leadership decisions and recommendations about the centre's financial viability?

Our financial records inform our business plan, and help create our projections and achieve our financial goals. It has been critical that I think of Co-op as a business and use that mindset to be strategic in forecasting. Paramount to our financial success has been the 'magic' number of children we are licenced for. By expanding our building a year ago, the addition of six children meant more income each year to invest in quality program delivery. This was used for funding additional educators to provide opportunities for our children to spend time in the community on a weekly basis, offer in-house professional development on curriculum matters for all staff and renovate our outdoor spaces in the near future incorporating a variety of calming, hidden, open-ended spaces where the environment provides endless teachable moments. It was a worthy renovation for the longevity of our service.

What challenges have you encountered and how did you overcome these problems?

The greatest financial challenge for Co-op has been utilisation. In my first years, Co-op was running below the anticipated 95 per cent of our budget. For us at the time there weren't many three- and four-year-old children in the community. This meant restructuring the children's groupings, including building a kindergarten room for three-five year olds. I became so resourceful, because I was trying to save every penny I could. All of sudden you realise you don't need a $2000 budget for art and craft, that storage cupboards full of matching boxes aren't necessary. Today, sustainability is embedded into Co-op, and it's occurring naturally.

There have been moments where I felt physically sick reading profit and loss reports. Regular monitoring of records increases predictability of finances, and today it is highly unusual that the financial records for each month would be a surprise to me. Grants were an important part of survival for Co-op and still are. As we recognised the time that it took to create high-quality grant applications, we prioritised our board members' roles for two people to be grants officers. This enabled us to share out the workload and have more time dedicated towards important applications.

In understanding an EC centre as a business enterprise, what advice would you give to an aspiring leader?

It has been important for me to ensure that although Co-op has had some hard times over the years, that we don't become run down and unsightly. Gratitude has played a big part for my staff and me. We are grateful to work in a lovely community and pride ourselves on the high-quality education and care that we provide, not on how expensive or how new our equipment is. At times as a leader you can walk into other spaces and be envious of what others have. Take these moments as opportunities to reflect on how you would like your centre to be in the future—they may just be your next financial goals.

Pause–reflect–act 13.3

- Daniela speaks about the financial challenges she encountered due to low utilisation rates. Reflect on the factors that impact the utilisation of an EC centre.
- What strategies can you use to increase utilisation by attracting more enrolments to your centre? Consider, for example, how to make use of places such as public libraries and real estate agents who are aware of families with young children moving in and out of local areas.
- Non-payment of fees is a common issue across all EC settings, regardless of factors such as centre size, location and the socio-economic status of the families using the centre. What strategies can you put in place to prevent and minimise non-payment of fees? Reflect on strategies used by Daniela when considering your options.

Understanding income and expenditure cycles

In any organisation, its operational systems, structure, financial processes and financial health should be consistent with the organisation's vision, philosophy, policies and procedures. It is also critical to identify the various sources of income—and to balance these with expenditure. In the EC sector sources of income can include fees, sponsorship, research or infrastructure grants, fee subsidies for families and fundraising events. It is particularly important to monitor *enrolment* and *utilisation* (or occupancy rates) and to understand the need to monitor the fee payments from families to ensure they are paid by the due date.

Pause–reflect–act 13.4

- Assess your current level of financial literacy on the basic financial procedures necessary to lead an EC centre as a viable business.
- Make a list of areas where you need to learn more and improve your skills and understanding in relation to financial planning and budgeting.
- Consider how you will get access to relevant people and/or other resources to ensure your familiarity with business planning.

Although a centre may aim for full occupancy and achieve it, the budget usually reflects an 80 to 95 per cent utilisation of available places, not 100 per cent. This enables flexible enrolments through vacancies that may occur throughout the year, both planned and unplanned. Some organisations, for example, plan for a staggered enrolment process at the start of the year, leaving some places vacant for two, three, four or more weeks. However, some centres are unable to budget for extra staff to support the existing staff in orienting new children into the program, nor deliberately keep places vacant by staggering enrolments over a few weeks. Every day that a place is vacant impacts on the income for the year, and the daily fee structure must also be set to take into account unexpected changes.

The above example illustrates the tension between daily operations and the philosophical approach to prioritising what is best for children. It is our belief that children settle quickly as their parents form relationships with staff during the initial orientation period. As such, it is recommended that intentional leaders seek a solution that can appropriately finance the orientation period, particularly for children under three years, from a long-term perspective. This may include families withdrawing children for a variety of reasons, such as moving house at short notice and any time lag that occurs between a place becoming vacant and a new child filling that spot means a loss of income. The daily fee structure should be set to ensure that, along with other income streams, all of the centre's expenditure can be covered for the year while taking into account such variations. Income from government subsidies, for example, can vary with each payment (as it is based on the means testing of families) and combined family incomes can vary, particularly for parents working in casual jobs.

Maintaining full enrolments for the year is the shared responsibility of the leader and the staff because it is the centre's overall reputation that attracts a strong and viable waiting list. Planning for 80 to 90 per cent of places being utilised is budgeting conservatively to ensure financial stability over time. Then, any utilisation above the budgeted amount can go towards covering unexpected loss of income or expenditure during the specified period. Stoney and Mitchell (2010, pp. 1–2) discuss the 'iron triangle (see Figure 13.1) of early care and education finance. Paying close attention to the three sides of the iron triangle is key to sound fiscal management'.

Table 13.1 is based on data collected for the Investigating Quality research study (Harrison et al., 2008), involving six externally rated high-quality EC centres in New South Wales. Each centre was a not-for-profit, medium-sized centre, with a capacity to enrol between 40 and 86 children in any one day. Centres 1 and 2 were located in a university; Centre 3 was auspiced by a large charity; Centres 4 and 5 were stand-alone centres; and Centre 6 was part of an integrated service delivering a mix of children's educational and health services. On average, each centre's budget was close to one million dollars. An examination of these centres' recent annual budgets enabled us to see the high/low expenditure items in a stand-alone EC centre run like a small business enterprise.

Figure 13.1 EC education iron triangle

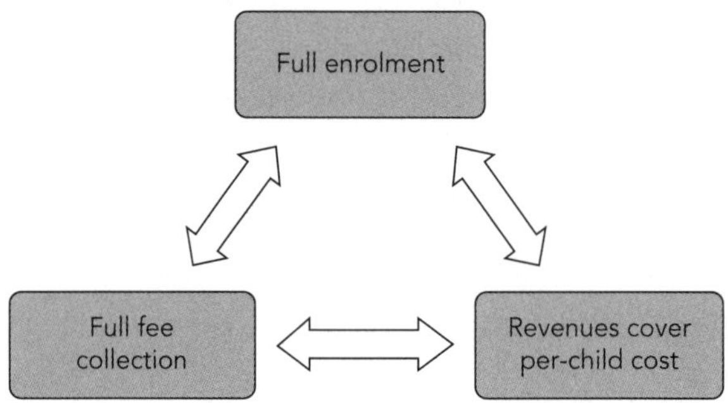

Source: Stoney & Mitchell, 2010.

Table 13.1 Budget information from six long day care centres

	Centre 1	Centre 2	Centre 3	Centre 4	Centre 5	Centre 6	Average
Licensed capacity	51	40	55	59	42	86	55.5
No. of families	75	50	110	160	86	225	118
Total budget ($)	1 077 167	906 670	1 128 664	732 848	621 544	1 320 617	964 585
	Proportion of the total budget allocated to each category of expenditure as identified (%)						
Staffing	90.2	89.3	71.7	83.8	83	88.4	84.4
Accommodation	3	1.6	3.6	5.8	6.7	4.4	4.2
Administration	2.2	1.4	16.5	3.4	3.9	2.2	4.9
Programs	3.8	6.4	2.8	3.6	1	1.6	3.2
Building	0.6	0.6	2.6	2.7	3.9	1.5	2
Profit	0.2	0*	2.7	0.7	1.7	0.8	1

Notes about the items listed in Table 13.1

- *Licensed capacity*: the total number of children each centre is licenced to enrol on any one day.
- *Number of families*: the number of families with children at the centre. It is possible to have two or more children from the same family. The large number of families in Centres 3, 4 and 6 reflect a high number of part-time users.
- *Staffing*: includes costs related to wages/salaries as well as superannuation, workers' compensation and professional learning.
- *Accommodation*: costs included gas, electricity, cleaning, security, non-program consumables and first-aid materials. Centres 1 and 2 are university-based centres and hence have lower accommodation, administration and building allocations.
- *Administration*: phone, Internet, advertising, licensing fees, professional membership, printing and stationery costs are included here.
- *Programs*: costs relate to consumables, equipment, furniture and furnishings, resources and laundry costs.
- *Building*: repairs, maintenance, insurance, rates, water and gardening costs.
- *Profit*: with the exception of Centre 2 (indicated by * in Table 13.1), which received additional financial support from an auspicing organisation, centres factored a profit margin into their budgets.

When planning the annual budget, EC leaders must consider the importance of quality, both to outcomes for children and families and, ultimately, to the centre's financial health. Quality is more than simply meeting minimum legislated child–staff ratios (Press, 2006) and staffing qualifications. Staffing costs are a major component in a centre's business plan, and the qualifications and experience of staff have a direct impact on those costs. Sylva, Melhuish, Sammons, Siraj-Blatchford and Taggart (2004a) established unequivocally that the higher the qualifications of staff, the better the outcomes for children. Consequently, a leader should be able to advocate for a long-term business plan that supports and retains staff who upgrade their qualifications.

A leader should also be able to articulate how the benefits of well-qualified staff outweigh any additional costs. It is often, in fact, both more cost-effective and educationally sound in the long term to retain staff with upgraded qualifications than to hire new staff who may attract lower salaries. While endeavouring to seek improvements to staffing ratios and resources, families, if included in the dialogue about operational costs, can become your greatest allies by supporting your decisions when presenting the budget for approval by management. An appropriate time to advise families of the fee structure and the need to increase fees each year as staff achieve higher qualifications is when they attend the waiting-list information session. A fee increase that includes retaining a valued staff member is seen in a more positive way when parents can understand the reasons for it. Additionally, remind management and staff of the significant value of long-term relationships for both children and families. With good ratios and well-qualified staff the productivity of the team is also increased and ultimately program quality is strengthened.

Pause–reflect–act 13.5

Use the information presented in Table 13.1 to reflect on the following questions:

- Centre 1 spends more than 90 per cent on staff; how can you justify this approach?
- Centre 3, which has the lowest allocation for staffing, has the highest administration costs. Which factors may be contributing to this approach?
- Look at the proportion of profit being targeted by each centre as identified in Table 13.1. Is this allocation too high/low?
- How would you justify making a profit if you are running a community-based, not-for-profit centre?

Avoiding pitfalls and managing risks

Leadership influences the way an EC organisation delivers its program and this, in turn, affects the financial health of the centre as a small business. Intentional leaders can make a difference by understanding, and responding appropriately to, the various external and internal factors that influence a centre's financial position. External factors that can impact on current and future cash flow include the health of the local economy and any changes to salary/wage rates, bank interest rates, local and global financial markets and government policy changes affecting EC settings. Internal factors may include changing family circumstances (such as an unexpected job loss for a parent), staffing changes (such as pregnancy and parental leave provisions), as well as management's ability to budget and plan effectively, taking into account relationships with families and the community.

In some regional areas in Australia, environmental factors such as floods or bushfires can be devastating for a small community-based EC setting; it can, for example, lead to a loss of income while waiting to claim payment from the building insurer. Another factor might be related to the accreditation process, whereby there is a requirement to plan and implement an environmental sustainability project to engage children and to raise awareness of issues such as floods or lack of rain impacting a community. The costs associated with this project may be substantial and, again, this requires adopting a long-term approach to business financing. Setting aside some of the organisation's surplus revenue for use for unexpected expenses is also a worthwhile consideration. For instance, supporting a family in need due to unemployment or ill health for a chosen period of time can benefit the family and enhance the organisation's social standing within the community in addition to contributing to the social capital of that community. A contingency fund could be established with defined eligibility criteria and procedures for applying for, and granting, temporary fee relief. Although management would usually be responsible for deciding on fee relief for a family, a pedagogical leader may be asked to contribute to the discussion.

Both long-term and short-term low occupancy rates are among the major financial risks of an EC organisation. It may be difficult to predict the timing or the impact of a major economic downturn such as the Global Financial Crisis of 2007–2008. This could mean that families cannot afford to send their children to EC settings. The quality of the program and the professional relationships developed by the leader and the staff, however, will be reflected in the families' satisfaction with the organisation. These relationships are important at all times, not only during a crisis. Social media may amplify the good, or poor, reputation of a centre as well as its business viability.

In Leaders in practice 13.2, Anthony Semann and Colin Slattery—who run a small business enterprise focusing on research, professional learning and organisational development—offer some guidance on how to avoid pitfalls and better manage risks when leading an EC organisation.

chapter 11 looks more closely at developing effective relationships with families, and the impact of social media is discussed in chapter 9.

LEADERS IN PRACTICE 13.2

Anthony Semann and Colin Slattery

Directors, Semann & Slattery, Sydney (NSW) and Melbourne (VIC)

How do you introduce the need to develop a business plan when running an EC organisation?

EC organisations are no different from any other business in that they are required to plan for the future. Business plans guide organisations across a range of functions including recruitment, marketing and finances. As consultants, we frequently see EC programs that, through a lack of planning, find themselves in financial crisis, including difficulties in managing the costs associated with delivering the program. In working alongside EC organisations, we explore with senior management the range of issues that may impact on operations and the plans or strategies that will assist them in making strategic business decisions. Such an approach often highlights that an 'organic' approach to business operations does not serve these organisations well. When planning for growth, the unexpected and tougher times are fundamental in running a successful EC organisation. It is unfortunate, however, that often it takes a crisis to alert individuals to the fact that business planning should be part of everyday organisational management, rather than a reactionary strategy to an existing or looming crisis.

What would you consider to be the key elements of a business plan for an EC setting?

First, understand the social and political contexts of the sector and community in which you operate. Undertaking an environmental scan is a good place to start in developing a business plan as this allows you to find out who (else) is operating in your community, where the sector is heading and what changes may be awaiting the sector.

In developing a business plan, it is also important to understand the demographics of your local community. This can be easily achieved by accessing census data. A business plan should include key outcomes and objectives for the organisation over a 12-month period, and identify any capital works to be initiated within the 12-month time frame and any potential human resources issues. A simple table that includes outcomes, strategies and resources is required (including people or finances) to map out responsibilities, time frames and progress. A quarterly review should track progress against these outcomes.

What would you identify as the pitfalls in the financial management of an EC setting and what steps could be taken to prevent these?

In everyday practice, a business plan comes alive through the centre budget. The development and management of an operational budget is the key to the success of any organisation. For many organisations, this means simply showing how income matches spending. However, this may fail to protect the organisation sufficiently from any fluctuations in income or in unexpected spending, so enough money should be held in reserve to cover unexpected or unplanned issues. Remember your budget should be an enabler, not a disabler. It should be developed knowing that you can undertake the everyday functions of the organisation while also saving money for future spending.

Understandably, there is much tension around the issue of profit making within the EC sector. Profit is often, incorrectly, linked to quality. That is, you can run a profitable business, pay staff well and still make money while delivering quality. Other challenges include market forces, such as including what other providers in the community are charging. It is important to benchmark what each service charges against other services. To do this effectively, you need to take into consideration variables such as staff salaries (for example, do you pay staff above the minimum award?), staff employment conditions (for example, do you provide staff with ample time to plan and document learning?) and the quality of the setting (for example, are the resources available for teaching and learning of good quality?).

Quality does matter, and quality does cost. You must always keep this in mind when developing your business plans and the budget. Investment in staff is vital to staff retention. The role of leaders is to build a healthy culture which rewards and recognises staff. Happy staff ultimately mean a healthy and viable workplace. One way to ensure this is to have the financial resources to implement the above points.

One final point: it is important that staff have an opportunity to participate in business planning and budget monitoring. It is hard to take responsibility for something one has little knowledge of. To that end, have you considered sharing some aspects of how the money is being spent with staff such as casual staff costs, buying resources and professional development? As staff begin to understand the mechanics of how a budget operates, they are more likely to have a greater appreciation of the financial aspects driving the quality of your organisation's operation.

Pause–reflect–act 13.6

Ensuring that a centre is full or at the budgeted capacity is critical for its economic viability. Taking into account advice provided by Anthony and Colin about avoiding pitfalls and managing risks when running EC settings, how would you respond to the following scenarios? Prioritise your approach in relation to the rights of the child.

- Can fees be made more affordable to ensure the centre is accessible to all children regardless of their parents' income? What are the implications of doing this in terms of program quality?

- What do you think about advertising a 'free day' once a month to entice families from disadvantaged backgrounds to send their child to your centre so they can experience an educational program? What are the pros and cons of this approach from the child's perspective?
- Is it appropriate to offer additional services such as haircuts, dinners or a laundry service to provide additional income for your centre? Give your reasons to explain your response.

Windows of opportunity

In most circumstances, both EC leaders and a centre's management are happy if the budget breaks even, or achieves a modest surplus, at the end of a financial year. As any extra expenditure usually represents an added cost to families, ambitious plans or dreams for the centre are often set aside. An intentional leader, however, must look for windows of opportunity to source the extra funding, services or labour needed for special projects or improvements. That is, there are possible solutions for EC settings to gain support for particular projects without it impacting on their budget expenditure. Consider for instance, that Technical and Further Education (TAFE) colleges and universities are willing to involve their students in community-based projects that fit in with the courses they offer by giving, for example, landscaping, horticultural and architectural advice. For example, if an EC setting wanted to upgrade its outdoor environment, it could allow students to do their practical experiences in planning and managing this upgrade at its setting. The EC setting could be responsible for paying the cost of the materials required, but not the labour to get the work completed. Funding available as community service grants from either the local council or a service club such as Lions or Rotary is also worth exploring.

Monitoring national, state and local government websites for opportunities to apply for funding for special projects should be a regular task for the EC leader. Funding is often available for capital works, environmental sustainability projects and community involvement. Developing funding applications can be quite arduous and funding is usually competitive, but programs may also allow for creativity and innovation on the applicant's part. The nature of the sponsor may also influence a decision to submit an application, as alignment with the centre's vision and philosophy is an important consideration. For example, sponsor by a fast food chain may not fit with a centre's healthy eating goals.

Most organisations will support an EC program project as long as a sound business plan and a formal agreement for the project have been developed. The plan should include compliance information, authorisation from management, the projected costs, sources of funding, lines of responsibility, insurance certificates and timelines, and opportunities for acknowledging the organisation in an ethical way.

Chapter summary

This chapter aimed to empower EC leaders to engage in the 'money matters' that are integral to running a successful centre. Less obvious compliance costs that are a result of legislative and financial accountabilities for the sector have also been highlighted. The 'Leaders in practice' sections included in this chapter provide suggestions for avoiding pitfalls and managing risks as well as how to make use of opportunities to strengthen your organisation as a small business enterprise. Upon reading this chapter it may now be evident that by enhancing financial awareness so much more can be achieved. In effect, dreams can be dreamed and business plans can be developed to make those dreams come true. It will not be all smooth sailing and ethical dilemmas will arise; advocacy will be needed, along with optimism. The leader must have an intention to become involved in the financial management of the organisation to ensure the pedagogical aims can be achieved and positive outcomes for children made possible—all within an integrated reporting model.

Key references

Adams, C. (2013). *Understanding Integrated Reporting: The concise guide to integrated thinking and the future of corporate reporting*. Oxford UK: Do Sustainability.

This book provides an overview of the integrated reporting system and approach.

Bryant, L. & Gibbs, L. (2013). *The manual: Managing a children's service*. Sydney: Community Child Care Cooperative NSW.

This book is a useful resource for approved providers and supervisors managing EC settings in New South Wales.

Morgan, G. & Emanuel, B. (2010). *The bottom line for children's programs* (5th ed.). Massachusetts: Steam Press.

This book has been written by American authors for EC settings located in the USA. It is being highlighted because it contains user-friendly templates and examples on money matters that can be modified for local contexts in Australia.

Online resources

Alliance for EC Finance

The authors of this website are financial consultants to the sector and post their discussion papers to be downloaded or read online at no cost. While the issues being discussed refer to experiences in the USA, there are many elements that are consistent with the experience in the Australian EC sector.

www.earlychildhoodfinance.org

Business help from the Australian Government

Australian government departments and agencies offer small business training and resources through their websites. Here are some examples:

Australian Taxation Office: ww.ato.gov.au/businesses/content.asp?doc=/content/00103072.htm

Australian Government Department of Industry, Innovation and Science: www.business.gov.au

Safe Work Australia: www.safeworkaustralia.gov.au/sites/SWA

14 PLACES AND SPACES FOR ADULTS FOR THINKING AND LEARNING

CHAPTER LEARNING OBJECTIVES

After studying this chapter you will understand that:

- Leaders in EC settings can define and influence the functional aspects of the indoor and outdoor spaces as well as the aesthetics and ambiance.
- Leaders' decisions on how indoor and outdoor spaces are arranged impact on the adults' engagement within the workplace.
- Physical spaces influence relationship building, thinking, learning and professional practice in ethical ways.
- Adults' health, well-being and job satisfaction are affected by how workplaces are designed and organised.
- The aesthetics and ambiance of the EC setting can influence, support and inspire the organisational ethos.
- The building design reflects the valuing of children, adults and learning in EC settings.

Key concepts

'Perezhivanie'
purpose built
re-purposed buildings
theory of binding and bonding
thinking environment

Overview

This chapter explores the impact of the EC workplace environment on the adults who work within these spaces. It is evident that the spaces for adults need to be functional, comfortable and well-designed to promote job satisfaction and to create a cohesive, harmonious workplace for teaching and learning. The two stories profiled in this chapter provide examples of how the environment influences and inspires both adults and children. Many centres plan, arrange and use their space very well. New centres are also being built with a focus on aesthetics and good design. This chapter offers suggestions for future consideration when reviewing and rebuilding your environments as places where adults can learn as well as offering a retreat where they can think and learn alone or with others.

Thinking about spaces for adults

Intentional leaders can lead the processes of planning, designing, building or refurbishing an EC educational space from the start. During the early stages, the leader can provide an account of the physical, intellectual and psychosocial needs of staff as well as those of the children and their families. Become involved with the design and organisation of the spaces within the setting by informing the architects and designers about the important elements of an EC educational workplace environment including the 'behavioural determinants of design' (Moore, 1979, p. 19). The environment does influence, for better or for worse, the working conditions for staff; this then impacts on their job satisfaction and their physical and emotional health and well-being. How the physical spaces in EC settings can either support staff or make it difficult to complete daily tasks easily and safely is incorporated into workplace health and safety policies in Australia (for example, see New South Wales Government WorkCover, 2011; NSW WorkCover, 2011; Work Safe Victoria, 2008).

Well-planned spaces are conducive for the complex requirements of staff when working with children and families. EC places are not just teaching and learning spaces. Relationships, which are fundamental to EC education, need places where professional relationships among staff, parents and other community members can be built and flourish along with the teaching and learning that takes place with children. 'Relational places creates connections and its aesthetic quality is dependent on the quality of the connections' (Giaminnutie, 2013, p. 27). Organisational or institutional characteristics—such as open spaces, functional furniture and other furnishings such as lights, windows, floor covering, curtains and cushions—add to the aesthetic appeal of the place. In some EC settings, carrying out the basic, everyday functions of the organisation—including developing relationships—is difficult, particularly in **re-purposed buildings**.

re-purposed buildings are settings located in a building that was originally built for another purpose, such as a family home or a neighbourhood community centre. To comply with legal and legislative requirements, the original buildings have been modified.

Mechanical or functional aspects of design (such as spaces designated for different experiences) should be planned for by ensuring ease of storage of resources and ease of movement. Design and style of furniture, equipment being used in these spaces (such as beds, benches, blocks and books) and floor coverings (such as bamboo floor boards, slate tiles and wool carpets) interact together in influencing the aesthetics of lighting, acoustics, temperature control, ventilation and accessibility of the EC setting. When taken together, each of these elements contributes to job motivation and job satisfaction (Jayaweera, 2015; Naharuddin & Sadegi 2013). Leaders can play a key role in planning the placements of these elements to ensure staff can enjoy their work, find satisfaction and carry out their responsibilities with enthusiasm.

LEADERS IN PRACTICE 14.1

Candace Fitzgerald

Early Childhood Teacher, Arnhem Land (NT)

My journey so far in teaching has been far from not being challenging and boring. It has been completely the opposite, by embarking on a not so 'traditional' career path for a first year teacher. Following my graduation from Macquarie University, my initial teaching plan was to work as a casual teacher in EC centres or primary schools around the Sydney metropolitan area. Instead, I have ended up 4045 km away from Sydney, in a school located in a remote place up north in a town with a population of approximately 1200.

During my fifth year at Macquarie University, studying a Bachelor of Education (Birth to 12 years), I was one of three students who completed the final practicums up in the Northern Territory at the local school in a remote Aboriginal community. I loved it so much that the following year I decided to pack up and move to this community. The remote school was located approximately three hours from Darwin in Arnhem Land, on the other side of Kakadu National Park. Arnhem Land is the home of traditional landowners, which requires non-Aboriginal people to get a permit to work or visit the land. The school caters for all ages of children with a crèche, a playgroup, a preschool, a primary school and a high school. During the first six months of my employment as a teacher, I was managing and running the playgroup, followed by a transition into the primary school for the rest of the year.

Many lessons have been learnt from engaging and working in this very 'foreign' setting that I have not grown up in and where they speak a different language. There are, however, two particular lessons I have learnt that I wish to highlight from this experience in this locality:

1 Building relationships with parents and children is the key to education

Relationship building can take a while, and depending on the cultures of the families you interact with, it may take longer. When I first started managing the playgroup I needed to hold myself back from my personal beliefs, such as asking parents questions about their child, shaking hands or talking loudly. All the things that may be very inviting for parents in urban settings were very intrusive for the parents I was working with, who were Aboriginal. It took me at least a month to see the trust being built between the children, the parents and me. Once the trust had been created, it was as if a wall was knocked down between us and I had been adopted into the community. First I was given a skin name, and from that point onwards the parents, particularly the women, taught me a lot about their culture and life. More importantly, I was able to develop meaningful relationships over time. This in turn reflected through my planning for activities and lessons because of my deeper understanding of their culture, as well as knowing how to communicate with parents to better understand their children.

2 Educating children and interacting with parents is not limited to the four walls of your EC centre or school

For some cultures, to set foot into a large, air-conditioned, clinical building can be very intimidating and an unwelcoming experience. When I initially was running the playgroup in the community, the attendance of children and parents was very low and I needed to find a way to encourage more people to attend. In collaboration with my colleague, who had lived in the community all her life and knew what community members wanted, we decided to take the playgroup to the community instead of them coming to us. We developed a mobile playgroup a couple of times a week where we took 'the classroom' into communal areas within the community. As a result, children's attendance grew because families could come and go, it was close to their homes, and teaching and learning occurred outdoors—on the land. I was so surprised at the difference in not only the attendance, but the difference in how comfortable both parents and children were being in the 'outside classroom'. I used a similar technique when teaching in the primary school. When a child's attendance was low or I wanted to share a good news story, I would reach out to the parents by personally visiting them at their homes instead of waiting for them to approach me. These EC strategies also helped to increase high school attendance and relationships.

Teaching is a career that can go far and beyond cities, buildings and fences. Putting yourself out there and letting go of traditional 'white man' environments where children are typically given an education is something I think all teachers should reflect upon within their own practices when teaching. Get out there and be a part of your community to make a difference in the child's world.

Pause–reflect–act 14.1

How we choose to work in an environment is linked to our understanding of social and cultural sensitivities of that place and its surrounding community.

- Consider Candace's experiences to gain an understanding of the value of creating a social environment within the physical environment that nurtures relationships.
- In Australia's culturally diverse society, how might you work with young children and their families at your centre in ways that respect their values and beliefs?

An environment that is well planned, designed and organised, where workplace and personal needs and comfort have been considered, sends a clear message to staff (and families) that they and their work are valued. Being valued leads to staff having the opportunity of building positive workplace relationships. Establishing a cohesive, harmonious workplace for staff should be one of the leader's key goals in an EC setting that delivers high quality programs for children. This is especially important for infants and young children, as staff, whether they realise this or not, set the scene for nurturing secure emotional connections through their daily engagements with each other and the children and their families. Vygotsky (1994) describes the influence of the emotional environment and experiences as the '**perezhivanie**' created by staff, which impacts on children's psychosocial development:

perezhivanie is the term used by Vygotsky (1994) to describe the emotional atmosphere created by the adults in children's play spaces.

> The emotional experience [perezhivanie] arising from any situation or from any aspect of his [her] environment, determines what kind of influence this situation or this environment will have on the child. It is a lived experience … inclusive of the surrounding conditions and how these conditions affect the person, how they are perceived and felt by them and how they cope with them. (Vygotsky, 1994, pp. 338–9)

The need to ensure children are dwelling within a positive, respectful and secure emotional environment makes a compelling argument for ensuring staff are happy and enjoy good working conditions where their emotional well-being as well as their physical needs are provided for along with the children's.

In an attempt to analyse the diverse emotional responses of human beings to built environments where people come together—such as schools, workplaces, shops, museums and hospitals—Stenglin (2008) identified the **theory of binding and bonding**: 'Binding theorises the way people's emotions can be affected by the organisation of space', and bonding 'is concerned with the potential spatial design has for social interaction: in particular the building of solidarity and affiliation' (p. 426). There is a need to bring people together to facilitate communication across EC settings. In seeking to achieve common goals, leaders can benefit from Stenglin's research by understanding how to share this information with architects and designers with confidence. This is one way leaders can influence the creation of effective places and spaces for adults to think and learn in EC settings.

theory of binding and bonding is concerned with the interpersonal dimension of organising spaces, and captures people's feelings or emotional responses to places.

Staff need comfortable places inside EC settings for a variety of different purposes including administrative tasks, research data analysis and writing, confidential meetings with parents, and places where they can sit still and reflect on children's learning. In effect, leaders can be influential in supporting staff in performing their multifaceted role satisfactorily through designing and allocation of appropriate spaces (Naharuddin & Sadegi, 2013). An intentional leader would aspire to ensure staff have a safe place that is also functional and pleasant to work in, with a great team of staff and appropriate resources. A sense of place is 'the particular experience of a person in a particular setting, feeling stimulated, excited, joyous, expansive' (Steele 1981 cited in Cross, 2001, np). A workplace environment has an effect on staff happiness and satisfaction. If staff feel unhappy, uneasy and insecure they want to leave the space, not linger in that space (Stenglin, 2008). Likewise, Preziosi (1979 in Giamminutie 2013, p. 53) states that binding 'recognises the emotional functions of the built environment, and space generates emotions, creates meaning and creates conditions for belonging'.

According to de Botton (2007) if there are visible signs of 'celebrations of tenderness' (p. 7) for the adults as well as the children, these elements can enhance feelings of well-being. This kind of ethos within an EC setting can be as inspirational for adults as they are for children. Based on interviews she conducted in the USA, Cross (2001, p. 3) developed a typology consisting of six types of relationship to place: 'biographical, spiritual, ideological, narrative, commodified, and dependent'. This typology can be used to analyse people's associations and attachments to various places, and these relationships to place can change over time. She concluded that 'people with a sense of cohesive rootedness have a strong sense of attachment, identification, and involvement' (p. 9) to a particular place. When applying this kind of understanding to an EC workplace environment, everyone should feel comfortable that they belong there. It is anticipated that EC leaders will seek to create workplaces that instil not only a sense of place, but one where everyone feels a sense of pride in identifying with their EC setting.

Pause–reflect–act 14.2

Think about the EC environments that you have experienced:

- Were there designated learning spaces that could be used as a place for adults' thinking and learning?
- Was the setting tranquil and calm or full of hustle and bustle throughout the day?
- What was the emotional ambiance or the 'perezhivanie' of this setting and how did it influence your work?
- Did staff have long periods of time to work with children without interruption?
- What was the communication like between the adults, including the parents and staff?

Functional and inspirational? EC environments can be both

In EC settings, it is more likely that the practical, functional features will be the dominant aspect of designing buildings, as well as in defining the organisation of internal spaces, and the outdoor environment. Planning will most likely refer to the past or current design 'blueprint' for the EC internal and outdoor environments. Preference for the tried and true elements is apparent in settings around Australia. The institutional design characteristics for internal spaces and fitout inclusions are commonly available and acceptable, especially where there is a focus on compliance with building codes and regulation requirements. Considerations of innovative or aesthetically pleasing designs in EC architecture and landscaping based on the work that is to be carried out in these spaces may not always be a priority. Leaders can, however, be creative and courageous by working out how to comply within an innovative and aesthetically pleasing design.

In the EC setting, aesthetically pleasing design elements refer to the style and configuration of the spaces, selection and organisation of furniture, furnishings and resources; and the colour palette. Although practitioners are aware of the importance of creating what de Botton (2007) describes as 'visible celebrations of tenderness' (p. 7), or invitations for engagement with children, we overlook the need for staff to have the same thoughtful inclusions in their environments. All of these elements in the design of the whole setting should be reflective of the values and philosophy of the EC setting as defined by the people and their cultural contexts, including the community, the location and the local landscape.

There is also a need to venture away from the EC aesthetic, which has not changed over the decades since the 1960s. It is an aesthetic that makes EC settings look the same no matter the location, suburb, region or state. Adhering to the aesthetic and design choices of the past has a way of creating an institutional aesthetic, a look so traditional 'that [it] has no story to tell' (Libeskind Ted Talk, 2009). One could say traditional EC environments have 'no story to tell' beyond their functional purpose. This is not a message we want the community to receive. We want the community to have an interest in EC education as it has a very important story to tell. For staff, children and families, the place must convey the message that what happens in that space or location is important.

All inhabitants must feel that they belong in this space: that it is a shared space with a collective responsibility for teaching and learning; and that it reflects the respect and values of the place and its people. An EC setting has a role to play within the community. It is a place for children and adults to think, learn and grow in various ways, including doing research, being a mentor and being mentored. It is also a place where young citizens are learning to be members of a civil society. In enabling learning, respecting and relating, leaders can ensure the setting has a better fit-for-purpose by prioritising thinking and learning which are at the heart of the organisation's mission. This attention to design also reflects how the organisation positions itself within its community by valuing education (Cairns, 2015).

Places and spaces for adults for thinking and learning

> To live in an environment that has to be endured or ignored rather than enjoyed is to be diminished as a human being (Gualdie, cited in Greenman, 2005, p. 1).

When visiting EC settings, you may see places where there has not been much attention paid to the comfort of staff or visitors. There are very few EC settings that have well-designed workspaces and staffrooms where staff can have lunch or take a break, read and think quietly. The administrative aspects of the work required in an EC setting may also be overlooked in the planning and designing process. This means there is little or no place to hold meetings or have confidential conversations with staff or families and have easy access to computers, printers and other technological devices.

Much is written on the need to pay attention to the environment on behalf of the children, and less is written about taking into account the responsibilities and comfort of the adults who work in educational spaces. EC programs that are conducted in church or community halls, or mobile programs that visit communities from time to time, have makeshift internal arrangements for both the learning and functional spaces such as kitchens, bathrooms and storerooms. Working spaces for the adults are at best inadequate—if they have a place for this at all. In 'pack-away' programs offered at multiple venues and locations, staff complete their written work in their mobile vans or at home. The furniture and equipment are packed away and stored in cupboards or in vans at the end of the day, then everything gets unpacked the next day as their teaching and functional spaces are used in the evenings and on weekends for community programs. This must be such a physically exhausting and daunting task for staff in these programs.

The wise leader, however, would view the EC setting as a place of possibilities for innovative practice. Conceptually, much can be achieved by creating what Nancy Kline (2016, p. 27) has described as a '**thinking environment**', where people get together to support each other to 'think for themselves and think well together'. With some imagination, spaces or places to think and learn alone or together can be created within existing space either inside the existing building or outdoors. Thinking environments 'make it possible for people's thinking to move further, go faster, plumb insights, banish blocks and produce brand-new, exactly needed ideas in record time' (ibid). Kline offers a refreshing set of 10 principles that can be used to frame the work of EC leaders in empowering staff to become effective thinkers. Her approach cautions us about the dangers of saying there is no time to stop and think because 'we are too busy doing it' by asserting that 'to take time to think is to gain time to live' (Kline, 2016, p. 21).

thinking environment is an environment that empowers people and enables leaders to create environments where others can flourish.

Pause–reflect–act 14.3

Thinking about workspaces for the adults in EC settings that you have visited:

- How were different spaces designed and arranged for a particular fit-for-purpose? Think about the babies' room, the kitchen and the outdoor spaces used by toddlers.
- How did staff feel about the ease of access to the resources needed in these settings?
- As a leader, what modifications would you recommend to make these settings better for adults' thinking and learning?

Current thinking about EC education should be reflected in the planning and architectural design of new EC spaces. Haberer (cited in OWP/P Architects, VS Furniture & Bruce Mau Design 2010, p. 69) reflects a practical point of view about learning space design: 'it seems obvious but is often forgotten: Teaching and learning should shape the building, not vice versa'. More recently, with the increase in the building of privately owned centres there has been more innovation in the design and thought given to the style and aesthetics of the **purpose built** buildings for EC education and care. No doubt there are difficulties in consulting with the future inhabitants of the space as staff are usually employed long after the building is completed and fitted out.

purpose built EC settings have been designed with much care and forethought. This may have involved architects with expertise in spaces for children as well as adults. Input from an EC leader can also make a difference in creating dedicated places and spaces for adults to think and learn.

Moore (1979), in defence of architects, concurs: 'On the urban scale we are more often dealing with anonymous users. We cannot identify specific people of whom we can ask pertinent questions and with whom we can develop sets of requirements' (p. 18). Moreover, due to the lack of research on the design and development of EC settings, it is difficult to know to what extent the needs of staff or other adults (and not to mention the children) are considered by management or the owners of the property. Sometimes, make-do spaces for staff are created and these spaces often double up as a storerooms or storage spaces. Learning spaces also have to double up as eating and sleeping spaces and this multitasking of spaces imposes a series of physical tasks on staff, which adds to the daily work load and as a consequence impacts on job satisfaction.

Deasy and Lasswell (1990) acknowledge that there is a need to consult with the end users of the space, and they also acknowledge that 'it is notoriously difficult to translate such generalisations into design specifics' (p. 15). They go on to say that designing for 'a different set of functional requirements as well as a different set of social and psychological relationships' is not always straightforward (p. 15), even if the designer is part of the discussion in defining the goals. So it would seem it is difficult to achieve success in planning a well-designed workplace in an EC setting. Nevertheless, being aware of the difficulties and the need for allowing for dedicated workspaces requires consideration by leaders. This is one way of minimising inefficient use of space, and maximising the possibility of planning for flexible work spaces that can be used in a variety of different ways.

The function of spaces determines the design along with the budget constraints in some ways, which in turn influences the ambiance or the lack thereof in an EC setting. Overall, purpose built EC settings reflect a strong sense of positive orientation or comfort between the occupants and the place. According to Stenglin (2008, p. 444), 'this means it encourages users to remain in a space for longer periods of time, and thereby increases the likelihood they will engage with the objects, furnishings and people occupying that space'.

Consider the question, 'What is it that staff need in regards to the physical environment in which they work?' In Australia, the needs of staff with regard to working with children are provided for within typical open spaces in halls or large open-plan rooms. Ideally, smaller, more innovative and intimate spaces for small-group or project work with fewer distractions would be more desirable. Current designs for progressive educational spaces internationally do provide for small project working spaces or alternate spaces to the main classroom. For example, consider the design of the preschools in Reggio Emilia. In these preschools, there are places for projects to remain in situ for the children, to be worked on over time rather than being packed away at the end of the morning.

Spaces for drama, movement or music, construction, eating and sleeping are not necessarily planned for satisfactorily in an EC environment. Staff have to provide for these multiple experiences by moving furniture and equipment around to create open spaces. This is not an efficient use of an educator's time and effort. When moving furniture and equipment regularly, there are also risks to staff's long-term physical health and well-being to consider. Work health and safety risk management plans need to be taken into consideration due to constant and repetitive movements and tasks that have to be performed in multipurpose built environments. Re-thinking space allocation could alleviate some of the problems related to spaces having to be packed and unpacked every day. The intentional leader, in collaboration with staff and the designer, needs to re-imagine the use of space to alleviate these problems in the long term if these requirements were not originally planned for in the design of the building.

Pause–reflect–act 14.4

If you *have* been inside a purpose built EC setting, reflect on the spaces allocated for staff use only and identify key features that were positive and negative in relation to its net impact on the people involved at the centre.

If you *have not* been in an EC setting that has designated adult work spaces, identify a suitable place and arrange a visit. Prior to the visit, make a list of questions you would like to ask about how they make good use of these spaces in their centre. For example:

- How old is the building and which spaces are dedicated for use by staff and/or parents?
- In terms of the layout of the buildings and grounds, what proportion of space is allocated for staff thinking and learning?
- How satisfied were the staff with these spaces?

When thinking about the comfort of children and staff in older, more traditional EC settings, some thought needs to be given to heating, cooling and ventilation. These comfort and ambient aspects are also not easily achieved in open spaces, large classrooms and older buildings. Large spaces are cold in winter and hot in summer and are costly to heat and cool. Makeshift solutions such as fans and heaters are costly to run, inefficient and environmentally unsustainable. Another element of comfort and aesthetics is lighting. Optimal and focused artificial lighting, as well as access to natural light, have the potential to add positively to working conditions and an adult's sense of health and well-being (NSW Government WorkCover, 2011; Work Safe Victoria, 2008). Based on a study on hotel workers in the UK Jayaweera (2015) provided insights into the 'environmental conditions that significantly affected job satisfaction' (p. 275). According to Jayaweera (2015), having the right environmental factors, both physical and psychosocial, will lead to [an] increase [in] performance.

Staff and children need to be housed in comfortable conditions, with temperature control, ventilation and lighting to create an ambient atmosphere that enhances teaching and learning as well as everyone's sense of well-being. ***When reading the following 'Leaders in practice', reflect on these aspects and consider how Lisa Syrette prioritised various aspects in her EC setting and how she explains the reasons for this.***

LEADERS IN PRACTICE 14.2

Visit Oxford Ascend to hear more from Lisa.

Lisa Syrette

Manager, Caretaker's Cottage Child Care Centre, Australian Institute of Sport, Canberra (ACT)

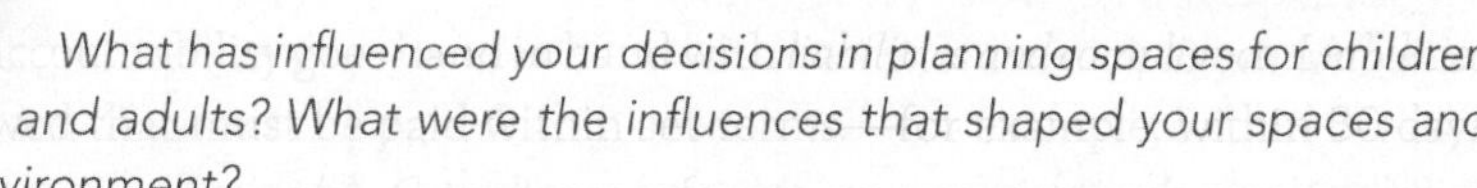

What has influenced your decisions in planning spaces for children and adults? What were the influences that shaped your spaces and environment?

Personal philosophy is important in planning spaces. I believe in aesthetics, sustainable practices and homelike spaces. Our image of children has also influenced our decisions. Concepts such as agency, freedom of movement, and seeing children as capable and competent are all factors in decision-making. Added to this is the importance of involving children in decisions, and we did consult with children extensively when planning our outdoor areas.

Staff well-being is important to me. When educators feel valued they give their best. I believe that being, belonging and becoming applies to educators and families as well as children. For a number of years we invested time and resources in improving spaces for children, but hadn't given the same attention to the adult spaces. It was a good opportunity to be reflective about this. Alain de Botton's 'visible signs of tenderness' remains a key concept, and something I refer to often. For us, it means our environments and resources are valued and cared for, and in turn that sends a message to children, families and educators that we value them and care for them.

What have you found to be the most effective decisions you have made? Who has benefitted and why?

A number of years ago we had the opportunity to build a new staff space, which means we now have a staff break room and a staff office. The benefits for staff well-being have been enormous. The staffroom is a work-free zone, away from the activity of the centre, so educators feel refreshed after breaks. A separate staff office means that the work of pedagogical planning and documentation is seen as valuable as well.

More recently, we opened our playground so that we have one space that children can share at all times. The change in children's play and relationships has been exciting to watch. Siblings can spend more time together and we have noticed that the morning drop-off rituals are happier as children can be dropped off together. Older children have mentoring and leadership opportunities and we have noticed that children are choosing peers based on shared interests rather than age. Relationships are developing between all educators and all children. I think that the sense of 'team' has developed, and communication between educators has improved as well.

Have there been any challenges to your decisions?

The shared outdoor space was challenging for educators. They needed to change the way they viewed supervision and responsibility for children. They also needed to revisit ideas of risk versus hazard and children's agency. Parents had some concerns about access to all areas as well, but we put in place some good communication strategies to ensure that parents were well informed.

What changes might you make after having lived with the organisation of the environment for a period of time?

The environment is always evolving. Opening the outside environment has changed our spaces and our thinking so much we are looking at how we can open up inside. The other challenge I have set is to think about how we can establish our outdoor space so that it doesn't need 'setting up' and 'packing away' every day.

What would you keep the same and why?

The one thing I would keep the same in relation to environments is our attitude. While there are things I love about our spaces, our thinking is always evolving and our community is changing regularly. What works for us now may not work in one, two or ten years. So openness to critical reflection in relation to environments is the only thing I wouldn't change.

Pause–reflect–act 14.5

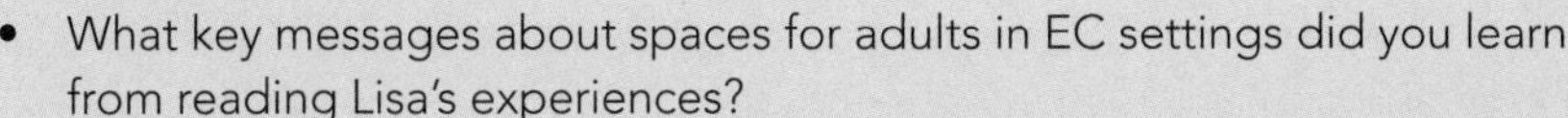

- What key messages about spaces for adults in EC settings did you learn from reading Lisa's experiences?
- Discuss the values that influenced Lisa's decision-making about thinking and learning spaces for adults at her EC setting?
- What are your thoughts about having a 'work-free zone' in EC settings?

Go to oxfordascend *to hear Lisa's thoughts.*

The staff room: the space for physical and social–emotional well-being

Something as basic as a staffroom, with secure storage facilities for personal belongings, and a place to eat, rest and relax, is an amenity for staff not necessarily found in every EC setting or workspace in other sectors (Park, 2010). For instance, research by Park (2010) with nurses in a hospital setting identified the importance of having 'a place to hang coats and hats and to change clothing; a clean well-appointed bathroom with shower; a well-equipped kitchen area for preparing meals and a dining area and furniture' (p. 11). Nursing staff also identified the need for a place to sit comfortably, relax and put their feet up with furniture that is clean, attractive and comfortable. The opportunity to 'share experiences and feelings' (Gray-Toft & Anderson, 1981, cited in Park, 2010, p. 11) is also considered a necessity. In this sense, a well-designed staff room in an EC setting is not just a space with amenities for cooking and dining—it is also a communal space at work where staff can see each other every day. Opportunities to communicate in a space such as this assist in building community.

Park (2010) also identified that the provision of a staff room can be considered through an ecological lens of design, and this is similar to the approach we have adopted in leading change within EC settings (Chapter 8). In this instance, from the perspective of 'productivity':

> Organisational Ecology addresses the interrelation of the physical setting and the social system as a key thriving/constraint factor of an organisation ... factors such as social and emotional support, communication, feeling valued, lower turnover rate, cost reduction, improved [output] quality, fatigue reduction, lower [task] errors all impact on increased job satisfaction. (Becker 2007, cited in Park 2010, p. 13)

Staff in most workplaces need the same retreat facilities identified in Park's research. Reflecting on such research, intentional leaders are asked to consider their attitudes and ability to pursue the establishment of an appropriate staff room in each EC setting. The benefits of providing a retreat for rest and relaxation for all staff, away from the classrooms and with some privacy in the workplace, can enhance the overall quality of the programs delivered as well as the well-being of everyone involved.

Pause–reflect–act 14.6

Think of the staff rooms in EC settings you have been in, and consider the following aspects:

- Were they pleasant spaces to be in as adults, with attractive furnishings inviting staff to come in?
- What signs were there to indicate staff attitudes about the use of this place?
- What messages are reflected by the presence of notes on the sink about cleaning your coffee mugs; unpacking the dishwasher; birthday/holiday greetings; music, fruit flowers and magazines, and so on?
- What is your ideal vision of an EC staff room? Give your reasons to justify your design.

As a leader what would you say were important inclusions within the built environment to support staff in the operational aspects of an EC setting?

Places for staff and families

Inclusion of designated places or spaces for staff and families to meet in comfort, with adult-sized seating is not part of the Australian National Law and Regulations (ACECQA, 2011a) covering EC settings. Since it is not mandated in this way, in many EC settings there is no formal meeting space for a confidential conversation. According to Greenman (2005, p. 7),

> Our EC environments say a great deal about our assumptions about the work and our expectations for staff. Do we expect staff to be simply nurturing or actively thinking, planning, creating, working collaboratively and meeting with parents [families]?

Staff meetings and professional development usually take place in classrooms with adults sitting on children's chairs. Staff meetings, if conducted in a professional space, however, have the potential to raise expectations for engagement and realisation of productive learning outcomes. After a long day, it is unreasonable to expect staff to be able to focus and contribute in a meaningful while sitting for an hour or more on children's chairs or on the floor. The quality of the discussion can be improved if seating arrangements in staff meetings are more comfortable.

Meetings with colleagues to discuss matters related to their work or about children's development or their professional development requires some privacy. It is important that meetings take place in a conducive environment. Meeting with families to discuss a child's progress while sitting on children's furniture in an empty classroom is not comfortable, nor is it private. The office space is often the default choice, with the director or coordinator or administrative staff needing to vacate the room. Interviews with prospective employees usually take place in the office as well. Depending on the number of people on the interview panel, a small office might be too small to hold everyone comfortably. This does not create a good impression with a prospective employee, but the office is usually the only private space in the centre. Very little is written or researched about the organisational culture or the aesthetics of an EC setting, except those in Reggio Emilia, Italy (Giamminuti, 2013). Most descriptions of an effective meeting space only require that the space be comfortable. Staff meetings, professional development workshops, family meetings and formal interviews are the operational aspects of a teaching and learning space.

Spaces that are flexible but not necessarily always used for multiple experiences regularly are more appropriate for the complexity of children's learning. Having designated learning spaces can enable staff to gain satisfaction in their work as they are not working as furniture removalists for most of the day. Instead, their time can be spent more productively with the children. The ambiance of the environment and the temperature, ventilation, lighting, design and aesthetics contribute to a positive workplace environment, which impacts on the relationships and physical and emotional health and well-being of both children and adults. Job satisfaction is an important goal for every employee and it is the leader's role to ensure this is made possible.

Meeting spaces and places for retreat for the adults who work in EC educational places may, one day, be included in the design and building of new and refurbished settings. Spaces for discussions, collaboration, documenting and recording all need to be available, along with meeting and retreat spaces, to afford privacy and comfort. This will mean acknowledging the complexity of the role of the teacher and other staff in an EC program. It is high time for EC leaders to flex their influence with developers, designers and architects to evaluate the work that is required to support the establishment of attractive and effective thinking and learning spaces for the adults involved.

Chapter summary

Planning for professional spaces, where educators and families can meet each other or retreat during work time in EC settings, requires critical attention by today's leaders. When collaborating or documenting professional work or wanting to have some respite during a busy day, staff need to have appropriate spaces at their place of employment. This will mean acknowledging the complexity of the individual and collective responsibilities of EC teachers, leaders and all other staff in an EC setting. Spaces for teaching and learning, both indoors and outdoors, need to be considered in the light of current thinking and practice about curriculum and children's ways of thinking and being.

Key references

de Botton, A. (2007). *The architecture of happiness*. UK: Penguin.

De Botton introduces the reader to the history and language of architecture and the impact that various elements of architecture have on people. Buildings and the spaces within buildings can create a sense of emotional and physical well-being, a sense of despair, safety and security or a sense of discomfort. De Botton describes these influences in a philosophical framework, and this is useful when planning, designing and organising EC settings.

Giamminuti, S. (2013). *Dancing with Reggio Emilia: Metaphors for quality*. NSW, Australia: Pademelon Press.

This book takes the reader on a virtual tour of the caring spaces and learning places in two of the world-famous EC settings in Reggio Emilia. Giamminuti describes in detail two different experiences of entering and engaging with the children and the adults in each setting. In conversations with the children, the reader discovers through Giamminuti's lyrical descriptions that the stairs in Sculo Pablo Neruda do speak to the children about what is to happen in this space.

Greenman, J. (2005). Places for childhood in the 21st century: A conceptual framework. *Beyond the journal, Young children on the Web,* May.

Greenman was the first EC practitioner to write about spaces and places for children in his seminal book *Caring Spaces Learning Places: Environments for Children that Work*, published in 1986. Two decades later, this article reminds educators to plan environments for children with the understanding that the context, the community and the lives of children change over time and these changes should be considered in the planning and organisation of EC settings.

Kline, N. (2016). *Time to think: Listening to ignite the human mind*. London: Cassell.

This book was originally published in 1999 and continues to be in high demand. It is ideally suitable for helping others to learn how to think for themselves. Based on 10 principles, it provides practical guidance for organisations and individuals that can be applied in any situation.

Stenglin, M. (2008). Binding: a resource for exploring interpersonal meaning in three-dimensional space. *Social Semiotics*.18(4), 425–47.

This article provides an in-depth exploration of the emotional impact that environments have on people. We can immediately gain a sense of attraction or repulsion, a sense of security or insecurity on entering or being in a space. The theory of binding and bonding explains the emotional responses that people have to buildings, spaces and the outdoor environment. With this knowledge it is clear that environments are not benign, and it would serve well to understand how to create spaces to promote a sense of well-being.

Online resources

Clore Duffield Foundation (2015). *Spaces for learning: A new handbook for creating inspirational learning spaces, UK*.

This is an online resource for those who are planning learning spaces for children. From planning through to consultations about the ambience, flooring, lighting and furniture, this resource is a useful guide to ensure all elements have been considered. These foundations can provoke thinking about planning places and spaces for adults.

www.cloreduffield.org.uk

Influences on Architectural Design

For those interested in the principles of architecture, this architectural presentation explains graphically the theory of binding and bonding, with visual images and the terms used by architects.

www.id2012.weebly.com/uploads/5/1/2/4/5124834/conceptualization_2.ppt

Libeskind, D. (2009). *17 words of architectural inspiration*.

In this presentation, architect Daniel Libeskind shares his views about the elements of architecture and the impact that buildings, spaces and places have on people. He shows visual images that help the viewer gain a layperson's understanding of the impact architecture has on people and their emotions.

www.ted.com/talks/daniel_libeskind_s_17_words_of_architectural_inspiration

McGuickin, G. & Libeskind, D. (2015). *The people's architect*.

This online resource provides the viewer with an overview of Libeskind's architecture and the philosophy behind his thinking about designs. This information creates a sense of why it is important to be thinking more deeply about the spaces created for adults and children in EC settings.

www.decoist.com/daniel-libeskind-architecture

Safework NSW: www.safework.nsw.gov.au/
Worksafe Victoria: www.worksafe.vic.gov.au/
Safe Work Australia: www.safeworkaustralia.gov.au/

15 CAREER DEVELOPMENT AND SUCCESSION PLANNING

CHAPTER LEARNING OBJECTIVES

After studying this chapter you will understand that:

- Being and becoming leaders in the EC sector comprises both leadership *with* learning and leadership *for* learning.
- Leadership growth requires a commitment to lifelong learning.
- Creation of a culture of learning is a key responsibility of leaders.
- Engagement in professional learning through diverse strategies is important.
- Induction to the profession involves identifying, encouraging and supporting novice educators to become leaders.
- Leadership growth and succession planning in strategic ways can involve specialisation.

Key concepts

aspiring leaders
career ladder
novice educators
professional learning and development
professional learning community

Overview

Leadership literature continues to promote the importance of engaging in continuous learning in career development and the key role leaders can play in nurturing aspiring leaders. Under NQS Quality Area 7, there is an expectation that in creating a positive organisational culture, 'individual plans are in place to support learning and development' of all staff at each EC setting (ACECQA, 2017). This chapter focuses on professional learning and development (PLD) as a leadership endeavour where intentional leaders engage in learning for self-development and in supporting others to also enhance their capabilities. This includes playing a key role in identifying, assessing and supporting other EC educators to engage in PLD in strategically planned ways. A conceptual model of professional learning reflecting a variety of strategies is presented. 'Leaders in practice' sections profiling two educators at different stages in their careers are also incorporated into this chapter to inspire and illustrate possibilities for career planning. Given the absence of linear predictable career pathways that can systematically foster EC leadership, the importance of succession planning in diverse ways is emphasised.

Being and becoming leaders

For those who are passionate about working in the EC education sector, it is more than 'just a job'; it is a professional career. This view was affirmed by the Productivity Commission (2011b), which noted that 'intrinsic motivation is an important factor in the employment decisions of ECEC workers' (p. 76). Importantly, those with teacher education qualifications were 'much more likely to choose a long-term career in ECEC, working in a number of different services over a course of a 20 year career' (p. 76). Given the speed and complexity of societal developments today, Aubrey (2015) wisely reminds EC educators that 'continuous change requires continuous learning to understand the changing relationships with the community and the organisation concerned' (p. 3). What does this mean in terms of being and becoming an EC leader?

Leadership is not a matter of management from a distance, or balancing numbers and people to fit with compliance requirements. Intentional leaders do not simply develop programs and environments like a butterfly collection, nor do they cling to a focus on maintaining the status quo and adhere to safe practice. An EC leader demonstrates passion, wisdom, vision, a broad spectrum of insight, and respect for children, families, colleagues and themselves. This approach to leadership entails a commitment to, and a curiosity about, learning as a lifelong process. Importantly, this view is reflected within Australian government policy under Quality Area 7 of the NQS, both in terms of a leader's self-development and their capacity to empower others and drive continuous improvement at their settings (ACECQA, 2017).

professional learning and development (PLD) refers to continuous study in terms of understanding professional knowledge and skills and then using these to advance professionally by refining and renewing practices as an EC educator.

An organisation that values staff engagement in **professional learning and development** (PLD) actively seeks to foster ways to continually acquire and build professional knowledge and skills as an educator. By promoting this philosophy at a centre, a **professional learning community** can be created because there is an ongoing commitment to learn by all involved (see Quality Standard 7.2 in ACECQA, 2017). In essence, intentional leaders are learners who value lifelong learning for themselves and simultaneously foster the learning of others. Importantly, leaders enjoy the challenges that arise from such a vision, and can demonstrate both 'leadership *with* learning' and 'leadership *for* learning':

professional learning community comprises educators involved in PLD by actively seeking to foster ways of building professional knowledge and skills within an organisation or a region.

- *Leadership* with *learning* indicates that leaders are themselves engaged in learning as a way of extending and deepening their own knowledge, skills and understandings. According to Dubrin et al. (2006), self-awareness and self-discipline are fundamental to leadership development. They explain self-awareness by referring to the work of Argyris (1991), who developed the concept of single and double loop learning to emphasise the importance of feedback from others in developing oneself. Argyris (1991, as cited in Dubrin et al., 2006) described single loop learners as those who are not interested in seeking feedback and as people who 'engage in defensive thinking' (p. 452). In contrast, double loop learners understand the benefits of feedback, regardless of whether it is positive or negative. As Dubrin and colleagues explain, double loop learning reflects in-depth exploration and analysis using 'feedback to confront the validity of the goals or the values implicit in the situation'. Likewise, 'self-discipline', the second component of developing oneself as a leader, is essential to mobilise 'one's effort and energy to stay focused on attaining an important goal' (Dubrin et al., 2006, p. 453). They also note that leaders can be distracted 'because of the pressures of everyday activities' (p. 454). It is important, therefore, to be diligent in consciously monitoring your self-development requirements.

- *Leadership* for *learning* underpins the relational nature of leadership, as it is concerned with facilitating the learning of others. There is sufficient empirical evidence to show that a leader's approach to PLD can influence the way staff respond to learning (see, for example, Duignan, 2006; Hadley et al., 2015; Waniganayake et al., 2008). The connection between leading learning for oneself and for others is crucial in not only being an authentic leader, but also in realising the leadership potential of others in an organisation.

It is also appropriate to make reference to Rinaldi (2006) who, while reflecting about a professional learning community located in the USA and inspired by the Reggio Emilia approach, stated:

> Personal and professional development, like education, should not be seen as static or unchangeable qualities, achieved once and for all, but rather as a process, an ongoing path that we follow from birth throughout our lives, now more than ever. Personal and professional development and education are something we construct ourselves in relation with others, based on values that are chosen, shared and constructed together. (p. 137)

These comments capture the essence of learning as being relational and lifelong. Moss (2004, p. 2) reinforces this perspective by adding that 'the concept of the worker as co-constructing learner and researcher opens up new, complex and exciting possibilities'. It is here that intentional leaders can play a critical role, demonstrating their own excitement in learning by facilitating opportunities to learn together in small teams or large groups as appropriate.

Pause–reflect–act 15.1

- As an EC leader, what steps are you taking to demonstrate your commitment to continuous learning?
- What do you do when you come back from a PLD session? How quickly should you implement changes in practice based on your new understandings?
- Within your EC setting, consider ways of getting to know people's ideas, beliefs and values about leadership.
- Having identified their perceptions about leadership, how can you address the gaps in knowledge and skills necessary to implement leadership more effectively within your organisation?

Understanding continuing professional growth

With increasing research evidence highlighting the benefits of professional learning (see, for example, Colmer, et al., 2014; Fleet et al., 2016; Hadley et al., 2015; Waniganayake et al., 2008), it comes as no surprise that governments have been urged to incorporate policy interventions that support participation in professional learning for EC educators (OECD, 2011, 2015; Productivity Commission, 2011b). In Australia, one of the foundational principles in the EYLF is the focus on educators' ongoing learning and reflective practice (Principle 5, DEEWR, 2009). Likewise, within Quality Area 7 in the NQS (ACECQA, 2017) centre management is charged with the responsibility of evaluating educators' performance by having individual professional development plans.

Much has been written about the professional growth of educators in various ways (see, for example, Cherrington & Wansbrough, 2007; Gibbs, 2011; Rodd, 2013). The terms 'professional development' and 'professional learning' were once described as in-service training to refer to professional learning undertaken while being employed in the sector. Waniganayake et al. (2008, p. 119) have highlighted the difficulties of arriving at 'a comprehensive definition of what is meant and understood by professional development and support' due to the diversity of learning methods, models, resources and strategies available. Formal certificate or diploma courses offered by various training agencies and universities, as well as informal networking, mentoring and coaching opportunities, can also be described as professional development or learning.

According to Edwards and Nuttall (2009, p. 2) the shift from professional development to professional learning may reflect an appreciation of lifelong learning. This approach requires educators to think beyond their current and immediate job needs or career stage and look more broadly at learning from a long-term perspective. Fleet and Patterson (2009), in critiquing the evolution of professional learning discourses in Australia, discuss the move from exploring small case-based observations to critical incidents as provocations that can motivate learning to using shared narratives or stories of effective practice and the use of practitioner inquiry projects. Their emphasis on providing 'emotionally safe spaces for the risk-taking inherent in personal professional disclosure' as well as 'the element of ownership as a key element of the principles of professional growth' (Fleet & Patterson, 2009, p. 20) are timely reminders for leaders embarking on creating a positive organisational culture to support professional learning within their organisations (ACECQA, 2011c, p. 169). These forays into sustained practitioner projects or professional inquiry models can lead to organisational change (Fleet et al., 2016).

Short, one-off seminars and workshops may have their place in transmitting specific skills or policy related information. From a long-term development perspective, however, it is important that leaders consider ways of creating opportunities for educators to revisit experiences as explained by Fleet and Patterson (2009)—to talk, think, listen, pause and imagine possibilities by engaging in deeper levels of learning, either on their own or with others. In highlighting collective learning, Fleet and Patterson (2009, p. 21) state 'the "group" not only contributes to its own learning through synergies of circumstances and collective energy, but has the potential of evolving into a critical mass of people who can create a local culture and effect sustainable inquiry'.

Why is professional learning necessary?

According to Moss (2004, p. 1), there are three key reasons why educators ought to engage in professional learning:

- to upgrade and keep abreast of new knowledge, skills and understandings
- to respond effectively to changing requirements in policy and practice
- to enhance career development and advancement.

mentoring and coaching are discussed in chapter 10.

These reasons reflect the long-term benefits of professional learning. Strategies used to engage in professional learning can vary, and include mentoring and coaching, which can be used to deal with challenges or problems that emerge in everyday practice.

Over time, with increasing experience in the sector, and without renewing their knowledge base, educators can become complacent. Ongoing participation in professional learning experiences can enhance the depth and breadth of an educator's expertise, which can, in turn, enhance the status of the profession and advancement as leaders. This view is reflected in the following comments made by participants in one study where professional learning was described:

> … as can be seen, as a 'sign of pride in your profession' (Focus Group in Western Australia) and/or a way of raising the status of the whole profession through an active demonstration of their interest in learning and renewing their professional knowledge base. (Focus Group in South Australia in Waniganayake et al., 2008, p. 119)

So, engagement in professional learning has wide implications, both individually and collectively, for educators, organisations and the sector.

Professional learning support strategies

Leaders must be aware and informed of a wide range of funding opportunities that can support staff's professional learning. According to the OECD (2015), in Korea, for instance, professional development for kindergarten teachers,

> includes a self-evaluation, peer-evaluation and satisfaction survey from parents. The self-evaluation helps teachers reflect on their practice, rather than contributing to their evaluation score. Evaluation results are then used to decide where teachers need training, to enhance their professional development or select teachers for a sabbatical learning year. (p. 228)

Previously, Waniganayake et al. (2008, p. 122) have proposed that Australia establishes 'a national minimum standard of five days per year of planned professional development and support for each children's services practitioner employed in a prior to school setting'. This recommendation may be adopted as a useful benchmark by intentional leaders to allocate funding and seek other ways to support staff's PLD within their organisation.

National Quality Standard 7.2 clearly articulates that creating a professional learning community within the organisation is a leadership responsibility (ACECQA, 2017). Research by Waniganayake et al. (2008) found that childcare centres in Australia accessed a wide variety of professional learning programs and strategies. This study also shows how centres have implemented creative solutions to barriers such as 'geographical isolation, cost of registration, accommodation and travel costs' (p. 124) by adopting a variety of strategies including closing the centre for a day to focus on professional learning with an external facilitator. In some instances, participation in all-day professional forums or conferences organised by local councils has also provided valuable professional learning and networking opportunities involving other professionals from schools, and health and community services.

The more traditional forms of PLD, which are delivered in disparate ways to diverse groups of educators from a variety of services, is being increasingly questioned in terms of effectiveness in garnering real change in practices (see Hadley et al., 2015). A move to 'customised' professional learning, which involves developing a program where the content of learning is determined specifically aligned with the centre's philosophy, goals and staff needs is becoming a more favourable approach to PLD. It has been found that this type of learning can foster 'a sense of ownership' because all aspects of planning, implementation and evaluation of the learning content included the learners (Waniganayake et al., 2008, p. 123; Hadley et al., 2015; Hadley et al., 2016).

In contrast, participation in generic sessions presented externally and involving educators from a variety of organisations may not necessarily be based on the analysis of professional learning needs of staff at a particular centre. Generic learning opportunities can include involvement in regional meetings or community project committees, or contributing to electronic discussion boards using online tools such as webinars, Twitter and wikis, can bring 'practitioners into contact with other professionals, especially those representing allied health, school education and welfare sector services' (Waniganayake et al., 2008, p. 123). It is possible that learning with others with different expertise and experiences outside the EC profession can provide creative insights, new ideas and alternative solutions because you are not necessarily trapped within an existing body of professional knowledge that is integral to your own profession.

Leaders can play a key role in matching appropriate options with staff interests and needs as well as priorities of the organisation (as identified in Figure 15.1). By adopting a long-term strategic approach to professional learning as a career advancement strategy, Raban et al. (2007) developed a professional learning model by incorporating self-reflection and guided practice involving a more experienced and skilled mentor. This model has now been extended to include a broader collective sphere of activity. This model can be of assistance to leaders aiming to facilitate professional growth in sustainable ways. Learning captured within each sphere can be described as follows:

- *Self-directed learning* comprises learning that individuals can do by themselves and is primarily aimed at self-development of the individual doing the learning.
- *Guided learning* involves learning with another person acting in the capacity of either a mentor or a coach. This person may be a peer or a colleague from another profession, and has appropriate expertise or knowledge and skills they are willing to share on a 1:1 basis.

Figure 15.1 Ways of learning as EC leaders

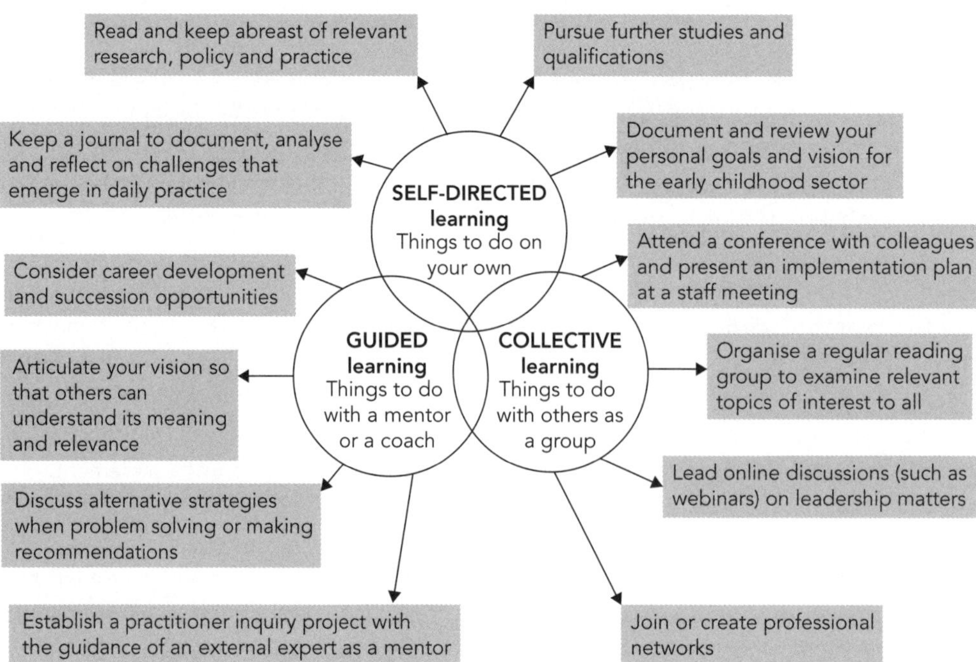

- *Collective learning* refers to participation in professional learning together with three or more people. These groups may be formal or informal, temporary or long-term as well as local or virtual using online strategies incorporating social media technologies such as blogs and wikis.

Examples of each of these learning strategies are presented in Figure 15.1 and can be expanded upon as appropriate to the needs and interests of those involved in any organisation. Likewise, how often individuals use any of these learning strategies, when and where they learn, and the nature or the content of the learning that is on offer can be defined as required by those involved in each context. To be sustainable, the options selected need to be relevant, properly costed and evaluated against individual staff development plans and organisational goals.

Pause–reflect–act 15.2

Look at the range of PLD options presented in Figure 15.1 and consider the following:

- Make a list of the types of professional learning activities you have experienced. You can add other examples under each of the three spheres of learning.

- Identify the positives and challenges you encountered during these experiences, and reflect on what these may suggest about your preferred learning style.
- Prepare a one- to two-year PLD plan for yourself by reflecting on the options presented.
- Now, adopting a leadership role, consider the PLD needs of colleagues in your organisation. Consider how you may use this model to encourage learning with your peers.
- Establishing an organisational culture of learning is not easy. Why? Reflect on the challenges of learning collaboratively within EC organisations.

Career pathways in the EC sector

Within the EC sector in Australia, it is difficult to identify a career pathway showing a linear track or a hierarchical system an individual could follow when seeking career advancement or promotion. In this type of **career ladder**, upward mobility is aligned with professional qualifications and salary increments in a systematic way. For some years, industrial awards systems developed through trade unions involved in safeguarding the conditions of employment of teachers and childcare workers in Australia have attempted to identify specific responsibilities that go with specific job titles. However, there is little or no consistency between awards in the use of different words to identify and describe employment positions within EC settings. This makes it difficult to navigate the industrial awards systems as an educator seeking direction in terms of career progression.

career ladder
a step-by-step system of career progression that enables educators to consider options, possibilities and pathways for becoming EC leaders.

The accreditation of EC teachers in Australia is a recent development. The policy and process differ between the states, with most states only requiring EC teachers who work in a prior-to-school setting to hold a registration card, including a police check and often some mandatory training in child protection and first aid (for example QLD, NT and SA). Some states, such as the ACT and Tasmania, require teacher accreditation only if employed in a primary school. However, WA has had a registration system for EC teachers working in prior-to-school settings since 2013. More recently, in New South Wales, the accreditation of EC teachers working in preschool and long day care centres began in July 2016 (see www.nswteachers.nsw.edu.au/current-teachers/early-childhood-teachers). Teachers are required to maintain their accreditation status by completing at least 100 hours of professional development, as well as submitting an online report every five years (if you are employed full-time, and seven years if you are part-time) to maintain their accreditation status.

It is possible that the number of years of experience may be reflected in the salary paid, as the rate of pay can increase according to the length of time or experience in the sector. However, an educator's qualifications may not be clearly aligned with the position, the roles and responsibilities, or how they are paid within an organisation.

Leadership specialisations

EC organisations vary in size, are run by a range of stakeholders, and have differing governance arrangements. The 'Leaders in practice' profiles in this chapter, and research on leadership by those such as Hayden (1996), Rodd (2013) and Waniganayake (2013), have shown that career advancement of EC leaders has usually been haphazard. Typically, university-qualified EC teachers have fallen into centre management positions because they were the most qualified person available in a particular setting when the director's job became vacant. In reality, it has been shown that many of these directors had little or no formal preparation to perform the leadership responsibilities expected of them. In part, this can be traced back to the nature of EC teacher education programs available prior to the 1990s, when leadership development was absent. Due to the lack of more recent research, however, it is difficult to know to what extent the inclusion of leadership and management units in EC degree and diploma programs in the past decade has prepared educators to implement leadership more effectively.

chapter 2 identifies different types of EC settings and chapter 4 discusses the implications in terms of governance.

The leadership model originally presented by Kagan and Bowman in 1997 illustrates at least five ways of specialising in EC leadership. With the passage of time, in keeping with contemporary workplace developments in the sector, Waniganayake (2011) has proposed extending the original model with two new conceptualisations that focus on leadership in research and entrepreneurship. For ease of reference, the full suite of leadership specialisations is presented in Figure 15.2. (Note that the scholars who were the authors of the chapters in

Figure 15.2 Leadership specialisations in EC

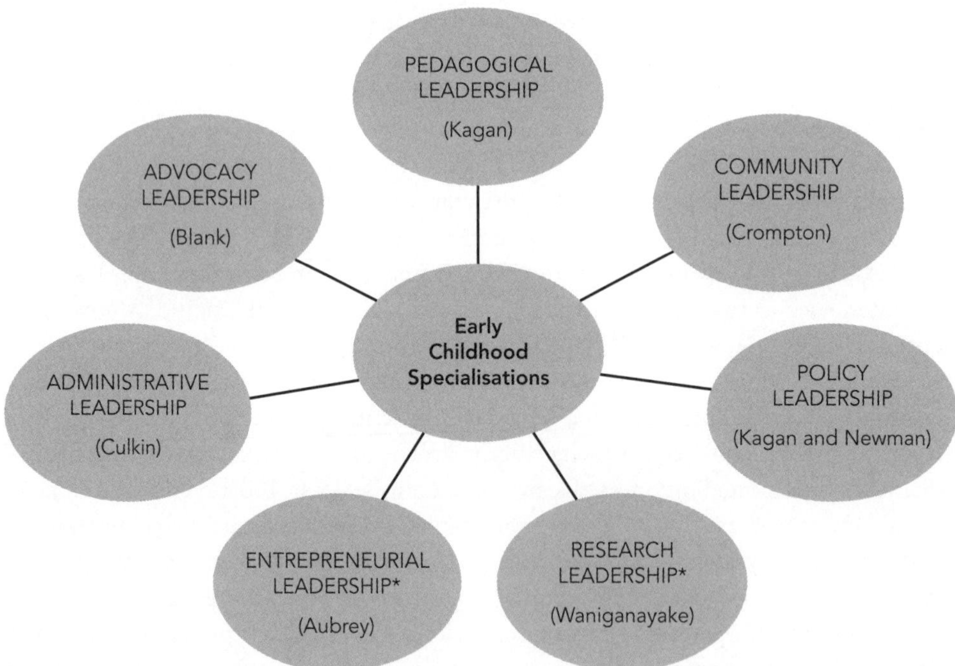

*These two specialisations were not included by Kagan and Bowman (1997).

Kagan and Bowman's book have been identified for easy reference to learn more about these areas of specialisations.)

Briefly, each specialisation indicates a focus on a particular sphere of leadership activity or function, as follows:

- *Administrative leadership:* This relates to essential administrative functions, including processing of enrolments, collection of fees, monitoring attendance and other data collection activities. Leadership involves collating and analysing data critically to improve efficiencies and strategic plans of the organisation.
- *Advocacy leadership*: These leaders are passionate about quality EC programs, the rights of children and upholding social justice principles in their practice. They draw public attention to concerns about equity, safety and well-being impacting on young children and their families, and those working in the sector.
- *Pedagogical leadership*: A focus on curriculum and pedagogy requires having a keen interest in learning. These leaders have a sound knowledge of diverse approaches on early years program design, implementation and evaluation.
- *Community leadership*: Awareness of local community strengths, needs and challenges is essential for leaders interested in engaging with those living in neighbourhoods and regions where EC settings can become a hub and a resource within their community.
- *Policy leadership*: Originally described as conceptual leadership, this specialisation has been revised to reflect the increasing importance of policy functions of contemporary EC leaders. These leaders not only have a vision, they also actively use policy reform to drive sector-wide changes.
- *Entrepreneurial leadership*: This new specialisation reflects the commercial side of EC settings, which may be perceived as small business enterprises. The importance of entrepreneurial work was highlighted in the research by Aubrey (2011) in England. The ability to work with professionals from multidisciplinary backgrounds is of particular interest to these leaders.
- *Research leadership*: This is another new area of specialisation, and reflects the increasing recognition of evidence-based policies and the value of researching diverse aspects of relevance to the sector. These leaders may have particular areas/topics that reflect their personal research and/or teaching interests and may be found within universities or other organisations with a strong research and development interest.

see chapter 5 on strategic planning.

see chapter 7 for more on advocacy.

see chapter 6 for details on pedagogical leadership.

see chapter 12 on community engagement.

chapters 2 and 3 explain the importance of context and identify potential areas of policy interest for leaders.

the EC setting as a small business is discussed in chapter 13.

The possibilities for specialisation as leaders can differ depending on a number of factors, including the structure and governance of the organisation where the leader is working and prevailing local conditions in each community or country. For example, research leaders may be located in diverse organisations that have research and development sections focusing on child and family matters. These may be government-sponsored organisations (for example, the Office of the Children's Commissioner, Australian Institute of Family Studies), non-government organisations (for example, Brotherhood of St Laurence in Melbourne and Sydney Day Nursery Children's Services) and large corporations (such as banks, hospitals and mining companies) concerned with supporting employees' balancing of work and family commitments.

More typically, research leaders may find employment in universities, as reflected in Leaders in practice 15.1, which profiles Karen Martin. Karen is the first Indigenous EC educator to be appointed to the position of Associate Professor of Early Childhood in Australia. In this profile, Karen shares her story of working as a researcher and teacher in the role of a university academic.

LEADERS IN PRACTICE 15.1

Dr Karen Martin

Associate Professor of Early Childhood, Griffith University (QLD)

I'm the youngest of seven children who grew up in a working class suburb of Brisbane (the capital city of Queensland). By the time I was 10, I cared for my three nephews and one niece. When I became a mother at the age of 15, I wanted more for my son and so, I completed a teacher assistant course in 1981. I'd found my niche. Over the following 12 years I obtained a Diploma of Teaching (Early Childhood) and a Bachelor of Education. I taught in Aboriginal EC services; developed policy and curriculum, and provided professional development to EC educators. In the late 1990s I worked in Indigenous education so my PhD is in Aboriginal knowledge and research.

In 2003 I returned to ECE and in 2008 became Associate Professor of Early Childhood. Currently I teach post-graduate students and undertake research in the areas of ECE and Aboriginal ECE, particularly curriculum and workforce. I am often invited to present at major conferences on these topics. This aligns with my roles as Deputy Chair of the Longitudinal Study of Indigenous Children Steering Committee and of the Griffith University Human Research Ethics Committee.

What are some of the key challenges you encounter in your job as an academic?

A key challenge I face constantly is the marginalisation of my work and knowledge as only being relevant to Aboriginal education, or Aboriginal people. Too often, people see my colour and not my credentials, my culture and not my scholarship, even though my PhD earnt a university medal.

When thinking about EC leadership, what qualities matter most?

Insight and foresight. Insight is the ability to understand and work within micro levels and their contexts. Foresight is the ability to work at a macro level and make connections to the micro contexts. Both enable you to see the little picture and the bigger picture at the same time.

How did you acquire your knowledge, skills and understandings about leadership?

I learnt mostly by calibrating my own ideas of leadership in observing others and by engaging in leadership roles. You soon learn about your own nature and that of others this way. I learnt that leadership is not uniform and to develop my own style over time.

Looking back at your career achievements, what are you most proud of as an EC educator?

I'm proud of being a leading educator in my own right and not simply because I'm an Aboriginal person. I'm proud of the recognition given to my work through awards and that it is often cited by others. I'm proud of now being at the level of my career that I can give back to the Aboriginal ECE sector. I call that my 'heart business'.

What advice would you offer those aspiring to become university leaders in EC?

Be clear about your reasons for taking the journey and be prepared for the challenges of working in higher education. Develop an expertise in more than one area within EC so you don't get marginalised. Have a network of respectful alliances as it can get lonely at times. Don't forget your EC values and push others out of your way. Your network is just as important as your scholarship, but, what's your 'heart business'?

How can we build the knowledge, skills and capacities of future leaders in the EC sector?

It's a lifelong journey that must include post-graduate studies—even better if this entails research. That's how you build your scholarship. Look for opportunities, big or small, to flex your leadership muscles and develop your own style of leadership. It's about transformations, not transactions. Transactions are encounters with ideas or people or places that do have some value, but it's not likely to be sustainable and or benefit a lot of people. Transformations are more powerful because they bring particular challenges to be considered, not merely addressed. The impact is not instant because change evolves, but it is sustainable. Leadership isn't always evident in leaders. Leaders are not always in the top roles.

Pause–reflect–act 15.3

- Identify two central themes about EC leadership that you can take away from reading Karen's story.
- In your work, how will you go about using these messages based on the story of an Australian Indigenous leader?

Novice educators and induction into the profession

Novice educators are new to the profession; they can be new graduates beginning their first job as a qualified educator in the sector. **Aspiring leaders** are educators who are interested in pursuing a position of leadership. Typically, they would have worked in the sector for at least two or more years, and have an interest in trying out roles that enable them to test their leadership potential. At the start of their careers novice educators may, or may not, be fully aware of their capacity or interest in becoming leaders. It is not unrealistic that when accepting a centre director's position, for example, a novice educator may need time to understand the expectations and responsibilities of leadership. Some educators, on the other hand, come into the sector aspiring to become leaders, while others acquire an interest in leadership through being inspired by those occupying leadership roles. Longevity in the sector or in a particular position or role, however, does not guarantee that someone is capable of working effectively as a leader.

novice educators
those who are new to the profession, or are beginning employment having completed a professional qualification as an EC educator.

aspiring leaders
are educators who are interested in becoming leaders and actively seek opportunities to try out leadership roles that enable them to test their leadership potential.

Previously, there has been a reluctance among educators to assume leadership roles in the EC sector (Ebbeck & Waniganayake, 2004; Rodd, 2013). University graduates who have completed an EC teaching degree in the past 15 years may have completed some modules on management and leadership. While this work may be sufficient to raise awareness of leadership in the profession, it is essential to find other ways to continue learning about leadership roles and responsibilities. Those occupying leadership roles can make a difference in guiding novice educators to perform leadership responsibilities in supportive ways. Setting aside time for regular professional conversations, providing resources, affirming good practice, debriefing when challenges occur, and fostering security and confidence can go a long way in successfully inducting a novice into leadership. *In Leaders in practice 15.2 Virginia Artinian highlights her first year of teaching and what she learnt from her degree, and experiences that helped shape where she is today.*

Visit Oxford Ascend to hear more from Virginia.

LEADERS IN PRACTICE 15.2

Virginia Artinian

Early Childhood Teacher (NSW)

To work with children is a privilege that should never be taken for granted. The last five years have taken me on a journey of learning the details of this relationship in the context of education and have shaped my vision for the future. I finished studying my Bachelor of Education: Early Childhood Education (birth to 12 years) degree last year, became a 'targeted graduate' and have invested my first year working with a class of Year 5 students at a Department of Education school in northern Sydney.

Looking back

My experiences during university life grew me holistically and shaped what I believe about education today. I quickly found myself seeking to support people who were new or on the 'outskirts'. I volunteered in the 'Mentors@Macquarie' program and worked with a team to facilitate the transition of many first-year students. My involvement and leadership in a Christian student society, 'Student Life,' taught me about developing and enlarging my vision, goal setting, strategic planning and the importance of continuous personal and professional development. I received many opportunities to engage in public speaking and developed a priority of being intentional in relationships with the view of supporting others. I worked at Macquarie University across four faculties in total while completing my degree. In these various roles, I sought to equip students studying education, mostly through individual tutoring. This taught me about working with others on a whole new scale as I was impacting the future teachers of society. During professional experience placements, I decided to get out of my 'comfort zone' and requested schools from varying demographics to ensure I got out of the 'middle class suburbia' bubble.

This year—2016

My current season of work as a Year 5 teacher has been a joy-filled and challenging experience. During Term 1, I felt as if there was a wall between the theories taught at university and the overwhelming amount of learning I had to do to become acculturated in this new setting. As time went by, I began to draw upon EC philosophy and pedagogy. Family-centred practice, the importance of aesthetics and aiming for students' holistic growth are probably the biggest three. I have kept a journal of my experiences in order to document what the roller coaster of beginning teaching is like and to give me clarity of thought when making decisions. I cannot reiterate how helpful underpinning reflective practice in my work and life has been.

The addition of mentoring time to support beginning teachers has been a leadership decision that has had a direct impact on my ability to succeed this year. My mentor has been a cornerstone in supporting and empowering me as I have sought to 'find my feet' in this new setting. I have had someone to ask how I am really going, provide ideas and resources for lessons, clarify the expectations of my role and share wisdom and advice. The executive leaders of my school have enabled me to work with my first year colleagues to create a teacher induction and transition program. It is only with their support that I am being empowered to use my ideas and vision in this capacity. This has been supported because of the broader landscape of leadership and the government's initiative of the Great Teaching, Inspired Learning (GTIL) reforms in New South Wales.

Looking ahead

My vision is to connect, support and empower children who experience marginalisation to live vibrant and fruitful lives with respect, equity, justice and hope. My passions stem from my Christian faith and worldview, where I am constantly challenged to think of what it truly means to 'love my neighbour as myself'. Professionally, this is working with my colleagues to support, connect and empower our students, with over 90 per cent learning English as a second language and many who are new to Australia. Outside of work, it means building relationships with children and families who have just arrived after fleeing the war in Syria. With people from my Armenian cultural community, we are taking initiatives to build relationships with people individually and connect them to society in ways that will empower them, restore their voices and bring out their best. It is a joy and privilege to gain new friends and share life together.

To be successful, I cannot do it alone. I need to work alongside others who share this vision and will be advocates, community builders and who will be present with these children. Teaching is an incredible career that gives us opportunities to use our leadership for the good of society and I am excited to be on this adventure.

Pause–reflect–act 15.4

- What attracted you to seek employment as an EC educator?
- Having read Virginia's story, what will influence you to continue working in EC settings teaching and advocating for children?
- What do you think about Virginia's perspectives of seeing her role and contribution as being broader than the 'classroom'?
- Both of the practitioners profiled in this chapter have university-based EC qualifications. Having read their stories, in your opinion, to what extent did their qualifications enhance their achievements in the sector?
- When looking for jobs as an EC leader, how have your studies made a difference?

Go to oxfordascend *to hear Virginia's thoughts.*

Succession planning

Succession planning involves thinking about the longevity of staff employed within an organisation or the sector in an orderly manner. Wright (2012, p. 20) defined succession planning as 'the process of assessing the current and forecasting the future environment, planning related transition policies and activities, and preparing the organisation to meet its current and future leadership needs'. The topic itself 'can stir up considerable emotion, fear, stress, conflict, and questions, and thereby create potential discomfort' for staff as well as management (Gothard & Austin., 2013, p. 273). Educators can come and go from organisations at different times due to various reasons. The sudden loss of an effective leader due to illness, death, disability or a business merger, termination or promotion can impact everyone in the organisation. This situation can be exacerbated by not having someone else with leadership skills or experience to draw upon during a crisis.

Instead of relying on a single individual, distributed leadership approaches (Ebbeck & Waniganayake, 2004; Harris, 2014; Heikka & Waniganayake, 2011) can enhance succession planning as it enables a range of people to implement leadership decision-making within an organisation on a continuous basis. Accordingly, succession planning is a collective responsibility that stems from individual goals and aspirations of how people see themselves growing within a career. At times, planning for career advancement can be built into annual performance reviews by inviting staff to identify their future career development goals including leadership aspirations (Nuttall, 2016). An analysis of individual goals in turn can pave the way to identifying organisational strengths and gaps in leadership advancement as a whole (Waniganayake et al., 2012).

Importantly, succession planning must be built into the strategic plans of any organisation (Titzer et al., 2013; Wright, 2012) so that it can continue delivering high-quality programs with minimal disruption due to the passing of the baton to a new leader. This includes identifying staff with leadership potential early and strategically supporting their development. Intentional leaders will actively seek to provide opportunities for their successors to experience, demonstrate and reflect upon leadership through action. Their presence in the background acts as a safety net, enabling the aspirants to 'test' their strengths or capabilities knowing that they are not alone—that a capable mentor is there to support them where appropriate and necessary.

Pause–reflect–act 15.5

- Why is succession planning important to include in your organisation's strategic plans?
- Do you favour pay increases for staff based on:
  - a Seniority that is associated with the number of years of experience in the EC sector?
  - b Type of formal EC qualifications completed regardless of the number of years of experience in the sector?
  - c Other qualifications and experience?

- What factors can you use to recognise and remunerate staff working in EC settings?
- How do you think the above impact on overall job satisfaction?
- What steps can you take to encourage aspiring leaders to consider succession within your organisation?

It is proposed that succession matters can be addressed through inspiration, care and strategic planning including:

- *An induction program:* designed to identify talents, interests and gaps in knowledge of new staff and monitor learning that takes place during the early stages of joining the organisation.
- *A performance appraisal system:* individual staff development plans can be used to assess the growth of leadership potential within the organisation.

These and other strategies to enhance leadership growth are included within NQS Quality Area 7 (ACECQA, 2017), and augur well in achieving high-quality programs in sustainable ways (Waniganayake et al., 2012, pp. 60–5).

Leaders must also know when it is time to retire from working in EC settings as some may find it difficult to let go of the power that comes with being in charge of an organisation. For instance, it is possible that some 'leaders are not personally prepared for the transition' into retirement (Wright, 2012, p. 18). However, retirement does not have to mean complete disappearance from professional engagement in the EC sector. To harness learning that comes with age, elders who retire from active service can demonstrate wisdom by being available to continue to nurture the next generation of leaders. Being role models in this way can be self-rewarding as well as motivational to others who look up to elders. This view embraces what Karen Martin (2007b, p. 17), profiled in this chapter, has described as the continuity of 'relatedness' to people, waterways, animals and plants underpinning Australian Aboriginal ways of living and learning. When working with children, Martin acknowledges the importance of agency and reciprocity in learning where 'children are trusted to be learners and at the same time as being teachers of teachers. Teachers are trusted to be learners and at the same time to teach children as well' (p. 18). She concludes by declaring 'This agency is the tracks we leave for our young ones, of the present and of the future. It is necessary to leave tracks that give them cause to be proud of us as ancestors who knew about the stories and lived them' (Martin, 2007b, p. 19). These comments show how connecting the past, the present and the future can make leadership both relevant and sustainable over time.

In this book, leadership is discussed as a professional responsibility of EC educators. Importantly, the ability to lead begins with a consideration of a leader's own values and beliefs about leadership and then being able to share these views with others. Consider, for example, how Karen Martin (personal communication, 17 February, 2012) explains her personal perceptions about leadership:

> For me, leadership is not about power, it is more about knowing who you are; where you come from and where you are going next. This means leadership

> is about looking after your relations and relationships, or your relatedness. Agency is only possible when this attention and responsibility is fulfilled and lived. Therefore, leadership by Aboriginal understanding, is only possible when relatedness is clear; relationships are active and agency is shared.

Martin's views on leadership have been shaped by her Aboriginality and her experiences of living and working as an educator in Australia. In her recent book, Martin (2016) brings together an anthology of professional journeys of Aboriginal EC practitioners. These stories illustrate the plurality of our lived experiences as educators. The extent to which each educator will be influenced in terms of the people, places and positions of leadership they encounter will vary, and there is much to be gained by sharing these discussions within organisations where educators work.

In responding to an increasingly complex and rapidly changing world, intentional leaders can engender a sense of courage, excitement, optimism, hope, resiliency and justice for all. When taken together, these characteristics can enhance an educator's capacity to lead complex organisations, especially during turbulent times. Moreover, within EC settings, nurturing future leaders through proactive succession planning strategies must be prioritised. Accordingly, intentional leaders are conscious about the power of learning and therefore can actively define the directions they want to take with their own learning and in guiding the learning of others. A focus on learning, therefore, is considered to be the essence of success and effectiveness of leadership.

Chapter summary

Intentional leaders play a key role in demonstrating leadership *with* learning and leadership *for* learning. Being an effective leader requires passion and a commitment to embracing learning as a lifelong process. There are many ways of learning to become a leader. Although there is no particular career pathway available for those aspiring to become leaders in EC, there are a variety of strategies that could be used in growing as a leader. Nurturing future leaders and succession planning must be top priorities for all EC organisations.

Key references

Edwards, S. and Nuttall, J. (Eds.). (2009). *Professional learning in early childhood settings*. (Vol. 3). Rotterdam: Sense Publishers.

This book comprises a range of chapters written by scholars with expertise and commitment to exploring professional learning from a diversity of perspectives.

Martin, K. (Ed.). (2016). *Voices visions: Aboriginal early childhood education in Australia*. Sydney: Pademelon Press.

This book is of importance for everyone interested in Aboriginal world views and knowledges impacting on ECE. Using examples from everyday practice, Karen and her co-authors explain Aboriginal ways of knowing, being and doing.

Waniganayake, M. (2013). Leadership careers in early childhood: Finding your way through chaos and serendipity into strategic planning. In E. Hujala, M. Waniganayake & J. Rodd, (Eds.), *Researching leadership in early childhood education* (pp. 61–78). Tampere: Tampere University Press. (See www.ilrfec.org/wp-content/uploads/2014/01/art_03Waniganayake.pdf)

This book chapter is based on a study of the leadership careers of eight EC practitioners in Australia. It discusses the supports and barriers that impacted on their professional growth and career advancement.

Online resources

Lobbying effectively

Watch this YouTube clip to see how one person, Irving Harris, convinced the foundation to invest in researching about ECED and lobbying governments for appropriate programs in the state of Illinois, USA.

www.youtube.com/watch?v=6_tBozslCC0

Robert McCormick Foundation

This foundation is committed to fostering communities of educated, informed and engaged citizens. Through philanthropic programs, Cantigny Park and museums, the foundation helps develop citizen leaders and works to make life better in our communities. It has many online resources/publications of relevance to leaders advocating for quality EC programs.

www.mccormickfoundation.org

GLOSSARY

accountability
Educators are answerable to children, families, the community and governments. In practice, this means being professionally responsible, and meeting legislative frameworks and relevant standards in providing quality EC programs for young children.

active listening
Hearing and understanding what another is saying, and communicating this understanding back so that that the receiver of your communication believes they have been heard.

activism
This refers to the questions, assumptions and discourses on which policy and practice are based and promoting through action how these might be implemented outside existing frames of reference.

advocacy
Advancing the values, needs and interests of an individual or group within existing frames of reference.

aspiring leaders
Educators who are interested in becoming leaders and actively seek opportunities to try out leadership roles that enable them to test their leadership potential.

Australian Constitution
Establishes the framework of the three main political institutions—the legislature, the executive and the judiciary—the relationships between them, and the powers of the Australian government in relation to the states and territories.

business plan
In their business plan, EC organisations outline the financial basics, including the resources available, goals: prioritising items to be achieved and a market analysis. It reflects the management's capacity to run a viable business.

career ladder
A step-by-step system of career progression that enables educators to consider options, possibilities and pathways for becoming leaders in EC.

centre advocacy/activism
Action aimed at influencing outcomes for centre staff or the centre itself.

checking financial statements
Involves regularly monitoring the financial activities of the EC organisation against the set budget and business plans to ensure business viability and to identify financial trends over time.

coaching
Usually, coaching involves explicitly modelling or directly instructing how to learn a new skill or knowledge. Coaching can also involve encouraging, practising and reviewing learning in an explicit way.

collaboration
Collaboration between staff and families brings different skills, knowledge and experience to a setting. Collaborating with families is essential for children to feel a sense of belonging.

communication
The process of verbally and/or non-verbally conveying and perceiving messages, which may or may not involve the use of power.

community
Includes all individuals, organisations and groups who connect because of a common purpose.

community coalition
A relationship developed with other like-minded people and organisations for the purpose of achieving an agreed goal.

conflict management
The process of productively working through content- or relationship-based communication issues, such that the conflict becomes an opportunity for learning and enhanced team effectiveness.

connections
Refers to the links and relationships developed within a community, an organisation or a network.

critical reflection
Engaging in critical reflection, requires questioning the assumptions, values, beliefs and ideology underpinning your work.

critically reading social policy
This process involves an understanding that policy is political and value laden, not neutral, and therefore requires an understanding of the values, interests, agendas and discourses that shape policy and can be targeted in advocacy and activist campaigns.

curriculum
A program or course of study, or the content of a course of study. It usually suggests that learning outcomes are predetermined in order to fulfil the prescribed intentions of the program or course.

decision-making
Intentional leaders make decisions after listening to families and considering the philosophy underpinning the EC programs at each setting.

discourse
Messages that define how something (e.g. EC education) is talked about. Discourses can shape values, beliefs and attitudes.

duty of care
This reflects the fundamental obligation of all EC staff to ensure children within their organisation are safe from harm at all times while at the centre. Failure to do so can suggest poor governance and warrants urgent attention by leaders.

emotional intelligence
The ability to perceive feelings in ourselves and others, to effectively control one's emotions, to be socially aware, and to communicate effectively and influence.

ethical practice
Continually working and making decisions through explicit, thoughtful consideration of legal and professional requirements, ethical principles and the organisation's philosophy.

ethical workplaces
EC organisations that provide socially just human resource policies and procedures for all staff.

ethics
The principles and values that guide an EC leader's professional behaviour and practice.

financial planning
Involves identifying and managing the financial risks of operating a centre as a small business enterprise to ensure financial stability.

governance
Within EC organisations, governance refers to the overarching formal structures and accountability procedures that inform leadership decision-making when working with young children and their families.

government
The political system set up to run a country, state/territory or a local municipality.

healthy (financial) bottom line
Typically refers to the financial viability of an organisation as a business, and reflects a good fit between income and expenditure.

innovation
Signifies that something revolutionary or a major advancement has occurred within an organisation.

Integrated Reporting Model
An approach to financial reporting that tells a story of the organisation's ethical contribution to society and effective disclosure of the six capitals (financial, manufactured, intellectual, human, social and relationships, and natural)

intentional leaders
These are educators who demonstrate courage in implementing leadership responsibilities in ethical ways. They act purposefully, learning and finding ways to collaborate with others to achieve collective goals.

legislative frameworks
Laws and regulations that EC educators are legally required to comply with.

management structures
EC organisations are managed under diverse systems, ranging in size and structure from a single organisation (i.e. 'stand-alone' centre) to a group comprising two or more centres.

marketing
Involves working strategically to develop a presence in the community that promotes the organisation, its programs, and the value of EC and ECE. This involves managing relationships, developing a profile and identifying opportunities for improving the service.

mentoring
A process of supported learning involving two or more educators engaged in professional dialogue. Mentors can be provided under formal professional learning programs or can emerge informally through networking while working within an organisation or more broadly across the profession.

mixed economy
There is diversity of ownership and management of organisations involved in delivering EC programs in Australia. The availability of this mix of private and community-based organisations within one country can be described as working within a mixed economy.

multidisciplinary teams
These comprise of a range of professionals from diverse backgrounds (such as teachers, nurses and social workers) working together to deliver various programs and services to children and their families.

networking
Establishing and maintaining professional relationships with others working in the

EC sector to promote collaborative learning in relation to pedagogy and curriculum. Contemporary leaders must also network with other professionals, especially those from school education, health and social welfare as they may also work with the same children attending EC programs.

novice educators
Those who are new to the profession, or are beginning employment having completed a professional qualification as an EC educator.

pedagogy
Pedagogy is often defined as the art and science of education. In an EC context it gives a focus to the educational theories, relationships, strategies and practices that educators can draw on when they make curriculum decisions and work with children in learning contexts to support and enhance their learning.

'perezhivanie'
This term is used by Vygotsky (1994) to describe the emotional atmosphere created by the adults in children's play spaces.

philosophies and theories
Curriculum models are underpinned by a range of theoretical and philosophical beliefs and assumptions that determine what will be included in a curriculum and what will be excluded or silenced. Philosophy and theory play a significant role in determining accepted teaching and learning practices and the resources and other provisions made available for children's play and learning in an EC setting.

planning team
A working group of ideally four to six people who represent the key stakeholders of the organisation. Together they coordinate the planning processes and ensure there is good coverage of views and ideas of people from across the organisation. The EC leader will be a part of this team and in some cases may take the leadership role.

policy
A statement of intent that can guide decision-makers about how to direct resources to achieve an intended outcome. Policy also reflects the political ideology and beliefs of the group with power to make decisions.

politics
The art and science of government; affairs of the state and civics.

power
The influencing of someone else's values, thoughts and actions. Power can be a positive force (e.g. when exercised within a social justice framework) or a negative force that is unethical.

productivity agenda
Government plans that focus attention and resources on national economic outcomes. Children are considered worthy of investment for the contribution they will make to a future productive nation.

professional and industry standards
Best practice, as deemed by industry bodies (e.g. Building Code of Australia) or professional bodies (e.g. Early Childhood Australia's 2016 Code of Ethics). These standards of practice can be legally enforceable only if they are incorporated in legislation or regulations.

professional autonomy
Being trusted with freedom to exercise professional judgment and take responsibility for making professional decisions.

professional boundary
Intentional leaders need to create a culture that supports staff to build respectful relationships with families that have clear boundaries and expectations of each other.

professional growth
Educators can continue to develop their capacity to lead through participation in a range of professional activities and support, as discussed throughout this book.

professional judgment
As an educator, the process of drawing on one's professional philosophy, professional knowledge base (e.g. theories and accountabilities) and understanding of a given situation (e.g. knowledge of child, family and staff involved) to make an informed decision that is considered to be quality practice and in the 'best interests of the child'.

professional learning and development (PLD)
PLD refers to continuous study in terms of understanding professional knowledge and skills and then using these to advance professionally by refining and renewing practices as an EC educator.

professional learning community
Comprises educators involved in PLD by actively seeking to foster ways of building professional knowledge and skills within an organisation or a region.

purpose built
Purpose built EC settings have been designed with much care and forethought. This may have involved architects with expertise in spaces for children as well as adults. Input from an EC leader can also make a difference in creating dedicated places and spaces for adults to think and learn.

quality
Quality education promotes children's rights, inclusion, development and well-being. What quality ECE looks like can vary among settings, in accordance with the philosophy and local context.

recruitment
The employment of appropriately qualified EC staff, in keeping with the organisation's vision, philosophy and strategic plans.

reflection
In EC contexts reflection demonstrates an educator/leader thinking about their own work, as well as when working with others, to improve their skills and knowledge in purposeful ways.

reflective action
Brings together the two components of thinking and doing, and thereby reflects the theory and practice connections.

reflexivity
Our ability to recognise our influence on our work.

re-purposed buildings
Settings located in a building that was originally built for another purpose, such as a family home or a neighbourhood community centre. To comply with legal and legislative requirements, the original buildings have been modified.

respectful relationships
Establishing respectful relationships requires the intentional leader to listen, to ask questions and to be open to a variety of ways of working with families.

retention
Strategies used to support staff, both individually and collectively as a team, by building on their strengths and addressing weaknesses.

rights of the child
The Convention on the Rights of the Child (CROC) (United Nations (UN), 1989) requires countries to act in the 'best interests' of the child. It was ratified by Australia in 1990. The rights of the child are embedded in the Code of Ethics (ECA, 2006) used by EC educators in this country.

small business enterprise
Typically employs fewer than 20 staff. This is the definition used by the Australian Bureau of Statistics (ABS) and has been applied in this book. Note that various regulators such as Fair Work Australia and the Australian Taxation Office adopt other criteria and these definitions may change according to government policy.

social capital
Incorporates the trust, reciprocity and networks that contribute to the social wealth and societal well-being created through community engagement.

social entrepreneurship
Combines ethical business decisions that support the viability of the organisation, identify creative opportunities and contribute positively to the rights of children.

spheres of influence
These reflect how leadership enactment can inspire and impact others. Within an organisation, leadership responsibilities may be formally defined in individual staff job descriptions. Individuals may also influence others through inspiration, encouragement and/or by demonstrating leadership informally in everyday work.

stakeholders
These are people who have an interest in the decision-making and operations of the setting. They may be involved in various activities at the setting either directly (e.g. staff, families or investors) or indirectly (e.g. neighbours, community representatives or allied health and welfare professionals who visit the setting).

strategic organisational development
An approach to organisational planning that takes account of the internal resources of the organisation and the external influences including the political, cultural and technical influences.

strategic planning
A medium- to long-term planning strategy that takes account of the organisation's internal and external operating environment.

SWOT analysis
Developed by Albert Humphrey from Stanford University in the USA, this process exposes the internal Strengths (S) and Weaknesses (W), and external Opportunities (O) and Threats (T) that characterise the organisation at a particular point in time.

theory of binding and bonding
This theory is concerned with the interpersonal dimension of organising spaces, and captures people's feelings or emotional responses to places.

thinking environment
An environment that empowers people and enables leaders to create environments where others can flourish.

vision
A statement that reflects an aspirational future for an organisation. The vision captures concisely who the organisation is and what it hopes to achieve.

workplace culture
Shared understanding of the beliefs and values that influence the work arrangements within an organisation.

workplace ethos
One aspect of the organisational culture reflecting its tone or broad characteristics, as reflected in its philosophy.

REFERENCES

ACECQA, *see* Australian Children's Education and Care Quality Authority

Adair, J. & Tobin, J. (2008). Listening to the voices of immigrant parents. In C. Genisha & A.L. Goodwin (Eds.), *Diversities in early childhood education. Rethinking and doing* (pp. 137–50). New York: Routledge.

Adams, C. (2013). *Understanding Integrated Reporting: The concise guide to integrated thinking and the future of corporate reporting*. Oxford: Do Sustainability.

Ahmed, F.A. (2014). Modeling the Relations among Parental Involvement, School Engagement and Academic Performance of High School Students. *International Education Studies*, 7(4), 47–56.

Ailwood, J. (2007). Mothers, teachers, maternalism and early childhood education and care: Some historical connections. *Contemporary Issues in Early Childhood*, 8(1), 157–65.

Alanis, M. [Alanis Business Academy] (2012, August 2). *How the communication process works | episode 20* [Video]. Retrieved from https://www.youtube.com/watch?v=q6u0AVn-NUM

Alavi, S.B. & Gill, C. (2016). Leading change authentically: How authentic leaders influence follower responses to complex change. *Journal of Leadership and Organisational Studies*, 1–15. doi: 10.1177/1548051816664681.

Antcliff, G., Andrews, K. & Hadley, F. (2007). *From strength to strength in children's services. What works for Children—Bridging the Gaps*. Paper presented at the Marymead Conference, Canberra, ACT.

Apple, M. (1992). The text and cultural politics. *Educational Researcher*, 21, 4–19.

Arcos Holzinger, L. & Biddle, N. (2015). *The relationship between early childhood education and care and the outcomes of Indigenous children: evidence from the Longitudinal Study of Indigenous Children*. Canberra: Centre for Aboriginal Economic Policy Research.

Argyris, C. (1991). Teaching smart people how to learn. *Harvard Business Review*, May–June, 99–109.

Atkinson, M., Doherty, P. & Kinder, K. (2005). Multi-agency working: models, challenges and key factors for success. *Journal of Early Childhood Research*, 3(1), 7–17.

Aubrey, C. (2007). *Leading and managing in the early years*. London: Sage Publications.

Aubrey, C. (2011). *Leading and managing in the early years* (2nd ed.). London: Sage Publications.

Aubrey, C. (2015). Editorial. *Early Education Journal*. 77, 1–2.

Australian Children's Education and Care Quality Authority. (2011a). *Guide to the Education and Care Services National Law and the Education and Care Services National Regulations 2011*. Retrieved from www.acecqa.gov.au/national-quality-framework/national-law-and-regulations.

Australian Children's Education and Care Quality Authority. (2011b). *Guide to the National Quality Framework*.

Australian Children's Education and Care Quality Authority. (2011c). *Guide to the National Quality Standard*. Retrieved from http://files.acecqa.gov.au/files/National-Quality-Framework-Resources-Kit/NQF-Resource-03-Guide-to-NQS.pdf.

Australian Children's Education and Care Quality Authority. (2016a). *Guide to the Education and Care Services National Law and the Education and Care Services National Regulations 2011*. ACECQA: Sydney. http://files.acecqa.gov.au/files/National-Quality-Framework-Resources-Kit/NQF-Resource-02-Guide-to-ECS-Law-Regs.pdf.

Australian Children's Education and Care Quality Authority. (2016b). *NQF Snapshot Q3 2016*. A quarterly report from the Australian Children's Education and Care Quality Authority. Retrieved from http://files.acecqa.gov.au/files/Reports/2016/NQF_Snapshot_Q3_2016.PDF

Australian Children's Education and Care Quality Authority. (2017). *Revised National Quality Standard*. Retrieved 26 April 2017 from http://files.acecqa.gov.au/files/Decision_RIS/RevisedNQSHandoutA4.pdf.

Australian Government Department of Prime Minister and Cabinet. (2016). *Closing the gap: Prime Minister's report 2016*. Retrieved from http://closingthegap.dpmc.gov.au/chapter-01/index.html.

Australian Government, Department of Education and Training. (2016). *Universal access to early childhood education*. Retrieved from www.education.gov.au/universal-access-early-childhood-education.

Australian Human Rights Commission and Early Childhood Australia (2015). *Supporting young children's rights: Statement of intent (2015–2018)*. Retrieved from www.humanrights.gov.au/sites/default/files/supporting_young_children_rights.pdf.

Australian Institute for Teaching and School Leadership (AITSL). (2012). *Animation—the Australian professional standards for teachers* (video). Retrieved from www.youtube.com/watch?v=iuKceiCvMEg&feature=player_embedded.

Australian Institute for Teaching and School Leadership. (2014). *Australian professional standards for teachers*. Retrieved from www.aitsl.edu.au/australian-professional-standards-for-teachers/standards/list.

Bacchi, C. (2009). Introduction. In *Analysing policy: What's the problem represented to be?* (pp. ix–xxii). Frenchs Forest, NSW: Pearson Australia.

Barnett, W.S. (2010). Benefits of early childhood interventions across the world (under) investing in the very young. *Economics of Education Review*, 29, 271–82.

Barron, D. (2012). Emotional intelligence and leadership. In Hurley, J. (Ed.), *Emotional intelligence health and social care* (pp. 75–87). London: Radcliffe Publishing.

Benevolent Society. (2008). *Strengths based practice in children's services project: Evaluation report*. Sydney: Families First NSW, Benevolent Society & Lady Gowrie Child Centre, Sydney.

Benevolent Society & Lady Gowrie Child Centre NSW. (2007). Sharing the learnings: Strengths based practice in children's services newsletter. 4(November), 1–6.

Bennett, J. (2011). Early childhood education and care systems in the OECD Countries: Issue of Tradition and Governance. *Encyclopedia on Early Childhood*

Development. Paris: OECD, Centre of Excellence for Early Childhood Development. Retrieved from www.child-encyclopedia.com/child-care-early-childhood-education-and-care/according-experts/early-childhood-education-and-care.

Bennett, N., Wise, C., Woods, P. & Harvey, J. (2003). *Distributed leadership: A literature review*. Retrieved from www.ncsl.org.uk/mediastore/image2/bennett-distributed-leadership-full.pdf.

Blackmore, J. & Sachs, J. (2007). *Performing and reforming leaders: Gender, educational restructuring and organisational change*. Albany: State University of NY Press.

Bloom, P.J. (2003). *Leadership in action*. Lake Forest, Illinois: New Horizons.

Bloom, P.J. & Sheerer, M. (1992). The effect of leadership training on child care program quality. *Early Childhood Research Quarterly*, 7, 579–94.

Bøe, M., Hognestad, K., & Waniganayake, M. (2016). Qualitative shadowing as a research methodology for exploring early childhood leadership in practice. *Educational Management Administration & Leadership*. Published online. doi:10.1177/1741143216636116.

Bøe, M., & Hognestad, K. (2015). Directing and facilitating distributed pedagogical leadership: Best practices in early childhood education. *International Journal of Leadership in Education*, 20(2): 133–48. doi:10.1080/13603124.2015.1059488.

Bollinger, K. (2009). Mentoring: A two way street. *Adult Learning*, 20(1/2), 39–40.

Borgia, E. & Schuler, D. (1988). *Action research in early childhood today*. Eric Digest.

Boswell, C. (1998). Developing a proposal: When opportunity knocks, will you be prepared? In B. Neugebauer & R. Neugebauer (Eds.), *The art of leadership. Managing early childhood organisations* (Vol. 1, pp. 146–8). Redmond, WA. USA: Child Care Information Exchange.

Botero-Lopez, V., Lawson, F., Bennett, M. & Semann, A. (2014). Exploring the role of the educational leader. Our journey. *Every Child*, 20(2), 4–5.

Bowes, J. & Grace, R. (Eds.) (2009). *Children, families and communities: Contexts and consequences* (3rd ed.). South Melbourne: Oxford University Press.

Bowes, J., Hayes, A. & Grace, R. (2009). Children, families and communities: Looking forward. In J. Bowes & R. Grace (Eds.), *Children, families and communities: Contexts and consequences* (3rd ed.) pp. 219–32. South Melbourne: Oxford University Press.

Bowes, J., Kitson, R., Simpson, T., Reid, J., Smith, M., Downey, B. et al. (2011). *Child care choices of Indigenous families. Research report to the NSW Department of Human Services (Community Services)*. Retrieved from www.iec.mq.edu.au/research/cfrc/research_approaches/vulnerable_and_at-risk_families/child_care_choices_of_indigenous_families.

Bown, K. & Sumsion, J. (2007). Voices from the other side of the fence: Early childhood teachers' experiences with mandatory regulatory requirements. *Contemporary Issues in Early Childhood*, 8(1), 30–49.

Bown, K., Sumsion, J. & Press, F. (2011). Dark matter: The 'gravitational pull' of maternalist discourses on politicians' decision making for early childhood policy in Australia. *Gender and Education*, 23(3), 263–80.

Brennan, D. (1998). *The politics of Australian child care: From philanthropy to feminism* (revised ed.). Cambridge: Cambridge University Press.

Brennan, D. (2007). The ABC of child care politics. *Australian Journal of Social Issues*, 42(2), 213–25.

Brennan, D. & Adamson, E. (2017). Early education and child care policy in Australia. In R. Grace, K. Hodge & C. McMahon. (Eds.) *Children, families and communities* (5th ed.) (pp. 318–36). South Melbourne: Oxford University Press.

Bretherton, T. (2010). *Developing the childcare workforce. Understanding 'fight' or 'flight' amongst workers*. Sydney, NSW: Workplace Research Centre, University of Sydney, Sydney.

Bridgman, P. & Davis, G. (Eds.). (2004). *The Australian policy handbook* (3rd ed.). Crows Nest, NSW: Allen & Unwin.

Bronfenbrenner, U. (1979). *The ecology of human development: Experiments by nature and design*. Cambridge: Harvard University Press.

Bronfenbrenner, U. (1994). Ecological models of human development. In M. Gauvain & C. Cole (Eds.). *Readings on the Development of Children* (pp. 37–43). New York: Freeman.

Bruno, H. (2007). Gossip-free zones: Problem solving to prevent power struggles. *Young Children*, 62(5), 26–7, 29–33.

Bryant, L. & Gibbs, L. (2013). *A director's manual: Managing an early education and care service in NSW*. Sydney: Community Childcare Ltd. (NSW).

Burke Harris, N. (2015, February 17) Video: *How childhood trauma affects health across a lifetime*. Retrieved from https://www.ted.com/talks/nadine_burke_harris_how_childhood_trauma_affects_health_across_a_lifetime

By, R.T., Burnes, B. & Oswick, C. (2012). Change management: Leadership, values and ethics. *Journal of Change Management*. 12(1): 1–5. doi:10.10180/14697017.2011.652371.

Cairns, S. (2015). *A new handbook for creating inspirational learning spaces*. London: Space for Learning Partners. Retrieved from www.cloreduffield.org.uk/userfiles/documents/SfL/Space-for-Learning.pdf

Caldwell, B. (2006). *Reimagining educational leadership*. Melbourne: Australian Council for Educational Research Press.

Caldwell, B. (2013). *Assessing the goodness of fit for Victoria of approaches to school governance in national and international jurisdictions*. Commissioned by the Strategy and Review Group. Department of Education and EC Development (DEECD). Final Report. Melbourne: DEECD.

Campbell, F., Conti, G., Heckman, J.J., Moon, S.H., Pinto, R., Pungello, E. & Pan, Y. (2014). Early childhood investments substantially boost adult health. *Science*, 343(6178), 1478–1485. doi:10.1126/science.1248429.

Cannella, G.S. (1997). *Deconstructing early childhood education: Social justice and revolution*. New York: Peter Lang.

Centre for Equity and Innovation in Early Childhood. (2006). *Cultural diversity*. CD-ROM resource. University of Melbourne. Melbourne: CEIEC. Retrieved from www.edfac.unimelb.edu.au/ceiec/resources/cdroms.html.

Chalke, J. (2013). Will the early years professional please stand up? Professionalism in the early childhood workforce in England. *Contemporary Issues in Early Childhood,* 14(3), 212–222. doi:10.2304/ciec.2013.14.3.212.

Chapman, T. (1988). She's got her ticket. On *Tracey Chapman* [CD] California, USA: Elektra Records.

Chaskin, R. (2001). Building community capacity: A definitional framework and case studies from a comprehensive community initiative. *Urban Affairs Review*, 36(3), 291–323.

Cheeseman, S. (2006a). Investigating pedagogical silences in Australian publicly funded programs for young children in Australia. Unpublished research report.

Cheeseman, S. (2006b). Pedagogical silences in Australian early childhood social policy. *Contemporary Issues in Early Childhood*, 8(3), 244–54.

Cheeseman, S. (2009). Belonging, being and becoming: How the Early Years Learning Framework (EYLF) can contribute to young children's lives. Paper presented at the KU Annual Seminar, Sydney University.

Cheeseman, S. (2010). UTS—Marrickville Council Pedagogical Leadership Project. Unpublished notes.

Cheeseman, S. (2016). Planning for children's learning: curriculum, pedagogy and assessment. In J. Ailwood, W. Boyd & M. Theobald (Eds.) *Understanding early childhood education and care in Australia.* Crows Nest, NSW: Allen & Unwin.

Cheeseman, S. & Torr, J. (2009). From ideology to productivity: Reforming early childhood education and care in Australia. *International Journal of Child Care and Education Policy,* 3(1), 61–74.

Cherrington, S. & Wansbrough, D. (2007). *An evaluation of Ministry of Education funded early childhood education professional development programmes.* Retrieved from www.educationcounts.govt.nz/publications/ece/11978.

City of Wodonga. (2010). *Building a child-friendly city. Report to children and young people from Wodonga City Council.*

Clark, A., Kjorholt, A.T. & Moss, P. (2005). *Beyond listening. Children's perspectives on early childhood services.* Bristol: The Policy Press.

Clark, A. & Moss, P. (2011). *Listening to young children: The mosaic approach.* (2nd ed.). London: National Children's Bureau Enterprises.

Clarke, D. & Hadley, F. (2009). *Establishing curriculum learning circles to increase pedagogical leadership.* Final report. Canberra, ACT: DEEWR.

Cleveland, G. & Krashinsky, M. (2005). *The non-profit advantage: Producing quality in thick and thin child care markets.* Scarborough, Toronto: University of Toronto.

Cloughessey, K. & Waniganayake, M. (2011). Educator responses to children with lesbian, gay, bisexual and transgender parents. *Reflections Gowrie Australia,* Summer (45), 14–16.

Cloughessy, K. & Waniganayake, M. (2014). Early childhood educators working with children who have lesbian, gay, bisexual and transgender parents: What does the literature tell us?. *Early Childhood Development and Care,* 184(8), 1267–1280. doi: 10.1080/03004430.2013.862529.

Cloughessy, K. & Waniganayake, M. (2015). 'Raised Eyebrows': Working with lesbian-parented families—experiences of childcare centre directors in Australia. *Children and Society,* 29(5), 37–387. doi:10.1111/chso.12065.

Clore Duffield Foundation. (2015). *Spaces for learning: A new handbook for creating inspirational learning spaces*, UK. Retrieved from www.cloreduffield.org.uk.

Clyde, M. & Rodd, J. (1993). A comparison of Australian and American centre-based caregivers perceptions of their roles. In S. Reifel (Ed.), *Advances in Early Childhood Education and Care*. Greenwich, CN: JAI Press.

COAG, *see* Council of Australian Governments

Cobb, C., Danby, S. & Farrell, A. (2005). Governance of children's everyday spaces. *Australian Journal of Early Childhood*, 30(1), March, 14–19.

Coleman, M. & Earley, P. (Eds.). (2005). *Leadership and management in education: Cultures, change and context*. Oxford: Oxford University Press.

Colmer, K. (2008). Leading a learning organisation: Australian early years centres as learning networks. *European Early Childhood Education Research Journal*, 16(1), 107–15.

Colmer, K. (2010). *Distributed leadership for professional learning*. Paper presented at the Early Childhood Australia Conference, Adelaide, Australia.

Colmer, K. (2016). *Leadership for professional learning during curriculum reform in early childhood centres in Australia*. A thesis submitted in fulfilment of the requirements of a PhD degree at Macquarie University, Sydney, Australia.

Colmer, K., Waniganayake, M. & Field, L. (2014). Leading professional learning in early childhood centres: Who are the educational leaders? *Australasian Journal of Early Childhood*, 39(4), December, 103–113.

Commonwealth of Australia. (1900). *The Australian Constitution*. Retrieved from www.aph.gov.au/senate/general/constitution/constit.pdf.

Commonwealth of Australia. (2010a). *The Education and Care Services National Law Act 2010*. Retrieved from www.legislation.vic.gov.au/Domino/Web_Notes/LDMS/LTObject_Store/LTObjSt5.nsf/DDE300B846EED9C7CA257616000A3571/A36B365963580A90CA25780E0011D8D4/$FILE/10-69aa001%20authorised.pdf.

Commonwealth of Australia. (2010b). *National Quality Standard for early childhood education and care and school age care: Draft assessment and rating instrument*.

Community Child Care Co-operative NSW. (2009a). Financial basics. *The manual: Managing a children's service* (pp. 100–24). Sydney: CCCNSW.

Community Child Care Co-operative NSW. (2009b). *The manual: Managing a children's service*. Sydney: CCCNSW.

Community Childcare Co-operative NSW. (2010). *Managing a child care service*. Sydney: CCCNSW.

Community Child Care New South Wales (CCCNSW). (2006). *Children's services and the law: A legal guide for the childcare sector*. Sydney: CCCNSW.

Costa, A.L. & Kallick, B. (2000). *Describing 16 habits of mind*. Alexandria, VA: ASCD.

Council of Australian Governments (COAG). (2009a). *Closing the gap: National partnership agreement on Indigenous early childhood development*.

Council of Australian Governments. (2009b). *Investing in the early years: A national early childhood development strategy*. Canberra: COAG.

Council of Australian Governments. (2009c). *National partnership agreement on the national quality agenda for early childhood education and care*. Retrieved from www.coag.gov.au/coag_meeting_outcomes/2009-12-07/docs/nap_national_quality_agenda_early_childhood_education_care.pdf.

Crompton, D. A. (2000). The art of power networking. *Child Care Information Exchange*, 1, 6–8.

Cross, J. (2001). *What is sense of place?* 12th Headwaters Conference Western State College, 2–4 November. Department of Sociology Colorado State University.

Crowburn, W. (1986). *Class, ideology and community education*. London: Croom Helm.

Cummings, T. & Worley, C. (2005). *Organization development and change* (8th ed.). Mason, OH: Southwestern.

Dahlberg, G. & Moss, P. (2005). *Ethics and politics in early childhood education*. London: RoutledgeFalmer.

Dahlberg, G., Moss, P. & Pence, A. (2007). *Beyond quality in early childhood education and care: Languages of evaluation* (2nd ed.). London: Routledge.

Davidoff, I. (n.d.). *Evidence of the child care market*.

Davies, B. (2011). *Leading the strategically focused school* (2nd ed.). London: Sage Publications.

Davis, K., Krieg, S. & Smith, K. (2015). Leading otherwise: using a feminist-poststructuralist and postcolonial lens to create alternative spaces for early childhood educational leaders. *International Journal of Leadership in Education. Theory and Practice*. 18(2): 131–48. doi.org/10.1080/13603124.2014.943296.

Deci, E. & Ryan, R. (2014). The importance of universal psychological needs for understanding motivation in the workplace. In M. Gagne (Ed.), *The Oxford handbook of work engagement, motivation, and self determination theory* (pp. 13–22). New York: Oxford University Press.

DEEWR, *see* Department of Education, Employment and Workplace Relations

Deasy, C. & Lasswell, T. (1990). *Designing places for people: A handbook on human behaviour for architects, designers and facility managers*. (2nd ed.). New York: Whitney Library of design.

Dees, G., Haas, M. & Haas, P. (1998). *The meaning of 'social entrepreneurship'*. USA: Kauffman Center for Entrepreneurial Leadership Ewing Marion Kauffman Foundation. Retrieved from www.redalmarza.cl/ing/pdf/TheMeaningofSocialEntrepreneurship.pdf.

de Botton, A. (2007). *The architecture of happiness*. UK: Penguin.

De Gioia, K. (2003). Beyond cultural diversity: Exploring micro and macro culture in the early childhood setting. Unpublished PhD thesis. University of Western Sydney.

De Gioia, K. (2009). Parent and staff expectations for continuity of home practices in the child care setting for families with diverse cultural backgrounds. *Australasian Journal of Early Childhood*, 34(3), 9–17.

Department of Education (2014). *National ECEC Workforce Census 2013*. Melbourne: Social Research Centre.

Department of Education, Employment and Workplace Relations (DEEWR). (2009). *Belonging, being and becoming: The Early Years Learning Framework for Australia*. Retrieved from www.docs.education.gov.au/system/files/doc/other/belonging_being_and_becoming_the_early_years_learning_framework_for_australia.pdf.

Derman-Sparks, L., LeeKeenan, D. & Nimmo, J. (2015). *Leading anti-bias early childhood programs: A guide for change.* New York: Teachers' College Press.

Derman-Sparks, L., Staff, A.T.F. & the ABC Task Force (1989). *Anti-bias curriculum: Tools for empowering young children* (7th ed.). Washington, D.C.: National Association for the Education of Young Children.

Dickson, J. (2011). *Humilitas: Lost key to life, love and leadership*. Grand Rapids, Michigan: Zondervan.

Dubrin, A.J., Dalglish, C. & Miller, P. (2006). *Leadership* (2nd Asia–Pacific ed.). Milton, Qld: John Wiley & Sons.

Duignan, P. (2006). *Educational leadership: Key challenges and ethical tensions*. Melbourne, Victoria: Cambridge University Press.

Dunlop, A. (2008). *A literature review on leadership in the early years*. Retrieved from www.scribd.com/document/205363958/A-Literature-Review-on-Leadership-in-the-Early-Years#

Dwyer, J. (2016). *Communication for business and the professions: Strategies and skills* (6th ed.). Melbourne, Victoria: Pearson Australia.

Dwyer, N. & Highfield, K. (2015). *Technology: Our tool not our master*. Deakin West, ACT: Early Childhood Australia.

Early Childhood Australia (ECA). (2016). *Code of ethics.* Retrieved from www.earlychildhoodaustralia.org.au/wp-content/uploads/2016/07/ECA-COE-Poster_2016.pdf.

Early Childhood Australia National Quality Standard Professional Learning Program. Retrieved from www.earlychildhoodaustralia.org.au/nqsplp/e-learning-videos/talking-about-practice/the-role-of-the-educational-leader/

Early Childhood Development Steering Committee. (2009). *Regulation impact statement for early childhood education and care quality reforms: COAG consultation RIS.*

Early Childhood Australia Learning Hub [Early Childhood Australia Inc. and the National Quality Standard Professional Learning Program funded by the Commonwealth of Australia]. (2012). *The role of the educational leader FULL version* [Video]. Retrieved from http://vimeo.com/55419391

Ebbeck, M. & Waniganayake, M. (2004). *Early childhood professionals: Leading today and tomorrow*. Sydney: Elsevier (originally published in 2003 by MacLennan & Petty).

ECA, *see* Early Childhood Australia

Edwards, S. & Nuttall, J. (Eds.). (2009). *Professional learning in early childhood settings* (Vol. 3). Rotterdam: Sense Publishers.

Egan, K. (2003). What is curriculum? *Journal of the Canadian Association for Curriculum Studies*, 1(1), 9–16.

Engle, P.L., Black, M.M., Behrman, J., de Mello, M.C., Gertler, P.J. & Kapiriri, L. (2007). Strategies to avoid the loss of developmental potential in more than 200 million children in the developing world. *The Lancet*. 369(9557), 229–42.

Fair Work Ombudsman [FairWorkGovAu]. (2015, 29 January). *Mediation—what it is and what happens* [Video].

Families First NSW. (2007). *Building connections. A handbook that supports early childhood professionals to develop relationships with culturally and linguistically diverse families and connect with appropriate support agencies*. Sydney, Australia: Families First NSW.

Farquhar, S. (1999). *Research and the production of 'worthwhile' knowledge about quality in early years education*. Paper presented at the 1999 AARE–NZARE Annual Conference, Melbourne, Australia. Retrieved from www.aare.edu.au/99pap/far99779.htm.

Fasoli, L., Scrivens, C. & Woodrow, C. (2007). Challenges for leadership in Aotearoa/New Zealand and Australian early childhood contexts. In L. Keesing-Styles & H. Hedges (Eds.), *Theorising early childhood practice: Emerging dialogues* (pp. 231–53). Castle Hill: Pademelon Press.

Fenech, M. (2007). The impact of regulation on quality in long day care in New South Wales: Teachers' perceptions and a critical analysis. Unpublished doctoral dissertation. Macquarie University, Sydney.

Fenech, M. (2011). An analysis of the conceptualisation of 'quality' in early childhood education and care empirical research: Promoting 'blind spots' as foci for future research. *Contemporary Issues in Early Childhood*, 12(2), 102–17.

Fenech, M., Giugni, M. & Bown, K. (2012). A critical analysis of the National Quality Framework: Mobilising for a vision for children beyond minimum standards. *Australasian Journal of Early Childhood,* 12(4), 5–14.

Fenech, M., Harrison, L., Press, F. & Sumsion, J. (2010). *Contributors to quality long day care: Findings from six case study centres*. Bathurst: Charles Sturt University.

Fenech, M. & Lotz, M. (2016, online first). Systems advocacy in the professional practice of early childhood teachers: From the antithetical to the ethical. *Early Years: An International Research Journal*. 1–16. doi: 10.1080/09575146.2016.1209739.

Fenech, M., Robertson, G., Sumsion, J. & Goodfellow, J. (2007). Working by the rules: Early childhood professionals' perceptions of regulatory environments. *Early Child Development and Care*, 177(1), 93–106.

Fenech, M., Salaman, A. & Hinton, A. (2016). What's best for my child? Building parents' understandings of early learning and quality early childhood education and care. Paper presented at the Early Childhood Australia National Conference 2016. 'This is childhood: Pedagogy and practice in the early years'. Darwin Convention Centre, 5–8 October.

Fenech, M. & Sumsion, J. (2007a). Early childhood teachers and regulation: Complicating power relations using a Foulcauldian lens. *Contemporary Issues in Early Childhood*, 8(2), 109–22.

Fenech, M. & Sumsion, J. (2007b). Promoting high quality early childhood education and care services: Beyond risk management, performative constructions of regulation. *Journal of Early Childhood Research*, 5(3), 263–83.

Fenech, M., Sumsion, J. & Goodfellow, J. (2006). The regulatory environment in long day care: A 'double-edged sword' for early childhood professional practice. *Australian Journal of Early Childhood*, 31(3), 49–58.

Fenech, M., Sumsion, J. & Shepherd, W. (2010). Promoting early childhood teacher professionalism in the Australian context: The place of resistance. *Contemporary Issues in Early Childhood*, 11(1), 89–105.

Fleet, A., De Gioia, K. & Patterson, C. (2016). *Engaging with educational change: Voices of practitioner inquiry*. London, United Kingdom: Bloomsbury Academic.

Fleet, A. & Patterson, C. (2009). A timescape. In S. Edwards & J. Nuttall (Eds.), *Professional learning in early childhood settings* (Vol. 3). Rotterdam: Sense Publishers.

Fleet, A., Soper, R., Semann, A. & Madden, L. (2015). The role of the educational leader: perceptions and expectations in a period of change. *Australasian Journal of Early Childhood,* 40(3), 29–37.

Foucault, M. (1977). *Discipline and punish: The birth of the prison* (A. Sheridan, Trans.). Harmondsworth: Penguin.

Foucault, M. (1978). *The history of sexuality: Volume 1* (R. Hurley, Trans.). London: Penguin Books.

Foucault, M. (1980). Truth and power. In C. Gordon (Ed.), *Power/knowledge* (pp. 109–33). Sussex: The Harvester Press.

Foucault, M. (1983). On the genealogy of ethics. In H. Dreyfus & P. Rabinow (Eds.), *Michel Foucault: Beyond structuralism and hermeneutics*. Chicago: The University of Chicago Press.

Freire, P. (1972). *Pedagogy of the oppressed*. Harmondsworth: Penguin.

French, F. (2008). *The smallest Samurai: A tale of old Japan.* London: Frances Lincoln Children's Books.

French, J.P. & Raven, B.H. (1986). The bases of social power. In D. Cartwright & A.F. Zander (Eds.), *Group dynamics: Research and theory* (3rd ed., pp. 259–70). New York: Harper and Row.

Fullan, M. (2016). *The NEW meaning of educational change*. (5th ed.). New York: Teachers College Press, Columbia University.

Fuqua, H., Payne, K.E. & Cangemi, J.P. (n.d.). *Leadership and the effective use of power*. Retrieved from www.nationalforum.com/Electronic%20Journal%20Volumes/Fuqua,%20Jr.,%20Harold%20E.%20Leadership%20and%20the%20Effectives%20Use%20of%20Power.pdf

Gammage, P. (2006). Early childhood education and care: Politics, policies and possibilities. *Early Years*, 26(3), 235–48.

Gangari Bamford Maguire and Associates. (n.d.). *Including Aboriginal Australia in your service*. Retrieved from www.earlychildhoodaustralia.org.au/eylfplp/pdf/including_aboriginal_australia.pdf

Garcia, J. L., Heckman, J., Leaf, D. E. & Prados, M. J. (2016). *The life-cycle benefits of an influential early childhood program. Working paper.* Retrieved from University of Chicago: https://econresearch.uchicago.edu/sites/econresearch.uchicago.edu/files/Garcia_Heckman_Leaf_etal_2016_life-cycle-benefits-ecp_r1.pdf

Giamminuti, S. (2013). *Dancing with Reggio Emilia: Metaphors for quality*. Castle Hill, NSW: Pademelon Press.

Gibbs, L. (2003). *Action, advocacy and activism: Standing up for children*. Marrickville, Sydney: Community Child Care Co-operative Ltd (NSW).

Gibbs, L. (2011). The lessons of the EYLF for professional learning and development. *Reflections—Gowrie Australia*, Winter(43), 4–7.

Giovacco-Johnson, T. (2009). Portraits of partnership: The hopes and dreams project. *Early Child Education Journal*, 37, 127–35.

Giugni, M. (2010). Talkin' up and speakin' out: Activism and politics in early childhood education for equity and social justice. In M. Giugni & K. Mundine (Eds.), *Talkin' up and speakin' out* (pp. 263–81). Castle Hill, NSW: Pademelon Press.

Gladwell, M. (2000). *The tipping point*. USA: Little Brown.

Glover, D. & Levacic, R. (2005). Financial and material resources for learning. In M. Coleman & P. Earley (Eds.), *Leadership and management in education. Cultures, change and context* (pp. 166–86). New York: Oxford University Press.

Godbee, G. (2007). *Accounting for managers*. Sydney: Macquarie University.

Goleman, D. (1995). *Emotional intelligence: Why it can matter more than IQ*. London: Bloomsbury.

Goleman, D. (1998). *Working with emotional intelligence*. London: Bloomsbury.

Goleman, D. (2000). Leadership that gets results. *Harvard Business Review,* 78(2), 78–90.

Gonzalez-Mena, J. (2001). Culture, identity and caregiving practices. *Every Child*, 7(3), 2.

Goodfellow, J. (2003). Practical wisdom in professional practice: The person in the process. *Contemporary Issues in Early Childhood*, 4(1), 48–63.

Gordon Training International. [gordontrainingint] (2010, January 21). *Leadership training—active listening* [Video]. Retrieved from https://www.youtube.com/watch?v=ESujTCel6lM.

Gothard, S. & Austin, M.J. (2013). Leadership Succession Planning: Implications for Nonprofit Human Service Organizations. *Administration in Social Work*, 37(3), 272–85, doi: 10.1080/03643107.2012.684741.

Grace, R., Bowes, J. & Elcombe, E. (2014). Child participation and family engagement with early childhood education and care services in disadvantaged Australian communities. *International Journal of Early Childhood,* 46(2), 271–98. DOI 10.1007/s13158-014-0112-y.

Grace, R., Cashmore, J., Scott, D. & Hayes, A. (2017). Effective policy to support children, families and communities. In R. Grace, K. Hodge. & C. McMahon. (Eds.). *Children, families and communities* (5th ed.) pp. 358–82. South Melbourne: Oxford University Press.

Grace, R., Hodge, K., & McMahon, C. (Eds.) (2017). *Children, families and communities: Contexts and consequences.* (5th ed.). Melbourne, Australia: Oxford University Press.

Grarock, M. & Morrissey, A.M. (2013). Teachers' perceptions of their abilities to be educational leaders in Victorian childcare settings. *Australasian Journal of Early Childhood,* 38(2), June: 4–12.

Green, J. & Bickley, M. (2013). Developing a 'learning community' for educational leaders. *Reflections*, 51, 6–7. Retrieved from http://reflections.realviewdigital.com/?xml=Reflections_V2&iid=77928#folio=14.

Greenman, J. (2005). Places for childhood in the 21st century: A conceptual framework. *Beyond the journal* Young children on the web,* 1–8 May.

Grieshaber, S. (2000). Regulating the early childhood field. *Australian Journal of Early Childhood*, 25(2), 1–6.

Grieshaber, S. (2002). A national system of childcare accreditation: Quality assurance or a technique of normalization? In G.S. Cannella & J.L. Kincheloe (Eds.), *Kidworld: Childhood studies, global perspectives and education* (pp. 161–80). New York: Peter Lang.

Gronroos, C. (1995). Relationship marketing: The strategy continuum. *Journal of the Academy of Marketing Science*, 23(4), 252–4.

Guilfoyle, A., Sims, M., Saggers, S. & Hutchins, T. (2010). Culturally strong childcare programs for Indigenous children, families and communities. *Australasian Journal of Early Childhood*, 35(3), 68–76.

Gunter, H. (2001). Critical approaches to leadership in education. *Journal of Educational Enquiry*, 2(2), 94–108.

Hadley, F. (2000). The community centred early childhood professional. Developing community linkages to support children and families. Unpublished masters research project. University of Western Sydney, Australia.

Hadley, F. (2007a). The 5th discourse: The connectivity role for early childhood services—Meaningful support for families. Unpublished doctoral dissertation. University of Western Sydney, Australia.

Hadley, F. (2007b). Building connections for diversity. *Reflections*, Spring, 4–7.

Hadley, F. (2007c). Families First northern Sydney children's services culturally and linguistically diverse project. Final report. Sydney: NSW: Families First NSW & Lady Gowrie Child Centre, Sydney.

Hadley, F. (2010). How do early childhood settings encourage families to belong? *Every Child Magazine*, 16(1), 10–11.

Hadley, F. (2012). Early childhood staff and families' perceptions: Diverse views about important experiences for children aged 3–5 years in early childhood settings. *Contemporary Issues in Early Childhood* 13(1), 38–49. doi: 10.2304/ciec.2012.13.1.38.

Hadley, F. (2014). 'It's bumpy and we understood each other at the end, I hope!' Unpacking what experiences are valued in the early childhood setting and how this impacts on parent partnerships with culturally and linguistically diverse families. *Australasian Journal of Early Childhood*, 39(2), 91–9.

Hadley, F. & De Gioia, K. (2008). Facilitating a sense of belonging for families from diverse backgrounds in early childhood settings. *Early Childhood Matters* (111), 41–6.

Hadley, F. & De Gioia, K. (2010). Come together. *Rattler*, Spring, 18–23.

Hadley, F. & Rouse, E. (in press). The family centre partnership disconnect: Creating reciprocity. *Contemporary Issues in Early Childhood.*

Hadley, F., Cheeseman, S., De Gioia, K., Highfield, K. & Degotardi, S., & Clarke, D. (2016). Stories of pedagogical leadership: Collaborative professional learning. In A. Fleet, K. De Gioia & C. Patterson (Eds.). *Engaging with educational change: Voices of practitioner inquiry.* London: Bloomsbury.

Hadley, F., Waniganayake, M. & Shepherd, W. (2015). Contemporary practice in professional learning and development of early childhood educators in Australia: Reflections on what works and why. *Professional Development in Education—Special Issue: The Professional Development of Early Years Educators*. 41(2), 187–202. doi: 10.1080/19415257.2014.986818.

Hand, K. & Wise, S. (2006). *Parenting partnerships in culturally diverse child care settings: A care provider perspective. Research paper No. 36*. Melbourne: Australian Institute of Family Studies. Retrieved from www.aifs.gov.au/institute/pubs/rp36/rp36.html.

Hard, L. (2006). Horizontal violence in early childhood education and care: Implications for leadership enactment. *Australian Journal of Early Childhood*, 31(3), 40–8.

Hard, L. (2008). *Understanding leadership enactment in early childhood education and care*. Saarbrucken: VDM Verlag.

Hard, L. (2009). Why is bullying an issue in the early childhood workforce? *Every Child*, 15(2), 24–5.

Hard, L. & Jónsdóttir, A.H. (2013). Leadership is not a dirty word: Exploring and embracing leadership in ECEC. *European Early Childhood Education Research Journal*, 21(3), 311–325. doi:10.1080/1350293x.2013.814355

Harding, B. & Harding, V. (2006). *The rainbow cubby house*. Sydney: National Library of Australia.

Hargreaves, A. (2009). Leadership succession and sustainable improvement. *The School Administrator*, 66(11), 1–5. Retrieved from www.aasa.org/SchoolAdministratorArticle.aspx?id=10134.

Harms, L. (2007). *Working with people: Communication skills for reflective practice*. South Melbourne: Oxford University Press.

Harris, A. (2004). Distributed Leadership and School Improvement. *Educational Management Administration & Leadership*, 32(1), 11–24. doi: 10.1177/1741143204039297.

Harris, A. (2008). *Distributed school leadership: Developing tomorrow's leaders*. London: Routledge.

Harris, A. (2009). *Distributed school leadership: Evidence, issues and future directions*. Sydney: Australian Council of Educational Leaders.

Harris, A. (2013). *Distributed leadership matters: Perspectives, practicalities and potential*. Thousand Oaks, CA: Corwin Press.

Harris, A., Day, C. & Hadfield, M. (2000). Effective leadership: Challenging the orthodoxy part 2. *Management in Education*, 14(2), 14–19.

Harris, A. & DeFlaminis, J. (2016). Distributed leadership in practice: Evidence, misconceptions and possibilities. *Management in Education*, 30(4), 141–6. doi:10.1177/0892020616656734.

Harris, A. & Spillane, J. (2008). Distributed leadership through the looking glass. *Management in Education*, 22(1), 31–4.

Harris, P. & Manatakis, H. (2013). Young children's voices about their local communities. *Australasian Journal of Early Childhood*, 38(3), 68–76.

Harrison, L., Press, F., Sumsion, J., Bowes, J. & Fenech, M. (2008). Investigating quality: A multi-modal investigation of current and proposed structures and processes determining and sustaining quality in Australian centre-based childcare. New South Wales: Australian Research Council Discovery Project DP 0881729.

Hattie, J. (2012). *Visible Learning for Teachers: Maximizing impact on learning*. New York: Routledge.

Hayden, J. (1996). *Management of early childhood services. An Australian perspective*. Sydney: Social Sciences Press.

Hayden, J. (1997). Administrators of early childhood services: Responsibilities, supports and training needs. *Journal of Australian Research in Early Childhood Education*, 2, 38–47.

Hayden, J., De Gioia, K., Fraser, D. & Hadley, F. (2002). *Community centred early childhood education: A health promoting approach to service delivery in NSW*. A report on the health promoting early childhood setting program. Final Report. Sydney: Government of New South Wales, Australia.

Hayden, J., De Gioia, K. & Hadley, F. (2005). ECD and health promoting: Building on capacity. *International Journal of Early Childhood*, 37(2), 67–76.

Hayes, K. (2004). Building leaders: mentoring, not managing. *Training and Development in Australia*, 10–13 April.

Heckman, J. (2000). *Invest in the very young*. Chicago, IL: Ounce of Prevention Fund and the University of Chicago. Retrieved from www.eric.ed.gov/ERICWebPortal/search/detailmini.jsp?_nfpb=true&_&ERICExtSearch_SearchValue_0=ED467549&ERICExtSearch_SearchType_0=no&accno=ED467549.

Heckman, J., Moon, S.H., Pinto, R., Savelyev, P.A. & Yavitz, A. (2010). The rate of return to the HighScope Perry Preschool Program. *Journal of Public Economics*. 94(1–2): 114–28. https://doi-org.simsrad.net.ocs.mq.edu.au/10.1016/j.jpubeco.2009.11.001.

Hedaa, L. & Ritter, T. (2005). Business relationships on different waves: Paradigm shift and marketing orientation revisited. *Industrial Marketing Management*, 34(7), 714–21.

Heikka, J. (2014). *Distributed Pedagogical Leadership in Early Childhood Education*. A cotutelle thesis submitted in fulfilment of the requirements of a PhD degree at Macquarie University, Sydney, Australia and the University of Tampere, Finland.

Heikka, J. & Hujala, E. (2013). Early childhood leadership through the lens of distributed leadership, *European Early Childhood Education Research Journal*, 21(4), 568–80.

Heikka, J., Halttunen, L. & Waniganayake, M. (2016). Perceptions of early childhood education professionals on teacher leadership in Finland. *Early Child Development and Care*. doi:10.1080/03004430.2016.1207066

Heikka, J. & Waniganayake, M. (2010). *Shared visions and directions on the roles and responsibilities of early childhood leaders: Perspectives from Finland*. Paper presented at the Early Childhood Australia Conference, Adelaide, Australia, September.

Heikka, J. & Waniganayake, M. (2011). Pedagogical leadership from a distributed perspective within the context of early childhood education. *International Journal of Leadership in Education,* 14(4), 499–512. doi: 10.1080/13603124.2011.577909.

Heikka, J., Waniganayake, M. & Hujala, E. (2013). Contextualizing distributed leadership within early childhood education: Current understandings, research evidence and future challenges. *Educational Management Administration & Leadership*, 41(1), 30–44. doi:10.1177/1741143212462700.

Ho, D. (2011). Identifying leadership roles for quality in early childhood education programmes. *International Journal of Leadership in Education*. 14 (1) 47–59.

Ho, D. & Tikly, L.P. (2012). Conceptualizing teacher leadership in a Chinese, policy-driven context: A research agenda. *School Effectiveness and School Improvement*, 23(4), 401–16.

Hogan, S. (2015). Are we expecting too much of leaders? *Early Education Journal*, 77, 4–5.

Hognestad, K. & Boe, M. (2015). Leading site-based knowledge development; a mission impossible? Insights from a study from Norway. In M. Waniganayake, J. Rodd & L. Gibbs (Eds.), *Thinking and learning about leadership. Early childhood research from Australia, Finland and Norway* (pp. 210–28). Sydney: Community Child Care Co-operative (NSW).

Hughes, M. (2015). Leading changes: Why transformation explanations fail. *Leadership*, 12(4): 449–69. doi:10.1177/1742715015571393.

Hughes, P. & MacNaughton, G. (2001). Consensus, dissensus or community: The politics of parent involvement in early childhood education. *Contemporary Issues in Early Childhood*, 1(3), 241–58.

Hughes, P. & MacNaughton, G. (2002). Preparing early childhood professionals to work with parents: The challenges of diversity and dissensus. *Australian Journal of Early Childhood*, 28(2), 14–20.

Hujala, E. & Puroila, A. (Eds.). (1998). *Towards understanding leadership in early childhood contexts: Cross-cultural perspectives*. Acta Universitatis Ouluensis, E Scientique Rerum Socialium 35. Oulu, Finland: Oulu University Press.

Hujala, E., Waniganayake, M. & Rodd, J. (Eds.). (2013). *Researching Leadership in Early Childhood Education*. Research Monograph. Tampere, Finland: Tampere University Press.

Huntsman, L. (2008). *Determinants of quality in child care: A review of the research evidence*.

Hutchins, T., Frances, K. & Saggers, S. (2009). Australian Indigenous perspectives on quality assurance in children's services. *Australasian Journal of Early Childhood*, 34(1), 10–19.

Influences on Architectural Design: id2012.weebly.com/uploads/5/1/2/4/5124834/conceptualization_2.ppt from online resources.

Irvine, S., Thorpe, K., McDonald, P., Lunn, J. & Sumsion, J. (2016). *Money, love and identity: Initial findings from the National ECEC Workforce Study. Summary report from the national ECEC Workforce Development Policy Workshop*. Retrieved from: https://eprints.qut.edu.au/101622/1/Brief_report_ECEC_Workforce_Development_Policy_Workshop_final.pdf.

Jayaweera, T. (2015). Impact of work environmental factors on job performance, mediating role of work motivation: A study of hotel sector in England. *International Journal of Business and Management*. 10(3), 271–8.

John, K. (2008). Sustaining the leaders of children's centres: The role of leadership mentoring. *European Early Childhood Education Research Journal*, 16(1), 53–66.

Johnston, J. & Duffield, C. (2002). Strategic public governance in Australian health: The 'unsmart', incapacitated state? *Australian Theory and Praxis*, 24(1), 125–44.

Jones, C. (2016). *Investigating job satisfaction among early childhood teachers using self-determination theory.* Unpublished Masters in Research thesis, Macquarie University, Australia.

Jones, C., Hadley, F. & Johnstone, M. (2017). Retaining early childhood teachers: What factors contribute to high job satisfaction in early childhood settings in Australia? *New Zealand Research in Early Childhood Education*, 20(2): 1–18.

Jones, C. & Pound, L. (2008). *Leadership and management in the early years*. London: Open University Press.

Jones, E. & Nimmo, J. (1994). *Emergent Curriculum*. Washington DC: NAEYC.

Kagan, S.L. (2015a). Introduction: Why governance? Why this volume? In Kagan, S.L. & Gomez, R.E. (Eds.). *Early childhood governance: Choices and consequences*. (pp. 3–8). New York: Teachers College Press, Columbia University.

Kagan, S.L. (2015b). Conceptualizing ECE governance: Not the elephant in the room. In Kagan, S.L. & Gomez, R.E. (Eds.). *Early childhood governance: Choices and consequences*. (pp. 9–29). New York: Teachers College Press, Columbia University.

Kagan, S.L. & Bowman, B.T. (Eds.). (1997). *Leadership in early care and education*. Washington, DC: National Association for the Education of Young Children.

Kagan, S.L. & Gomez, R.E. (Eds.). (2015). *Early childhood governance: Choices and consequences*. New York: Teachers College Press, Columbia University.

Kagan, S.L. & Hallmark, L.G. (2011). Cultivating leadership in early care and education. *Childcare Information Exchange*, 140, 7–11.

Kangas, J., Venninen, T. & Ojala, M. (2016). Distributed leadership as administrative practice in Finnish early childhood education and care. *Educational Management Administration & Leadership*, 44(4): 617–31. doi: 10.1177/1741143214559226.

Katz, L.G. (1995). *Talks with teachers of young children: A collection*. Norwood, NJ: Ablex.

Khan, H. & Ede, D. (2009). How do not-for-profit SME's attempt to develop a strong brand in an increasingly saturated market? *Journal of Small Business and Enterprise Development*, 16(2), 335–54.

Kieff, J. (2009). *Informed advocacy in early childhood care and education: Making a difference for young children and families*. New Jersey: Pearson Education.

King, D. L., Case, C. J. & Premo, K. M. (2010). Current mission statement emphasis: Be ethical and go global. *Academy of Strategic Management Journal*, July. Retrieved from http://findarticles.com/p/articles/mi_m1TOK/is_2_9/?tag=content;col1.

Kline, N. (2016). *Time to think: Listening to ignite the human mind*. London, UK: Cassell.

Knight, R. (2003, April 28). Managing conflict in your workplace [Video]. Retrieved from www.youtube.com/watch?v=ILUkGb4sZ0s.

Krieg, S., Davis, K. & Smith, K.A. (2014). Exploring the dance of early childhood educational leadership. *Australasian Journal of Early Childhood*, 39(1), 73–80.

Ladkin, D. (2010). *Rethinking leadership: A new look at old leadership questions*. Cheltenham, UK: Edward Elgar Publishing Ltd.

Lattimer, H. (2012). Agents of change: Teacher leaders strengthen learning for their students, their colleagues, and themselves. *The Australian Educational Leader*, 34(4), 15–19.

Lawrence, P. (2015). Leading change—insights into how leaders actually approach the challenge of complexity. *Journal of Change Management*, 15(3): 231–52. doi:10.10180/14697017.2015.1021271.

Layzer, J. & Goodson, B. (2006). The 'quality' of early care and education settings: Definitional and measurement issues. *Evaluation Review*, 30(5), 556–76. doi:10.1177/019384x06291524.

Leithwood, K. (2004). What we know about successful leadership. *The Practicing Administrator*, 26(4), 4–7.

Leithwood, K., Mascall, B. & Strauss, T. (Eds.). (2008). *Distributed leadership according to the evidence*. New York: Routledge.

Libeskind, D. (2009). *17 words of architectural inspiration* [Video]. Retrieved from www.ted.com/talks/daniel_libeskind_s_17_words_of_architectural_inspiration.

Linke, P. (2000). Infant brain research: What is it and what does it mean? *Every Child*, 6, 4–5.

Little, H. & Sweller, N. (2015). Affordances for risk-taking and physical activity in Australian early childhood education settings. *Early Childhood Education Journal,* 43(4), 337–45. doi: 10.1007/s10643-014-0667-0.

Lloyd-Smith, M. & Tarr, J. (2000). Researching children's perspectives: A sociological perspective. In A. Lewis & G. Lindsay (Eds.), *Researching children's perspectives* (pp. 59–69). Buckingham, UK: Open University Press.

Lower, J.K. & Cassidy, D.J. (2007). Child care work environments: The relationship with learning environments. *Journal of Research in Childhood Education*, 22(2), 157–69.

Lumby, J. & Morrison, M. (2010). Leadership and diversity: Theory and research. *School Leadership and Management*, 30(1), 3–17.

Luthans, F. (2002). The need for and meaning of positive organizational behaviour. *Journal of Organizational Behavior*, 23, 695–706.

Macfarlane, K. & Lewis, E. (2012). United we stand: Seeking cohesive action in early childhood education and care. *Contemporary Issues in Early Childhood,* 13(1), 63–73. doi:10.2304/ciec.2012.13.1.63.

MacMillan, K., Money, K., Money, A. & Downing, S. (2005). Relationship marketing in the not-for-profit sector: An extension and application of the commitment–trust theory. *Journal of Business Research*, 58(6), 806–18.

MacNaughton, G. & Hughes, P. (2011). *Parents and professionals in early childhood settings*. Maidenhead, Berkshire: Open University Press.

MacNaughton, G., Smith, K. & Lawrence, H. (2003). *ACT Children's Strategy: Consulting with children birth to 8 years of age*. Melbourne: Centre for Equity and Innovation in Early Childhood. Retrieved from www.edfac.unimelb.edu.au/ceiec/research/program1/program1.5.html.

Mair, J. & Marte, I. (2006). Social entrepreneurship research: A source of explanation, prediction, and delight. *Journal of World Business*, 41, 36–44.

Marotz, L. & Lawson, A. (2007). *Motivational leadership in early childhood education*. Melbourne, Australia: Thomas Delmar Learning.

Marsden, J. & Tan, S. (2010). *The rabbits*. Sydney: Lothian Children's Books.

Marsh, S. (2014). *Locating and imagining leadership that improves learning in New South Wales Independent schools*. An unpublished thesis completed in fulfilment of the requirements for the degree of a Doctor of Philosophy. Sydney: Macquarie University.

Marsh, S., Waniganayake, M. & De Nobile, J. (2014). Improving learning in schools: the overarching influence of 'presence' on the capacity of authoritative leaders. *International Journal of Leadership in Education*, 17(1): 23–39. doi:10.1080/13603124.2013.778334.

Marsh, S., Waniganayake, M. & De Nobile, J. (2016). Leading with intent: Cultivating community conversations to create a shared understanding. *School Effectiveness and School Improvement*, 27(4): 580–593. doi: 10.1080/09243453.2015.1136337.

Martin, K. (2007a). Here we go 'round the broombie tree: Aboriginal early childhood realities and experiences in early childhood services. In J. Ailwood (Ed.), *Early childhood in Australia. Historical and comparative contexts*. Frenchs Forest, NSW: Pearson Education Australia.

Martin, K. (2007b). Ma(r)king tracks and reconceptualising Aboriginal Early Childhood Education: An Aboriginal Australian perspective. *Childrenz Issues*, 11(1), 15–20.

Martin, K. (Ed.). (2016). *Voices visions: Aboriginal early childhood education in Australia*. Sydney: Pademelon Press.

Maton, K.I., Schellenbach, C.J., Leadbeater, B.J. & Solarz, A.L. (Eds.). (2004). *Investing in children, youth, families, and communities: Strengths-based research and policy*. Washington DC: American Psychological Association.

McCain, M., Mustard, J. & Shanker, S. (2007). *Early years study 2. Putting science into action*. Toronto, Canada: Council for Early Childhood Development.

McCashen, W. (2005). *The strengths approach: A strengths based resource for sharing power and creating change*. Bendigo, Victoria: St Luke's Innovative Resources.

McCrea, N.L. (2015). *Leading and managing early childhood settings: Inspiring people, places and practices*. Cambridge, United Kingdom: Cambridge University Press.

McGuickin, G. (2016, March 15). Daniel Libeskind: The people's architect. *Design Ideas*. Retrieved from http://www.decoist.com/daniel-libeskind-architecture/

McFarlane, A. (2015). *Exploring the organisational cultures of early childhood centres*. Unpublished thesis submitted in fulfilment of the requirements for the degree of Master of Research, Macquarie University, Sydney.

McNaughton, D., Hamlin, D., McCarthy, J., Head-Reeves, D. & Schreiner, M. (2008). Learning to listen: Teaching an active listening strategy to preservice education professionals. *Topics in Early Childhood Special Education*, 27(4), 223–231. doi: 10.1177/0271121407311241.

McTell, R. (1969). Streets of London. On *The Best of Ralph McTell*.

Mead, S. (2007). *Million dollar babies: Why infants can't be hardwired for success*. Washington DC: Education Sector.

Mevawalla, Z. (2009). *Advocacy and power: Early childhood leaders' perceptions*. Unpublished honours dissertation. Institute of Early Childhood, Macquarie University.

Mevawalla, Z. & Hadley, F. (2012). The advocacy of educators. *Australasian Journal of Early Childhood* 37(1), 74–80.

Meyer, P.J. (2003). *Attitude is everything: If you want to succeed above and beyond*. Waco, TX: Meyer Resource Group, Incorporated.

Miller, K.I. (2015). *Organizational communication: Approaches and processes* (7th ed.). Stamford, CT: Cengage Learning.

Mintzberg, H. (1994). *The rise and fall of strategic planning: Reconceiving roles for planning, plans and planners*. New York: The Free Press.

Mitchell, A. (1998). Way beyond bake sales—fundraising success stories. In B. Neugebauer & R. Neugebauer (Eds.), *The art of leadership. Managing early childhood organisations* (Vol. 1, 155–8). Redmond, WA. USA: Child Care Information Exchange.

Moore, G. (1979). Architecture and human behaviour: The place of environment-behaviour studies in architecture. *Wisconsin Architect*, September, pp.18–21.

Moore, T. (2008a). *Evaluation of Victorian children's centres: A literature review*. Melbourne: Centre for Community Child Health.

Moore, T.G. (2008b). Rethinking universal and targeted services, *CCCH Working Paper 2*, August. Parkville, Victoria: Centre for Community Child Health.

Moran, M., Porter, D. & Curth-Bibb, J. (2014). *Funding Indigenous organisations: Improving governance performance through innovations in public finance and management in remote Australia*. Closing the gap Clearinghouse. Melbourne: Australian Institute of Health and Welfare and Australian Institute of Family Studies.

Morgan, G. & Emanuel, B. (2010). *The bottom line for children's programs* (5th ed.). Massachusetts: Steam Press.

Moss, P. (2004a). Structures, understandings, and discourses: Possibilities for re-envisioning the early childhood worker. *Contemporary Issues in Early Childhood Education Research Journal*, 15(1), 5–20.

Moss, P. (2004b). The early childhood workforce: Continuing education and professional development. *UNESCO Policy Briefs on Early Childhood*, 28(November–December).

Moss, P. (2009). *There are alternatives! Markets and democratic experimentalism in early childhood education and care*. The Hague: Bernard Van Leer Foundation.

Moss, P. (2010). We cannot go on as we are: The educator in an education for survival. *Contemporary Issues in Early Childhood*, 11(1), 8–19.

Moss, P. & Pence, A. (Eds.). (1994). *Valuing quality in early childhood services: New approaches to defining quality*. London: Paul Chapman Publishing Ltd.

Mujis, D., Aubrey, C., Harris, A. & Briggs, M. (2004). How do they manage? A review of the research on leadership in early childhood. *Journal of Early Childhood Research*, 2(2), 157–69.

Mullen, C.A. (2008). Editor's overview: Assessing mentoring effectiveness and building support systems. *Mentoring & Tutoring: Partnership in Learning*, 16(4), 359–62.

Murray, J. & McDowall Clark, R. (2013). Reframing leadership as a participative pedagogy: the working theories of early years professionals. *Early Years—An International Research Journal*. 33(30), 289–301. doi:10.1080/09575146.2013.781135.

Murray, P., Poole, D. & Jones, G. (2006). *Contemporary issues in management and organisational behaviour*. South Melbourne, Australia: Thomson.

Myers, R.G. (2004). In search of quality in programmes of early childhood care and education. *EFA Global Monitoring Report 2005, The Quality Imperative*.

Myers, T. (2005). Establishing relationships—the key to marketing for better schools. *Independent Education*, 35(1), 32–3.

Naharuddin, N. & Sadegi, M. (2013). Factors of workplace environment that affect employees performance: a case study of Miyazu Malaysia. *International Journal of Independent Research and Studies*. 2(2), 66–78.

Nanus, B. (1992). *Visionary leadership*. San Francisco, CA: Jossey-Bass.

National Childcare Accreditation Council. (2005). *Quality improvement and accreditation system handbook*. Sydney: NCAC.

Neugebauer, R. (1996). *How to stimulate word of mouth Child Care Information Exchange*. Redmond, WA: Child Care Information Exchange.

Neugebauer, R. (1998). Keys to success in raising funds. In B. Neugebauer & R. Neugebauer (Eds.), *The art of leadership. Managing early childhood organisations* (Vol. 1, pp. 138–45). Redmond, WA: Child Care Information Exchange.

Neuman, M.J. (2005). Governance of early childhood education and care: Recent developments in OECD countries. *Early Years*, 25(2), 129–41.

Neuman, M.J., Josephson, K. and Chua, P.G. (2015). A review of the literature: Early childhood care and education (ECCE) personnel in low- and middle-income countries. Paris: UNESCO.

New South Wales Department of Community Services. (2007). *Service analysis and business development resource manual for NSW DoCs funded children's services*. Retrieved from www.community.nsw.gov.au/__data/assets/pdf_file/0020/322283/SABD_MANUAL.PDF.

New South Wales Government. (2016). *Education and Care Services National Regulations*. Retrieved from: www.legislation.nsw.gov.au/#/view/regulation/2011/653.

New South Wales Government WorkCover (2011). *Managing the work environment and facilities: Code of practice*. Safe Work Australia. Retrieved from www.safework.nsw.gov.au/__data/assets/pdf_file/0016/50074/managing-work-environment-facilities-code-of-practice-3567.pdf.

Newman, L. & Pollnitz, L. (2002). *Ethics in action: Introducing the ethical response cycle*. Watson, ACT: Australian Early Childhood Association.

Newman, L. & Pollnitz, L. (2005). *Working with children and families: Professional, legal and ethical issues*. Frenchs Forest, NSW: Pearson Education.

Nicholson, G., Newton, C., McGregor-Lowndes, M. & Sheldrake, M. (2008). Governance training needs in community organisations. *Just Policy*, 49(December), 5–7.

Nicholson, J. & Maniates, H. (2016). Recognising postmodern intersectional identities in leadership for early childhood. *Early Years: An International Research Journal*. 36(1), 66–80. doi:10.1080/09575146.2015.1080667.

Nolan, A., Cartmel, J. & Macfarlane, K. (2012). Thinking about practice in integrated children's services: Considering transdisciplinarity. *Children Australia*, 37(3), 94–9.

Northouse, P.G. (2015). *Introduction to leadership: Concepts and practice*. Los Angeles: Sage

Novinger, S. & O'Brien, L. (2003). Beyond 'boring, meaningless shit' in the Academy: Early childhood teacher educators under the regulatory gaze. *Contemporary Issues in Early Childhood*, 4(1), 3–31.

Nupponen, H. (2006a). Framework for developing leadership skills in child care centres in Queensland, Australia. *Contemporary Issues in Early Childhood*, 7(2), 146–61.

Nupponen, H. (2006b). Leadership concepts and theories: Reflections for practice for early childhood directors. *Australian Journal of Early Childhood*, 31(1), 43–50.

Nuttall, J. (2016). Leadership for professional practice development in early childhood education: From 'performance management' to 'system development'. *Australian Educational Leader*, 38(2), 14–17.

Nuttall, J. & Edwards, S. (2007). Theory policy and practice: Three contexts for the development of Australia's early childhood curriculum documents. In L. Keesing-Styles & H. Hedges (Eds.), *Theorising early childhood practice. Emerging dialogues*. Castle Hill, NSW: Pademelon Press.

OECD, *see* Organisation for Economic Co-operation and Development

Office of the United Nations High Commissioner for Human Rights (UNHCHR). (2007). Good governance practices for the protection of human rights. New York: United Nations. Retrieved from www2.ohchr.org/english/issues/development/governance.

Oldroyd, D. (2005). Human resources for learning. In M. Coleman & P. Earley (Eds.), *Leadership and management in education: Cultures, change and context* (pp. 187–207). Oxford: Oxford University Press.

Olsson, L.M. (2009). *Movement and experimentation in young children's learning. Deleuze and Guattari in early childhood education*. Oxford: Routledge.

Onyx, J. & Bullen, P. (1998). Measuring social capital in five communities in NSW: An analysis. *CACOM Working paper* (Vol. 41). Sydney, Australia: Centre for Australian Community Organisations and Management (CACOM), University of Technology.

Ord, K., Mane, J., Smorti, S., Carroll-Lind, J., Robinson, L., Reed, A-A, Brown-Cooper, P., Meredith, E., Rickard, D. & Jalal, J. (2013). *Developing pedagogical leadership in early childhood education*. Wellington, New Zealand: NZ Childcare Association.

Organisation for Economic Co-operation and Development. (2006). *Starting strong II—Early childhood education and care*. Paris: OECD.

Organisation for Economic Co-operation and Development. (2012). *Starting strong III—A quality toolbox for early childhood education and care*. Paris: OECD.

Organisation for Economic Co-operation and Development. (2015). *Starting strong IV—Monitoring quality in early childhood education and care*. Paris: OECD.

Orland-Barak, L. & Hasin, R. (2010). Exemplary mentors' perspectives towards mentoring across mentoring contexts: Lessons from collective case studies. *Teaching & Teacher Education,* 26(3), 427–37.

Osgood, J. (2004). Time to get down to business: Responses to early years professionals to entrepreneurial approaches to professionalism. *Journal of Early Childhood Research,* 2(1), 5–24.

Osgood, J. (2006). Deconstructing professionalism in early childhood education: Resisting the regulatory gaze. *Contemporary Issues in Early Childhood,* 7(1), 5-14. doi:10.2304/ciec.2006.7.1.5.

Owings, W.A. & Kaplan, L.S. (2012). *Leadership and organizational behavior in education.* Boston: Pearson.

OWP/P Architects, VS Furniture & Bruce Mau Design. (2010). *The third teacher: 79 ways you can use design to transform teaching & learning.* New York: Abrams.

Packard, B.W.L. (2003). Web-based mentoring: Challenging traditional models to increase women's access. *Mentoring & Tutoring: Partnership in Learning,* 11(1), 53–65.

Panousieris, G. (2008). Governance and diversity: Encouraging and enabling participation from marginalised and minority community groups. *Just Policy,* 49(December), 90–3.

Park, G. (2010). DEA 6530 Planning and Managing the Workplace Cornell University. Design Dilemmas: Staff break room. http://iwsp.human.cornell.edu/files/2013/09/Course-Overview-ysk7ns.pdf.

Pascal, C. & Bertram, T. (2011). Listening to young citizens: The struggle to make real a participatory paradigm in research with young children. *European Early Childhood Education Research Journal,* 17(2), 249–62.

Pence, A.R. & Benner, A. (2000). British Columbia's ministry for children and families: A case study in progress. In J. Hayden (Ed.), *Landscapes in early childhood education: Cross national perspectives on empowerment* (pp. 361–74). New York: Peter Lang Publishers.

Penn, H. (2005). *Unequal childhoods: Young children's lives in poor countries.* London: Routledge.

Pisapia, J.R. (2009). *The strategic leader: New tactics for a globalizing world.* Charlotte, NC: Information Age Publishing Inc.

Pocock, B. (2003). *The work/life collision.* Sydney, Australia: The Federation Press.

Pocock, B. & Hill, E. (2007). The childcare policy challenge in Australia. In E. Hill, B. Pocock & A. Elliott (Eds.), *Kids count* (pp. 15–37). Sydney: Sydney University Press.

Porter, L. (2008). *Young children's behaviour. Practical approaches for parents and teachers* (3rd ed.). Marrickville: Elsevier.

Power, K. (2002). *Storylines of Indigenous women and leadership in early childhood education.* Unpublished PhD dissertation. University of New England.

Press, F. (2006). *What about the kids? Policy directions for improving the experiences of infants and young children in a changing world.* Sydney: Crown in right of the State of New South Wales, the State of Queensland and the National Investment for the Early Years.

Press, F., Sumsion, J. & Wong, S. (2010). *Integrated early years provision in Australia: A research project for the Professional Support Coordinators Alliance (PSCA).* Bathurst: PSC National Alliance.

PricewaterhouseCoopers. (2011). *Five lessons for driving innovation and entrepreneurial spirit.* Retrieved from http://resources.greatplacetowork.com/article/pdf/lessons_for_driving_innovation_and_entrepreneurial_spirit.pdf.

Productivity Agenda Working Group. (2008). *A national quality framework for early childhood education and care: A discussion paper.*

Productivity Commission. (2010). *Early childhood development workforce.* Issues paper, November. Canberra: Australian Government.

Productivity Commission. (2011a). *Childhood development workforce: Draft report.* Retrieved from www.community.nsw.gov.au/docswr/_assets/main/documents/childcare_building_blocks9.pdf.

Productivity Commission. (2011b). *Early childhood development workforce: Research report.* Retrieved from www.pc.gov.au/inquiries/completed/education-workforce-early-childhood/report.

Productivity Commission. (2014). *Childcare and early childhood learning: overview.* Inquiry Report No. 73. Canberra: Australian Government. Retrieved from www.pc.gov.au/inquiries/completed/childcare/report.

Purdie, N., Milgate, G. & Bell, H.R. (Eds.). (2011). *Toward culturally reflective and relevant education.* Melbourne: ACER Press.

Putnam, R. (1995). Bowling alone: America's declining social capital. *Journal of Democracy,* 6(1), 65–78.

Raban, B., Waniganayake, M., Nolan, A., Deans, J., Brown, J. & Ure, C. (2007). *Building capacity: Strategic professional development for early childhood practitioners.* Melbourne: Thomson Social Science Press.

Raven, B.H. (1993). The bases of power: Origins and recent developments. *Journal of Social Issues,* 49(4), 227–51.

Rinaldi, C. (2006). *In dialogue with Reggio Emilia: Listening, researching and learning.* London: Routledge.

Regenstein, E. (2015). Glancing at governance. In S.L. Kagan & R.F. Gomez (Eds). *Early childhood governance: Choices and consequences.* (pp. 33–44). New York: Teachers College Press, Columbia University.

Robards, B. (2010). Negotiating identity and integrity on social network sites for educators. *International Journal for Educational Integrity,* 6(2), 19–23.

Robbins, S.P., Bergman, R., Stagg, I. & Coulter, M. (2009). *Foundations of management* (3rd ed.). Frenchs Forest, NSW: Pearson Education Australia.

Robert R. McCormick foundation. 2013. *Irving Harris & early childhood education—321 FastDraw* [Video]. Retrieved from www.youtube.com/watch?v=6_tBozslCC0

Roberts, J. (2008). Governance is as governance does! *Just Policy,* 49(December), 97–9.

Roberston, J. (2011). Partnership in Leadership and Learning. In J. Roberston & H. Timperley (Eds.). *Leadership and Learning.* (pp. 213–26). London: Sage.

Robinson, K. (2002). Making the invisible visible: Gay and lesbian issues in early childhood education. *Contemporary Issues in Early Childhood*, 3(3), 415–34.

Robinson, K. (2013). *Innocence, knowledge and the construction of childhood: The contradictory nature of sexuality and censorship in children's contemporary lives*. London: Routledge.

Rodd, J. (1994). *Leadership in early childhood: The pathway to professionalism*. Maidenhead: Open University Press.

Rodd, J. (1997). Learning to be leaders. Perceptions of early childhood professionals about leadership roles and responsibilities. *Early Years*, 18(1), 40–4.

Rodd, J. (2006a). *Leadership in early childhood* (3rd ed.). Crows Nest, NSW: Allen & Unwin.

Rodd, J. (2006b). Working together to find solutions and resolve differences. In J. Rodd (Ed.), *Leadership in early childhood* (3rd ed., pp. 104–28). Crows Nest, NSW: Allen & Unwin.

Rodd, J. (2013). *Leadership in early childhood: The pathway to professionalism* (4th ed.). Crows Nest, NSW: Allen & Unwin.

Rodd, J. (2015). *Leading change in the early years: Principles and practice*. Maidenhead, Berkshire: Open University Press.

Rohrmann, T. & Emilsen, K. (2015). Editorial for the special edition on men in early childhood. *European Early Childhood Education Research Journal*, 23(3), 295–301. doi: 10.1080/1350293X.2015.1043804.

Rosen, M. (2007). *This is our house*. London: Walker Books.

Roscommon County Childcare Committee (2016, November 10). *10 how can we model pedagogical leadership in early childhood care and educational settings* [Video]. Retrieved from https: www.youtube.com/watch?v=xYvEk6nj0DI.

Roscommon County Childcare Committee (2016). Videos / Podcasts – Roscommon childcare committee. Retrieved from www.roscommonchildcare.ie/videos-podcasts/

Rouse, E. & Spradbury, G. (2016). The role of the educational leader in long day care—how do they perceive their role? *Early Child Development and Care*, 186(3) 497 –508. doi: 10.1080/03004430.2015.1036419.

Rytmeister, C. & Marshall, S. (2007). Studying political tensions in university governance: A focus on board member construction of role. *Tertiary Education and Management*, 13(4), 281–94.

Sachs, J. (2003). *The activist teaching profession*. Buckingham: Open University Press.

Schminke, M., Ambrose, M. & Neubaum, D. (2005). The effect of leader moral development on ethical climate and employee attitudes. *Organizational Behaviour and Human Decision Processes*, 7(2), 135–51.

Semann, A. (2011). If you keep on doing what you've done, you will keep on getting what you've got: A time for brave ideology and courage during times of change. Paper presented at the Kindergarten Parents Victoria and Gowrie Victoria, Melbourne.

Sergiovanni, T. (1984). Leadership and excellence in schooling. *Educational Leadership*, 41(5), 4–13.

Sergiovanni, T. (1992). *Moral leadership: Getting to the heart of school leadership*. San Francisco: Jossey Bass.

Sergiovanni, T. (1994). Organisations or communities? Changing the metaphor changes the theory. *Educational Administration Quarterly*, 30(2), 214–26.

Sergiovanni, T. (1998). Leadership as pedagogy, capital development and school effectiveness. *International Journal of Leadership in Education*, 1, 37–46.

Seung-Hee, C.S., Kyong-Ah, K., Hyun-Joo, J. & Soo-Young, H. (2013). Head Start classrooms and children's school readiness benefit from teachers' qualifications and ongoing training. *Child Youth Care Forum, 42*, 525–53. doi: 10.1007/s10566-013-9213-2.

Shakiba, E. [Eleanor Shakiba]. (2014). *How to speak assertively with I statements by Eleanor Shakiba* [Video] Retrieved from www.youtube.com/watch?v=sswGv9iH-4o.

Shawar V.R. & Shiffman, J. (2016). Generation of global political priority for EC development: the challenges of framing and governance. *The Lancet*. doi.org/10.1016/50140-6736(16)31574-4.

Shepherd, W. (2004). Children's services: Dangerous places for children? *Rattler*, Autumn, 23–6.

Shonkoff, J.P. & Phillips, D.A. (Eds.). (2000). *From neurons to neighbourhoods: The science of early child development*. Washington: National Academy Press.

Shore, R. (2001). Making sense of the brain debates. *Every Child*, 7(3), 4–5.

Sims, M. (2007). The determinants of quality care: Review and research report. In E. Hill, B. Pocock & A. Elliott (Eds.), *Kids count: Better early childhood education and care in Australia* (pp. 220–41). Sydney: Sydney University Press.

Sims, M., Forrest, R., Semann, A., & Slattery, C. (2015). Conceptions of early childhood leadership: Driving new professionalism? *International Journal of Leadership in Education*, 18(2), 149–166. doi:10.1080/13603124.2014.962101

Sims, M. & Waniganayake, M. (2015). The performance of compliance in early childhood: Neoliberalism and nice ladies. *Global Studies in Early Childhood*, 5(3), 333–345. doi:10.1177/2043610615597154

Sinclair, A. (2016). *Leading Mindfully*. Sydney: Allen & Unwin.

Sinclair, C. (2003). Mentoring online about Mentoring: Possibilities and practice. *Mentoring & Tutoring: Partnership in Learning*, 11(1), 79–94.

Siraj-Blatchford, I. & Hallett, E. (2014). *Effective and caring leadership in the early years*. London: Sage.

Siraj-Blatchford, I. & Manni, L. (2007). *Effective leadership in the early years sector: The ELEYS study*. London: Institute of Education, University of London.

Siraj-Blatchford, I. & Siraj-Blatchford, J. (2009). *Improving development outcomes for children through effective practice in integrating early years services*. London: Centre for Excellence and Outcomes in Children and Young People's Services.

Siraj-Blatchford, I. & Woodhead, M. (Eds.) (2009). *Effective Early Childhood Programmes*. Early Childhood in Focus, No.4. Milton Keynes: Open University.

Skattebol, J. & Ferfolja, T. (2007). Voices from an enclave: Lesbian mothers' experience of childcare. *Australian Journal of Early Childhood*, 32(1), 10–18.

Slattery, C. (2009a). Report on the childcare staff mentoring study in the Australian Capital Territory. Canberra: Semann & Slattery.

Slattery, C. (2009b). Troubling times at the top: The dark side of leadership. Sydney: Semann & Slattery.

Slocum-Bradley, N. & Bradley, A. (2010). Is the EU's governance 'good'? An assessment of EU governance in its partnership with ACP states. *Third World Quarterly*, 31(1), 31–49.

Social Research Centre (Melbourne. Vic.). (2014). *National early childcare education and care workforce census*. Retrieved from www.researchconnections.org/childcare/resources/27946.

Special Taskforce on Domestic and Family Violence in Queensland. (2015). *Not Now Not Ever Report: Putting an end to domestic and family violence in Queensland*. Brisbane.

Spillane J.P. (2006). *Distributed leadership*. San Francisco: Jossey-Bass.

Spillane, J.P., Halverson, R. & Diamond, J. B. (2004). Towards theory of leadership practice: A distributed perspective. *Journal of Curriculum Studies*, 36(1), 3–34.

Stamopoulos, E. (2001). School staff positions on P1 composite classes. Unpublished PhD dissertation. Edith Cowan University.

Stenglin, M. (2008). Binding: a resource for exploring interpersonal meaning in three-dimensional space. *Social Semiotics*. 18(4), 425–47.

Stephens, K. (1998). Courting the media with special events. In B. Neugebauer & R. Neugebauer (Eds.), *The art of leadership. Managing early childhood organisations*, 2, (340–344). Redmond, WA: Child Care Information Exchange.

Stonehouse, A. (1989). Nice ladies who love children: The status of the early childhood professional in society. *Early Child Development and Care*, 52(1), 61–7.

Stoney, L. & Mitchell, A. (2010). *The iron triangle: A simple formula for financial policy in ECE programs*. Retrieved from www.earlychildhoodfinance.org/finance/finance-strategies.

Streuli, N., Vennam, V. & Woodhead, M. (2011). 'Increasing choice or inequality? Pathways through early education in Andhra Pradesh, India.' Working Paper 58: *Studies in Early Childhood Transitions*. The Hague: Bernard van Leer Foundation.

Sumsion, J. (2006). From Whitlam to economic rationalism and beyond: A conceptual framework for political activism in children's services. *Australian Journal of Early Childhood*, 31(1), 1–9.

Sumsion, J., Barnes, S., Cheeseman, S., Harrison, L., Kennedy, A.M. and Stonehouse A. (2009). Insider perspectives on developing Belonging, being & becoming: The early years learning framework for Australia. *Australasian Journal of Early Childhood*, 34(4), 4–13.

Supernanny. (2004). [TV Series]. *Supernanny TV series*. Ricochet Entertainment, Warner Bros. Television Productions UK.

Sylva, K., Melhuish, E., Sammons, P., Siraj-Blatchford, I. & Taggart, B. (2004a). *The effective provision of pre-school education (EPPE) project: Final report: A longitudinal study funded by the DfES 1997–2004*. London: Institute of Education, University of London.

Sylva, K., Melhuish, E.C., Sammons, P., Siraj-Blatchford, I. & Taggart, B. (2004b). The effective provision of pre-school education (EPPE) project: Technical paper 12—The final report: Effective pre-school education. London: DfES/Institute of Education, University of London.

Taguchi, H.L. (2010). *Going beyond the theory/practice divide in early childhood education. Introducing an intra-active pedagogy.* London: Routledge.

Talks, C. [Carolyn Talks]. (2014, January 30). *Leading with emotional intelligence in the workplace* [Video]. Retrieved from https://www.youtube.com/watch?v=OoLVo3snNA0.

Tayler, C., Tennent, L., Farrell, A. & Gahan, D. (2002). Use and integration of early childhood services: Insights from an inner city community. *Journal of Australian Research in Early Childhood Education*, 9(1), 113–23.

The House of Tiny Tearaways. (2005). [TV series]. *UK independent production company.* Outline Productions.

Thomas, A. (2011). Not-for-profit organisations: Better governance, better outcomes. *Keeping Good Companies*, March, 31–54.

Thomas, M. (2010). What do the worldwide governance indicators measure? *European Journal of Development Research*, 22(1), 31–54.

Thomas, L. & Nuttall, J. (2014). Negotiating policy-driven and state-mandated expectations of leadership: The discourses accessed by early childhood educators in Australia, *New Zealand Research in Early Childhood Education.* 17, 101–14.

Thornton, K., Wansbrough, D., Clarkin-Phillips, J., Aitken, H. & Tamati, A. (2009). *Conceptualising leadership in early childhood education in Aotearoa New Zealand.* Wellington: New Zealand Teachers Council.

Tian, M., Risku, M. & Collin, K. (2015). A meta-analysis of distributed leadership from 2002 to 2013: Theory development, empirical evidence and future research focus. *Educational Management Administration & Leadership*, 44(1), 146–64. doi:10.1177/1741143214558576.

Titzer, J., Tooley, S. & Shirey, M. (2013). Nurse manager succession planning: synthesis of the evidence. *Journal of Nursing Management*. 21(7): 971–9.

Tobin, J., Arzubiaga, A. & Figueroa Fuentes, P. (2007). Entering into dialogue with immigrant parents. *Early Childhood Matters*, 108, 34–8.

Tomlinson, G. (2012). *Video – active listening skills.Wmv* [Video]. Retrieved from: https://www.youtube.com/watch?v=7PFX23Ynkfs.

Torrance, D. (2013). Distributed leadership: Challenging five generally held assumptions. *School Leadership & Management*, 33(4), 354–72. doi:10.1080/13632434.2013.813463.

Ulhøi, J.P. (2005). The social dimensions of entrepreneurship. *Technovation*, 25(8), 939–46.

UNICEF. (2008). *The child care transition. A league table of early childhood education and care in economically advanced countries.* Innocenti Report Card 8. Retrieved from www.unicef-irc.org/publications/pdf/rc8_eng.pdf.

United Nations (UN). (1989). *Convention on the rights of the child.* Retrieved from www.ohchr.org/en/professionalinterest/pages/crc.aspx.

Van de Veer, R. & Valsiner, J. (Eds.) (1994). *Lev Vygotsky: The Vygotsky reader.* Oxford: Blackwell.

Vermeer, H. J., van IJzendoorn, M.H., Ca´rcamo, R.A. & Harrison, L.J. (2016). Quality of child care using the environment rating scales: A meta-analysis of international studies. *International Journal of Early Childhood*, 48, 33–60. doi:10.1007/s13158-015-0154-9.

Vitiello, V.E. & Kools, M. (2010). Good governance of early childhood development programmes in developing countries. The need for a comprehensive monitoring system. Florence, Italy: UNICEF, Innocenti Research Centre.

Vygotsky, L. (1994). The problem of the environment. In R. van der Veer & J. Valsiner (Eds.). *The Vygotsky reader*, pp 338–54. Oxford: Blackwell.

Wagner, K. (2006). *Finance for nonfinancial managers: 24 lessons to understand and evaluate financial health*. USA: McGraw-Hill.

Waniganayake, M. (2011). Early childhood leadership at crossroads: Current concerns and future directions. In M. Veisson, E. Hujala, P. Smith, M. Waniganayake & E. Kikas (Eds.), *Global perspectives in early childhood education: Diversity, challenges and possibilities* (pp. 297–311). Frankfurt: Peter Lang GmbH.

Waniganayake, M. (2013). Leadership careers in early childhood: Finding your way through chaos and serendipity into strategic planning. In E. Hujala, M. Waniganayake, & J. Rodd, (Eds.), *Researching leadership in early childhood education* (pp. 61–78). Tampere: Tampere University Press.

Waniganayake, M., Colmer, K. & Palkhiwala, S. (2012). Quality area 7: Leadership and service management. In B. Raban (Ed.), *The National Quality Standard—Towards continuous quality improvement: A practical guide for students and professionals* (pp. 59–69). Melbourne, Australia: Teaching Solutions.

Waniganayake, M. Rodd, J. & Gibbs, L. (Eds.). (2015). *Thinking and Learning about Leadership: Early childhood research from Australia, Finland and Norway*. Research Monograph #2. Sydney: Sydney: Community Child Care Cooperative NSW.

Waniganayake, M., Harrison, L., Cheeseman, S., De Gioia, K., Burgess, C. & Press, F. (2008). *Practice potentials: Impact of participation in professional development and support on quality outcomes for children in childcare centres*. Canberra: Professional Support Coordinators Alliances, Access Macquarie and the Department of Education, Employment and Workplace Relations.

Waniganayake, M., Morda, R. & Kapsalakis, A. (2000). Leadership in child care centres: Is it just another job? *Australian Journal of Early Childhood*, 25(1), 1–6.

Warin, J. & Adriany, V. (2015). Gender flexible pedagogy in early childhood education. *Journal of Gender Studies*. Published online. doi:10.1080/09589236.2015.1105738.

Weaver, A. (2010). Facebook and other Pandora's boxes. *Access*, 24(4), 24–32.

Welch, A. (2010). Making education policy. In R. Connell, C. Campbell, M. Vickers, A. Welch, D. Foley & N. Bagnall (Eds.), *Education, change and society* (2nd ed., pp. 235–50). South Melbourne: Oxford University Press.

Wenger, E. (2010). Communities of Practice and Social Learning Systems: the Career of a Concept. In C. Blackmore (Ed.) *Social learning systems and communities of practice*. (pp. 338–54). Open University, London: Springer.

Whalley, M. (2001). Working as a team. In G. Pugh (Ed.), *Contemporary issues in the early years. Working collaboratively for children* (3rd ed.). London: Paul Chapman Publishing.

Whalley, M. (2006). Leadership in integrated centres and services for children and families: A community development approach. *Childrenz Issues*, 10(2), 8–13.

Whitebook, M. (2003). *Early education quality: Higher teacher qualifications for better learning environments: A review of the literature*. Berkeley, CA: Center for the Study of Child Care Employment.

Whitebook, M. & Sakai, L. (2003). Turnover begets turnover: an examination of job and occupational instability among child care center staff. *Early Childhood Research Quarterly*, 18(3), 273–93.

Wong, D. (2010). Understanding mentoring: Definitions, functions, approaches, contexts and implications for early childhood practitioners. Unpublished paper. Institute of Early Childhood, Macquarie University.

Wong, S. (2006). *Early childhood education and care in New South Wales: Historicising the present*. Unpublished Doctoral thesis. Macquarie University.

Wong, D. & Waniganayake, M. (2013). About Mentoring: Exploring its meaning, dimensions, and implications for Early Childhood. In E. Hujala, M. Waniganayake, & J. Rodd (Eds.), *Researching Leadership in Early Childhood Education*. Tampere: Tampere University Press. http://ilrfec.org/publication/researching-leadership-in-early-childhood-education/

Woodrow, C. & Busch, G. (2008). Repositioning early childhood leadership as action and activism. *European Early Childhood Education Research Journal*, 16(1), 83–93.

Woodrow, C. & Press, F. (2007). Repositioning the child in the policy politics of early childhood. *Education Philosophy and Theory*, 39(3), 312–25.

Woods, P.A. & Woods, G.J. (2013). Deepening distributed leadership: A democratic perspective on power, purpose and the concept of the self. *Leadership in Education*, 2, 17–40.

Work Safe Victoria (2008). Compliance Code: Workplace amenities and work environment. Victoria: Work Cover Authority: Retrieved from www.worksafe.vic.gov.au/__data/assets/pdf_file/0004/9229/Workplace_amenities_CC.pdf.

Wright, D. (2012). A Qualitative Look at Leadership Succession in Human Service Organizations. *International Leadership Journal*, 4(3), 18–28.

Wyver, S., Tranter, P., Naughton, G., Little, H., Sandseter, E.B. & Bundy, A. (2010). Ten ways to restrict children's freedom to play: The problem of surplus safety. *Contemporary Issues in Early Childhood*, 11(3), 263–77.

Young, H. (2015). Knowledge, experts and accountability in school governing bodies. *Educational Management and Leadership*, 45(1), 1–17. doi: 10.1177/1741/143215595415.

INDEX